NBER
Macroeconomics
Annual 1989

Editors
Olivier Jean Blanchard and
Stanley Fischer

THE MIT PRESS
Cambridge, Massachusetts
London, England

Send orders and business correspondence to:
The MIT Press
55 Hayward Street
Cambridge, MA 02142

In the United Kingdom, continental Europe, and the Middle East and Africa, send orders and business correspondence to:
The MIT Press Ltd.
126 Buckingham Palace Road
London SW1W 9SD England

ISSN: 0889-3365/89
ISBN: hardcover 0-262-02296-6
      paperback 0-262-52145-8

Contents

Editorial, NBER Macroeconomics Annual 1989

This fourth edition of the NBER Macroeconomics Annual contains seven papers. Two deal with topics in the news. Charles Bean and James Symons review the record of Mrs. Thatcher's first ten years in office. Frank Levy documents and analyzes changes in U.S. income and earnings distributions. Two papers deal with perennial issues in macroeconomics. David and Christina Romer reexamine and extend Friedman and Schwartz's evidence on the relation between money and output. John Campbell and N. Gregory Mankiw reexamine the evidence on consumption and the consumption function. Two papers explore new directions of research and start confronting them with data. Kevin Murphy, Andrei Schleifer, and Robert Vishny examine the role of increasing returns in economic fluctuations. Stephen Williamson examines the macroeconomic implications of different types of financial arrangements. Finally, in a shorter paper, James Stock and Mark Watson summarize their work on the construction of coincident and leading indicators. We limit ourselves in this introduction to brief descriptions of the papers themselves; an important contribution of the conference however is in both the formal and informal comments which follow each paper.

At the beginning of Mrs. Thatcher's eleventh year in office, Charles Bean and James Symons present a careful review of Britain's economic record since 1979 that avoids partisan excess in either direction. During that decade, inflation has fallen, the public sector deficit has turned into a large surplus, and the rate of productivity growth has risen to the extent that, in recent years, it is second only to Japan among the major industrialized countries. These improvements have however been accompanied by a large increase in the unemployment rate (which did begin to fall sharply in 1988) and a significant widening of the income distribution.

Bean and Symons focus on four topics: the decline in inflation and the role of the Medium Term Financial Strategy; unemployment; the increase in productivity growth; and the distribution of income. In each area, they wrestle quite successfully with the difficulty facing all attempts at evaluating policies—the absence of a clear counterfactual. They deploy economic models, simple regressions, the extensive literature, and expert forensic skill to build their case.

During the Sixties and Seventies the woman in the street in Britain and elsewhere was inclined to blame much of the poor performance of the British economy on the unions. Economists would point to such facts as the relatively low number of days lost to strikes in the UK and look for other causes. Bean and Symons side with the person in the street in placing heavy emphasis on changes in labor relations and union behavior as responsible for higher productivity growth. They attribute part of the widening of the income distribution—which is true of the distributions of both pre-tax income and family income—to the ending of incomes policy. They suggest, however, that other factors must have been at work, noting the similarity of changes in the income distribution in the UK and the U.S. during that period. They are cautious in evaluating the prospects for continued high productivity growth in the UK, and are concerned that maintenance of high productivity growth may require increased investment in training and human capital. Their overall evaluation of the record to date is a favorable one, though.

The basic facts on which Frank Levy concentrates in his paper on recent trends in U.S. earnings and family income have made headlines in recent years. They have led some to announce the disappearance of the American middle class, and have led a presidential candidate to make "good jobs at good wages" a central campaign theme. One of the main contributions of Levy's paper is carefully to establish the facts: Income per worker in the U.S. has grown very slowly since 1973; much of the growth in aggregate income is due to a larger labor force and increased participation. The average income of male workers is roughly the same as in 1973 and the male income distribution has "hollowed out," with more weight going to both the high and low income groups. Female workers have fared better and there is also no evidence of hollowing out in the female income distribution. Finally, there is indeed greater inequality of family incomes. Levy also points to a number of related facts. Among them: the relative and absolute income of the elderly has risen significantly; the relative position of the poorest one-third of children has declined sharply; the relative income of less educated workers has declined.

Levy stops short of a formal analysis of the causes of those shifts in earnings and income distribution. He suggests however that both supply and demand shifts are responsible for the recent trends. The contrast between the European and American experiences in the Eighties suggests that the U.S. has absorbed the very large increase in the labor force in part because real wages have not increased much. But demand shifts have played a role, in that the decline of manufacturing has had an adverse effect on the income of the less well educated young who have moved into services.

The paper by Christina and David Romer is an interesting and innovative contribution to the recently revived debate on whether money matters. That issue seemed to be settled a quarter of a century ago, after the appearance in 1963 of Milton Friedman and Anna Schwartz's classic *Monetary History of the United States, 1867–1960,* and related work by them, Karl Brunner and Allan Meltzer, and others. Most macroeconomists then accepted the view that money mattered, in the sense, for example, that the Fed could engineer a recession by sharply cutting the growth rate of money, or equivalently by sharply raising interest rates.

That consensus dissolved in the 1980s, mostly as a result of two developments: first, empirical work along the lines pioneered by Christopher Sims, using formal statistical techniques, suggested that the quantitative evidence was in fact much weaker than had been claimed by Friedman and Schwartz. Second, the logical possibility that the relation between money and income may reflect a causal relation from income to money was given a new life with the development of real business cycle theories, which concluded that they could explain most of the important business cycle facts while maintaining the assumption of money neutrality. (Both of those aspects were the subject of the paper by Eichenbaum and Singleton in the 1987 Macroeconomics Annual).

Romer and Romer go back to Friedman and Schwartz's classic volume and reexamine their results—particularly their argument that the Great Depression earned its name because of poor monetary policy. They give a number of reasons why one may doubt some of Friedman and Schwartz's conclusions. They then suggest a method which embodies the spirit but not the letter of Friedman and Schwartz's approach. The method is simple. They look, in the record of deliberations of the Fed's Open Market Committee for all the occasions when the Fed decided that inflation had to be reduced. On every such occasion, they show that inflation was effectively reduced, and that output was lower than would have been predicted on the basis of normal behavior. As the discussion points out, their approach relies on the use of dummies rather than either money or interest rates, and thus does not tell us how monetary policy actually works. Skeptics may still argue that inflation, rather than the resolve of the Fed, is what triggers the ensuing recession. Nevertheless, their work represents an important methodological and empirical contribution.

Ten years ago, a paper by Robert Hall had a profound effect on empirical work on consumption. He suggested that, if the purpose of research was to test particular theories of consumption behavior, the best strategy was not to estimate consumption functions as had been done until then, but rather to test optimality conditions. This led to simpler and more focused tests. Largely as a result of his paper, the last ten years have seen a flurry of empirical work on consumption. In their paper, Campbell and Mankiw review and extend this empirical work and offer a characterization of aggregate consumption behavior. Aggregate consumption, they argue, can be viewed as the results of consumption decisions by two types of consumers. Roughly half of the consumers are forward looking and behave according to the life cycle hypothesis; they are, however, very reluctant to substitute consumption across periods in response to interest rate movements. The other half are "rule-of-thumb" consumers, consuming all of their income. They show how this characterization can explain three important empirical regularities. First, expected changes in income are associated with expected changes in consumption. Second, expected real interest rates are not associated with expected changes in consumption. Third, periods of low saving are typically followed by high growth in income.

It is clear that Campbell and Mankiw's interpretation should not be taken literally. It is likely that each consumer is in part forward looking and in part following simple rules-of-thumb. It is also clear that the division between the two types of consumers may not be invariant to changes in financial markets; what Campbell and Mankiw call rule-of-thumb consumers may be what others have called credit- or liquidity-constrained consumers. Nevertheless, the characterization they offer provides a useful description of the data, one that can be used to think about the effects of tax cuts, for example, or subsidies to savings.

The role of increasing returns in the macroeconomy is one of the hottest topics of research in macroeconomics today. In the 1987 edition of the *Macroeconomics Annual*, Romer examined the role of increasing returns in growth. In this edition, Kevin Murphy, Andrei Shleifer, and Robert Vishny look at the role of increasing returns in generating business cycles. They construct a model which has two basic elements. The first is a downward sloping supply curve. They derive it from competitive pricing, with marginal cost declining with aggregate output. They note that this is a strong assumption, stronger than the more usual assumption of declining average cost. They suggest that an alternative derivation is one which assumes constant marginal cost but allows for imperfectly competitive pricing, where the markup of price over cost declines with the level of output. The second element of their model is that the goods which are produced are durable. This has two implications: the first is that the demand for goods at any point in time is very elastic, as buyers can time the purchase of the good to take advantage of low prices. The second implication, which has a long history in macroeconomics, is that recessions create forces which eventually lead to an expansion: a long period of low production leads to a decline in the stock, which eventually leads to an increase in demand to replenish the stocks.

Under those assumptions, the economy goes through cycles, which resemble actual cycles in many ways; they come from the endogenous alteration of high activity-high productivity and low activity-low productivity periods. The authors compare their results to the "real business cycle approach," which is in many ways similar to it, except for its maintained assumption of constant returns to scale and exogenous productivity movements. In another useful contribution, they discuss issues which must be confronted by any model that relies on productivity changes to explain fluctuations. One such issue is that of the positive co-movement of employment across sectors which characterizes the business cycle. They discuss the role of limited labor mobility in explaining positive co-movements in employment across all sectors that result from movements in productivity in only a few of those sectors. Another issue they discuss is where in the economy these productivity changes actually take place; by looking at the behavior of relative prices, they conclude that, if prices reflect marginal cost, productivity shocks are taking place at the end of the chain of production.

The model of cycles proposed by Murphy, Shleifer, and Vishny is stimulating, but is unlikely to convince all macroeconomists. Indeed, one way of reading their paper is that it shows how stringent the conditions are for such cycles to emerge. There is no question, however, that the elements they identify, namely various forms of increasing returns and the role of durable stocks, play an important role, if not in generating cycles, at least surely in explaining their characteristics.

The implications of asymmetric information for financial arrangements and macroeconomic fluctuations are another recent topic of research. Stephen Williamson, in his paper, takes the theory to the data. He chooses to focus on Canada and the U.S. from 1870 to 1913. What makes that period particularly interesting are the differences in the financial structures of those two countries. While Canada had a well diversified branch banking system, and Canadian banks could issue large denomination notes unbacked by government securities, the U.S. banking system was one of unit banking, and all notes had to be fully backed by government bonds.

Williamson first constructs a theoretical model designed to capture those differences. The model, which is a dynamic general equilibrium model with asymmetric information, is, by nature, complex. But its basic structure is simple. The returns from investment by entrepreneurs are not directly observable; they can however be verified at a cost. This leads to the creation of financial intermediaries who borrow from primary lenders and lend to entrepreneurs using an optimal, debt-like, contract. The entrepreneur promises a fixed payment to the financial intermediary. If the entrepreneur later declares it cannot meet the payment, then bankruptcy occurs and the entrepreneur consumes zero. To the extent that risks are idiosyncratic, financial intermediaries can diversify and offer riskless lending to the lenders. Williamson then formalizes unit banking in the U.S. by assuming that, in the U.S., restrictions on financial intermediaries prevent them from being able to diversify and offer riskless lending. He formalizes restrictions on the backing of bank notes by assuming that this prevents some lenders from lending at all. He then characterizes the behavior of output, prices, and bank liabilities. Interestingly, he shows that the two restrictions tend to decrease, through their effect on investment, fluctuations in output. More intermediation leads to larger, but welfare-improving, fluctuations. Having derived those implications, Williamson goes back to the data. While his model does not fit the evidence in prices, the data support one major implication of the model: Canadian output varies relatively more than U.S. output, and this does not seem to be attributable to composition effects.

Like the paper by Murphy, Shleifer, and Vishny, this paper is more of a foray into uncharted territory than a definitive treatment of issues. But it breaks substantial theoretical and empirical ground and, in so doing, shows how endogenizing the structure of financial institutions may shed light on a number of macroeconomic issues.

In the last paper in this volume, James Stock and Mark Watson summarize their work on coincident and leading indicators. The initial set of leading indicators was developed in 1937 by Burns and Mitchell. The indicators used today are the result of fifty years of trial and error, with little help from formal time series econometrics. The challenge taken up by Stock and Watson is to see whether modern econometrics can help.

They construct three indices, an index of coincident indicators (CEI), an index of leading indicators (LEI), and a recession index. The CEI extracts the common component of four monthly aggregate series, industrial production, real personal income, sales, and employee hours. This is based on the implicit theory that there is an underlying common component, the cycle, which is best captured by looking at a number of aggregate variables. The LEI in turn is designed to forecast growth in the CEI over the following six months. Through a process of elimination, Stock and Watson end up choosing seven series which, they conclude, together yield the best prediction of growth in the CEI. Interestingly, four of the seven variables are prices rather than quantities. Three are interest rates: the first is the yield on 10-year government bonds, the second is the spread on 6-month private versus public bills, and the third is the spread between the yield on 10-year and 1-year government bonds. The fourth variable is the trade-weighted nominal exchange rate. Finally, Stock and Watson compute a recession index that assesses the probability of a recession six months hence. As of the time their paper was written, this last index showed no sign of an impending recession. As was the case for the current NBER leading indicators, Stock and Watson's indicators will need to be time tested. As the authors are very much aware, doing well in a sample is no guarantee of success in the future. Their work however contains the promise of a reliable, statistically well grounded, set of coincident and leading indicators.

The Conference at which these papers were presented and discussed was efficiently organized by Kirsten Foss and Ilana Hardesty. David Cutler and Janice Eberly acted as editors of the papers, the comments and as rapporteurs for the general discussion. Their assistance was invaluable.

Olivier Jean Blanchard and Stanley Fischer

Abstracts

Ten Years of Mrs. T.

CHARLES BEAN AND JAMES SYMONS

We argue that the 1970s were characterized by attempts to maintain a coopera-tive, low-unemployment equilibrium in the face of considerable union power, through the use of incomes policies and neo-corporatist machinery. The 1980s saw a shift away from this, toward direct measures to limit union power. This, together with the adoption of tight macroeconomic policies, explains the initial rise in unemployment. Empirical evidence suggests that its persistence through-out the decade is due to the effect of prolonged unemployment on the search behaviour of the outsiders, rather than the insider mechanism emphasized by Blanchard and Summers, and others.

The reduction in union power also helps to explain the acceleration in produc-tivity growth. The craft nature of much of the British union movement has led to a multiplication of bargaining units within firms. Bargaining in isolation a union can perceive overmanning and other restrictive practices as being in its interests, resulting in low wages and productivity. A fall in union power results in a reduction in these inefficiencies and leads not only to a rise in productivity but also in wages. Cross-section empirical evidence supports the thesis that the productivity acceleration has been greatest where multi-unionism is present. We also show how this explains the widening in pre-tax as well as post-tax earnings.

Recent Trends in U.S. Earnings and Family Incomes

FRANK LEVY

Since 1973, U.S. wage rates have shown slow growth bordering on stagnation. During this period, the real *annual* earnings distribution of prime age men has shown both little average growth and increased inequality. The distribution of real annual family incomes has similarly shown little average growth and in-creased inequality. By contrast, the distribution of real annual women's earnings has shown modest growth and a slight trend toward equality. When wage trends are disaggregated by group, the data show a sharp deterioration in the real wages of young, less educated men and a sharp increase in the wage rates of younger, better educated women. Disaggregation of the family income distribution shows that growing family income inequality is driven, in part, by the growing number of families who are are either headed by a single woman or are husband-wife families with two earners.

Does Monetary Policy Matter? A New Test in the Spirit of Friedman and Schwartz
CHRISTINA D. ROMER AND DAVID H. ROMER

This paper uses the historical record to isolate episodes in which there were large monetary disturbances not caused by output fluctuations. It then tests whether these monetary changes have important real effects. The central part of the paper is a study of postwar U.S. monetary history. We identify six episodes in which the Federal Reserve in effect decided to attempt to create a recession to reduce inflation. We find that a shift to anti-inflationary policy led, on average, to a rise in the unemployment rate of two percentage points, and that this effect is highly statistically significant and robust to a variety of changes in specification.

We reach three other major conclusions. First, the real effects of these monetary disturbances are highly persistent. Second, the six shocks that we identify account for a considerable fraction of postwar economic fluctuations. And third, evidence from the interwar era also suggests that monetary disturbances have large real effects.

Consumption, Income, and Interest Rates: Reinterpreting the Time Series Evidence
JOHN Y. CAMPBELL AND N. GREGORY MANKIW

This paper proposes that the time-series data on consumption, income, and interest rates are best viewed as generated not by a single representative consumer but by two groups of consumers. Half the consumers are forward-looking and consume their permanent income, but are extremely reluctant to substitute consumption intertemporally. Half the consumers follow the "rule of thumb" of consuming their current income. The paper documents three empirical regularities that, it argues, are best explained by this model. First, expected changes in income are associated with expected changes in consumption. Second, expected real interest rates are not associated with expected changes in consumption. Third, periods in which consumption is high relative to income are typically followed by high growth in income. The paper concludes by briefly discussing the implications of these findings for economic policy and economic research.

Building Blocks of Market Clearing Business Cycle Models
KEVIN M. MURPHY, ANDREI SHLEIFER, AND ROBERT W. VISHNY

We compare "real business cycle" and increasing returns models of economic fluctuations. In these models, business cycles are driven by productivity changes resulting either from technology shocks or from movements along the increasing returns production function. We stress four crucial building blocks that give both types of models hope of fitting the data. These building blocks include durability of goods, specialized labor, imperfect credit and elastic labor supply. We also present new evidence on co-movement of both outputs and labor inputs across sectors and on the behavior of relative prices over the business cycle. We conclude that the increasing returns model is easier to reconcile with the data than the real business cycle model.

Restrictions on Financial Intermediaries and Implications for Aggregate Fluctuations: Canada and the United States 1870–1913
STEPHEN D. WILLIAMSON

During the period 1870–1913, Canada had a well-diversified branch banking system while banks in the U.S. unit banking system were less diversified. Canadian banks could issue large-denomination notes with no restrictions on their backing, while all U.S. currency was essentially an obligation of the U.S. government. Also, experience in the two countries with regard to bank failures and banking panics was quite different. A general equilibrium business cycle model with endogenous financial intermediation is constructed that captures these historical Canadian and American monetary and banking arrangements as special cases. The predictions of the model contradict conventional wisdom with regard to the cyclical effects of banking panics. Support for these predictions is found in aggregate annual time series data for Canada and the United States.

New Indexes of Coincident and Leading Economic Indicators
JAMES H. STOCK AND MARK W. WATSON

The system of Leading and Coincident Economic Indicators, currently maintained by the U.S. Department of Commerce (DOC), was developed as part of the NBER research program on business cycles over fifty years ago. This paper uses recent developments in econometric methodology and computing technology to take a fresh look at this system. The result is three experimental indexes. The first, constructed using a dynamic factor model, is numerically similar to the current index of coincident indicators maintained by the DOC. The second, an alternative index of leading indicators, is designed to forecast the growth in the DOC index over a six month horizon. The third—a "Recession Index"— estimates the probability that the economy will be in a recession six months hence. Only two of the seven series in the proposed leading index are used by the DOC to construct their index. Of these new series, interest rates (a public-private risk premium and the slope of the yield curve) are found to be particularly useful predictors of future economic activity.

Charles Bean and James Symons
LONDON SCHOOL OF ECONOMICS AND UNIVERSITY COLLEGE,
LONDON UNIVERSITY

Ten Years of Mrs. T.

Introduction

Throughout the Sixties and Seventies Britain's economic performance deteriorated. Economists queued up with their prognoses, but without any noticeable effect. Then came Mrs. Thatcher. Her favourite economist was Adam Smith with a respectful nod to Milton Friedman, and since 1979 her government has set about rolling back the frontiers of the state. In doing so she broke decisively with the postwar consensus on the role of the state in the economy.

Early assessments of the Thatcher economic revolution, such as Buiter and Miller (1981, 1983), were perhaps too early to appraise the success of the new regime. A more complete assessment on ten years should be possible, and there has been a veritable flood of eulogies and epitaphs (e.g., Burns, 1988; Layard and Nickell, 1989; Matthews and Minford, 1987; Maynard, 1988; Walters, 1986). Yet in some ways the waters are as murky as ever, for while it is relatively easy to document what has happened, it is harder to say what would have happened under alternative policies. Would the benefits have been greater or the costs smaller under an alternative set of policies? That, unfortunately, is a question to which we can never know the answer.

However, we can at least assess the Thatcher programme against its stated objectives. Table 1 provides snapshots of the British economy at the start of Mrs. Thatcher's administration (which coincides with the peak of the previous cycle), at the trough of the recession in 1981 and in 1988 (which may well turn out to be another business cycle peak).

From a macroeconomic perspective the immediate objective in 1979 was to achieve a steady and sustained reduction in the rate of inflation through monetary control. To limit upward pressure on interest rates,

peak of the previous cycle), at the trough of the recession in 1981 and in 1988 (which may well turn out to be another business cycle peak).

From a macroeconomic perspective the immediate objective in 1979 was to achieve a steady and sustained reduction in the rate of inflation through monetary control. To limit upward pressure on interest rates, the monetary targets were part of an overall framework—the Medium Term Financial Strategy (MTFS)—which envisaged a decline in the government's borrowing requirements over a number of years. The government also promised a reduction in government spending and taxes but, unlike the Reagan programme, there was to be no dabbling in the black arts of the Laffer curve. Tax cuts would come only when the government's financial position allowed.

The primary objective—the achievement of a low and relatively steady rate of inflation—clearly has been achieved, current "blips" aside. Similarly the public sector borrowing requirement (PSBR) has swung from a large deficit to what is now quite a sizable surplus, and for this reason has now been renamed the public sector debt repayment (PSDR). The share of government spending in total output, and with it the share of taxes, however, has changed rather little until the last year or two. (This is not simply due to increased transfer payments stemming from higher unemployment; the share of government expenditure on goods and services in GDP was 19.8% in 1987 against 19.7% in 1979.) The next section of the paper discusses in more detail this aspect of the government's record, and in particular the role of the PSBR targets in the MTFS.

Table 1   SELECTED UK ECONOMIC STATISTICS

	1979	1981	1988
GDP[a]	100.0	96.7	121.0
Manufacturing output	100.0	85.9	107.8
Output/head	100.0	99.9	121.3
Manufacturing output/head	100.0	99.5	148.1
Unemployment rate	4.9	9.4	8.6
Long-term unemployment rate (more than 12 months)	1.2	2.1	3.5
Retail price inflation	13.4	11.9	4.9
Real earnings	100.0	105.3	126.0
Real earnings (Male manuals, lowest decile)	100.0	102.1	107.0
Profit share (% of GDP[b])	20.4	16.5	21.0
Public Sector Debt Repayment (% of GDP[c])	−6.4	−4.1	2.4
Government expenditure (% of GDP[c])	43.4	46.1	38.6
Tax Revenue (% of GDP[c])	34.1	37.8	37.2
Current account (% of GDP[c])	−0.3	2.7	−3.1

Notes: (a) Average of income, output and expenditure measures
        (b) At factor cost
        (c) At market prices
Source: Economic Trends, Employment Gazette, and New Earnings Survey

As far as the real side of the economy goes, the picture is mixed. Furthermore the perspective is very different viewed from 1979 (favoured by critics of Mrs. Thatcher) and 1981 (preferred by supporters). The annual growth rate of output is an anaemic 2.1% judged from the former, but a healthy 3.3% from the latter. There is no doubt that the record on unemployment has until recently been rather bad, while that on productivity has been relatively good. The unemployment rate, which peaked at 11.8% in 1985, has reached levels second only to those experienced during the Great Depression. Almost all of this increase in unemployment is due to an increase in duration rather than an increased probability of unemployment, resulting in a large increase in those who have been unemployed for a year or more. Reasons for this rise in unemployment are discussed in Section 2 of the paper.

Productivity growth of 2.2% per annum (4.5% in manufacturing) since 1979 may not seem startling to the average Japanese (or German) reader, but it does represent a significant improvement over Britain's past record, both in absolute and relative terms. The sources and sustainability of this resurgence in productivity are discussed in Section 3.

Alongside this acceleration in productivity has been a sharp rise in average real (pre-tax) earnings. However as Section 4 details, the inequality between both pre- and post-tax incomes has risen greatly during the Thatcher years, with the result that the real incomes of those at the bottom end of the income distribution have hardly risen at all. Gains there may have been from the Thatcher years, but they have been shared very unequally.

1. Inflation and the Public Finances

The immediate objective of the government after its election in 1979 was the eradication of inflation. To this end it instituted a Medium Term Financial Strategy (MTFS) embodying guidelines for both monetary and fiscal policies over a rolling four-year horizon. In particular the MTFS envisaged a steady reduction in nominal GDP growth through a gradual reduction in the rate of growth of the money stock (£M3), accompanied by a declining path for the PSBR.

Targets for £M3 were not new, having been first introduced by the Labour government in 1977. The MTFS, however, was different in providing target ranges for a number of years ahead. Unfortunately, in the first two years of the strategy, £M3 vastly overshot its target range (18.4% in 1980 and 16.3% in 1981 as against targets of 7–11% and 6–10%) leading both to a further tightening of monetary policy and to upward revision of the ranges in ensuing MTFSs. This led some observers to

claim that monetary conditions were far too loose and the rampant inflation (retail price inflation peaked at 22% in May 1980) was a consequence
of this monetary laxity.

With hindsight it is clear that this was incorrect and that the country
was in the grip of a tight monetary squeeze. The rate of growth of the
monetary base slowed from 12.1% in 1979 to 2.6% in 1981. Furthermore
the nominal exchange rate appreciated by no less than a quarter between
the beginning of 1979 and the end of 1980, resulting in a similar loss of
competitiveness. Some of this is certainly due to North Sea oil—in particular the revaluation of oil rents in the wake of OPEC II—but a variety
of studies using different approaches all point to a real appreciation from
oil of around 8–12% (see Bean 1987, for a survey). Although there are
some difficulties in squaring a monetary explanation of the rest of the
appreciation with the ex post behaviour of interest differentials (see
Buiter and Miller 1983), it seems reasonable to attribute a significant part
of the remaining 13–17% to the monetary squeeze.

In any case the outturn for nominal GDP growth seems to have been
pretty much as the government would have hoped. Burns (1988) reports
internal figures lying behind the 1980 MTFS which envisaged a reduction in nominal GDP growth from 17.5% in the financial year 1979–80 to
9.6% in 1982–83. The outturn for 1982–83 was in fact 9.2%. Where things
went somewhat awry was in the split between inflation and real output
growth in 1980 and 1981. Since then, despite continued misbehaviour of
the monetary aggregates due to financial innovation, nominal GDP
growth has been fairly steady, ranging between 7% and 10% per annum.

1.1 THE PSBR TARGETS

That some sort of monetary deceleration would be associated with the
disinflation process is relatively uncontroversial, although it is open to
debate whether the disinflation could have been less painfully accom-
plished. A natural alternative for instance would have been an exchange
rate target, perhaps within the EMS. An incomes policy might have
provided a second nominal anchor (more on this below). An interesting
issue, however, is the role played by the targets for the PSBR in the
MTFS. Were they important in the disinflationary process and, if so,
how?

In the original 1980 MTFS, the PSBR, as a percentage of GDP, was set
to decline steadily from 4.7% in 1979–80 to 1.5% in 1983–84. However,
as Table 2 shows, it took the government considerably longer to reduce
the PSBR than was originally intended in the 1980 MTFS. In fact progress
has been even less dramatic, for the PSBR treats the proceeds from
privatisation as a form of negative capital expenditure rather than a way

of financing the deficit. The Public Sector Financial Deficit/Surplus (PSFD/PSFS) instead treats privatisation proceeds as a form of finance and thus gives a more accurate picture of the pressures government policy is putting on the capital markets. Table 2 shows that this changed remarkably little until the rapid growth of the last few years swelled tax receipts.

The overrun of the PSBR targets in the wake of the deeper-than-expected recession of 1980–81 is an indication that they did not constitute an unconditional rule for fiscal policy. However, it is clear that the permitted overrun was less pronounced than could have been expected under previous administrations. Table 2 also contains the OECD's cyclically corrected measure of the budget deficit which gives an indication of the "discretionary" changes in fiscal policy (although it does *not* necessarily provide a good measure of the impact of policy on demand). This shows policy tightening in 1980 and, especially, 1981 when the economy was undergoing its severest slump since the early Thirties. Thus while fiscal policy has not been unconditional, it has been considerably less responsive to short-run fluctuations in activity than in the past, reflecting the government's emphasis on medium and long-term objectives.

1.2 INTEREST RATES AND THE MTFS

So much for what happened to the PSBR. What has the fiscal part of the MTFS achieved? It is helpful to start by recording what the government *thought* it would achieve. The 1980 MTFS gave the following rationale:

Table 2   THE PUBLIC FINANCES (% OF GDP AT MARKET PRICES)

	PSDR	PSFS[a]	Cyclically Adjusted PSFS	Oil Revenues	Permanent Income PSFS
1970	0.0	1.3	5.0	0.0	6.8
1975	−9.6	−7.2	1.1	0.0	−0.3
1978	−4.9	−5.0	−1.0	0.4	−0.1
1979	−6.4	−4.3	0.9	1.3	0.2
1980	−5.1	−4.5	2.1	1.8	−0.1
1981	−4.1	−3.1	5.3	3.0	0.2
1982	−1.8	−2.7	5.6	3.3	0.2
1983	−3.8	−3.4	3.7	3.4	−0.6
1984	−3.2	−4.0	3.2	4.3	−2.3
1985	−2.1	−2.7	3.6	3.8	−0.6
1986	−0.6	−2.1	3.1	1.5	0.8
1987	0.4	−1.1	3.0	1.1	2.2

Note: (a) Excludes certain other financial transactions as well as privatisation proceeds.
Sources: Economic Trends, Financial Statement and Budget Report, OECD Economic Outlook, (various) and Begg (1987).

It is not the intention to achieve this reduction in monetary growth by excessive reliance on interest rates. The consequence of the high level of public sector borrowing has been high nominal interest rates and greater financing problems for the private sector. If interest rates are to be brought down to acceptable levels the PSBR must be substantially reduced as a proportion of GDP over the next few years (Financial Statement and Budget Report, 1980–81).

It is clear that the government's primary argument for the PSBR targets was to prevent the crowding-out of investment that might occur if the private sector was asked to absorb increasing quantities of government debt. This rationale was severely criticised at the time by such diverse economists as Dornbusch, Friedman, Laidler, and Kaldor (see Treasury and Civil Service Committee 1981), and does not look stronger with hindsight. Nominal short-term interest rates have never fallen much below 9% since 1979 and are currently almost as high as when the government took office. Real short-term interest rates—approximately zero in 1978—have averaged around 4% over the last five years. Furthermore, this is not because of a fiscal-inspired recovery in investment; investment in 1978 stood at 18.5% of GDP while over 1983–87 it averaged only 16.8%.

Of course, other things have changed since 1980. In particular the level of world real interest rates has risen dramatically. But this merely serves to emphasize the fundamental weakness in the basic argument; namely that real interest rates are determined primarily in international capital markets. Empirical evidence suggests that the effects of changes in the relative supplies of different assets has relatively little effect on real interest differentials (e.g., Frankel 1985), and once this is recognised the original rationale for the PSBR targets looks distinctly shaky.

1.3 SOLVENCY AND THE MTFS

An alternative rationale advanced for the PSBR targets is that it enhanced the credibility of the government's monetary targets. According to this line of argument, sustained budget deficits now must be associated with either budget surpluses or increased monetisation in the future. A lower rate of monetary growth today can thus engender expectations of higher future inflation unless accompanied by a reduction in the fiscal deficit (Sargent and Wallace 1981).

Is this argument relevant to the UK? Start by recalling that the government budget identity implies that for a given debt-income ratio, b, the rate of inflation, π, is given by

$$\pi = v[d+(r-n)b]-n \quad (1)$$

where v is the velocity of high-powered money (assumed constant for simplicity), d is the primary deficit as a proportion of GDP, r is the real interest rate and n is the rate of growth of the economy $(r > n)$. It follows that the nominal deficit must certainly fall if inflation is to be permanently lower, as also must the primary deficit. If these cuts are not made at the same time as any cut in monetary growth, there is a danger that private agents will be led to expect higher monetary growth and inflation in the future rather than fiscal retrenchment.

The first point to note is that seigniorage has never been an important source of revenue in the UK because the velocity of circulation is so high (roughly 20). During the Seventies seigniorage averaged 0.8% of GDP, and half that in the Eighties. Since a 10 percentage point reduction in inflation calls for a reduction of the primary deficit of around .5 percentage point, and the political costs of inflation are high, it is much more likely that a future government would resort to conventional taxation rather than the printing presses in order to cover the increased debt service resulting from a lower rate of monetary expansion today. Consequently an essential ingredient of the Sargent-Wallace argument—that future primary deficits are fixed independently of the rate of monetary growth—would seem to be missing.

More relevant, however, is the existence of long-dated nominally-denominated debt. Unanticipated disinflation represents a windfall subsidy to bondholders which has to be financed from somewhere. Consequently the primary deficit would need to fall for as long as the overhang of high real interest payments on existing long-dated nominally-denominated debt lasts, if the debt-income ratio were not to rise. The problem with this line of argument is that the government could avoid a squeeze on the primary deficit by carrying out a swap of indexed for non-indexed debt prior to initiating its disinflationary programme. Nominal interest payments would then decline with inflation.

An associated argument is that the existence of nominally-denominated debt encourages governments to indulge in bouts of unanticipated inflation to expropriate bondholders. The mere announcement of a low inflation path may thus not be credible. Sticking to the PSBR targets was one way of building up the credibility of its monetary programme. The problem is that, as before, the authorities can avoid this problem of time inconsistency by issuing indexed debt before initiating the disinflationary programme while it still lacked credibility. Now although the government has been issuing indexed stock since 1980 it still constitutes only 11% of the face value of the outstanding debt, and thus falls well short of a full debt swap. Possibly the government had not realised that it could avoid the pains of building up credibility through this simple device; it seems more likely that both the government and the private sector (which seemed reluctant to absorb large quantities of indexed debt) simply did not regard the time inconsistency problem as serious.

A third line of argument is that the initial levels of the deficit were unsustainable. The primary deficit between 1978 and 1980 averaged around 2.33% of GDP. Given a net debt-income ratio of a fraction over 40% and a real growth corrected interest rate of 1–2%, equation (1) implies a steady-state inflation rate of around 50%. Although such a situation does not require that adjustment be made today, correction of an unsustainable financial plan has to begin sometime.

To see whether existing fiscal plans were ex ante unsustainable, start by noting that the government comprehensive balance sheet requires that (Buiter 1985):

$$G \equiv \begin{cases} \text{Present value of exhaustive consumption spending} \\ + \text{ present value of transfers, grants and subsidies} \end{cases}$$

$$= \begin{cases} \text{Public sector net assets (financial and real)} \\ + \text{ present value of taxes} \\ + \text{ present value of seigniorage} \\ + \text{ present value of public sector capital formation programme} \end{cases} \equiv W.$$

If R is the real long-term interest rate, then the indefinitely sustainable flow of government spending is given by the annuity value of net worth, RW, and a measure of the fiscal elbow room the government is bequeathing to its successors is given by the "permanent income deficit" (Buiter 1985), $g - RW$, where g is the flow of real consumption spending and transfers. If this is negative then future governments will have to reduce future spending or increase net worth, e.g., by raising taxes.

Begg (1987) has calculated a time series for this quantity, assuming a constant share of non-oil taxes in output and his figures have been updated for Table 2. Compared to the conventional PSFD/PSFS there are three important adjustments. First, the debt burden is evaluated at the long-term real interest rate. Second, North Sea oil taxes are replaced by their permanent income equivalent (based on the prevailing real oil price). Third, half of the public sector investment programme in dwellings and public corporations are deducted on the (conservative) assumption that this half yields cash returns to the government at the market rate. The figures indicate that the permanent income deficit was roughly zero in 1979, suggesting no obvious sustainability with existing taxation and spending plans.

Finally a number of industrial countries have carried through successful disinflationary programmes without fiscal retrenchment. Ireland
(Dornbusch 1989) and Italy (Giavazzi and Spaventa 1989) are two cases
in point. Both of these countries have net debt-income ratios in excess of
90%. In addition the United States has managed to combine low inflation
with growing public debt, albeit from a low base. Fiscal correction may
often be an essential part of a disinflationary programme, particularly
where capital markets are thin and seigniorage is important, but it is not
obvious that it was necessary in the British case.

1.4 THE MTFS AND THE CHANGE IN REGIME

So what have the PSBR targets achieved? We think two things. First, at a
rather mundane level, the setting of PSBR targets has brought the two
sides of the public accounts, expenditure and revenue, together. In the
UK, public spending plans have always been laid out in the autumn,
whereas taxation decisions have been made at budget time in the spring,
with only a rather tenuous link between the two processes. There is now
a greater awareness that spending and taxation are two sides of the same
coin and the increases in the spending of one department must come out
of another department's allocation, or increased taxation.

The second achievement was to establish the credibility of the government as a "tough" one that would not accommodate inflationary wage
demands through expansionary macroeconomic policies. In particular
the 1981 budget was a watershed in which policy tightened despite
high and rising unemployment. At a time when the monetary targets
were being overshot by a considerable margin, this was an important
signal of an irrevocable break with the past (see Buiter and Miller 1983
and Begg 1987, for a similar view). However, it was not simply a
disavowal of Keynesian stabilisation policies that represented a break
with the past. Equally significant was the fact that it signalled the end
of attempts to sustain a cooperative low unemployment equilibrium
through the use of neo-corporatist policies. This is a theme we develop
in the next section.

2. Unemployment

The reduction in inflation, the stabilisation of the public finances, and
the resurgence in productivity (discussed in Section 3) are the most
conspicuous economic successes of the Thatcher years. The most obvious failure has been the level of unemployment, plotted in the first panel
of Figure 1. Critics have blamed this on the government's contractionary
fiscal and monetary policies. But the defence of the government has

been to argue that, while deplorable, the unemployment is a consequence of private sector decisions and not government actions.

We begin by putting the UK's unemployment experience in an international context. Most of the industrialised countries went through a bout of
disinflation during the first half of the Eighties. Were the effects of this
worse in the UK than elsewhere? Table 3 reports inflation and unemployment rates in 1980 and 1985 in the UK and a number of other countries.
The final column, the "sacrifice ratio," reports the ratio of the cumulated
excess of the unemployment rate over its 1980 level during this period to
the reduction in inflation. Of course, since unemployment could have
risen because of adverse supply-side developments as well as coun-
terinflationary macroeconomic policies, this does not necessarily provide
an accurate measure of the costs of disinflation, but it does at least provide
a rather crude indicator of comparative macroeconomic performance.

Compared to Japan, Sweden and the U.S.—three countries with very
different economic and institutional structures—British performance
was rather poor. However, her comparative performance is rather better
compared to the rest of the European Community; Germany for instance
fared especially badly under the sacrifice ratio criterion. However, the
most obvious comparison, in terms of similarity of initial conditions, is
with Italy. Viewed in this light, British performance looks somewhat less
satisfactory.

The fact that unemployment may be widespread in the European
Community does not, however, necessarily absolve the Conservative

Figure 1 FACTORS AFFECTING THE NATURAL RATE

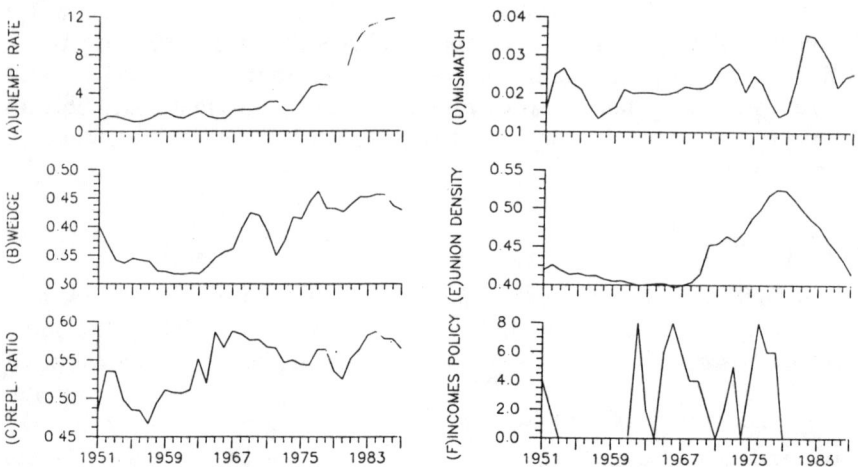

government from all responsibility. Many of the policies followed by Mrs. Thatcher have been emulated by other European governments, so the common unemployment experience could simply reflect common policies, as well as common exogenous shocks which may have also tended to raise the equilibrium rate of unemployment. We must therefore delve a little deeper into the forces behind the movements in the British unemployment rate.

2.1 THE DETERMINANTS OF THE NATURAL RATE

We start by considering factors that may have raised the natural rate of unemployment (meaning the rate of unemployment at which wage-setters' intended markup of wages over prices is consistent with price-setters' intended markup of prices over wages). The following list includes most of the obvious candidates: the tax and import price wedge; the benefit system; skill and regional mismatch; and union power. Time series of these variables are also plotted in Figure 1 and are discussed further below.

2.1.1 Taxes and Import Prices   Workers care about the purchasing power of wages post-tax, while for firms the relevant variable is the cost of labour in terms of the price of its output. Anything that changes the "wedge" between post-tax consumption wages and own-product labour costs could affect equilibrium unemployment. An argument that is often

Table 3   COMPARATIVE INFLATION AND UNEMPLOYMENT
PERFORMANCE

	Inflation[a]		Unemploy-ment[b]		"Sacrifice Ratio"[c]
	1980	1985	1980	1985	
Germany	4.9	2.3	3.0	7.2	6.8
France	11.6	5.9	6.3	10.2	2.1
Italy	21.5	9.2	7.5	10.1	0.7
Japan	3.9	1.5	2.0	2.6	1.0
Sweden	11.9	6.9	2.0	2.8	0.4
United Kingdom	19.1	5.8	6.4	11.2	1.8
United States	9.1	3.0	7.0	7.1	1.0

Notes: (a) GNP/GDP deflator.
(b) Standardised unemployment rate.

(c) $\left[\sum_{1981}^{1985} (\text{Unemployment}_i - \text{Unemployment}_{1980}) \right] / [\text{Col.}(1) - \text{Col.}(2)]$

Source: OECD Economic Outlook, December 1988.

advanced to explain the initial rise in unemployment in 1974–75 is that it was the outcome of attempts by labour to maintain the consumption wage in the face of the deterioration in the terms of trade due to the first oil price shock.

Panel (b) of Figure 1 shows an upward movement in the total wedge from the mid-1960s due primarily to increasing income tax rates, while in the 1973–75 period we see a second widening in the wedge due to the terms of trade deterioration. There are, however, good reasons for believing that an increase in the wedge should not permanently raise equilibrium unemployment. The reason is that in most optimising models the wedge affects unemployment only via the consumption wage. This has increased manyfold since the Dark Ages, but without much altering the unemployment rate. Thus one might expect changes in the wedge to have at most a transitory effect (a finding that is confirmed by Newell and Symons 1985).

2.1.2 Benefits An increase in the generosity of unemployment benefits should make workers more willing to risk unemployment or be more selective about accepting job offers if they are unemployed. Panel (c) of Figure 1 plots the ratio of supplementary benefit to the lowest decile of manual earnings after taxes (since most unemployed can expect to go into lowly paid manual jobs). While there was a big increase in the replacement ratio in the mid-Sixties, it has since risen little, and there is nothing with which to associate the upward movement in unemployment. Of course, the way benefits are administered may be more important and, in particular, the vigour with which the work-test is enforced. Layard and Nickell (1987) suggest that, until recently at least, attitudes had indeed become more lenient in this regard. Furthermore, as discussed below, the characteristics of the benefit system may be important in understanding the dynamics of unemployment.

2.1.3 Mismatch One common explanation of the increase in unemployment lies in the impact of new technology, especially computers, and the effect of increasing competition in traditional industries from Japan and the NICs. This has made the human capital of a large portion of the work force redundant, especially manual workers in the traditional manufacturing industries like cars and shipbuilding. If firms in the South East want skilled computer operators, a large pool of unemployed welders on Tyneside will be of little help to them in filling vacancies. But, if retraining and relocation is costly, the unemployed may choose to remain where they are in the hope of getting their old jobs back in due course. An increase in the mismatch between the type/location of vacancies and the type/location of unemployment can therefore be expected to reduce the efficiency of the process of matching unemployed workers to jobs, resulting in higher equilibrium unemployment.

Appealing as this line of argument may be, it does not receive strong empirical support. A direct measure of mismatch can be based on a comparison of the share (in total unemployment) of unemployment in a particular category (skill/location/industry) with the share (in total vacancies) of vacancies of the same category. Such measures do not reveal increased skill or regional mismatch (in fact the latter appears to have been falling in recent times); only industrial mismatch seems to have increased (Jackman and Roper 1987). Because this index of industrial mismatch is only available for a short period, our empirical work below employs a measure with similar time series properties based on (a distributed lag of) the weighted standard deviation of employment growth rates across nine major employment categories. This variable is plotted in panel (d) of Figure 1 and exhibits a very marked increase over 1979–81, after which it falls back. However if industries respond differently to a common aggregate demand shock, movements in this variable could reflect aggregate demand shocks as well as sector-specific real shocks.

2.1.4 Unions Increased union power will tend to raise equilibrium unemployment in most models, even where there is bargaining over employment. To see this consider the following canonical case of a closed economy composed of n identical imperfectly competitive firms, each of which faces an inverse demand function $P_i = \delta Y_i^{-\epsilon}$ ($\epsilon < 1$; $i = 1, ., n$) and possesses a Cobb-Douglas technology $Y_i = N_i\alpha$ ($\alpha < 1$). Here Y_i is output, P_i the firm's relative price, N_i is employment and the demand shift parameter, δ, is a decreasing function of the general price level. The firm bargains with a single union over wages and employment. Union utility is given by the utilitarian utility function $N_i V(W_i) + (M - N_i)\tilde{V}$ where $V(W_i)$ is the utility of an employed worker, W_i is the real consumption wage, $\tilde{V}$ is (expected) utility for an unemployed union member and M is the membership. Wages and employment in each firm are given as the outcome of a generalised Nash bargain between management and the union:

$$Max\ [V(W_i) - \tilde{V}]^\beta N_i^\beta (\delta N_i^{\alpha(1-\epsilon)} - W_i N_i)$$

where we have assumed that the status quo points for the union and firm are $M\tilde{V}$ and zero respectively and β is interpreted as a measure of union power. The first order conditions are then:

$$\beta V'/(V-\tilde{V}) = N_i/(\delta N_i^{\alpha(1-\epsilon)} - W_i N_i)$$

$$\beta + [\alpha(1-\epsilon)\delta N_i^{\alpha(1-\epsilon)} - W_i N_i]/[\delta N_i^{\alpha(1-\epsilon)} - W_i N_i] = 0.$$

Now in a symmetric equilibrium $W_i(=W)$ and $P_i(=1)$ are the same for all firms. Then if $\tilde{V}=(1-u)V(W)+uV(B)$, where u is the unemployment rate and B is benefits, and assuming for simplicity that $V(W)=W^\gamma/\gamma$ with $\gamma<1$, it follows that the equilibrium unemployment rate is given by:

$$u = [1-\alpha(1-\epsilon)]\beta\gamma/[\beta+\alpha(1-\epsilon)](1-\rho^\gamma)$$

where ρ is the replacement rate, B/W. Real wages are given by:

$$W = [\beta+\alpha(1-\epsilon)]/(1+\beta)[M(1-u)]^{1-\alpha}.$$

It follows that an increase in union power (an increase in β) will, in general equilibrium, tend to be associated with (i) a rise in unemployment (and therefore also in labour productivity) and (ii) a rise in real wages. The argument extends to other environments, including the "right-to-manage" model, in which bargaining takes place over only wages.

The impact of union power on unemployment will be ameliorated if there is a secondary sector in which wages are determined competitively and wherein workers who lose their jobs in the unionised sector can find alternative employment. However, if some of these workers choose to remain unemployed because the wage in this sector is less than their reservation wage, an increase in aggregate unemployment will still result.

Union density is the most obvious choice as a measure of union power. As panel (e) of the figure shows, this rose steadily during the Seventies, but fell back during the Eighties. Of course, union power is a multi-faceted concept, depending on institutional structure and the legal environment as well as simple density, but the series is consistent with the commonly held view that union power and influence was at its height under the Labour governments of the Seventies.

In addition to the question of quantifying union power, there is also the issue of how it is used. Decentralised bargaining by one union-firm pair may impose externalities on other bargaining units (Blanchard and Kiyotaki 1987). Moderation in wage and price setting will then raise employment and welfare, but is not individually rational. This problem would not arise in a fully competitive economy, and one approach is thus to limit union and firm monopoly power with the aim of approximating the competitive ideal, viz. the United States. Neither does the problem arise in a fully centralised economy, such as in Scandinavia, where the externalities are internalised. A halfway house with decentralised unions and firms with market power is the worst of all worlds (see Calmfors and Driffill 1988). Unfortunately it appears to be the one inhabited by the UK, as well as some other members of the European Community.

During the Sixties and Seventies successive British governments sought to limit the adverse effects of the decentralised exercise of market power through the development of corporatist machinery, such as the tripartite National Economic Development Council, and the use of incomes policy. Such policies are best thought of as tools to lower the equilibrium rate of unemployment. This is easily seen in the model above where the imposition of a (binding) side constraint $W_i < \bar{W}$ necessarily produces a lower equilibrium unemployment rate, u_{IP}:

$$u_{IP} = u/[1 + \mu u \bar{W}(1 - \rho^\gamma)/\beta\gamma]$$

where μ is the multiplier on the incomes policy constraint and u is the unemployment rate without an incomes policy.

However, the corporatist machinery and incomes policies in particular, proved a very blunt weapon for sustaining the cooperative equilibrium. An important characteristic of the British union movement is the considerable degree of autonomy accorded to local shop stewards in representing their members' interests. This meant that some groups of workers were able to negotiate extra payments through more favourable overtime arrangements, etc., and thus exploit the moderation of other groups, provoking discontent among workers in less favourable positions. In addition, the imposition of incomes policies invariably hit those groups of workers due to settle contracts in the near future especially hard, since it limited the extent to which they could recoup losses due to past unanticipated inflation. Finally firms sometimes found incomes policies inconvenient, as they limited the extent to which wages could be raised to attract scarce labour or reward productivity increases. As a result incomes policies were only politically feasible as a temporary measure.

The long history of incomes policy is summarised in the final panel of Figure 1. This series is due to Desai, Keil, and Wadhwani (1984) and tries to measure the intensity as well as the occurrence of an incomes policy, by comparing the intended rate of inflation embodied in the policy with the existing rate. The most recent experience of an incomes policy—the "Social Contract" under the Callaghan government—was initially rather successful in facilitating the first bout of disinflation during 1976–78 without a significant rise in unemployment, but came badly unstuck during the "Winter of Discontent" in the first few months of 1979. This was a significant, perhaps crucial, factor in the first election victory of Mrs. Thatcher later that year.

In the light of this experience, as well as on ideological grounds, the Thatcher government resolved to have nothing to do with incomes policies in particular and neo-corporatism in general. The private sector was to be free to make its own decisions, but would have to live with the consequences. The government chose direct legislative measures to curb union power, in particular the three Employment Acts of 1980, 1982, and 1984. The 1980 Employment Act outlawed mass secondary picketing and provided employers with legal remedies against secondary action. The 1982 Employment Act removed the previous blanket immunity of unions in tort, and made union funds liable to sequestration in cases of unlawful disputes. At the same time disputes for political reasons were outlawed, union labour-only requirements were forbidden, and employers were empowered to dismiss striking workers without facing unfair dismissal claims. The 1984 Employment Act introduced a variety of measures to increase the democratic accountability of union leaders, in particular mandatory secret ballots of the membership before undertaking strike action. Finally, other measures, such as reducing employment protection provisions and the scope of wage councils, also tended to weaken unions.

2.2 PERSISTENCE

So far nothing has been said about the role of the demand contraction in generating high unemployment. Because the effect of a demand shock on unemployment should last only as long as it takes any nominal inertia to work its way out of the economy or for the credibility of macroeconomic policies to be established, some persistence mechanism whereby high unemployment today raises the natural rate in future periods is also required if demand is to play much of a role in explaining continued high unemployment. Two main channels have been proposed, one focussing on the behaviour of those with jobs (the insiders); the other highlights on the behaviour of the unemployed (the outsiders). These provide a mechanism whereby temporary demand (or supply) shocks can have long-lasting effects on unemployment and output.

Blanchard and Summers (1986), Gottfries and Horn (1987), and Lindbeck and Snower (1988) have analysed the first channel. The idea, roughly speaking, is that the insiders fix real wages to ensure their continued employment. If an adverse shock reduces the number of insiders (assuming the unemployed cease to be members of the union), the next period's employment, absent further unforeseen shocks, will be lower by the same amount.

While this theory has a ring of truth, it cannot easily explain the outward shift in the unemployment-vacancy relationship which occurred in most high unemployment countries, and is especially pronounced in the United Kingdom. None of the extant insider models incorporate turnover, but one would expect the operation of the insider effect to be associated with a movement along a given unemployment-vacancy curve rather than an outward shift. To explain this one needs to understand why the rate at which unemployed workers are matched to vacant jobs has fallen so much. The insider mechanism thus cannot be the whole story.

The idea behind the second channel is that a history of continued unemployment itself reduces the chances of an unemployed person finding a job. This mechanism has been stressed especially by Layard and Nickell (1986, 1987). To begin with there is clear evidence that in all countries the exit rate from unemployment is much lower for the long-term unemployed than for the freshly laid off. In Britain the rate is but one-tenth of its initial value for those who have been unemployed over four years. Furthermore, as was made clear in the introduction, most of the rise in British unemployment has been due to reduced overflow and increased duration rather than the increased frequency of spells of unemployment.

Although this decline in exit rates could just be a consequence of heterogeneity among the unemployed, there are a number of ways in which genuine duration dependence might arise. First, the human capital of the unemployed depreciates, making them less attractive to employers. Second, firms may use the unemployment history of a worker as a screening device so that long duration is taken as a signal of low productivity. Finally, the unemployed might become progressively more disillusioned and apathetic as duration lengthens, leading to less intensive search activity.

There is some evidence which suggests that this mechanism helps account for the outward shift in the unemployment-vacancy relationship (Budd, Levine, and Smith 1986; Franz 1987) as well as why the downward pressure on wages is so limited at the present time (Layard and Nickell, 1987). Clearly, however, its importance is likely to vary with the generosity and, especially, the duration of unemployment benefits. We test this proposition below.

2.3 EMPIRICAL EVIDENCE

There have been an enormous number of studies of British and European unemployment. Most of these provide estimates of, at a minimum, a labour demand/price-setting relationship and a labour supply/wage-setting relationship. However, the identifying assumptions underlying such models are not to everybody's taste. Rather than provide yet another set of estimates of a small macro model, we instead provide estimates of a reduced form unemployment equation, leaving the reader to put his or her own interpretation on the underlying structure. Specifically we assume that:

$$u_t = \lambda u_t^* + (1-\lambda)u_{t-1} + \epsilon_t \quad (2)$$

where u_t^* is the "long-run" natural rate and is a function of the variables discussed above, u_{t-1} captures insider and outsider persistence mechanisms (as well as any dynamics inherent in the matching process), and ϵ_t reflects the effect of demand shocks which drive the unemployment rate away from its instantaneous natural rate. In a New Classical model with incomplete information this would simply be proportional to the price "surprise." In a world in which wages and prices are set to clear labour and goods markets ex ante, but are fixed ex post because of menu or transaction costs, it would reflect instead a quantity "surprise." In either case, under rational expectations, the forecast errors should be orthogonal to available information. (We also tried proxying nominal demand shocks directly with the change in the rate of inflation and the change in the rate of growth of nominal income; this left the coefficients on the other variables virtually unchanged.) The error term could, of course, reflect other factors driving the natural rate, but which have been omitted from the equation. Finally, both a rise in taxes and a fall in import prices will be associated with a decline in the demand for domestically produced goods, and hence may be correlated with the error. For this reason the change in the tax-import price wedge is entered into the equation lagged; in practice only the income tax component turns out to be important.

In addition to the variables already discussed we include the proportion of the working population born after 1930. One of us has suggested that labour has become more willing to risk unemployment as fewer workers are able to recall the experience of mass unemployment during the interwar years (Newell and Symons 1988). However, the trended nature of this variable means that it may also act as a control for any omitted but trended variable which affects the natural rate. In any case one would want to be wary of projecting its effects into the future.

To maximise the rather limited information in the data, we have included the interwar years in the sample. There is some evidence of heteroskedasticity across the war years, for which the estimates have been corrected, but little evidence of parameter instability (a Chow test gives $F(5,42)=0.87$). Finally a non-nested test suggests that it is better to specify the equation with the logarithm, rather than the level of the unemployment rate as the dependent variable. Our estimated equation is:

$$\Delta \log u = \underset{(2.46)}{-0.847} + \underset{(1.46)}{0.369D} + \underset{(3.40)}{13.6\Delta TY_{-1}} + \underset{(1.54)}{0.738RR} + \underset{(0.57)}{1.62MM}$$

$$+ \underset{(1.94)}{1.83UD} - \underset{(1.72)}{0.018IPD} + \underset{(1.10)}{0.322POP} - \underset{(2.49)}{.195\log u_{-1}}$$

t-statistics in parentheses.
Sample period: 1923–38, 1948–87.
Standard error 1923–38 = 0.198; Standard error 1948–87 = 0.171
LM test for second-order serial correlation: $\chi^2(2) = 4.61$
where D is a dummy on 1923–38, TY is the income tax rate, RR is the replacement ratio, MM is industrial mismatch, UD is union density, IPD is the incomes policy dummy, POP is the proportion of the working population born after 1930, Δ is the difference operator and all variables are defined net of their 1955 values. While most of the variables are not especially significant, which is unsurprising given the limited sample information, in all cases they do at least have the anticipated signs. A particularly notable feature is the high degree of persistence embodied in the equation (further legs are not significant).

This equation contains most of the contending explanations for an increase in the natural rate, yet leaves much of the rise in unemployment in 1980 and 1981 unexplained, for there are two very large positive residuals in these years which it seems natural to identify with the severe contraction in the growth of nominal demand discussed in Section 1. Conditional on this identifying assumption (which should give an

Table 4   CAUSES OF THE RISE IN UNEMPLOYMENT AFTER 1978
(% POINTS)

Due to:	1980	1982	1984	1986
Dynamics	1.4	2.0	2.4	2.6
Benefits	−0.5	−0.4	0.0	0.2
Mismatch	0.1	0.5	0.7	0.7
Working population born after 1930	0.1	0.4	0.8	1.3
Unions	−0.1	−0.9	−2.1	−3.6
Incomes policy	1.2	2.4	3.3	3.6
Income taxes	−2.4	−1.7	−1.1	−0.7
Demand	1.0	3.1	2.5	3.1
Total	0.8	5.3	6.5	7.0

upper bound on the effect of demand) Table 4 gives a breakdown of the rise in unemployment after 1978 into its constituent parts. This is obtained by dynamic simulation of the estimated equation, setting each independent variable in turn to its 1978 level.

The picture is as follows. At the start of 1979 unemployment was below its underlying long-run natural rate u_t^*, so unemployment would have shown some tendency to rise in any case (see the first row of the table). To this must be added the effects of the demise of incomes policy as manifested in the "Winter of Discontent." These two factors together raise unemployment by 45 percentage points by 1982. On top of this is a further 3 percentage points coming from the demand contraction. The weakening of the unions since then has acted to reduce unemployment, but the persistence mechanisms have ensured that this beneficial effect has been offset by the continuing effects of the demand shock as well as the end of incomes policy. In fact by 1986 the effect of incomes policy and union density exactly offset; one could say the Iron Lady obtained the same effect by decimating the unions as Jim Callaghan obtained by collaborating with them!

Unfortunately data for all the explanatory variables is not available for 1988. However, by 1987 the long-run employment rate u_t^* is some 3.5 percentage points *below* the actual unemployment rate. Consequently even in the absence of further beneficial supply-side developments, or positive demand shocks, some fall in unemployment in 1988 could have been expected. This may help to explain events in the last year.

How does this assessment relate to other studies? Both Bean and Gavosto (1989) and Newell and Symons (1988), using rather different structural frameworks, attribute around 3.5 percentage points of the rise in unemployment from the late Seventies to the early Eighties to nominal demand shocks. Layard and Nickell (1986) attribute an even stronger role to demand; they calculate that virtually all of the rise in unemployment is attributable to the demand shock. None of these studies find an important role for benefits or mismatch. There is some comfort in the fact that these studies produce similar results to the approach adopted here.

A striking feature of Table 4 is the persistence of the effects of the demand shock. This persistence seems far too large to be attributed to the ordinary lags inherent in the process of matching workers to jobs: is it due to insider or outsider mechanisms? It is difficult to say much about this from time series evidence on one country alone. Accordingly we have examined differences in the degree of persistence across countries to see whether they are better explained by insider or outsider phenomena. Although the insider mechanism need not be confined to unionised industries—it could occur anywhere incumbent labour has some monopoly power—one would expect it to be more pronounced in countries with a high level of unionisation, other things being equal. Conversely where replacement ratios are high and, in particular, where the period for which benefits are payable is long, the outsider mechanism should be relatively strong.

The basic data for this exercise is drawn from the CLE-OECD databank, augmented by data on benefit levels and duration drawn from Emerson (1986) and OECD (1988). In the spirit of equation (2), we conduct a panel regression of the standardised unemployment rate on its lagged value, where union density, replacement rates, benefit duration, and the Bruno-Sachs 1985 corporatism ranking are interacted with the lagged unemployment rate. To proxy the long-run natural rate in each country we incorporate a country specific constant, as well as union density and the replacement ratio which exhibit time series as well as cross-section variation. We also include a common time trend to control for unmodelled shifts in the natural rate (results are similar if country specific trends are included instead). The countries in the sample are Austria, Belgium, Canada, Denmark, Finland, France, Germany, Ireland, Japan, the Netherlands, Norway, Spain, Sweden, Switzerland, the United Kingdom, and the United States. The sample period runs from 1961 to 1986. We obtain (omitting country constants):

$$\Delta u = (0.0052 CORP + 0.00054 DUR + 0.239 RR - 0.263 UD - 0.151) u_{-1}$$
$$(2.01) \qquad\quad (5.60) \qquad\qquad (2.82) \qquad\; (3.41) \qquad\; (6.53)$$

$$+\; 0.313 RR \quad+\; 1.59 UD \quad+\; 0.031 t$$
$$(1.20) \qquad\quad (3.43) \qquad\quad (5.02)$$

where *CORP* is the Bruno-Sachs corporatism ranking, *DUR* is the number of weeks for which benefits are payable (set at 260 for benefits of indefinite duration), and the other variables are as defined above. *t*-statistics are in parentheses.

The results are striking. Adjustment is apparently more rapid in corporatist economies (a *low* value of *CORP* corresponds to a highly corporatist economy), but controlling for this, high unionisation actually appears to *speed up* adjustment, contrary to the insider thesis (although higher unionisation does raise the level of the natural rate, as one would expect). Per contra, the higher the replacement rate and, especially, the longer the duration of benefits, the slower is adjustment. Raising duration from 26 weeks to two years raises the coefficient on lagged unemployment by 0.042, which for an "average" country raises the mean lag from 5.3 years to 7.5 years. While this regression is crude, it does suggest that the primary source of unemployment persistence may come via the outsider rather than the insider effect.

2.4 THE VERDICT ON UNEMPLOYMENT

So is the unemployment record to be counted on the debit side of the government's ledger? Could it have done better? Some would argue for continued efforts to build consensus through the development of cor-poratist machinery, aided by the use of more flexible (tax-based?) incomes policy. Supporting a cooperative equilibrium in this fashion would in their opinion have been preferable to the painful and divisive process of breaking down power groups. A successful incomes policy would also have served as a second nominal anchor during the disinflation process.

Whether such policies could have worked is open to debate. What is certain, however, is that they were not on offer to the electorate in 1979, for it was difficult to see how an increasingly divided Labour party could deliver a pact with the unions after the disastrous "Winter of Discontent." Mrs. Thatcher declared, "There Is No Alternative," and from a purely political perspective she was probably right.

3. PRODUCTIVITY

3.1 AN INTERNATIONAL PERSPECTIVE

The defeat of inflation was by no means the only objective of the Thatcher administration. Tax cuts to reward enterprise, deregulation and privatisation to promote efficiency, and measures to limit the influence of trade unions were supposed to enhance the supply performance of the economy. A low and stable rate of inflation would simply provide the right macroeconomic environment. What evidence is there of improved performance on the supply side?

Table 5 presents data on the rate of growth of labour productivity in

Table 5 PRODUCTIVITY GROWTH (GNP/GDP PER WORKER; % PER ANNUM)

	1967–73	1973–79	1979–83	1983–87
United Kingdom	3.3	1.1	2.1	2.3
United States	0.9	0.0	0.2	1.4
France	4.4	1.3	1.6	2.1
Germany	4.4	2.2	1.3	1.7
Italy	4.9	1.7	1.0	2.5
Japan	8.4	3.0	2.5	3.5

Source: Economic Trends and OECD Economic Outlook.

the UK and its five main industrial competitors. Prior to 1973 Britain's productivity growth rate lagged behind all of them except the U.S. The second half of the Seventies saw a marked slowdown in all countries, but Britain's performance since 1979 has been relatively good, being exceeded only by that of Japan.

Table 6 puts these growth rates into perspective by comparing absolute productivity levels to those of the U.S. at various dates in the postwar era, using the OECD's estimates of 1980 purchasing power parities. This shows that, although British productivity prior to Mrs. Thatcher had been improving relative to the U.S., performance relative to the other four countries had been poor. The picture is broadly consistent with the Gerschenkron thesis; those countries that exhibited particularly rapid productivity growth during the postwar period were also those that lagged furthest behind. France, Germany, Italy, and Japan all started the postwar era with severely depleted capital stocks. Consequently they also had the biggest potential for growth. Why was Britain overtaken by her European partners? While the other countries appeared to be closing in on the U.S., Britain seemed to be converging to a lower level.

The following simple "catch-up" regression makes this point forcibly. The sample is a panel of the nineteen countries in the CLE-OECD data bank running from 1950 to 1980, i.e., prior to Mrs. Thatcher. The dependent variable is the rate of growth of productivity in the country in question relative to the rate of growth of productivity in the leading country (ΔRP). This is related to (the logarithm) of lagged relative productivity (RP_{-1}) and a string of variables which might explain asymptotic differences in productivity levels. These are (all measured relative to the lead country): days lost through industrial action per worker to control for the degree of conflict between labour and capital (STR); the proportion of the 20–24 age group in higher education to control for differences in the level of human capital (EDN); the share of taxes in total income to

Table 6   RELATIVE OUTPUT PER WORKER (US=100, AT 1980
           PURCHASING POWER PARITIES)

	1951	1960	1970	1980
United Kingdom	55.2	56.7	60.4	66.5
France	38.9	48.2	63.9	80.7
Germany	37.1	50.9	63.5	77.9
Italy	34.1	57.9	67.9	79.4
Japan	16.0	23.5	46.1	62.8

Source: OECD *National Accounts.*

control for any effect on the effort levels of both workers and managers (TAX); and union density as a proxy for union power (UD). In addition, for the UK only, there is a constant (D) to allow for any unexplained difference in long-run productivity levels. Note that physical capital per worker is not included as a regressor. Obviously this is central to explaining productivity differences in the short-run. However, in the long run capital is endogenous and, assuming perfect capital mobility and access by all countries to an identical production technology, differences in capital per worker should reflect cross-country differences in total factor productivity due to variables such as tax rates and skill levels. The estimated equations can thus be thought of as simple reduced forms. Estimation by SUR (for brevity, diagnostics for individual countries are not presented) gives, with t-statistics in parentheses:

$$\Delta RP = -.0439RP_{-1} - .0008STR + .0353EDN - .0042TAX - .0024UD - .0128D$$
$$(9.86)\phantom{RP_{-1}}\ (0.33)\ (4.48)\ (2.92)\ (0.58)\ (7.33)$$

Given the simplicity of the model, the results are suprisingly sensible. Most of the variables enter as one would expect; viz. higher taxes lower long-run relative productivity, an expansion in higher education tends to raise relative productivity and the productivity "gap" is eliminated at around 4% per annum. The dummy for the UK is highly significant and implies an asymptotic productivity level some 30–35% below other countries with a similar structure. This is despite controlling for some of the most frequently cited reasons for Britain's poor relative performance: high taxes, low skills, bad industrial relations, and excessive union power. Countries such as Sweden have high tax rates and high union density, but also a high relative productivity level. What is so special about the United Kingdom? Any explanation for Britain's poor productivity performance—and its possible reversal under Mrs. Thatcher—must come to grips with this peculiarity. With this as background let us therefore turn to a closer examination of recent experience.

3.2 THE PRODUCTIVITY REBOUND

The acceleration in productivity growth is not apparently due to a revival in investment, which has grown strongly only very recently, but rather to rapid total factor productivity (TFP) growth. We use a measure that caters both for labour hoarding and imperfect competition in product markets. Start by assuming a CRS technology of the form $Y=HF(AN,BK)$ where H is effective hours worked per shift, A is labour-augmenting technical progress and B is capital-augmenting technical progress. Following Hall (1986), *TFP* growth ($\hat{X}$) is given by:

$$\hat{X} \equiv \hat{Y} - \hat{H} - \mu S_N \hat{N} - (1 - \mu S_N)\hat{K} = \mu S_N \hat{A} + (1 - \mu S_N)\hat{B} \quad (3)$$

where a caret denotes a growth rate, μ is the ratio of price to marginal cost, and S_i is the share of factor i. As a simple correction for the possibility that observed hours, H_0, may exceed effective hours, we employ the correction suggested by Muellbauer (1986):

$$h = h_N + (H_0 - H_N)/H_N - \beta H_N/(H_0 - H_N)$$

where lower case letters denote logarithms, H_N is a measure of normal hours, and β is a parameter to be estimated. Since the overtime hours term $(H_0 - H_N)/H_N$ is procyclical, this last term should also control for labour hoarding along the heads dimension.

For each two-digit industry, over the period 1969–86, we estimate the regression:

$$\Delta[y - h_n - (H - H_N)/H_N - k]_t = \alpha - \beta \Delta[H_N/(H_0 - H_N)]_t + \mu[S_N \Delta(n - k)]_t + u_t$$

using the rate of growth of total domestic output[1] and the rate of growth of world output as instruments for the endogenous (labour-share-weighted) capital-labour ratio. We then use the associated estimates to calculate $\alpha + u_t$. We allow for shifts in the drift parameter, α, at the beginning of 1974 and again at the beginning of 1980.

For brevity we shall not report the full regression results for each industry here. The mean estimates of μ is 1.52. Most industries are fairly close to this, although the individual standard errors are sometimes quite large. However, there are a few industries which produce unreasonable estimates of μ. For this reason we have employed a Bayesian estimator in which the prior distribution of μ is normal with a mean of 1.33 and a standard deviation of 0.5, while the prior distribution on the other parameters is diffuse. This is sufficient to eliminate any a priori implausible estimates of μ, which might otherwise contaminate the estimates of TFP growth.

1. Domestic output will be correlated with the equation error if economy-wide productivity shocks are an important source of economic fluctuations. Under the maintained hypothesis that the rate of growth of world output is a valid instrument, the hypothesis that domestic output is uncorrelated with the equation error can be tested with the aid of the usual Lagrange-Multiplier instrument orthogonality test. For only two out of the twenty-six industries is the χ^2 statistic significant at the 95% level and for the twenty-six industries taken together the test statistic is 31.3, distributed as $\chi^2(26)$.

The associated TFP growth rates over key sub-periods appear in Table 7. Two points are worth making. First, although politicians and the media began to draw attention to the productivity miracle only in the mid-Eighties, for some industries the revival can be dated as early as 1980. Industries like metal manufacture and shipbuilding are cases in point. Second, the productivity revival is not confined to manufacturing, although it is more pronounced there. Construction, distribution, transport, banking, and other services all show an acceleration.

We have also calculated a second set of estimates of TFP growth for industries in the manufacturing sector. These are based on the same methodology except that they use different capital stock estimates. A number of authors have suggested that the official capital stock figures may overstate the rate of capital accumulation during the second half of

Table 7   TOTAL FACTOR PRODUCTIVITY GROWTH BY INDUSTRY (PER CENT PER ANNUM)

	1969–73	1973–79	1979–82	1982–86
Agriculture	3.2	0.5	7.5	2.8
Coal	−0.9	−0.6	1.8	5.6
Oil and natural gas	22.6	71.8	−16.7	11.8
Oil processing	−5.8	−4.1	−0.6	−0.7
Electricity, gas, and water	7.4	2.5	1.2	3.9
Manufacturing Industries:				
Metal manufacture	2.4	3.0	13.9	6.0
Other mineral products	6.6	1.5	2.0	4.2
Chemicals	5.8	1.1	3.1	5.5
Other metal products	1.2	−0.8	1.0	0.5
Mechanical engineering	3.3	0.7	3.5	2.4
Electrical engineering	7.8	3.8	5.9	6.5
Motor vehicles	1.3	−0.9	6.6	4.4
Ships and aircraft	5.7	−1.9	7.1	5.1
Food	2.5	1.1	4.3	1.9
Drink and tobacco	2.9	0.8	0.9	3.4
Textiles	4.5	1.4	3.3	4.9
Leather, footwear, and clothing	3.9	4.9	3.4	7.3
Timber	5.6	−1.4	0.2	−0.3
Paper	4.0	1.7	3.3	2.6
Rubber	4.2	3.6	4.0	7.9
Construction	2.8	0.0	1.8	3.9
Distribution	3.2	0.1	1.9	2.7
Transport	6.5	1.3	2.8	4.1
Communications	3.9	3.4	2.6	4.8
Banking	0.6	0.4	2.2	2.7
Other services	−2.6	−1.6	1.5	0.3

the Seventies and the early Eighties when there was extensive unre-
corded scrapping following the two oil price shocks. Conversely, the rate
of capital accumulation during the mid-Eighties is likely to have been
understated as some imputed retirements would already have taken
place.

Quantifying the size of this effect is no easy matter, but Wadhwani
and Wall (1986), provide an alternative time series from 1972 to 1982 for
total manufacturing using a firm's historic cost accounts, which suggests
a cumulative overprediction of around 14% between 1974 and 1982.
They provided us with alternative estimates of the rate of capital accumulation from 1972 until 1982 by industry. These were then used in place of
the official figures for this period and the estimates for after 1982 adjusted upwards to take account of the lower based.

For brevity, the results (available on request) are not reported here.
However, the (unweighted) mean annual TFP growth rates over 1973–
79, 1979–82, and 1982–86 are, respectively, 1.3%, 3.6%, and 4.0%. The
corresponding figures for Table 7 are 1.2%, 4.2%, and 4.2%. Thus the
attenuation in the estimated acceleration in TFP growth is really very
modest. Furthermore, the correlation across industries of the two different measures of the TFP acceleration between 1969–79 and 1980–86 is
also very high at 0.95. This suggests that explanations for differences in
productivity performance across industries may not depend too critically
on the choice of measure. However, to be on the safe side the estimates
reported below employ both measures.

Finally, technical progress both before and after 1980 seems to be
primarily labour-augmenting. Suppose that in industry i, $A_i = \bar{A} + \tilde{A}_i$,
and $B_i = \bar{B} + \tilde{B}_i$, where $\bar{A}$ and $\bar{B}$ are the economy-wide average levels of
labour and capital-augmenting technical progress respectively. Then (cf.
equation (3)):

$$\hat{X}_i = (\mu S_N)_i \bar{A} + (1 - \mu S_N)_i \bar{B} + (\mu S_N)_i \tilde{A}_i + (1 - \mu S_N)_i \tilde{B}_i.$$

Provided $\tilde{A}_i$ and $\tilde{B}_i$ are uncorrelated with $(\mu S_N)_i$, consistent estimates of $\bar{A}$
and $\bar{B}$ can be obtained from a cross-section regression of TFP growth on
(μS_N) and $(1 - \mu S_N)$. Table 8 reports the results of such a regression for
mean TFP growth over 1969–79 and 1980–86 for the TFP measures. In
each case the estimate of $\bar{B}$ is near zero and totally insignificant suggesting that technical progress is indeed labour-augmenting. This suggests
that in trying to understand the sources of the productivity revival one
should focus on factors likely to enhance the efficiency of labour rather
than capital.

3.3 EXPLANATIONS FOR THE PRODUCTIVITY REBOUND

Muellbauer (1986) cites five main hypotheses for the acceleration in productivity growth after 1980. Two of these have already been implicitly addressed and dismissed: the effects of labour hoarding and the mismeasurement of capital due to early retirements. The three other hypotheses are:

(i) A Schumpeterian "gale of innovation" due to the spread of the microchip and the introduction of computerised technology;
(ii) A "batting-average" effect whereby the deep recession of 1980–81 led to the closure of the least efficient plants, thus raising the average productivity of those who remained in business;
(iii) An improvement in industrial relations as a result of the weakening of the union movement.

To these three hypotheses we might add two others:

(iv) A "kick-in-the-pants" effect whereby a tightening of product market conditions and increased threat of takeover led to the elimination of managerial slack;
(v) Increased effort by workers and managers resulting from cuts in income taxes.

Three of these explanations have in common that the severity of the 1980–81 recession was itself a primary cause of the productivity boom. The most telling way to test this hypothesis is to examine the consequences of the even greater recession of 1929–31. Between 1933 and 1936

Table 8 TECHNICAL PROGRESS IS LABOUR-AUGMENTING

Dependent Variable	μS_N	$(1-\mu S_N)$	$\bar{R}^2$
(1) $\hat{X}_1(1969\text{--}79)$	0.0209 (4.78)	−0.0123 (0.77)	0.116
(2) $\hat{X}_1(1980\text{--}86)$	0.0387 (9.73)	−0.0076 (0.05)	0.243
(3) $\hat{X}_2(1969\text{--}79)$	0.0250 (7.49)	0.084 (0.73)	0.028
(4) $\hat{X}_2(1980\text{--}86)$	0.0375 (8.17)	−0.020 (0.95)	0.232

Notes: White t-statistics in parentheses.
Rows (1) −− (2) use basic TFP measure.
Rows (3) −− (4) use alternative capital stock measure

manufacturing productivity grew 4.7% per annum; some 1.7 percentage points faster than it had prior to 1929, but over 1936–38 productivity actually fell slightly. We conclude that the Great Depression did not deliver a productivity breakthrough in Britain. This seems to hold a fortiori for other countries during the interwar period. Finally and more recently, there are a number of European economies which experienced deep recessions in the Eighties, but did not experience a spurt in productivity growth. However, while there seems to be no necessary link between deep recessions and subsequent rapid productivity growth, it is nevertheless still possible that any, or all, of the five mechanisms may have played a role in Britain's productivity revival.

There may be something to the "gale of innovation" explanation although it is inevitably difficult to quantify. The *New Earnings Survey* shows that the relative wages of computer personnel and those in information technology have risen more than most during the Thatcher years, which is at least consistent with the "microchip" hypotheses. On the other hand to the extent that such new technology is embodied in capital one would expect its adoption to be associated with a burst of investment, yet investment in plant and machinery remained very depressed until 1984. To be sure, there are some industries where the adoption of new technology has totally altered the character of production. Yet often this technology had been available for some time, and it was only a change in the climate of industrial relations which permitted its introduction. The introduction of direct computerised typesetting and the consequent elimination of the "hot metal" printworkers in the newspaper industry is a classic example. Finally one would surely have expected such a microchip-led spurt of productivity growth to be a worldwide phenomenon, yet as the international comparisons made clear, an acceleration in productivity growth during the Eighties is a primarily British phenomenon.

The second hypothesis, the batting average-effect, looks increasingly less plausible as time passes. This produces a once-and-for-all change in the level of productivity, and should thus have come to a halt after 1982 as the economy entered the recovery phase. So it is difficult to explain the continued rapid productivity growth of the last few years with this hypothesis. Furthermore Oulton (1987) shows that while the level of productivity is in general higher in large plants, the 1980–81 recession was associated with a shift in employment *away* from large plants. Consequently there was, if anything, a reverse batting average-effect in which the high productivity producers were eliminated.

Let us now turn to the fourth hypothesis, the kick-in-the-pants effect. When managerial effort cannot be accurately monitored, inefficiencies are likely to arise. These are likely to be greater when the threat of bankruptcy or takeover is low. Governments during the Sixties and Seventies showed themselves willing to finance the operating deficits of the nationalised industries and to subsidise declining private firms and industries. Whatever the merits of this from a social point of view, it is likely to have reduced pressure on managers. Mrs. Thatcher's government slashed industrial subsidies, and set the nationalised industries the target of breaking even with the ultimate aim of returning them to the private sector. Furthermore the removal of exchange controls and increasing capital market integration has made firms more open to takeover than before.

It is virtually impossible to quantify the importance of this channel. Some rather weak evidence against its significance is provided by Table 8, for if improved management were the key, then one might expect capital productivity as well as labour productivity to have improved. Yet the table suggests that even after 1979 most of the TFP growth seems to have been labour-augmenting in nature. One should not push this too far, however, because managerial inefficiencies might well be mostly manifested in the way labour is deployed. Furthermore, to some extent increased managerial efficiency is simply the counterpart of the reduction in union power that underlies the "industrial relations" hypothesis.

The tax-cut argument must also hinge on increased managerial effort, for the reduction in marginal tax rates at average earnings levels has been fairly modest, even to the present (see Dilnot et al. 1987). By contrast the top rate of tax has been halved from 83% in 1979 to 40% today. As we shall see, the before-tax incomes of high earners have at the same time risen, which some have taken as an indication that effort is highly responsive to marginal tax rates (Minford and Ashton 1988). However, the findings of Holland (1977) suggest that even for managers and the professions, the responsiveness of effort to changes in taxes is negligible (see also Dilnot and Kell 1988). Cuts in marginal tax rates at the upper end of the earnings distribution may have stimulated entrepreneurship—the rate of new business formation in 1987 was some 40% higher than in 1979—but that can scarcely have had a measurable effect on the productivity figures which are dominated by firms that were already in existence in 1979.

Any explanation of the productivity rebound must therefore focus on the role of labour, and there is little doubt that the third hypothesis, a change in the climate of industrial relations, is a strong candidate (e.g., Metcalf 1988, and the many references therein; Layard and Nickell 1989). However, there is less agreement on the precise channel and whether changes in structure due to legislation or changes in the economic environment should take the credit.

The legal measures to reduce the power of unions were discussed above in Section 2. It is easy to see that the recession of 1980–81 is also likely to have reduced the relative bargaining strength of unions. On one hand increased unemployment raises the prospective cost to the worker of layoff or redundancy. On the other hand the ability of management to meet high wage demands will have been limited by increased product market pressures arising from falling demand generally and in the tradeables sector by the appreciation of sterling. The difference, of course, is that this weakening in the relative position of unions would not be expected to persist as the economy recovered. By contrast the reduction in union power wrought by politico-legal changes might well be more permanent.

3.4 MODELLING THE PRODUCTIVITY REBOUND: THE IMPORTANCE OF MULTI-UNIONISM

While it is easy to document possible reasons for a reduction in union power, it is, from a theoretical perspective, less clear how this can explain events, for as we saw in Section 2.1.4., one would expect a reduction in union power to be associated with a *fall* in own-product wages. Yet even the real wages of unskilled workers have been rising in the last decade.

The discussion of Section 2.1.4 also suggests one solution. There we showed that, in a unionised economy, the presence of an incomes policy would result in lower unemployment, real wages and productivity than would be delivered under free collective bargaining. The demise of the Social Contract during the "Winter of Discontent" in early 1979 signalled the end of centralised incomes policies and allowed wage bargainers to move to a privately efficient point involving higher productivity and higher wages. The difficulty with this thesis is that while it could help to explain the rapid productivity growth, rising real wages, and falling employment observed during 1980–82, it is a little difficult to believe that the rapid productivity growth since then is simply the consequence of the unwinding of incomes policies. Furthermore, what is involved is a movement along a given production frontier, while the calculations in Section 3.3 suggested that what is required is an outward shift of that frontier in the guise of labour-augmenting technical progress.[2] So it

2. With bargaining over wages and employment, a change in union power, or the removal of the constraints imposed by incomes policies, would lead to a change in μ. If, however, μ is held constant as in the calculations underlying $\hat{X}_1$ and $\hat{X}_2$, this would be interpreted instead as a change in TFP growth. Measured TFP growth $\hat{X}$ is then given by:

$$\hat{X} = \hat{X}^* + (\mu' - \mu)S_N(\hat{N} - \hat{K})$$

where $\hat{X}^*$ is true total factor productivity growth and μ' is the new ratio of price to marginal cost. If the capital-labour ratio is rising at 3% per annum one would need $(\mu' - \mu) \approx -0.5$ to produce a spurious acceleration in TFP growth of one percentage point. Hence it requires a very large fall in μ to rationalise the data.

seems that an increase in the efficiency with which labour is used must be a central part of any explanation of the productivity rebound.

The only authors that we are aware of who tackle this issue seriously are Jackman, Layard, and Nickell (1989, ch. 5). They suggest that the Seventies were characterised by bargaining over both wages and effort. By contrast, in the Eighties they argue that the restoration of the right-to-manage took effort out of the province of negotiation. In their model effort and wages are both higher in general equilibrium when effort is not an object of the bargain, while unemployment is unchanged. The problem with this line of argument, however, is that it does not explain *why* effort should have ceased to be an object of negotiation in the Eighties, since from the point of view of the firm and the union, it is in their mutual interest to negotiate over as wide a set of variables as possible. Yet the argument is important in focussing on the importance of changes in efficiency, because the industrial relations evidence quoted by Metcalf (1988) suggests that a major ingredient of the productivity revival has been an end to overmanning, demarcation, and similar restrictive practices. The theoretical conundrum is to explain: first, how these could ever have been rational to begin with and second, why other countries with similar, or higher unionisation rates were not equally affected.

A key ingredient is, we believe, the preponderance of multi-union firms and internecine divisions within single unions. For historical reasons much of the British trade union movement is organised along craft rather than firm or industry lines. Table 9, drawn from the 1984 *Workplace Industrial Relations Survey*, reports the prevalence of multi-unionism for both manual and non-manual workers. Furthermore it is not just the

Table 9   MULTI-UNIONISM IN 1980 AND 1984 (ALL ESTABLISHMENTS, %)

	Manual Workers		Non-Manual Workers	
	1980	1984	1980	1984
Number of unions				
1	65	65	43	39
2 or more	35	35	57	61
Number of bargaining units				
1	77	82	57	61
2 or more	20	18	42	37
Unknown	2	1	1	2

Source: Millward and Stevens (1986).

prevalence of multiple bargaining units within the firm that is notable. Shop stewards typically have a considerable degree of autonomy (e.g., Flanagan, Soskice, and Ulman 1983, p. 364).

In our view it is this unique complexity of British union organisation that helps to explain the Thatcher productivity "miracle." Independent of any extra transaction costs arising from the need for management to deal with a number of unions or work force representatives, agreements between management and one group of workers may create externalities for another group. In particular, in isolation a group of workers may perceive restrictive practices as good for the employment of its members, while from the perspective of the firm and its work force as a whole, they lower productivity and discourage employment.

In an appendix we make this idea more precise in a model that combines elements of the union and policy coordination literatures. Typically, although for reasons not well understood, unions negotiate over manning levels rather than employment directly, which is left to the discretion of management (see Oswald and Turnbull 1985). An overmanning requirement has two effects on employment. First, it raises employment directly by increasing labour requirements for given output and production techniques; second, it raises the cost of labour in efficiency units leading to a reduction in the level of output and substitution away from that sort of labour to other sorts of labour or more capital intensive forms of production. The first effect dominates if, and only if, the elasticity of demand for the type of labour governed by the overmanning requirement is less than unity.

When the work force is fragmented into a number of bargaining units representing labour types that are not close substitutes for each other, this condition is more likely to be fulfilled. If this is the case, a union acting in isolation will perceive overmanning arrangements as a way of protecting jobs, and one which does them less harm than lowering wages. However, this results in a fall in the marginal product of other types of labour, so reducing the demand for those types at given wages and with given manning arrangements. The result is an inefficient equilibrium with low wages and low productivity.

How does this help to explain the productivity "miracle"? If the unions acted as one, this would internalise the externalities imposed on other types of labour by overmanning requirements; indeed in the model of the appendix, the coordinated equilibrium involves no overmanning whatsoever. However, this is *not* what we believe has happened, for as Table 9 shows, the extent of multi-unionism hardly changed between 1980 and 1984. (There has been a growth in single union deals but their number is still small; see Bassett 1986.) There has not been a major change in the underlying structure. However, a reduction in union power, whether wrought by the recession or legislation, has the effect of reducing the degree of overmanning and thus shifts the non-cooperative equilibrium *toward* the cooperative one. Furthermore, in general equilibrium it turns out that the resulting increase in efficiency and productivity is actually associated with an *increase* in real wages (provided some conditions on tastes and technology are satisfied), despite the fall in union power.

3.5 EMPIRICAL EVIDENCE

The thesis developed above suggests that productivity gains are likely to have been greatest in firms with multiple bargaining units, and where there is scope for individual shop stewards to defend sectional interests even where there is only one union. Direct information on the prevalence of multiple bargaining units can be extracted from the *Workplace Industrial Relations Survey.* However, this does not cover the second aspect, the degree of shop steward independence within single unions. Since job diversity is likely to be greater in large plants, one would also expect the acceleration in TFP growth to have been most pronounced in large plants. Furthermore, as noted by Millward and Stevens (1986), there is a very strong relationship between establishment size and the prevalence of multiple bargaining units. Eighty-five percent of establishments with fewer than a hundred employees were covered by a single bargaining unit, while for establishments with a thousand or more employees the proportion is only 46%. Given the limited degrees of freedom available we therefore choose to use a measure of average plant size as a single control for both the presence of multiple bargaining units and the degree of individual steward autonomy in our empirical work.

Table 10 reports the results of tests of the hypothesis that the differences in TFP growth across industries are correlated with plant size. The regressand is the change[3] in average TFP growth between 1974–79 and 1980–86 for each of the two-digit manufacturing industries in Table 7 (some of the regressors are not available outside manufacturing); results are reported for both the TFP measures. The independent variables are

---

3. In its basic form the model predicts that uncoordinated bargaining with multiple bargaining units should reduce the *level* of productivity below what would be achieved with a single union. This suggests that the dependent variable should be the level of the rate of TFP growth between, say, 1979 and 1986, rather than the change in the rate of TFP growth. In fact when the rate of TFP growth 1974–79 is included as a regressor, it attracts a small coefficient of around −0.1 and is invariably insignificant, suggesting that the difference formulation is indeed appropriate. The most likely interpretation is that the presence of lagged TFP growth controls for inter-industry differences in TFP growth not captured by the other regressors.

the share of employment in the industry accounted for by establishments of more than five hundred employees (our plant size variable), the proportion of manual workers in the industry covered by a collective agreement, and a demand shock variable.

We have employed two proxies for the last variable. The first is the percentage fall in employment in the industry between 1979 and 1982 (measured as a negative number). Metcalf (1988) and Layard and Nickell (1989) both employ this variable in their investigations of the productivity revival. Metcalf interprets this as a "fear factor"—which could be the result of a weakening of unions as well as tightening product market conditions. Layard and Nickell, however, associate this specifically with the impact of the 1980–81 recession. This is problematic if the increase in productivity was the result of the legislation to weaken unions. This is not adequately controlled for in the rest of the equation. In that case the coefficient on the employment shock variable will be biased downward, leading one to overestimate the importance of the recession in generating the productivity revival. We have therefore also used the percentage fall in output in the industry over the same period as an alternative demand shock variable. Since this variable will, if anything, be positively correlated with the equation error it should enable us to bound the effect of the recession. The top half of Table 10 reports results using the employment fall as an explanatory variable, while the bottom half reports results using the output fall.

Despite the small sample size, the results are surprisingly good. The

Table 10   SOURCES OF ACCELERATION IN TFP GROWTH, 1980–86 ON 1973–79

Dependent Variable	Constant	Collective Agreement	Shakeout	Proportion of Large Firms	$\bar{R}^2$
(1) $\Delta \hat{X}_1$	−0.0762 (1.97)	0.0840 (1.48)	−0.0802 (2.43)	0.0567 (2.98)	0.72
(2) $\Delta \hat{X}_2$	−0.0810 (2.79)	0.0829 (1.95)	−0.1113 (4.50)	0.0439 (3.08)	0.81
(3) $\Delta \hat{X}_1$	−0.0724 (1.68)	0.0889 (1.40)	−0.0499 (1.60)	0.0628 (2.74)	0.66
(4) $\Delta \hat{X}_2$	−0.0761 (2.15)	0.0861 (1.66)	−0.0806 (3.16)	0.0559 (2.98)	0.71

Note: Rows 1–2 use the percentage fall in employment between 1979 and 1982 as the demand shock variable. Rows 3–4 use the percentage fall in output between 1979 and 1982 as the demand shock variable.
Rows 1 and 3 use the basic TFP measure.
Rows 2 and 4 use the alternative capital stock measure.

equations explain a high degree of the cross-section variation in total TFP growth rates, and in all four regressions the explanatory variables have the anticipated signs and, in the case of the shock and firm size variables are usually highly significant. The shock variable remains important even when the output rather than the employment fall is used. Furthermore, when the first two regressions are estimated by Instrumental Variables using the output fall as an instrument for the potentially endogenous employment fall, the point estimates of the coefficients are virtually identical. This suggests that the employment fall is *not* picking up any effect from anti-union legislation.

Focussing attention on the final set of estimates, we see that a 10% fall in output between 1979 and 1982 was associated with a 0.8 percentage point increase in TFP growth, while firms with more than 500 employees on average experienced a 0.6 percentage point increase in TFP growth. Finally a 10% increase in union coverage is associated with a 0.9 percentage point increase in TFP growth. These results are certainly consistent with our basic hypothesis.

How do these results compare with other studies? Both Metcalf, and Layard and Nickell using three-digit industry level data find the employment shock significant, although neither find any relationship between productivity growth and unionisation.[4] Layard and Nickell do, however, report evidence from a panel of firms which suggests that unionisation matters. Neither Metcalf nor Layard and Nickell include a variable like plant size so their results do not shed light on the particular hypothesis under investigation here.

There are, however, a wealth of studies investigating Britain's relatively poor productivity performance prior to the Thatcher revolution which do shed light on the industrial relations explanation of the productivity miracle. Davies and Caves (1987) compare productivity in UK and U.S. three-digit manufacturing industries in 1967–68 and 1977, and find that relative productivity performance is often especially bad in large plants, which they ascribe to either poor industrial relations or bad management. Pratten (1976) finds that of the 27% productivity differential in 1972 between German and UK plants of the same international company, some 12 percentage points are directly attributed to restrictive practices, overmanning, and industrial disputes. (Since these will also discourage capital formation the total effect on productivity will be even greater.) Finally a major study by Prais (1981) of ten industries during the

4. Metcalf uses the level rather than the change in productivity growth over 1980–85 as the dependent variable. This greatly weakens the effect of the union variables by failing to control for underlying differences in productivity growth rates across industries (see footnote 3). Layard and Nickell's results, however, do not suffer from this problem.

Sixties and Seventies found that overmanning and restrictive practices were a major constraint in six of them and that large plants especially suffered from industrial relations difficulties. However, Prais also found that in the other four industries, inadequate training and skills were the chief factor retarding productivity, which has important implications for the sustainability of the productivity revival.

3.6 CAN THE PRODUCTIVITY MIRACLE CONTINUE?

Our estimates in Section 3.1 suggested that prior to the election of Mrs. Thatcher, the UK was converging to a level of productivity some 30–35% below its main industrial partners. It may be that Britain has at last turned the corner and begun to eliminate that differential, holding out the prospect of continued rapid productivity growth and rising real incomes for some time to come. Such an optimistic assessment is premature, however.

To begin with it is not obvious how durable are the productivity gains of the last few years. To the extent that the decline in union power is a cyclical phenomenon reflecting high levels of unemployment, rather than the result of legislative changes, economic growth and declining unemployment may put a halt to the continued elimination of overmanning. Indeed the simple one-shot game in the appendix suggests that the productivity gains of the last few years might even be reversed as the uncoordinated equilibrium starts to shift away from the cooperative equilibrium. We think this is unlikely, for once workers have experienced the higher income generated by a more efficient, productive economy they are unlikely to want to revert to the status quo ante, and it may be easier to maintain an already established equilibrium necessitating a degree of cooperation than to establish a cooperative equilibrium in the first place. But the new equilibrium may be fragile, and it may prove difficult to coordinate further moves toward a fully efficient equilibrium without changes in organisational structure. Yet as noted above the extent of multi-unionism has changed little. Except for the legislative changes embodied in the Employment Acts, there does not appear to have been any marked changes in underlying structure which are likely to foster continued erosion of the productivity differential between the UK and its competitors.

Second, even if this assessment is too pessimistic, the studies by Prais (1981), Daly, Hitchens, and Wagner (1985), and Steedman and Wagner (1987) suggest that a lack of technical skills is increasingly important as a factor leading to poor relative productivity performance. Steedman (1987) and Prais and Wagner (1988) elaborate on this and show that, despite government initiatives, the gap between the vocational skill levels of British workers and their French and German counterparts seems to be widening rather than closing. At the end of the day, even if the productivity revival does not run out of steam on its own, a lack of human capital is very likely to bring it to a halt.

4. Income Distribution

While there may have been real gains under the Thatcher regime, they have so far not been shared widely, for the Thatcher years have coincided with a remarkable widening of the income distribution in the UK, reversing a long-established trend. This is true not only after taxes, but also of raw pre-tax earnings, which is rather more surprising. This widening occurred both within and between occupations. Perhaps the most significant divergence was between white and blue collar workers (Table 11, row 1), but there has been an important increase in earnings dispersion within each grouping as shown by the last four rows of Table 11.

Who in particular prospered? Within the non-manual occupation, the *New Earnings Survey* shows a very striking increase by business and administration professionals (some 22 relative points between 1979 and 1988). Within this broad category the most successful occupations have been finance specialists, managers and executives, and accountants—in general those concerned with the running of private business. But all the higher-status non-manual occupations showed increases in both relative earnings and employment.

The increase in dispersion is quite general throughout all occupations except for government employees. There also seems to be a positive correlation across occupations between growth of relative earnings and the dispersion of earnings within the occupation. However earnings dispersion increased absolutely even for manual workers, for whom both relative earnings and employment fell.

Table 11   CHANGES IN THE DISTRIBUTION OF EARNINGS

	1969	1979	1988
Non-manual males relative to manual males	1.34	1.22	1.43
Upper decile as proportion[a] of median, manual males	1.47	1.39	1.48
Lower decile as proportion[a] of median, manual males	0.73	0.73	0.69
Upper decile as proportion of median non-manual males	1.91	1.69	1.80
Lower decile as proportion of median non-manual males	0.61	0.63	0.58

Note: (a) Refers to straight-time earnings. Other rows employ weekly earnings.
Source: New Earnings Survey (various).

An obvious question is whether this increase in the dispersion of pre-tax earnings is part of a global phenomenon, or whether it is peculiar to the UK, and hence possibly a consequence of government policy. The paper by Frank Levy in this volume shows a remarkably similar widening, for instance, of the earnings distribution in the U.S. during the Eighties. While there are some similarities with behaviour in other industrialised countries, it is clear that Britain is something of an outlier. Thus the OECD (1987) concludes that whereas the manual/non-manual differential narrowed by around 5–10% in most OECD countries during the Seventies (with the notable exception of Germany where the opposite occurred), since then it has been mostly static or else risen only slightly. The size of the British increase is clearly quite exceptional. These remarks apply equally well to managerial staff in particular (OECD, op. cit., chart 3.3). While time series data on the dispersion of manual wages is not readily available across countries, the skilled/unskilled differential for manual workers displays a similar pattern, with only the UK among the European countries showing a very pronounced widening in the Eighties (OECD, op. cit., chart 3.4).

So what has caused this increase in earnings dispersion? One possibility is the operation of a strong substitution effect toward increased labour supply resulting from reductions in income taxes. One of Mrs. Thatcher's first acts was to reduce drastically the top rates of income taxes, and this has been followed in recent years by cuts in the basic rate (down to 25% from 33% in 1979). Despite this, personal income tax receipts have actually increased from 17.4% of GDP in 1979 to 18% in 1987, which might look like evidence of a movement down the inefficient part of a Laffer curve. Given the concentration of the tax cuts at the top end of the income distribution, one would expect to see greater increases in labour supply at the top end and therefore an increase in the spread of weekly earnings. However, if all that is involved is an increase in the supply of hours one would also expect to see a *narrowing* of the dispersion of hourly wages. The second and third rows of Table 11 relating to movements within manual occupations employ hourly wage rates and thus contradict the hypothesis. Information on hours worked for non-manuals is not available (and indeed it is not clear that it would be meaningful for many occupations if it were), so it is possible that the behaviour of differentials within non-manuals, as well as the non-manual/manual differential (which also uses weekly earnings for manuals), is simply a consequence of changes in relative hours. On the whole we think this is unlikely, however. It is possible that the behaviour of all the differentials, including those within the manual group, reflects increased effort where pay is performance related, but for the reasons set out in Section 3.3, increased effort at higher incomes is unlikely to be the explanation. The available evidence just does not suggest that the elasticity of the supply of effort is sufficiently large for the relevant groups. Having said that, we should note that striking similarity with the U.S., which has also experienced a reduction in the progressivity of the tax system. Were the same phenomenon to happen in other tax-cutting countries (Sweden?) then one would be led to put more weight on this explanation. As the Ian Fleming character Auric Goldfinger remarked, "Once is happenstance, twice is coincidence, but three times, Mr. Bond, is enemy action."

We believe rather that two other factors have been in operation. The first is the unwinding of the incomes policy. As we noted in Section 2, incomes policies were in operation for around 60% of the time between 1961 and 1979. Many of these policies were of the fixed sum, rather than fixed percentage, variety and thus automatically gave higher percentage increases to lower paid workers (such provisions were often essential in gaining TUC assent). Consequently, the narrowing of earnings differentials prior to 1979 is hardly surprising. Furthermore, the OECD (1987) attribute much of the narrowing that occurred in other European countries over this period to the operation of incomes policies.

The second factor is a by-product of our explanation of the productivity rebound. We attributed much of this to the ending of overmanning and restrictive practices. This not only raises the efficiency of the labour directly concerned, but will also raise the marginal product of other factors (provided they are cooperant). Consequently one would expect to see the earnings of capital, managers, skilled workers, and so forth also rising. In the appendix we show that a reduction in union power which leads to the end of overmanning not only raises the wages of the unionised workers in general equilibrium, but is also likely to lead to an increase in the relative wages of other sorts of labour, i.e., the latter are the major beneficiaries of the elimination of inefficient practices.

Given the increased participation of married women in the labour force, it is perhaps more useful to focus on what is happening to households rather than individuals when it comes to considering the welfare implications of developments in the income distribution. Table 12 compares the household income distribution before and after the operation of the tax and benefit system. Final incomes are now significantly less equal than before Mrs. Thatcher took office in 1979: it is as if the top quintile of households has imposed a tithe of 1% of the national cake on each of the lower quintiles. The Gini coefficient for final incomes has risen from 32% to 36%. Paradoxically, because of bracket-drift, the highest quintile could legitimately claim that it is taxed at a higher rate on original income than in 1979: final household income is now 82% of original income as against 84% in 1979. Looked at from a different perspective, the tax and benefit system has transformed a seven point increase in the Gini coefficient for original incomes between 1979 and 1986 into a four point increase in the coefficient for final incomes.

So much for household shares; what of spending power? Adjusting the shares in Table 12 for changes in real GDP and household size, we find that real final income per head grew between 1979 and 1986 by 24%, 11%, and 10% for the top three quintiles. However for the lower two quintiles real income actually *fell* by 4% and 12% respectively. Now this increase in income inequality need not indicate that lifetime inequality has increased, for what matters is permanent rather than current income. It is possible that the increased inequality in Table 12 merely reflects the fact that unemployment is presently at a high level, or that the variability of (household) earnings over the life cycle has increased. We can examine this hypothesis by looking at consumption rather than income, since this should be related to expectations of lifetime earnings. Looking therefore at the distribution of real household expenditure rather than income (using the *Family Expenditure Survey*) we find that the lowest decile and quartile grew by only 3% and 6% respectively between

Table 12   DISTRIBUTION OF ORIGINAL AND FINAL INCOME

	1975	1979	1986
Original Income			
Quintile Group			
Bottom	0.8	0.5	0.3
2nd	10	9	6
3rd	19	19	16
4th	26	27	27
Top	44	45	51
Gini Coefficient	43	45	52
Final Income			
Quintile Group			
Bottom	7.1	7.1	6.3
2nd	13	12	11
3rd	18	18	17
4th	24	24	24
Top	38	38	42
Gini coefficient	31	32	36

Note: "Final Income" includes such benefits in kind as the National Health Service and the state education system.
Source: Economic Trends, December 1988.

1979 and 1986. For the lowest decile, real expenditure fell by 9% for one-adult households, and by 6% for single-pensioner households. Poor families with children suffered particularly: real expenditure for single-adult households with children fell by 16% at the lowest decile (and by 23% at the lowest quartile). Real expenditure for the standard one man, one woman, two children-household fell by 4% at the lowest decile. Not everyone has prospered in Mrs. Thatcher's Britain.

5. Conclusions

There are many aspects of the Thatcher revolution we have left untouched, but most of the important macroeconomic events of the last decade can in our view be traced to the fundamental switch away from neo-corporatist solutions to Britain's economic problems. Has Mrs. Thatcher been a Pareto-improvement? The verdict must depend on what would have happened without her. Some would argue that successful corporatist policies would have allowed a lower unemployment rate and a more painless disinflationary process. Under such policies the income distribution would almost certainly not have widened in the way it has. Whether they would have also led to the productivity revival is more debatable.

Supporters of the government argue—with good reason—that these policies had been tried and found wanting. The basic structure of the British economy was simply not conducive to Scandinavian-style solutions. There really was no alternative. If the successes of the Thatcher years—the reduction in inflation and improvement in productivity are continued into the foreseeable future, then the costs in terms of the increased unemployment and poverty of the last decade will probably turn out to be worthwhile. If the productivity revival comes to a halt and unemployment remains high, then the issue is less clear cut.

Appendix: A Model with Multiple Unions

The demand curve facing the firm is given by $P = \delta Y^{-\epsilon}$, where notation is as in Section 2.1.4 unless otherwise specified and firm subscripts are omitted for brevity. Two types of labour, each with their own union, are used to produce output via a well-behaved, CRS technology $Y = F(A_1 N_1, A_2 N_2)$, where N_i is employment of type i labour, and A_i represents an "over-manning" coefficient that is the subject of bargaining ($0 < A_i < 1$). The idea is that management and union can negotiate to have more men on a machine than is strictly necessary to operate it. Union utility is given by the utilitarian form $N_i V(W_i) + (M_i - N_i)\tilde{V}$, where M_i is the total membership of each union, and for simplicity $V(W) = \frac{W^\gamma}{\gamma}$.

The key assumptions are that while bargaining can take place over wages and manning levels, bargaining over employment directly is not feasible, and that there is no layoff pay. Together these ensure that, under some circumstances, it may be optimal to negotiate manning agreements involving the employment of totally surplus labour.

The profit maximising employment levels, for given A_i, W_i, then satisfy the usual marginal productivity conditions

$$\frac{\partial F}{\partial N_i} \equiv F_i = W_i / A_i P(1-\epsilon) \qquad (i=1,2) \quad (A1)$$

Straightforward algebra establishes that:

$$\partial n_i / \partial w_i = -[S_i + (1-S_i)\sigma\epsilon]/\epsilon = -\eta_i, \text{ say} \quad (A2a)$$

$$\partial n_i / \partial a_i = \eta_i - 1 \quad (A2b)$$

$$\partial n_i / \partial a_j = -\partial n_i / \partial w_j = S_j(1-\sigma\epsilon)/\epsilon = \varphi_j, \text{ say} \quad (i \neq j) \quad (A2c)$$

where $S_i = F_i N_i / F$ is the "competitive share" of labour type i, $\sigma = F_1 F_2 / F_{12} F$ is the elasticity of substitution, and lower-case letters denote logarithms.

Management negotiates with each union in turn over wages and manning treating the outcome of the other bargain as given. Along a union indifference curve we know that, for union i:

$$da_i / dw_i = [WV_i' / (V_i - \tilde{V}_i) - \eta_i]/(1-\eta_i) = 1 + [\gamma V_i / (V_i - \tilde{V}_i) - 1]/(1-\eta_i) \quad (A3)$$

and hence

$$d^2 a_i / dw_i^2 = \gamma V_i' \tilde{V}_i / (V_i - \tilde{V}_i)^2 (\eta_i - 1) \gtrless 0 \text{ as } (\eta_i - 1) \gtrless 0. \quad (A4)$$

Management is indifferent between any combination of wages and manning levels that leaves the efficiency cost of labour, W_i / A_i, unchanged. Hence the firm's isoprofit lines have $da_i / dw_i = 1$.

There are two possible scenarios depending on whether $\eta_i \gtrless 1$. A low elasticity of labour demand ($\eta_i < 1$) is the only case where an interior solution with overmanning can exist. The contract curve then satisfies:

$$V_i(W_i) = \tilde{V}_i(1-\gamma) \quad (A5)$$

which is independent of the manning level. Shifts in bargaining power, for given $\tilde{V}_i$, affect only manning arrangements and not the wage. This is, of course, an artifact of the particular specification of preferences. With a high elasticity of labour demand ($\eta_i > 1$), equation (A5) constitutes a set of minima rather than maxima. It follows that the equilibrium outcome of the bargain must then involve no overmanning.

In order to examine both the partial equilibrium within the firm, and the general equilibrium in the whole economy, it is helpful to choose a particular bargaining solution. For instance suppose wages solve a generalised Nash bargain, where $M_i\tilde{V}_i$ is the status quo point for the union:

$$\text{Max } [V(W_i) - \tilde{V}_i]^\beta \, N_i^\beta [\delta F(A_1 N_1, A_2 N_2)^{1-\epsilon} - W_1 N_1 - W_2 N_2] \quad (A6)$$

for $i = 1,2$. Then for an interior solution, the bargaining outcome is characterised by the contract curve (A5) and the division of the rents condition:

$$\beta \gamma V_i / (V_i - \tilde{V}_i) - \beta \eta_i - W_i N_i / \Pi = 0. \quad (A7)$$

For a boundary solution with $A_i = 1$ only the latter condition is required.

Henceforth focus on the case where $\eta_i < 1$ and there is an interior solution with overmanning. We know that for given $\tilde{V}_i$, the wage is determined by (A5) independently of manning levels. Hence the best response of each bargaining unit to the manning level chosen by the other bargaining unit is given by:

$$\bar{W}_i N_i = \beta(1 - \eta_i)[\delta F(A_1 N_1, A_2 N_2)^{1-\epsilon} - \bar{W}_1 N_1 - \bar{W}_2 N_2] \quad (A8)$$

where the bars are added to emphasise that the negotiated wage is independent of the manning level. Consequently along the optimal response for bargaining unit 1 we have:

$$da_1/da_2 = -\beta \bar{W}_2 N_2 / (1+\beta) \bar{W}_1 N_1 + \varphi 1 / (1+\beta)(1 - \eta_1) \quad (A9)$$

and similarly for bargaining unit 2, mutatis mutandis. The sign of the right-hand side of this equation depends on the particular parameter values, but the important thing is that a reduction in union power (or a negative demand shock) shifts the response function in the direction of reduced overmanning. Specifically suppose that the production function is symmetric (in the sense that $F(N_1, N_2) = F(N_2, N_1)$) and both sorts of labour face the same outside opportunities. Then, for $i = 1,2$, we have in intra-firm equilibrium:

$da_i/d\beta = -1/2\beta^2(1-\eta) < 0$ (A10a)

$da_i/d\delta = -[1+2\beta(1-\eta)]/2\beta\delta(1-\eta) < 0$ (A10b)

where $\eta=\eta_1=\eta_2$ is the common labour demand elasticity.

It may seem that although the model can explain the productivity rebound, it cannot simultaneously explain the increase in wages. However, it must be remembered that, in general, equilibrium $\tilde{V}_i$ is endogenous. Assuming type i labour receives the same wage in all firms and that $\tilde{V}_i=(1-u_i)V(W_i)+u_iV(B)$ where u_i is the unemployment rate for type i labour, we know from (A5) that:

$u_i = \gamma/(1-\rho_i^\gamma)$ (A11)

where $\varPi_i$ is the replacement ratio for type i labour. A natural benchmark is when this is fixed, e.g., because benefits are indexed to earnings. Changes in relative bargaining strength then have no effect on unemployment and only affect wages and productivity. For a common reduction in relative bargaining strength across all firms we obtain:

$dw/d\beta = da/d\beta = 1/\beta[(1-\epsilon)-2\beta\epsilon(1-\eta)]$ (A12)

Hence a reduction in union power leads to a rise in wages and productivity if and only if $2\beta\epsilon(1-\eta)>(1-\epsilon)$. Furthermore, for this benchmark case, productivity improvements are *fully* reflected in real wages, in contrast to the partial equilibrium result.

Now suppose that instead of bargaining independently with management, the two unions got together and bargained over wages and manning levels simultaneously. To keep things simple assume again that the production function is symmetric and that the "superunion" weights the welfare of the two types of labour equally. This symmetry ensures that we need only consider symmetric solutions with $W_1=W_2=W$ and $A_1=A_2=A$. In that case the superunion's indifference curve has elasticity

$da/dw = 1 + [\gamma V/(V-\tilde{V})-1]/(1-\eta-\varphi)$.   (A3)

Generically this is the same as (A3). However, since $\eta+\varphi=1/\epsilon>1$ there is necessarily no overmanning in the cooperative equilibrium.

A straightforward extension, relevant to Section 4, is to introduce a third, non-unionised factor of production. This could be capital or could be highly skilled or managerial labour. Provided this factor is a substitute for the two sorts of unionised labour, the reduction in overmanning that accompanies a reduction in union power will tend to be associated with an increase in the return to that factor if it is in fixed supply.

For instance consider the special case where the elasticity of substitution between the three inputs is the same. Then the elasticities of labour demand with respect to wages and the overmanning coefficients continue to be described by equations (A2) ($A_3=1$ if the third factor is non-unionised). Now consider a reduction in union power. In a general equilibrium where the replacement ratio for unionised labour is kept constant, an increase in productivity and real wages for both types of union labor results (provided certain conditions on the parameters are fulfilled). However, if W_{12} is the equilibrium wage for unionised labour and W_3 is the payment to the third factor it is easily shown that:

$$dw_3/dw_{12} = (S_1+S_2)(1-\sigma\epsilon)/[(S_1+S_2)(1-\sigma\epsilon)-(1-\sigma)]. \quad (A13)$$

Hence for a small elasticity of substitution a reduction in union power is not only associated with an increase in the real wages of unionised labour, but also a shift in differentials in favour of the third factor.

We are grateful to Charles Goodhart, Nils Gottfries, Mervyn King and participants of seminars at the Institute for International Economics in Stockholm, The London Business School and the University of Southampton, as well as the NBER Conference itself, for many helpful suggestions. We would also like to thank Danny Blanchflower, Donald Roy, Martin Wall and Sushil Wadhwani for assistance with data and to Guglielmo Caporale for research assistance.

A longer version of this paper is available as a Centre for Labour Economics Discussion Paper.

REFERENCES

Bassett, P. 1986. *Strike Free.* London: Macmillan.
Bean, C. 1987. "The Impact of North Sea Oil." in R. Dornbusch and R. Layard (eds.). *The Performance of the British Economy.* Oxford: Oxford University Press.
Bean, C. and A. Gavosto. 1989. "Outsiders, Capacity Shortages and Unemployment in the United Kingdom." forthcoming in J. Dreze, C. Bean, and R. Layard (eds.). *Europe's Unemployment Problem.* Cambridge: MIT Press.
Begg, D. 1987. "Fiscal Policy." in R. Dornbusch and R. Layard (eds.). *The Performance of the British Economy.* Oxford: Clarendon Press.
Blanchard, O. and N. Kiyotaki. 1987. "Monopolistic Competition and the Effects of Aggregate Demand." *American Economic Review.* Vol. 77, pp. 647–66.
Blanchard, O. and L. Summers. 1986. "Hysteresis and the European Unemployment Problem." *NBER Macroeconomic Annual.* pp. 16–78.
Bruno, M. and J. Sachs. 1985. *The Economics of Worldwide Stagflation.* Oxford: Oxford University Press.
Budd, A. P. Levine, and P. Smith. 1987. "Long Term Unemployment and the

Shifting U/V Curve: A Multi-Country Study." *European Economic Review.* Vol. 31, pp. 296–305.

Buiter, W. 1985. "A Guide to Public Sector Debt and Deficits." *Economic Policy.* Vol. 1, pp. 14–79.

Buiter, W. and M. Miller. (1981). "The Thatcher Experiment: The First Two Years." *Brookings Papers on Economic Activity.* Vol. 2, pp. 315–79.

Buiter, W. and M. Miller. 1983. "Changing the Rules: Economic Consequences of the Thatcher Regime." *Brookings Papers on Economic Activity.* Vol. 2, pp. 305–65.

Burns, T. 1988. "The UK Government's Financial Strategy." in W. Eltis and P. Sinclair (eds.). *Keynes and Economic Policy: The Relevance of the General Theory after Fifty years.* London: Macmillan.

Calmfors, L. and J. Driffill. 1988. "Bargaining Structure, Corporatism, and Macroeconomic Performance." *Economic Policy.* Vol. 6, pp. 13–62.

Daly, A., D. Hitchens, and K. Wagner. 1985, "Productivity, Machinery and Skills in a Sample of British and German Manufacturing Plants: Results of a Pilot Inquiry." *National Institute Economic Review.* No. 111, pp. 48–61.

Davies, S. and R. Caves. 1987. *Britain's Productivity Gap.* Cambridge: Cambridge University Press.

Desai, M., M. Keil, and S. Wadhwani. 1984. "Incomes Policy in a Political Environment: A Structural Model for the UK 1961–80," in A. Hughes Hallet (ed.). *Applied Decision Analysis and Economic Behaviour: Advanced Studies in Theoretical and Applied Econometrics.* Hingham, Mass.: Martinus Nijhoff Publishing.

Dilnot, A., G. Stark, I. Walker, and S. Webb. 1987. "The 1987 Budget in Perspective." *Fiscal Studies.* Vol. 8, No. 2, May, pp. 48–57.

Dilnot, A. and M. Kell. 1988. "Top-Rate Tax Cuts and Incentives: Some Empirical Evidence." *Fiscal Studies.* Vol. 9, No. 4, November, pp. 70–93.

Dornbusch, R. 1989. "Credibility, Debt and Unemployment: Ireland's Failed Stabilisation." *Economic Policy.* Forthcoming.

Emerson, M. 1986. "What Model for Europe." Harvard University. Mimeo.

Flanagan, R., D. Soskice, and L. Ulman. 1983. *Unionism, Economic Stabilisation and Incomes Policies: European Experience.* Washington, D. C. Brookings Institution.

Frankel, J. 1985. "Portfolio Crowding-Out, Empirically Estimated." *Quarterly Journal of Economics.* Vol. 100.

Franz, W. 1987. "Hysteresis, Persistence and the NAIRU: An Empirical Analysis for the FRG," in R. Layard and L. Calmfors (eds.). *The Fight Against Unemployment.* Cambridge, Mass.: MIT Press.

Giavazzi, F. and L. Spaventa. 1989. "Italy in the Eighties: An Unconventional Story." *Economic Policy.* Forthcoming.

Gottfries, N. and H. Horn. 1987. "Wage Formation and the Persistence of Unemployment." *Economic Journal.* Vol. 97, pp. 877–84.

Hall, R. 1986. "Market Structure and Macroeconomic Fluctuations." *Brookings Papers on Economic Activity.* Vol. 2, pp. 285–322.

Holland, D. 1977. "The Effect of Taxation on Incentives of Higher Income Groups." *Fiscal Policy and Labour Supply.* London: Institute for Fiscal Studies.

Jackman, R., R. Layard, and S. Nickell. 1989. *Unemployment.* Oxford: Oxford University Press. Forthcoming.

Jackman, R. and S. Roper. 1987. "Structural Unemployment." *Oxford Bulletin of Economics and Statistics.* Vol. 49, pp. 9–36.

Layard, R. and S. Nickell. 1986. "Unemployment in Britain." *Economica*. Vol. 53, pp. S121–70.

Layard, R. and S. Nickell. 1987. "The Labour Market." in R. Dornbusch and R. Layard (eds.). *The Performance of the British Economy*. Oxford: Oxford University Press.

Layard, R. and S. Nickell. 1989. "The Thatcher Miracle?" *American Economic Review*. Papers and Proceedings. Forthcoming.

Lindbeck, A. and D. Snower. 1988. "Cooperation, Harassment, and Involuntary Unemployment: An Insider-Outsider Approach." *American Economic Review*. Vol. 78, pp. 167–88.

Matthews, K. and P. Minford. 1987. "Mrs. Thatcher's Economic Policies 1979–87." *Economic Policy*. No. 5, pp. 57–102.

Maynard, G. 1988. *The Economy Under Mrs. Thatcher*. London: Basil Blackwell.

Metcalf, D. 1988. "Water Notes Dry Up." London School of Economics, Centre for Labour Economics. Discussion Paper No. 314.

Millward, N. and M. Stevens. 1986. *British Workplace Industrial Relations, 1980–84*. Gower, Aldershot.

Minford, P. and P. Ashton. 1988." The Poverty Trap and the Laffer Curve—What Can the GHS Tell Us?." London School of Economics, Centre for Economic Policy Research. Discussion Paper No. 275.

Muellbauer, J. 1986. "Productivity and Competitiveness in British Manufacturing." *Oxford Review of Economic Policy*. Vol. 2(3), Autumn, pp. 1–25.

Muller, P. and R. Price. 1984. "Structural Budget Indicators and the Interpretation of Fiscal Policy Stance in OECD Economies." *OECD Economic Studies*.

Newell, A. and J. Symons. 1985. "Wages and Employment in the OECD Countries." London School of Economics, Centre for Labour Economics. Discussion Paper No. 219.

Newell, A. and J. Symons. 1987. "Corporatism, Laissez-Faire and the Rise in Unemployment." *European Economic Review*. Vol. 31, pp. 567–614.

Newell, A. and J. Symons. 1988. "The Passing of the Golden Age." London School of Economics, Centre for Labour Economics. Discussion Paper No. 347.

OECD. 1987. *Employment Outlook*. Paris.

OECD. 1988. *Employment Outlook*. Paris.

Oswald, A. and P. Turnbull. 1985. "Pay and Employment Determination in Britain: What are Labour 'Contracts' Really Like?" *Oxford Review of Economic Policy*. Vol. 1(2), pp. 80–97.

Oulton, N. 1987. "Plant Closures and the Productivity Miracle in Manufacturing." *National Institute Economic Review*. No. 121, pp. 53–59.

Prais, S. 1981. *Productivity and Industrial Structure*. Cambridge: Cambridge University Press.

Prais, S. and K. Wagner. 1988. "Productivity and Management: the Training of Foremen in Britain and Germany." *National Institute Economic Review*. No. 123, pp. 34–47.

Pratten, C. 1976. *Labour Productivity Differentials Within International Companies*. Cambridge: Cambridge University Press.

Sargent, T. and N. Wallace. 1981. "Some Unpleasant Monetarist Arithmetic." *Federal Reserve Bank of Minneapolis Quarterly Review*.

Steedman, H. 1988. "Vocational Training in France and Britain: Mechanical and Electrical Craftsmen." *National Institute Economic Review*. No. 126, pp. 57–70.

Steedman, H. and K. Wagner. 1987. "A Second Look at Productivity, Machinery,

and Skills in Britain and Germany." *National Institute Economic Review.* No. 122, pp. 84–96.
Treasury and Civil Service Committee. 1981. *Report on Monetary Policy.* London: HMSO.
Wadhwani, S. and M. Wall. 1986. "The UK Capital Stock—New Estimates of Premature Scrapping," *Oxford Review of Economic Policy.* Vol. 2(3), Autumn, pp. 44–55.
Walters, A. 1986. *Britain's Economic Renaissance.* Oxford: Oxford University Press.

Comment

WILLIAM D. NORDHAUS
Yale University

Thatcherism has one feature in common with Reaganism. Whatever the verdict of historians about the ultimate wisdom of the economic policies for the nations involved, the policies have been a boon for economic science, providing natural experiments in the impact of changing macroeconomic policies and philosophies.

The paper by Bean and Symons provides a useful and provocative survey of major recent developments in the British economy. In evaluating the Thatcher experiment, I will focus on two particular issues of the 1980s: the inflation-unemployment experience and the trends in productivity and output.

Inflation and Unemployment

Observers of recent inflation and unemployment, in Britain as well as continental Europe, have been struck by the rising trends in unemployment along with the apparent stickiness of wage inflation in the latter half of the 1980s. The experience is devastating to modern rational-expectations theories or models which assume that the economy moves quickly toward its long-run equilibrium. Moreover, it provides little comfort to conventional modern natural-rate Phillips-curve theory, which cannot explain why inflation does not continue to decline with rates of unemployment that are presumably well above the natural rates.

With respect to new classical theories, economic policies in the U. S. and the U. K. after 1979 provided good laboratories to test the credibility hypothesis, which states that credible and publicly stated policies to curb inflation would lead to a more rapid and less costly reduction in inflation than would traditional approaches. Tests for the United States indicate that the structural wage-price equations were remarkably stable during the monetary experiment from 1979 to 1982.

An analogous test is presented by Bean and Symons in Table 3, where they calculate "sacrifice ratios" for the U.K. and other countries. At the outset, it should be noted that these tests are not comparable with other calculations (such as those of R. J. Gordon), for they take the benchmark unemployment rate as the *actual* unemployment rates in 1980 rather than the *natural* unemployment rates over the period; for the United States, this approach underestimates the sacrifice ratio by a factor of approximately two. In addition, they examine the unemployment-sacrifice ratio rather than the output-sacrifice ratio.

Setting aside analytical difficulties, the numerical results are hardly comforting to the credibility hypothesis. The U. K. sacrifice ratio ranks third out of seven even though most would agree that the U. K. had the most draconian anti-inflation policies of any of the countries. It is interesting to note as well that the country with the most deeply imbedded hostility to inflation, Germany, has the highest sacrifice ratio—a finding that is inconsistent with the well-known Lucas international evidence on inflation and unemployment.

It should be noted that modern neo-Keynesian natural-rate Phillips-curve theories have great difficulties in explaining wage-price movements over the 1980s in the U. K. and in much of Europe. Attempts to find stable Phillips curves have proven elusive, except perhaps for Japan and the U. S.[1]

This crisis has produced a wide variety of approaches. The most popular approach is to allow for "hysteresis" in the natural rate of unemployment—that is, to allow the natural rate to track the actual unemployment rate. The paper by Bean and Symons follows this tradition and includes a number of variables that might plausibly affect the natural rate. As I read their results (presented implicitly in Figure 1 and Table 4), the natural rate in Britain rose from under 2 percent before 1970 to a peak of 13 percent in the early 1980s and since then has fallen to around 7 percent.

The general line of reasoning of the hysteresis approach is troubling. There seems little reason to question the fact that standard Phillips curves appear highly unstable in Britain and other European countries during the 1980s. The most straightforward reaction to that fact would be to conclude that the underlying Phillips curve mechanism is mis-

1. A study outlining the difficulties of standard Phillips curves and showing the drift in the implicit natural rate of unemployment is David T. Coe, "Nominal Wages, the NAIRU, and Wage Flexibility," *OECD Economic Studies*, No. 5, Autumn 1985, pp. 87–126.

specified. Natural-rate theories have little appeal if the natural unemployment rate is as variable as the actual unemployment rate.

The usual approach, however, is to attempt to model the natural rate
as a function of a number of variables that could plausibly affect the
labor market. I find the argument presented in Bean and Symons even
less convincing than the hysteresis models developed in other studies.
One difficulty lies in the basic relation, equation (2), or in the actual
equation estimated (p. 31). It is misleading to label this a reduced form,
for the equation is not derived from a set of structural equations. Moreover, it seems misspecified in omitting any wage and price variables.
Most significantly, it completely omits any variables that could be instruments for the aggregate demand.

The results are also unconvincing. The results of the U. K. equation (p.
31) are inconsistent with the pooled cross-section results (on p. 33). The
crucial union density variable has different signs in the two equations.
Another variable which seems ad hoc is the aging variable (*POP*), which
represents the proportion of the population born after 1930 and who are,
according to Bean and Symons, "more willing to risk unemployment as
fewer workers are able to recall the experience of mass unemployment
during the interwar years." Does this variable show up in unemploy-

Figure 1 POTENTIAL OUTPUT (LABOR AND THATCHER) AND ACTUAL
OUTPUT

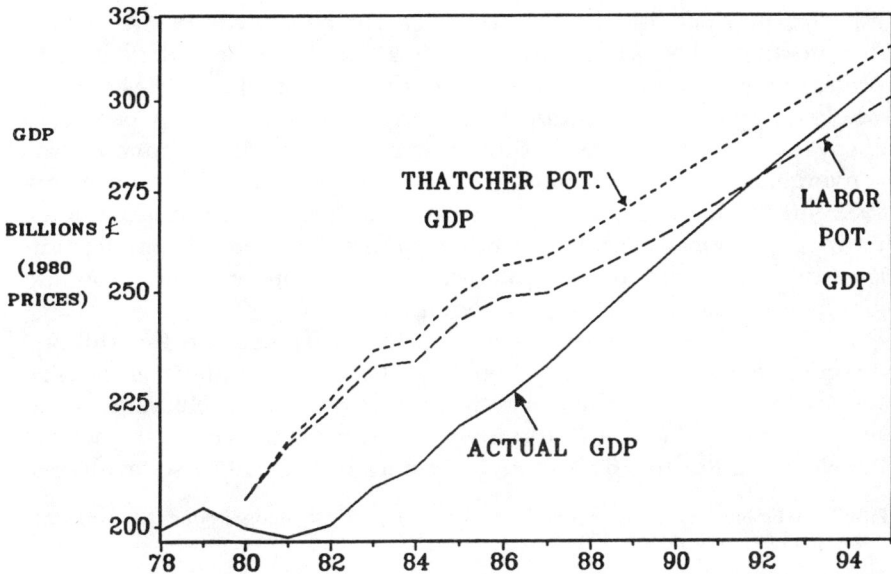

ment rates of different cohorts? Why do those unemployed since 1980 not begin to develop unemployment-aversion as well?

In addition, there is some ambiguity about whether the tax variables are influencing the demand or supply side. Finally, it seems inappropriate to assume that the demand effects can be captured by a stationary error term and by the lagged unemployment rate. The Thatcher years changed the pattern of policy from Stop-Go-Stop-Go to Stop-Stop-Stop-Stop; if policy affects aggregate demand, this implies that either the autoregressive structure of the errors or the coefficient on the lagged unemployment rate would change during the Thatcher years.

In the end, I believe that the equations are capturing a change in the unemployment-wage-price structure that is associated with a depression economy. After all, depressions are qualitatively different from normal times. Perhaps labor markets, along with price and wage behavior, behave differently during periods of extended slack; perhaps our models simply will not extrapolate into depression epochs. One reason for the change in structure might be a downward rigidity of the nominal wage rate, which bends the long-run (or at least the medium-run) Phillips curve at very low inflation rates. Another possible regime shift is the mass migration of workers from the labor force. I am selling no particular theory of regime change; rather, I am suggesting that we cannot use "good-time" models to understand the dynamics of wages, prices, and unemployment in bad times.

The other fascinating fact about the Thatcher regime is the improvement in productivity during the 1980s. To begin with, there is little dispute about the fact that the U.K. succeeded in reversing its lagging productivity growth better than most other industrial countries. On the whole, I agree with the interpretation in the Bean-Symons paper. I had always been struck by the fact that Britain was the only exception to the convergence hypothesis among large countries, as I remarked in my 1982 study.[2] If in fact Mrs. T was able to break the cartels, unions, university tenure systems, and other groups that were preventing Britain from converging toward the technological frontier, then we should join in a chorus of "She's a jolly good lady."

While this line of reasoning is plausible, I do not find the authors' empirical evidence supports their hypothesis. The authors emphasize the role of multiple unions as an important factor in inhibiting efficient reorganizations. While the argument seems plausible on its face, we are unable to judge the quantitative significance of British-style unions.

2. William D. Nordhaus, "Economic Policy in the Face of Declining Productivity Growth," *European Economic Review*, 1982.

Surely, the change in multiple unions shown in Table 9 is insufficient to cause the widespread productivity gains. The only direct evidence is presented in Table 10, which indicates that unions are favorable to TFP growth. Would not Thatcherism have *lowered* TFP through its union-busting campaign?

While much has been made of the startling gains to productivity in Britain, we might ask whether the game was worth the candle. Say that we agree with the Olsen hypothesis that it was necessary to break the chains of labor and business cartels in Britain; say that this required a blood-letting depression such as we have witnessed; and say that Mrs. T was just the person to draw the blood. We can still weigh costs and benefits.

Figure 1 gives a simple account of the dilemma. We show in that figure British potential output under Thatcher (calculated from actual GDP assuming an Okun's Law coefficient of 2 and a potential unemployment rate of 4 percent). We assume that Mrs. T's policies were able to raise British productivity growth by .5 percent per year for a decade.[3] The alternative path of potential output is shown in Figure 1 as "Labor Potential GDP." Finally, we show the actual path of output through the forecast for 1989 and bring actual output back to potential output over the coming decade.

Figure 2 shows the cumulative losses and gains from this calculation. If we do not discount future output, then the gains from the higher productivity growth will offset the losses from the depression sometime in the first decade of the next century. If we discount the future output gains at 6 percent per annum, then the losses of the 1980s will never be regained.

This calculation of the gains and losses from Thatcherism is obviously dependent upon the precise assumptions about future productivity growth. But is does remind us that whatever productivity gains have been achieved in Britain did not come cheaply. Put differently, even though *productivity growth* may have been higher in the 1980s under Mrs. T, *output* was probably lower than it would otherwise have been. And it is useful to note that the Cheerful Economics of Mr. R in America managed to raise productivity growth sharply without the same prolonged depression that still haunts Britain.

3. The assumption about the productivity rebound is crucial to the figure. This number is obtained by assuming that one-half of the rebound in British productivity from 1973–79 to 1979–87 (see Bean and Symons, Table 5) is due to the Thatcher reforms. Alternatively, if it is assumed that the differential growth between the U.K. and other countries is halved (see the equation on p. 36), then the productivity acceleration is about .5 percent per annum.

Figure 2 CUMULATIVE GAINS OR LOSSES FROM THATCHERISM

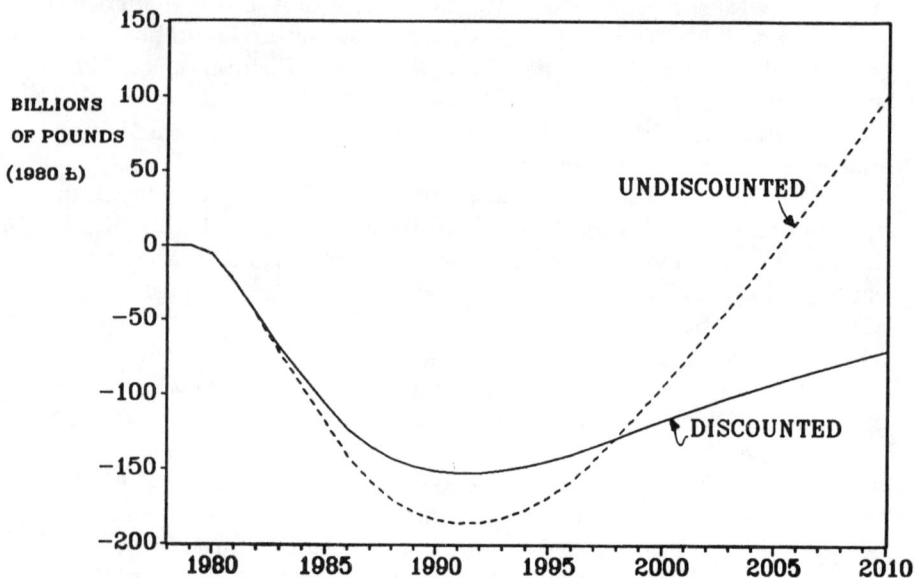

The authors remind us that the stated purpose of Thatcherism was to reduce inflation. Given the heavy output losses shown in Figure 2, I am reminded of some words of James Tobin, who was reflecting upon the postwar experience in the United States:

The whole purpose of the economy is production of goods or services for consumption now or in the future. I think the burden of proof should always be on those who would produce less rather than more, on those who would leave idle men or machines or land that could be used. It is amazing how many reasons can be found to justify such waste: fear of inflation, balance-of-payments deficits, unbalanced budgets, excessive national debt. . . . Too often the means are accorded precedence over the ends.[4]

In the end, putting aside the non-economic issues such as the evils of socialism, we can judge the Thatcher period by whether the austerity of the period beginning in 1980 (and not yet ended in 1989) will raise British national income and output. Given the steep economic losses of the 1980s, it will be many years before a higher productivity growth will provide sufficient gains to offset the cumulative losses. Perhaps Britain

4. James Tobin, *National Economic Policy: Essays,* pp. vii–viii.

will never recover the losses of the 1980s. All this serves as a reminder that depressions and class wars resemble conventional wars and strikes in being negative-sum games in which the losses of the suffering generation are never recouped.

Comment

WALTER ELTIS
Director General of the National Economic Development Office, London

The paper by Charles Bean and James Symons provides one of the most statistically balanced and thought provoking analyses of what has been achieved in Mrs. Thatcher's first ten years. Some matters of emphasis are of course open to criticism. Thus when Bean and Symons write:

The most obvious failure [of the Thatcher years] has been the level of unemployment . . .[p. 21] The unemployment rate, which peaked at 11.8% in 1985, has reached levels second only to those experienced during the Great Depression (p. 15).

they fail to put the complete 10-year unemployment record into perspective.

Official United Kingdom unemployment fell from 11.8% in 1985 to 11.1% in 1986, 10.0% in 1987, 8.1% in 1988, and 7.5% in May 1989. United Kingdom unemployment is therefore now lower than in France, Italy, and most of the other EC economies. It is a little surprising that their table which puts "the UK's unemployment experience in international context" [Table 3 on p. 23] should quote comparative data only for 1985 when United Kingdom unemployment peaked at 11.8% instead of a later year when it was relatively low by West European standards. The 11.8% at which unemployment peaked was very far below the 21.3% unemployment of 1931.

It is widely agreed that the rapid rate of fall of United Kingdom unemployment owes something to increased strictness in the administration of unemployment benefit rules with the result that some of the recorded fall reflects the removal of names from the register as a consequence of administrative action; but there is a variety of evidence which points to increasing tightness in the labour market over much of the United Kingdom, so a very significant fall in unemployment has unquestionably occurred.

But this has been quite recent. The growth of the United Kingdom economy accelerated sharply in 1986 to a rate between 4% and 5% per annum (according to the output measure of GNP which has proved the most accurate), and that is the principal reason why unemployment has fallen so sharply. Manufacturing productivity has also advanced very rapidly in these two years (by 16%), which reflects the improvement in the United Kingdom's overall supply side performance.

The superior growth and unemployment performance in 1986–88 has been partly due to an unsustainably rapid growth of demand. During 1988, real United Kingdom consumption grew by 6.5% and real investment by 10% to produce a growth of real domestic demand of over 7.5% of which about 3% had to be met from overseas, and this has produced a £12 billion deterioration in the current account of the balance of payments. At the same time the underlying rates of wage and price inflation have accelerated and the government has had to take corrective action to slow the growth of demand. This may produce a cyclical peak in 1989 or 1990 (not 1988 as Bean and Symons suggest because 1989 output is so far running some 4% above 1988 levels) so that statistics for a complete cycle from the 1979 peak to a further peak in 1989 or 1990 will in due course become available. This genuine 10–11 year cycle is likely to include further above average growth in 1988–90 and show faster overall annual growth rates than the Bean and Symons statistics which include all the negative data from the 1979–81 recession but not yet all the positive data from the subsequent boom.

There is of course a considerable possibility that the United Kingdom authorities will be able to achieve a slowdown in the growth of demand to a sustainable rate in 1989–90 without actually creating a cyclical downturn, and this will be easier to achieve if the acceleration of growth in 1986–88 contains a significant element that stems from sustainable supply side improvements. Bean and Symons document the extent to which marginal rates of United Kingdom taxation on high personal incomes were reduced in 1980 and on corporate profits in 1983 and any beneficial effects on supply from these will be quite significantly lagged, so it is not implausible that the main favourable effects only came through after 1985. There was also extensive deregulation to assist small businesses, which have grown very rapidly. Bean and Symons themselves, in the most interesting part of their paper, attach considerable weight to the favorable influence on labour productivity of trade union legislation that reduced restrictive practices and union power. There has been a reinforcing consideration which helps to explain why many private sector trade unionists have entirely voluntarily cooperated with management to an increasing degree in the 1980s.

In the pre-Thatcher cycle between the cyclical peaks of 1973 and 1979 the real net of tax earnings of the average worker increased at an annual rate of only 0.9% per annum while the net pre-tax rate of return on capital of non-North Sea companies fell from 8.9% to 5.6%. From 1979 to 1988 the net of tax earnings of the average worker rose at the far faster annual rate of 3.0% with the result that the real incomes of those in work rose by approximately one-third in Mrs. Thatcher's first nine-and-a-half years. At the same time the pre-tax net rate of return of non-North Sea companies rose from 5.6% in 1979 to 10.2% in 1987 (which has probably risen by a further fifth since). A consequence of the rapid productivity recovery which Bean and Symons began to track has therefore been that workers in work and companies have been able to enjoy very rapid simultaneous increases in both wages and profits. The near stagnation of wages and the decline of real rates of return on capital in 1973–79 encouraged zero sum behaviour by trade unions where one group of workers was mainly able to gain extra real incomes at the expense of profits or of other workers via the exercise of the short-term power to disrupt production. As the Thatcher boom in which real wages and profits have both risen rapidly developed, the conditions for positive sum behaviour have gradually emerged and labour relations have now moved toward a situation where all parties realise that they stand to gain far more from sustained increases in production and productivity than from relative income shifts achieved via threats to disrupt the productive process. The unwillingness of most workers in the private sector to support strike action may well owe something to the large gains they have been able to achieve via cooperation to achieve continual advances in productivity and improvements in international competitiveness. Bean and Symons recognise the importance of this line of argument and they add, "Once workers have experienced the higher incomes generated by a more efficient, productive economy, they are unlikely to want to revert to the status quo ante."

It is widely perceived that there have also been considerable gains in the quality of management, but Bean and Symons remark (p. 42):

. . . *if improved management were the key, then one might expect capital productivity as well as labour productivity to have improved. Yet the table [8. on p. 40] suggests that even after 1979 most of the TFP [Total Factor Productivity] growth seems to have been labour-augmenting in nature.*

They rightly say that "one should not push this too far," and especially since the extent to which productivity growth is capital-augmenting is extremely difficult to measure. This is partly because technical progress which is capital-augmenting ex ante will lead to a consequent substitution of capital for labour so that much of what occurs ex post will be indistinguishable from the consequences of labour-augmenting technical progress. This will be precisely the case if the elasticity of substitution between labour and capital is unity, and if it is closer to 0.6 or 0.7 as is widely supposed, subsequent substitutions will still disguise most of the precise effects of capital augmentation. The difficulties are of course compounded by the distortions which influence the relation between marginal products and factor returns in most industries. For these reasons, and because the statistical findings which Bean and Symons use to reject capital-augmenting technical progress (in Table 8) are rather tenuous, the suggestion that productivity advances in the United Kingdom have been exclusively labour augmenting need not be accepted. The official data show real investment net of capital consumption in manufacturing industry totalling a mere £64 millions or less than 0.1% of the capital stock in the four years 1984, 1985, 1986, and 1987. The output of manufacturing industry rose 13% in these four years, and to be able to produce 13% more with negligible recorded net investment is compatible with the presence of a good deal of capital-augmenting technical progress. If this has indeed been present on a considerable scale, the hypothesis that assets have been more efficiently managed in a wide range of industries ceases to be unacceptable; it may be added that extremely cooperative trade unions have allowed managers to manage these assets far more effectively than in the 1970s.

This Comment has focused on the microeconomic aspects of Bean and Symons' account. So far as the macroeconomic management of the economy is concerned, the government has succeeded in reducing price inflation from the more than 10% rates of the 1970s to an underlying 4% to 5% from 1982 onward, but it has so far failed to arrive at a consistent macroeconomic framework for the guidance of policy. Virtually every target announced has had to be quite rapidly modified, for essentially pragmatic reasons. In 1988–89 the United Kingdom has a budget surplus of between 3% and 4% of GNP (when the most recently enunciated principle to guide budgetary policy called for a balanced budget). Despite this and negligible public expenditure growth, the expansion of real demand accelerated to an unsustainable 7.5%. Precise monetary targets have not had a direct influence on policy since about 1985, quite largely because only the demand function for the narrowest measure of the money supply MO has shown any stability. In practice the government has endeavoured to maintain a stable inflation rate via well judged movements in short-term interest rates that have a considerable impact on the exchange rate which in turn influences the inflation rate. This pragmatic approach came adrift in 1987–88 when interest rates and therefore the exchange rate were set too low to stabilise inflation and the rate of growth of real demand. The United Kingdom has nonetheless enjoyed eight years of uninterrupted growth since 1981 and considerable stability in inflation. The government has judged that this together with supply side-oriented reductions in personal and company taxation provide the best available environment for companies and their workers to take long term decisions which can be expected to promote growth and international competitiveness.

If substantial supply side improvements have begun to come through from about 1985 onwards as this Comment suggests, then these are probably the most important outcomes of the policies of Mrs. Thatcher's governments. It is moreover entirely plausible that the buoyancy of investment and consumption that has followed from supply side successes and the consequent growth of new small businesses has had a positive impact on aggregate demand that even a budget surplus of more than 3% of the national income has so far failed to restrain.

Discussion

Charles Bean replied to Nordhaus that the regressions were intended as reduced forms, so that there was no need to include aggregate demand explicitly, and that even so results are similar if the change in GDP is included in the regression. He also suggested that the change in productivity was not due to a move away from multi-unionism, but that a decrease in union power meant that the distortions from multi-unionism were less important. In response to Eltis, Bean noted that they only had data through 1987, and that the recent increase in output can be attributed almost wholly to increases in consumption.

Robert Gordon questioned Nordhaus's cost-benefit analysis of the Thatcher years. He indicated that the comparison depends on the comparability of the US economy in the 1930's with the economy in the postwar and on the comparability of the postwar US and UK economies, neither or which he found convincing. He noted that inflation showed little persistence in the prewar period, while it is very persistent in the postwar, and that the US appears to have a stable natural rate of unemployment, unlike in the UK.

Robert Hall questioned why the move to free markets is associated with adverse changes in income distribution, contrary to the classical view. He speculated that reducing inflation has costs which offset the structural benefits of free markets. Matthew Shapiro responded that most of the changes in income distribution were due to changes in tax rates that accompanied the move to free markets, though Bean noted that in the UK even the pretax income distribution has widened.

John Campbell questioned that relation between market power and multi-unionism. He noted that the integration of the European market in 1992 may lower the amount of monopoly power and thus lead to a more US-style union sector. Bean agreed with this view.

William Brainard thought it was inappropriate to examine British disinflation independent of the world disinflation. Olivier Blanchard asked whether the decrease in manning restrictions should have a once-and-for-all effect on productivity, or whether they were preventing British catch-up in the world economy and thus would have a permanent effect. Bean replied that he thought the removal of manning restrictions had a once-and-for-all effect.

Eltis questioned whether the recent output increase was really due to consumption. He noted that while consumer spending is up, corporate and government saving have increased a well. William Nordhaus defended his indictment of Thatcher policy. If the hysteresis view of unemployment is incorrect, then Thatcher produced a depression to lower inflation. If the hysteresis view is correct, then deflationary policy has very long-lasting effects. Robert Hall suggested that the authors use their data to identify the bias in technological change. The bias can be uncovered, he suggested, by examine the relation between the Solow residual in Table 15 and the shares of capital and labor.

Frank Levy[1]

UNIVERSITY OF MARYLAND

Recent Trends in U.S. Earnings and Family Incomes

1. Introduction

In his recent survey of economic growth, Angus Maddison (1987) referred to "the postwar golden age which ended in 1973 . . . (p. 649)." Maddison was discussing the growth of GDP but his description applies equally well to the growth of individual incomes. Since 1973, industrialized countries have faced the income losses of two oil price shocks and experienced sharp slowdowns in the growth of multi-factor and labor productivity.

The impact of these events can be understood by considering the stylized frontier that describes the point-in-time trade-off between the growth rate of employment and the growth of the marginal product of labor (Figure 1). For most countries, the decline in labor productivity growth shifted the frontier inward. The oil price shocks had a similar, but more episodic, effect by raising import prices and so reducing the purchasing power of the product wage.

Different countries dealt with their newly restricted choices in different ways. Many European economies continued to enjoy real wage growth at the cost of historically high unemployment (Blanchard and

1. School of Public Affairs, Morrill Hall, University of Maryland, College Park, Maryland 20742. 301–454–7242. This paper is an extension of two earlier papers: "Incomes, Families, and Living Standards," Chapter 4 in Robert E. Litan, Robert Z. Lawrence, and Charles L. Schultze (eds.), *American Living Standards: Challenges and Threats* (Brookings Institution, 1988) and "Earnings and Education: Recent U.S. Trends" (with Richard Michel), paper prepared for the Joint Economic Committee of the U.S. Congress, forthcoming, 1989). The author wishes to thank Patrick Purcell of the Urban Institute for extensive research assistance, Carol Newman of the Brookings Institution for programming assistance and Stanley Fischer, Robert Lawrence, Richard Michel, Kevin Murphy, Charles Schultze, and Larry Summers for comments on various drafts. He also wishes to thank the Ford Foundation, the Urban Institute and the Brookings Institution for financial support.

Figure 1 THE TRADE-OFF BETWEEN THE GROWTH RATE OF
EMPLOYMENT AND THE GROWTH RATE OF LABOR'S
MARGINAL PRODUCT

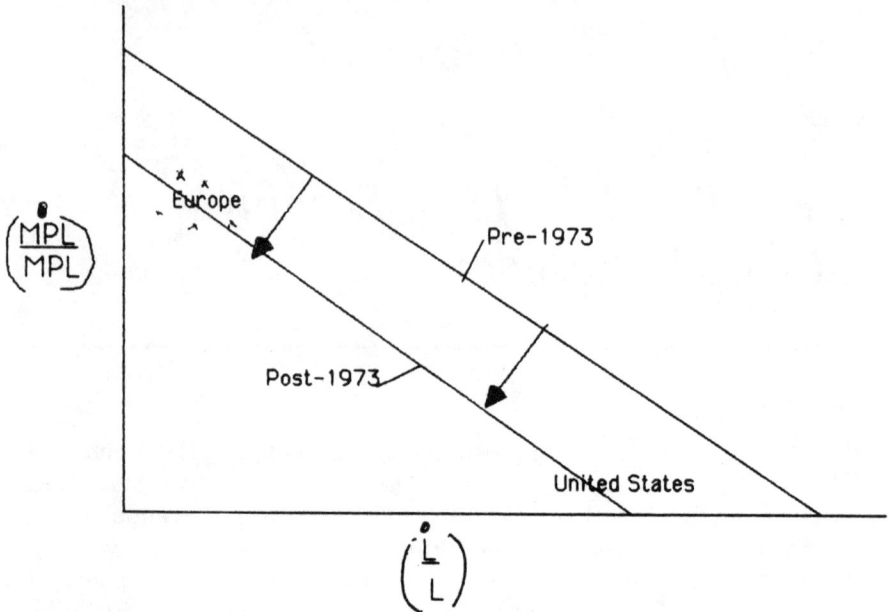

Summers 1986; and Lawrence and Schultze 1987). In the United States, civilian employment increased by 24.5 million persons (+29%) between 1973 and 1986 but at the cost of very low real wage growth.[2] In the U.S., moreover, general wage stagnation was accompanied by greater inequality in annual earnings for men (but not for women) and greater inequality in family incomes.

The combined effect of stagnant wages and greater inequality on U.S. men's earnings is displayed in Figure 2 which compares annual earnings distributions of prime age men (ages 25–55) for 1973 and 1986. The data, taken from the Current Population Survey (CPS), refer to pre-tax money earnings (the CPS records neither taxes nor fringe benefits) and the sample consists of men who worked at least one hour during the year.[3]

2. The reader may ask whether the increase in U.S. employment is, by itself, sufficient to explain low wage growth without appeal to the restricted frontier of Figure 1. I discuss this question in Section 2.

3. For purposes of this paper, earnings are defined as the sum of CPS items measuring an individual's wage and salary income, self-employment income and farm income. Where this sum is negative (reflecting business losses among the self-employed), it has been arbitrarily reset to $1.00.

Figure 2 EARNINGS OF 25-55-YEAR-OLD MEN: 1973, 1986 (MEN AGE 25–34
WITH 12 OR FEWER YEARS OF EDUCATION SHOWN IN SUB-
BARS)

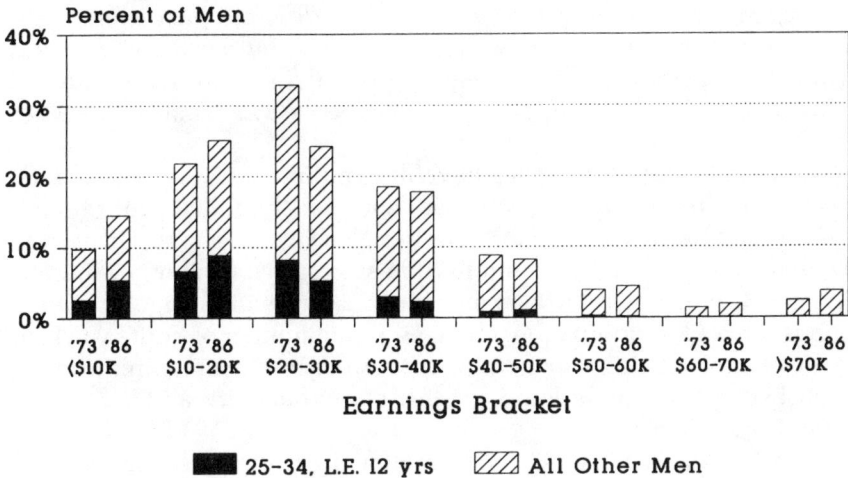

Earnings in 1987 dollars. Inflation-adjusted using PCE Index.

The data, like all other income data in this paper, are expressed in 1987
dollars using the implicit Personal Consumption Expenditure Deflator of
the Gross National Product Accounts.

Had real wages grown at, say, 2% per year after 1973, the 1986 distribution in Figure 2 would have been centered in the $30–$40,000 range.[4] In
the absence of such growth, the 1973 and 1986 distributions overlap to a
substantial degree and the overlap facilitates intertemporal comparisons.
When 1973 and 1986 are compared, the proportion of men earning less
than $20,000 and earning more than $50,000 have both increased while
the proportion of men earning $20–$50,000 has declined. In the language of popular debate, these changes in the distribution of male earnings are consistent with either of two meanings of vanishing middle
class jobs: an increased inequality of earnings (resulting in a distribution
with a smaller middle class), and a declining proportion of workers who

4. For example, in the 13 years from 1960 to 1973, labor productivity in the non-farm
   business sector grew at an average 2.4% per year and the median individual income of
   all men who worked year-round and full-time increased from $19,638 to $27,490 (in 1987
   dollars) (+40%) (Bureau of the Census, 1987b). The conjectural 2% figure in the text
   reflects the fact that under the best of conditions, the growth of output per worker
   would have been depressed by the entrance of the baby boom cohorts into the labor
   force.

earn enough to support a middle class standard of living—e.g., above $20,000.[5]

Figure 3 compares the 1973 and 1986 annual earnings distributions of prime age women (ages 25–55). Here, a quite different picture emerges. Women's annual earnings lie well below mens', but between 1973 and 1986, the proportion of women earning less than $10,000 has declined substantially while the proportion earning between $20 and $50,000 has increased.

A number of popular articles have drawn direct links between shifts over time in the real earnings distribution and the movement of labor between middle class, or "good jobs" (high wage jobs) and "bad jobs" (low wage jobs).[6] A moment's reflection suggests several other reasons why real earnings distributions may shift: changes in the age/education composition of the population, changes in the number of hours worked, changes in cohort size. Further, all of these factors operate in a context established by the underlying growth of productivity and macroeconomic shocks.

Figure 4 compares the 1973 and 1986 family income distribution. The Census defines a "family" as two or more persons related by blood, marriage, or adoption. Persons who live alone or cohabit with non-relatives are excluded from the distribution.[7] The resulting family distribution depends in part on individual earnings and in part on the number of earners per family, as well as the distribution of income sources other than earnings including interest, dividends, rents, private pensions, and government pensions and transfer payments. (Note, however, that the CPS does *not* record income from capital gains.)

In the family income distribution, as in the distribution of prime-age male annual earnings, there has been little real growth between 1973 and 1986. Over the period, median family income increased from $28,890 to $30,670 (5% per decade), a far slower rate than in earlier decades.[8] And as

5. The debate was prominent in the 1988 presidential campaign and included Michael Dukakis' references to "good jobs at good wages" and "two-paycheck prosperity," Richard Gephardt's commercial featuring the "$48,000 K-Car," Jesse Jackson's speeches on the victims of "economic violence" and Pat Robertson's speeches to South Carolina textile workers in which he argued that their industry was being destroyed by international bankers.

6. These articles are referenced in Section 3.

7. In Census statistics, these persons are included in a separate income distribution of "unrelated individuals."

8. These figures are from the U.S. Bureau of the Census (1987b) but they are adjusted by the implicit PCE deflator rather than the Consumer Price Index (CPI) used by the Census. CPI adjustment would show median family income *declining* by 1% per decade. I discuss family income growth in Section 5.

in the distribution of male earnings, stagnation of family incomes was accompanied by greater income inequality. During the period, the proportions of families with incomes below $10,000 and above $50,000 both increased moderately while the proportions of families with incomes between $10,000 and $50,000 declined moderately.

In this paper, I review recent trends in the level and distribution of individual earnings and family incomes in the United States. The remainder of the paper is divided into six sections. In Section 2, I review the trend in individual incomes for the post-World War II period. The trend is one of significant income growth through 1973 followed by very slow growth (i.e., stagnation) thereafter. I discuss some of the implications of the transition from growth to stagnation for U.S. life. In Section 3, I examine detailed post-1973 wage and earnings trends for selected demographic groups to see why some groups' earnings grew faster than the underlying trend while other group's earnings grew more slowly. Much of the growing "lower tail" in Figure 2 reflects the declining earnings of young, less educated men. By contrast, some of the upward shift in Figure 3 reflects higher hourly wages for college educated women. I propose an explanation of these trends based

Figure 3 EARNINGS DISTRIBUTION OF WOMEN (EARNINGS IN 1973 AND 1986; WOMEN 25–45 WITH 4 YEARS COLLEGE SHOWN IN SUB-BARS)

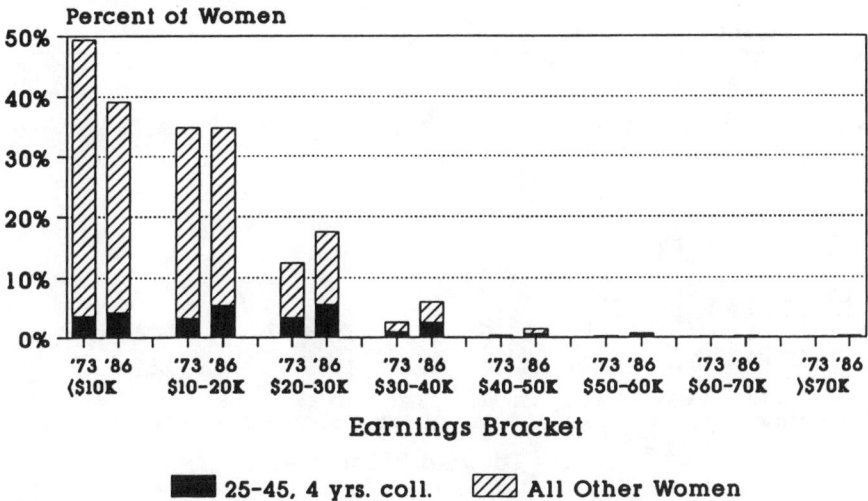

Earnings in 1987 dollars. Inflation-adjusted using PCE Index.

largely on shifts in the demand for different kinds of labor. Together, the detailed statistics and the explanation help clarify the good jobs-bad jobs debate.

In Section 4, I briefly sketch how the nation managed to increase per capita income, a traditional measure of living standards, even as earnings stagnated.

In Section 5, I review recent changes in the family income distribution. Family income inequality has increased to a degree but equally important are movements of various groups *within* the distribution. In a context of slow family income growth and moderately increasing inequality, the position of elderly families has improved significantly while the position of the poorest one-third of children has declined sharply.

In Section 6, I examine parts of the process by which changes in men's earnings inequality are transformed into changes in family income inequality. The complete transformation is complex and depends upon the distribution of unearned income, the propensity to marry, the propensity of married men to have working spouses, and the relationship between low male wages and the formation of female-headed families. I present some rough calculations on the first three items in this list.

Section 7 contains a short conclusion and some speculations on the future.

Figure 4 DISTRIBUTION OF FAMILIES BY INCOME 1973, 1986

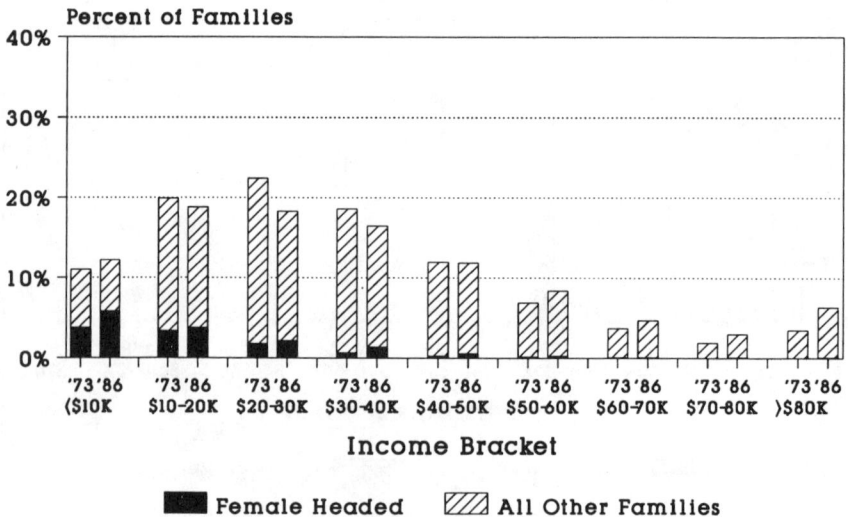

Income in 1987 dollars. Inflation-adjusted using PCE Index.

2. Earnings Growth and Stagnation.

A standard analytical tool in labor economics is the age-earnings profile, the relationship between earnings and age in a cross-sectional sample. The profile shows how earnings change with increased experience. But as a man or woman actually ages, changes in earnings will arise from two general effects. The first is the movement along the age-earnings profile, the effect of increased experience. The second is the effect of changes in the economy's real wage scale which can move the entire age-earnings profile up or down.

In periods of strong real wage growth, the second effect dominates the first through much of a man's career. Consider the cohort of men who were 35–44 in 1949 (Figure 5). The CPS reports the median income of

Figure 5 THE GROWTH OF MEN'S EARNINGS OVER TIME (1987 DOLLARS)

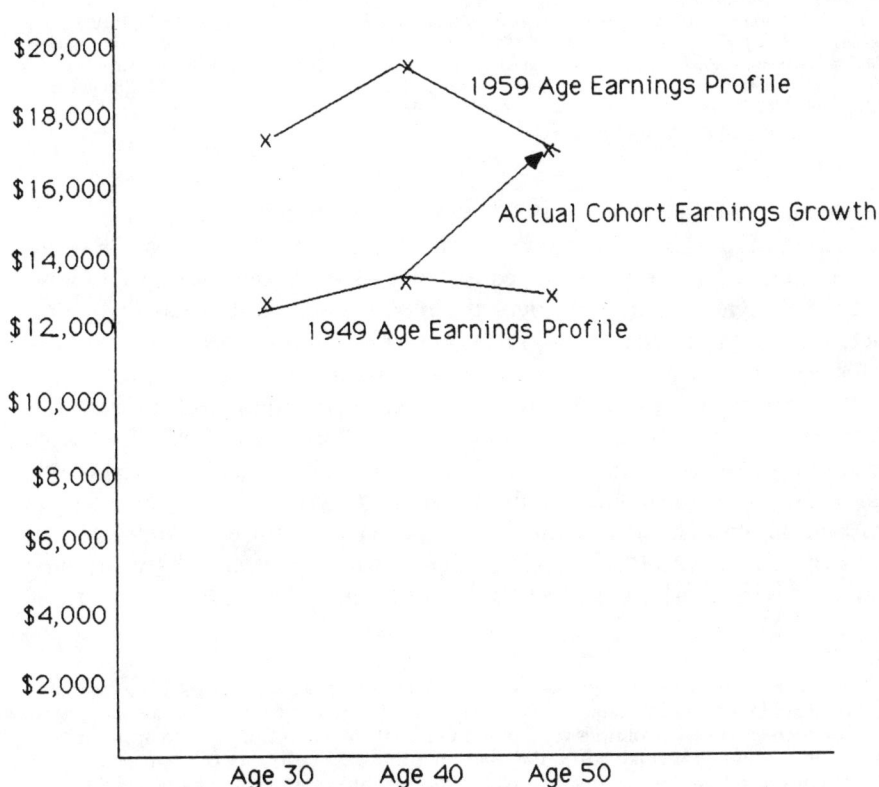

Source: Current Population Reports, Various Issues. Income at Age 30 refers to Median income of 25-34-year-old men, etc.

Table 1   THE STAGNATION OF WORKERS' INCOMES AFTER 1973
(1987 DOLLARS)

Men who were 50 in:	Their average income at age 50 (Full-Time Workers Only)		Growth in the income scale over the previous decade	
	Census	Adjusted	Census	Adjusted
1946*	$15,257	$15,529	—	—
1956	$18,558	$19,208	21.6%	23.7%
1966	$23,971	$25,168	29.2%	31.0%
(1973)	($30,578)	($32,701)	**	**
1976	$30,179	$32,752	25.9%	30.1%
1986	$32,960	$36,228	9.2%	10.6%

*1946 is used as a starting point because it is when the first published data were available.
**As noted in the text, the process of deep stagnation began at the end of 1973 with the first OPEC oil price shock. The growth rate of incomes between 1973 and 1987 on a *per decade basis* was 5.9% (Census) and 8.2% (Adjusted).
Source: Income statistics from U.S. Bureau of the Census, *Current Population Reports*, Series P-60, various issues. Income for adjustments from U.S. Department of Commerce, Bureau of Economic Analysis, *National Income and Product Accounts*, various issues. "Average Income of men at 50, Full-Time Workers Only" refers to the median income of all male year-round, full-time workers, ages 45–54. Conversion to 1987 dollars made using the Personal Consumption Expenditure Index.

these men to be $13,706 (in 1987 dollars) while the median income of 45–54-year-old men in the same year was $12,777 (in 1987 dollars). In terms of pure experience effects, the cohort of 35-44-year-old men should have seen little real income gain over the next decade. But when the cohort actually reached ages 45–54 (in 1959) their median income was $17,860 (+30%), the result of a rising real wage structure.[9]

We can approximate the real wage scale by following an earnings benchmark over time—the median annual income of 45-54-year-old men who worked year-round and full-time (Table 1) as tabulated by the CPS. By 1987, the oldest baby-boomers (born in 1946) had not yet turned 45; so earnings of men in the 45-54-year-old age range were at least partially protected from big changes in cohort size.[10] By focusing on men who work year-round and full-time, we can isolate the effects

9. In practice, the age-earnings profile for more educated workers keeps rising even after the profile for less educated workers has turned down. It follows that a small part of the increase in the example reflects the fact that the cohort of 35-44-year-old men in 1949 had higher average education than the cohort ten years older.
10. The protection is only partial because of the potential substitution between older and younger men in production.

of rising real wages while reducing the big income variations due to changing unemployment.[11]

The benchmark has two problems. The CPS did not cross-classify incomes by education in the 1950s and 1960s and so some of the benchmark's growth will reflect the rising educational levels of 45–54-year-old men rather than a rising (or falling) wage scale.[12] And as noted earlier, the CPS measures only income while it excludes the value of fringe benefits. In recent years, fringe benefits have become an increasing portion of compensation and for this reason, Table 1 contains two columns: income as published by the Census and Census income figures with approximate adjustments for fringe benefits.[13]

From 1950 to 1973, GDP per hour of work (labor productivity) grew at an average annual rate of 2.5% and provided the basis for real wage growth. In 1946 the average 50-year-old man working full-time had income of $15,257 (Table 1). This benchmark rose steadily so that by 1973, the year that ended with the first OPEC oil price shock, the average 50-year-old man working full-time had income of $30,578.

A small part of this growth reflected the increased education of 45–54-year-old men. Another small part reflected the movement of men out of "bad" jobs—particularly low wage agricultural jobs—and into "good" jobs. But the gains in Table 1 were largely a macroeconomic phenomenon that affected most occupations. For example, in 1969, white men who worked as "Craftsmen and Precision Workers" had mean earnings of $22,398, 16% above the real mean earnings of white men who worked as "Executives, Administrators, and Managers" in 1949 (Levy 1988a, Table 7.2).

At the end of 1973, the first oil price shock led immediately to unanticipated inflation and recession in the U.S. and by 1975, the Census benchmark had fallen by about 3%.[14] More important, 1973 marked the

---

11. CPS volumes in the 1950s and 1960s did not contain detailed *earnings* data and so Table 1 is based on individual *incomes* (which include interest and dividends, unemployment compensation, etc.). Among middle aged men who work year-round full-time, median income is a reasonably good approximation of median earnings.

12. I use the term rising wage scale to describe a situation in which workers with a given set of demographic characteristics are paid a higher hourly compensation than similar workers earned at an earlier time.

13. These corrections are made by inflating Census estimates of median individual income by the ratio of Other Labor Income (which includes employer contributions for private fringe benefits) to Wage and Salary Income where both figures are taken from the National Income and Product Accounts.

14. Median incomes for all 50-year-old men (as distinct from full-time workers) fell more sharply because unemployment rose sharply in the 1974–75 recession.

beginning of the sharp slowdown in the growth of multi-factor and labor productivity.[15]

The income loss from the 1973–74 oil price shock followed by slow-growing productivity meant that the benchmark did not regain its 1973 level until 1979. Then the Iranian revolution triggered the second major OPEC oil price increases and the cycle of unanticipated inflation and recession began again.[16] Between 1973 and 1986, the CPS benchmark grew by 5.9% per decade compared to 20–30% per decade in the 1950s and 1960s. Total compensation increased faster than wages and salaries as employers paid higher social security taxes and health insurance premiums. But when the benchmark is adjusted for these benefits, it grew by 8.2% per decade between 1973 and 1986, less than one-third of its earlier growth rate.

The role of rising labor productivity in earnings gains is easy to accept. The precise sources of earnings stagnation are more controversial. In Section 1, I argued that the post-1973 productivity slowdown worsened the trade-off between employment growth and the growth of labor's marginal product. The reader may ask whether slow-growing U.S. earnings reflected nothing more than rapid employment growth per se: that in Figure 1, the U.S. simply moved to the upper left on the pre-1973 frontier.[17]

Two kinds of evidence argue against this view. The first are the estimates of Kendrick (1984) and Denison (1985) that rapid post-1973 growth in the U.S. labor force (including declining labor force experience) accounts for only about .2% of a 1.5% slowdown in the annual growth of labor productivity. The second is the international nature of the productivity slowdown in which the growth of multi-factor and labor productivity growth slowed sharply after 1973 even in countries without rapid labor force growth (Denison 1985; Maddison 1987). In sum, the slowdown of productivity growth exerted independent downward pressure on U.S. real wages above and beyond the pressure of growing employment.

A second argument is that employee compensation has grown slowly because income is increasingly going to owners of property via interest payments, dividends, etc. Figure 6, originally prepared by the Joint Economic Committee (JEC) shows that before 1980, the growth of compensa-

15. Maddison (1987) presents the following estimates for the annual growth of joint factor productivity: U.S., 2.14% (1950–73), .52% (1973–84); Japan, 5.79% (1950–73), 1.21% (1973–84); Germany, 4.32% (1950–73), 1.55% (1973–84); United Kingdom, 2.14% (1950–73), 1.22% (1973–84). The growth of labor productivity *per se* fell in a parallel fashion.
16. More precisely, the 1979–80 oil price shock added unanticipated inflation to what was already a high rate of anticipated inflation.
17. This is equivalent to saying (as some people do) that the current slow growth in the U.S. labor force will auomatically bring an end to the productivity slowdown.

Figure 6 PRODUCTIVITY (BOX) AND REAL COMP(CROSS)

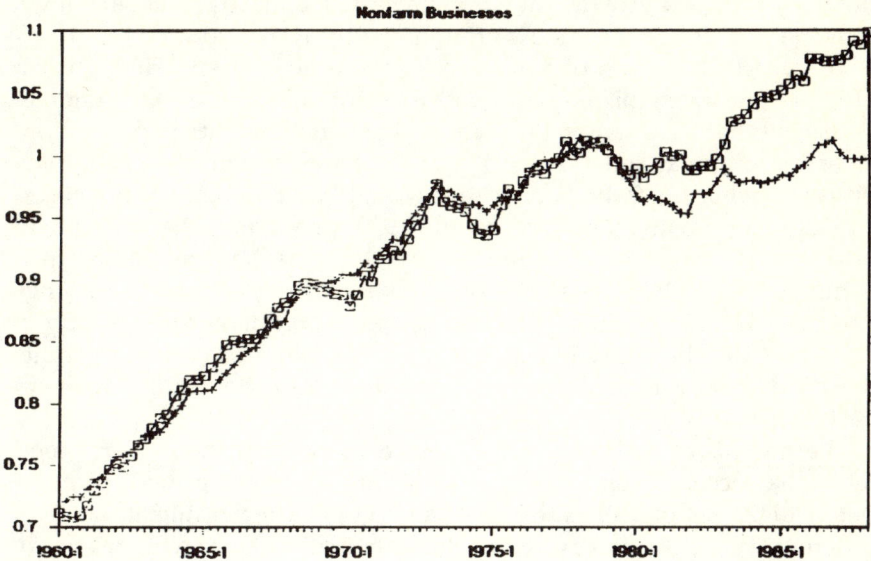

Nonfarm Businesses

Source: Joint Economic Committee

tion per hour closely tracked the growth of GNP per worker, but that since 1980, the compensation series has lagged behind the output series.[18] The biggest part of this divergence reflects the post-1980 difference between the GNP deflator (used to adjust GNP) and the CPI-X1 (used to adjust compensation).[19] At the same time, compensation's nominal share of GNP did fall from .385 in 1980 to .370 in 1986 while the share of property income (in particular, interest payments) rose correspondingly. The point is that over moderately long periods, rising output per worker is a necessary, but not sufficient, condition for rising real wages. This is most evident in the case of manufacturing where the pressure of recession and import competition have caused labor negotiations to focus on job security more than real wage gains, despite rising productivity. But even if 1986 compensation was raised by 4% (to adjust for the

18. I wish to thank Jim Klumpner of the JEC staff for Figure 6 and the discussion of the points of this paragraph.
19. Prior to 1982 the CPI-X1 was similar to the standard CPI (Consumer Price Index) except that it measured housing costs using rental equivalents rather than house prices. Beginning in 1982, the CPI-X1 became the "official" CPI. A different choice for adjusting compensation would not have produced such dramatic results. For example, between 1980 and 1986, the implicit GNP deflator rose by 37.3% while the Personal Consumption Expenditure component of the GNP deflator rose by 38%.

decline in GNP share) it would remove only a small portion the slow-down in earnings growth shown in Table 1. Ultimately, that slowdown must be explained by the slow growth of output per worker.

The pre-1973 growth of real earnings (and the corresponding growth of family incomes) played important roles in national life—for example, the sense that each generation would live better than its parents. Consider a young man who, at age 18, left his parents' home. As he left, he observed what his father's paycheck would buy and he kept the observation as a personal yardstick. In the 1950s and 1960s, the young man would have measured up quickly: by the time he was 30, his real earnings would have been 15–20% greater than his father's earnings had been 12 years earlier.[20] The young man would have known early in his career that he could live at least as well as he had seen his parents live. (I discuss a related issue—the expansion of the middle class—in Section 5.)

The growth of real wages also helped to cushion the loss of "good jobs" that occurs even in periods of strong economic growth (Schumpeter, 1942, Chapter 8). The loss of a good job often results in taking a different job at lower pay (e.g., Horvath 1987). When real wages are growing throughout the economy, a worker can imagine regaining his old real wage in a few years and relative earnings declines do not lead to absolute earnings declines, at least in the long run. But when real wages are stagnant, absolute earnings declines (and the permanent loss of "good jobs") are far more likely. I look at the issue of good and bad jobs in greater detail in the next section.

3. A Loss of Good Jobs?

In 1984, the Joint Economic Committee of the U.S. Congress published "The Great American Job Machine," a paper authored by Barry Bluestone and Bennett Harrison (1986). The authors argued that while the economic expansion of 1982–84 had created a large number of new jobs, most were in what they defined as the "low wage" category. By their calculations, 58% of the net new jobs created between 1979 and 1984 paid less than $7,012 per year (or $7,712 in 1987 dollars). "The Great American Job Machine" was an influential paper both for the media attention it received and the way it shaped the debate over the economy's performance. Even many of Bluestone and Harrison's critics

---

20. Richard Easterlin (1980) develops similar examples for point-in-time comparisons. As Table 1 suggests, the father's income would have grown over these 12 years as well.

to address the "good jobs" argument in Bluestone and Harrison's terms.[21]

In particular, both Bluestone-Harrison and many of their critics used shifts in the *distribution of real annual earnings* to draw inferences about changes in the relative number of *jobs with high hourly wages* ("good jobs").[22] This is, as I noted in Section 1, a big leap because shifts in the distribution of real annual earnings can arise from a number of different factors.

One factor is a changing composition of the work force. At a point in time, wage rates tend to rise with experience (holding education constant) and with education (holding experience constant). It follows that a shift in the age/education composition of the work force can shift the distribution of annual earnings even if workers of a given age and education earn precisely what their counterparts earned in previous years.

A second factor is hours worked. In popular debate, "good jobs" refer to jobs that pay high hourly wages but the good jobs debate has been based on the distribution of *annual* earnings data. One example of the problems this can cause is the upward trend in working women's annual hours of work: a trend that could shift the distribution of women's annual earnings upward even though wage rates had not changed.

Finally, macroeconomic events—unanticipated inflation, changes in the level of productivity, etc.—can shift the distribution of real annual earnings distribution even when the number of steel workers, fast food clerks, professors, etc. remains constant.

The annual earnings distributions of men and women shown in Section 1 (Figures 2 and 3) were potentially influenced by all of these factors.[23] To begin to disentangle these effects, Table 2 focuses on 1973, 1979, and 1986 mean annual earnings and estimated hourly wages of 25–55-year-old year-round full-time workers subdivided by sex, age, and selected educational levels (1987 dollars, PCE adjusted). Earnings distri-

21. A sample of critical commentary includes Kosters and Ross (1988), Samuelson (1987), Brookes (1987), and the Council of Economic Advisers (1988) while Norwood (1987) is slightly more agnostic. Another article relevant to the debate is Rosenthal (1985).
22. Here and elsewhere in this paper, I use the term "wages" to refer to the hourly rate of compensation of any employee, including those whose pay is contracted on a weekly, monthly, or annual basis.
23. The distributions in Figures 2 and 3 differ in several respects from the distributions used by the authors in the "good jobs" debate. Where Figures 2 and 3 focus on 25–55-year-old workers, those articles often focused on all workers age 16 and above. Where Figures 2 and 3 present the data in $10,000 increments, most articles in the debate use two real dollar cut-offs to divide annual earnings into a "low-medium-high" classification. In practice, different authors have chosen different cut-offs and this has further confused the issue.

Table 2   CHANGES IN MEAN INDIVIDUAL EARNINGS FOR MEN
AND WOMEN WHO WORK FULL-TIME, BY AGE AND
SELECTED EDUCATIONAL LEVEL: 1973, 1979, AND 1986
(1987 DOLLARS)

	Mean Earnings In: (Percent Earning $20,000 or Less)			Percent Change in:		
				Annual 1973– 1979	Earnings 1973– 1986	Wages 1973– 1986
	1973	1979	1986			
Men, 25–34						
4 yrs. H.S.	$26,364 (27.0%)	$24,701 (36.0%)	$22,226 (47.5%)	−6%	−16%	−17%
4 yrs. col.	$32,036 (14.7%)	$29,062 (23.6%)	$31,745 (22.6%)	−9%	−1%	−3%
Men, 35–44						
4 yrs. H.S.	$29,736 (19.0%)	$28,992 (24.5%)	$27,738 (28.4%)	−3%	−7%	−7%
4 yrs. col.	$43,331 (9.3%)	$40,555 (11.8%)	$40,194 (13.2%)	−6%	−7%	−9%
Men, 45–54						
4 yrs. H.S.	$30,621 (19.8%)	$29,773 (23.5%)	$29,520 (24.2%)	−3%	−4%	−8%
4 yrs. col.	$45,757 (8.4%)	$43,565 (10.9%)	$45,973 (11.5%)	−5%	—	+1%
Women, 25–34						
4 yrs. H.S.	$15,157 (83.1%)	$15,516 (81.0%)	$15,700 (77.0%)	+2%	+4%	−8%
4 yrs. col.	$20,733 (47.9%)	$20,116 (57.8%)	$23,333 (43.7%)	−3%	+13%	+5%
Women, 35–44						
4 yrs. H.S.	$16,006 (77.4%)	$15,963 (78.7%)	$17,373 (69.3%)	—	+9%	+1%
4 yrs. col.	$23,283 (41.1%)	$21,391 (51.4%)	$26,214 (34.5%)	−8%	+13%	+5%
Women, 45–54						
4 yrs. H.S.	$16,406 (77.3%)	$16,456 (76.6%)	$17,400 (67.2%)	—	+6%	+3%
4 yrs. col.	$23,075 (39.3%)	$21,549 (51.4%)	$25,001 (30.8%)	−7%	+8%	+2%

Source: Author's tabulations of CPS micro data files.

butions are typically skewed upward and so each mean is accompanied by the proportion of the sample who earn less than $20,000.[24] From 1973 through 1979, the data exhibit the slow earnings growth described in Section 2. Relationships among the *relative* earnings of different groups also remained stable. From 1979 through 1986, the average earnings level in the work force continues to show little growth but relative earnings begin to diverge sharply around the average.

The post-1979 dispersion in relative earnings contains three general elements. First, women's earnings, while lower than men's earnings, grew faster than men's earnings. For example, among year-round full-time workers, ages 25–34, with four years of college, women's annual earnings increased by 13% while men's annual earnings declined by 1%. A similar pattern holds among women and men of most other age and educational levels: women's earnings increased while men's declined.

The second pattern involved workers' education. Among workers of a given sex and age, the earnings of the less educated workers usually showed the slowest gains (or the biggest declines). For example, among 35–44-year-old women who worked year-round and full-time, the earnings of women with four years of college grew by 13% over the period while the earnings of women with four years of high school grew by 4%.[25]

Finally, among all year-round workers of the same sex, the earnings of young, less educated workers grew less (or declined more) than the earnings of all other groups.

A more detailed look at the data shows that (estimated) hourly wages *per se* usually grew more slowly over the period than full-time annual earnings. As noted above, the CPS defines a full-time worker as someone who works 35 hours or more per week, a definition which still permits variation in annual hours worked over time. Women classified as year-round full-time workers averaged 36.8 hours of work per week in 1973 but 41.8 hours of work per week in 1986. Similarly, male full-time workers averaged 43.1 hours of work per week in 1973 and 45.3 hours of work per week in 1986. The last column of Table 2 adjusts mean changes in year-round full-time annual earnings for mean changes in hours worked to approximate changes in hourly wages.[26] The resulting esti-

24. A more appropriate statistic for Table 2 would be median earnings but the computation of medians was too cumbersome for this paper.
25. For clarity, the Table 2 is restricted to persons with exactly 12 or 16 years of education. Tabulations not published here indicate a generally monotonic relationship between earnings changes and education within each age-sex group.
26. The CPS does not report an individual's annual hours of work. Rather it reports the individual's hours of work in a "normal week" and the number of weeks worked per year (where full-time workers must report working at least 50 weeks per year). In 1986,

mates of wage changes reproduce the three patterns noted above but at lower absolute rates of growth.

The gradual convergence of men's and women's earnings has been examined by a number of authors including Smith and Ward (1984) and Fuchs (1988). The standard demonstration of the convergence is based on the ratio of published median incomes of all women to all men who work year-around and full-time, a ratio which has grown from .57 in 1973 to .60 in 1979 to .65 in 1986 (U.S. Bureau of the Census 1987b). Because women who work year-round and full-time have increased their average hours worked, the standard demonstration is overstated. But the data in Table 2 demonstrate convergence even when hours are controlled.

The growing earnings gap between more and less educated workers has been less studied and is a reversal of past developments. In 1976, Richard Freeman published *The Overeducated American,* a book which highlighted the falling rate of return to a college diploma. In Freeman's description, America had reached a state of over-education in which:

. . . *the economic rewards to college education are markedly lower than has historically been the case and/or in which additional investment in college training will drive down those rewards—a society in which education has become, like investments in other mature industries or activities a marginal rather than highly profitable endeavor. (pp. 4–5).*

Published U.S. Census data supported Freeman's view. Consider the behavior over time of the following ratio:

$$\frac{\text{Median Income of 25–34-year-old men with 4 years of college}}{\text{Median Income of 25–34-year-old men with 4 years of H.S.}}[27]$$

Throughout the 1950s, the ratio stood at about 1.3. By the end of the 1960s the increasing number of college graduates had caused the ratio to fall to 1.25. And by 1973—roughly the time Freeman was writing—it had fallen to 1.15.

---

both numbers were reported as continuous variables. In 1973, the weeks worked variable was reported in classes with the top class being 50–52 weeks per year. For this reason, changes in annual hours worked were estimated from changes in hours normally worked per week, calculated separately for each age-education-sex group of year-round full-time workers.
27. We use income statistics in this comparison rather than earnings per se because the Census did not publish separate earnings statistics in the 1950s and 1960s.

The ratio remained between 1.15 and 1.2 for the rest of the 1970s. But then, as we have seen, the ground began to shift, most clearly under younger men (Table 2). Among 25–34-year-old men, the ratio grew to 1.30 in 1980 (a recession year) and kept increasing to 1.5 in 1986.[28]

Together, the data in Tables 1 and 2 begin to suggest a two-part story of post-1973 earnings changes. The first part is the combination of oil-price shocks and slow productivity growth which, together, slowed the rate of real wage growth for all workers. The second part is a set of shifts in the demand and supply of different kinds of labor which caused some workers' earnings to grow faster than the underlying trend and other workers' wages to grow more slowly. What remains to be determined is the relative importance of supply shifts and demand shifts in this story.

I begin to look at this question in Table 3 which extends Table 2 to look at the 1973 and 1986 mean earnings of all men and women, ages 25–55, who worked at least one hour for pay during the year (the basis for Figures 2 and 3). For purposes of comparison, Table 3 reproduces from Table 2 the percentage change in earnings for the subset of workers who worked year-round and full-time. Earnings patterns for all workers replicate earnings patterns for year-round full-time workers with slightly larger amplitudes; this suggests that groups who saw wage gains also saw gains in average hours worked, while groups that saw wage declines saw declining average hours as well. The fact that wages and hours were moving in the same direction suggests that relative wage movements were primarily driven by shifts in demand.[29]

Table 4 addresses the issue of supply and demand more directly by comparing changes in a group's mean annual earnings with changes in the group's size. These data also point to the importance of demand shifts in relative earnings movements. Among men or women of a given age, the number of college educated workers grew more quickly than the number of high school educated workers but high school workers' earnings grew more slowly. Similarly, among workers of a given age and education, the number of working women grew more rapidly than the number of working men but women's mean earnings increased while men's mean earnings declined or, in a few cases, remained constant.

28. This fact seems to have been discovered more or less independently by Levy and Michel (1987), Sum and Fogg (1987), Murphy and Welch (1988), and Freeman (personal communication).

29. Ideally, one would verify this fact by directly tabulating annual hours worked. As noted earlier, however, the 1973 Current Population Survey only contains data on hours normally worked per week (a continuous variable) and weeks worked per year (a classified variable). Among people who work part-year, weeks worked is coded in broad classes—e.g., 27–39 weeks—which mean that annual hours of work can be estimated only with great imprecision.

Table 3   MEAN EARNINGS OF ALL MEN AND WOMEN WITH $1 OR
MORE OF EARNINGS, 1973 AND 1986, (1987 DOLLARS)

	Mean Annual Earnings In: (Percent Earning $20,000 or Less)		Percent Change in Earnings for All Workers	(Percent Change in Earnings for Subset of Year-Round Full-Time Workers)
	1973	1986		
Men, 25–34				
4 yrs. H.S.	$24,267 (35.7%)	$19,410 (60.2%)	−20%	−16%
4 yrs. col.	$28,339 (27.7%)	$29,170 (32.5%)	+3%	−1%
Men, 35–44				
4 yrs. H.S.	$27,946 (25.5%)	$25,103 (41.8%)	−11%	−7%
4 yrs. col.	$41,926 (12.8%)	$38,374 (20.1%)	−8%	−7%
Men, 45–54				
4 yrs. H.S.	$28,102 (28.5%)	$27,133 (37.9%)	−3%	−4%
4 yrs. col.	$42,988 (14.7%)	$43,803 (18.4%)	+2%	—
Women, 25–34				
4 yrs. H.S.	$9,870 (94.9%)	$11,133 (89.9%)	+13%	+4
4 yrs. col.	$14,876 (78.1%)	$18,850 (64.1%)	+27%	+13%
Women, 35–44				
4 yrs. H.S.	$10,926 (92.2%)	$12,440 (85.8%)	+14%	+9%
4 yrs. col.	$14,878 (80.1%)	$19,837 (62.3%)	+33%	+27%
Women, 45–54				
4 yrs. H.S.	$12,233 (91.1%)	$13,220 (85.1%)	+8%	+6%
4 yrs. col.	$18,835 (72.0%)	$19,753 (59.5%)	+5%	+3%

Source: Author's Tabulations of CPS micro data files.

In sum, demand shifts do not explain *absolute* earnings gains and losses—oil price shocks and the productivity slowdown are the principal culprits here. But demand shifts help to explain relative earnings gains and losses—why some groups did better than the generally stagnant trend while others did worse.

A story of demand shifts begins by examining the distribution of workers across industries in the early 1970s where, for clarity, I have collapsed industries into four groups:

• Durable and Non-Durable Manufacturing
• Mining and Construction
• Agriculture

Table 4 CHANGES IN GROUP'S SIZE AND GROUP'S AVERAGE ANNUAL EARNINGS, FOR 25–55 YEAR-OLD MEN AND WOMEN WORKERS, 1973–1986

	Number of Workers in:		*Percent Change in Group Size*	*Percent Change in Annual Earnings*
	1973	*1986*		
	(millions)			
Men, 25–34				
4 yrs. H.S.	5.1m	8.1m	+58%	−20%
4 yrs. col.	1.8m	3.3m	+83%	+3%
Men, 35–44				
4 yrs. H.S.	3.8m	5.3m	+39%	−11%
4 yrs. col.	1.1m	2.6m	+136%	−8%
Men, 45–54				
4 yrs. H.S.	4.0m	3.8m	−5%	−3%
4 yrs. col.	1.1m	1.2m	+9%	+2%
Women, 25–34				
4 yrs. H.S.	3.5m	6.7m	+91%	+13%
4 yrs. col.	1.1m	3.0m	+172%	+27%
Women, 35–44				
4 yrs. H.S.	2.8m	5.8m	+107%	+14%
4 yrs. col.	.5m	1.7m	+240%	+33%
Women, 45–54				
4 yrs. H.S.	3.0m	4.0m	+33%	+8%
4 yrs. col.	.4m	.8m	+100%	+5%

Source: Author's tabulations of March 1974 and March 1987 CPS micro data files.

- The Service Sector including wholesale and retail trade, finance-insurance-and real estate, personal services, business and professional services, transportation-utilities-communication, and public administration
- Persons who were not employed during the year (for men only).[30]

Table 5 shows the 1973 distribution of men and women across these employment categories. In 1973, less educated men were concentrated in durable manufacturing and other goods producing industries while more educated men and women were concentrated in services. Among men with a high school education or less, about 45% were employed in durable manufacturing or other goods industries while about 40% were employed in the service sector. Among men with at least some college, about 60% were employed in the service sector. Among women, the proportion employed in the service sector ran from 54% (for women who had not graduated high school) to 97% (for women with more than four years of college).

At this point, it is useful to ask where the "good jobs" were in 1973: Which industries paid men[31] relatively high annual earnings (holding observed characteristics constant). In recent years, it has become a cliché that good jobs are in manufacturing while the bad jobs are in services. While the cliché is stated in general terms, it clearly refers to good and bad jobs for less educated workers (or all today's pre-law and pre-finance undergraduates are making a terrible mistake). But even if I restrict attention to less educated men, earnings patterns in the early 1970s were slightly more complex than the cliché suggests.

Table 6 contains estimates of two-digit industry effects on the annual earnings of men with four years of high school and, for comparison, men with four years of college.[32] The 1973 estimates for high school men show that annual earnings in Retail Sales were about 13% less than annual earnings in Durable Manufacturing, the kind of gap noted 20 years ago by Victor Fuchs (1968). But annual earnings were slightly higher in Transportation, Communications, and Utilities (with the high capital intensity described by Katz and Summers (1988)) and in Whole-

---

30. Later in this section, we will compare industrial distributions for women in 1973 and 1986. Women's labor force participation increased sharply during this period and this makes it hard to separate industrial shifts from increased labor supply. For this reason, we confine women's industrial distributions to working women.

31. We restrict this discussion to men because women were already highly concentrated in the service sector (the sector of "bad jobs" in the popular debate).

32. Estimates come from separate regressions for each educational group, controlling for age and industry. Age-industry interactions for 23–34-year-old workers (i.e., entry level workers) proved insignificant.

Table 5   DISTRIBUTION OF MEN AND WOMEN ACROSS INDUSTRIAL
SECTORS, 1973

	Mfg.	Mining and Constrctn.	Service Sector	Agr.	Persons Who Did Not Work*
All Men, 25–55, by education					
L.T. H.S.	.32	.16	.35	.07	.10
H.S. Grad.	.32	.12	.48	.04	.04
1–3 yrs. col.	.26	.08	.59	.02	.05
4 yrs. col.	.24	.06	.65	.02	.03
4+ yrs. col.	.14	.02	.80	.01	.03
Women, 25–55, by education					
L.T. H.S.	.35	.01	.54	.09	n/a
H.S. Grad.	.20	.02	.76	.02	n/a
1–3 yrs. col.	.12	.01	.86	.01	n/a
4 yrs. col.	.06	.02	.91	.01	n/a
4+ yrs. col.	.02	.01	.97	.00	n/a

*Data for women exclude persons who did not work during the year. See text for explanation.
Source: Author's tabulations of the March 1974 CPS micro data files.

Table 6   EFFECTS OF INDUSTRY ON THE ANNUAL EARNINGS OF
SELECTED 25–34-YEAR-OLD MEN (REFERENCE GROUP IS MEN
IN NON-DURABLE MANUFACTURING)

	Men with 4 Yrs. High School		Men with 4 Yrs. College	
Ref. Group	1973	1986	1973	1986
Earnings	$22,711	$19,853	$29,149	$29,240
Ag/For/Fsh.	−46.2%*	−83.3%*	−33.9%	−87.2%*
Mining	−.6%	+16.5%	−4.9%	+25.4%
Construction	−3.6%	−23.3%	−25.2%	−21.6%
Non-Durable Mfg.	—	—	—	—
Durable Mfg.	+4.0%	+.7%	−6.4%	+8.9%
Trans/Com/Utl.	+7.4%*	−1.0%	+.2%	+1.2%
Wholesale Trd.	+5.6%	−4.5%	−12.4%**	+4.4%
Retail Trade	−12.7%*	−31.5%*	−23.2%*	−32.1%*
FIRE	+6.9%	−11.8%	−9.9%**	−2.4%
Bsns/Rpr/Srv.	−11.9%*	−44.9%*	−27.3%*	−15.8%*
Pers. Srv.	−34.8%*	−45.5%*	−38.4*	−44.4%*
Prof. Srv.	−18.4%*	−37.5%*	−23.8%*	−25.8%*
Public Adm.	+2.2%	+3.2%	−6.5%	−5.7%*

* = coefficient from which percentage change was estimated was significant at the .05 level; ** =
significant at the .10 level.
Source: Estimates calculated from regressions of LN (annual earnings) on age and industry for 25–55-
year-old men with four yrs. high school and four yrs. college (separate regressions).

sale Trade. If anything, the 1973 earnings pattern for young men with four years of college fit the clichè slightly better.

The earnings patterns for less educated men point to the possibility of a disequilibrium in which at least some men were working in the service sector (outside Transportation, Communications, and Utilities) because vacancies in higher wage industries were not available.[33]

In the 13 years after 1973, vacancies in manufacturing, in particular did not grow appreciably. Manufacturing—particularly durable manufacturing—is sensitive to economic downturns. The years after 1973 saw two sharp downturns: 1973–75 and 1980–82 (Lawrence 1982). Beyond this, the post 1982 recovery was accompanied by an overvalued high dollar which further undercut both foreign and domestic demand for U.S. manufactured goods. Between 1973 and 1979, employment on manufacturing payrolls increased by 5%, much less than the growth in the male labor force. Between 1979 and 1986, employment on manufacturing payrolls declined by 10%. (Council of Economic Advisers, 1989).

Table 7 compares the 1973, 1979, and 1986 industrial distributions of men and women. Among 25–34-year-olds with a high school education, the proportion in manufacturing fell sharply from .34 to .24 with most of the drop coming after 1979. Conversely, among 25–34-year-old men with four years of college, the proportion of college educated men in manufacturing held steady at .20. The comparison is noteworthy because the absolute number of college educated men in this age group grew faster than the number of high school educated men (Table 4). This suggests that less educated young men were losing manufacturing jobs not only because of the slow growth of manufacturing employment but because the composition of that employment was shifting toward more educated workers.

In theory, the shift of younger, less educated men out of goods production might have been a voluntary response to more attractive alternatives in other sectors. The 1986 pattern of high school men's earnings by industry in Table 6 suggests this was not the case: the earnings gap between manufacturing and service sector industries was sharper and more uniform in 1986 than it had been in 1973. More plausibly, the contraction of manufacturing employment placed young, less educated men in a position of excess supply. To a limited extent, service sector

33. One might postulate a similar disequilibrium among college educated men except that industry-specific training makes substitution across industries more problematic (e.g., moving from being a retail manager to being an engineer).

industries acted as an absorbing buffer, but at the cost of a steep decline in service sector earnings, which led to the sharpened manufacturing/ services distinction noted above.[34] More generally, the movement of younger, less educated men out of manufacturing did not represent more service sector employment so much as more young men out of the labor force. The earnings statistics in Tables 2 and 3 exclude men who do not work during the year but the existence of such men also points to their being in excess supply. The result was a sharp decline in the relative earnings of young, less educated men in all sectors (Table 6) including manufacturing.[35]

When compared to young, less educated men, other groups of workers were in relatively stronger positions. Older, less educated men had the benefit of job seniority while better educated men and most women were heavily concentrated in the service sector and so were relatively insulated from the problems of manufacturing.[36] Better educated women, in particular, appear to have benefited from a moderate amount of occupational mobility (Bianchi and Spain 1986).

It follows that a resolution of the good jobs-bad jobs debate must make three points. The first point is the slow growth of earnings—a macroeconomic phenomenon—which affected earnings in all sectors. Today, a young man (or woman) with four years of college can accept what used to be called a good white collar job for $25,000 and wonder whether he will ever be able to afford a house like the one in which he grew up. In this sense, weak productivity growth (and the income losses of oil price shocks) have limited the number of jobs with "middle class paychecks" and have helped create a wide audience for the good jobs-bad jobs debate.

The second point is the shift in demand away from young, less educated male workers. In 1973, 64% of male high school graduates, ages 25–34, earned more than $20,000 per year (in 1987 dollars). By 1986, the corresponding proportion had declined to 40%. Shifts in demand occur all the time, of course, but reduced demand in a context of general stagnation has much more serious implications. Elsewhere, I have estimated that today's 30-year-old male high school graduate will have trouble out-earning his high school educated father if labor productivity

34. Earnings in Transportation, Communications, and Utilities also dropped as a result of deregulation.
35. A recent paper by Blackburn, Bloom, and Freeman (1989) similarly concludes that the decline in the earnings of young, less educated men, is much more a function of wage declines within industries than shifts of employment across industry.
36. Though it appears from Tables 5 and 6 that young, less educated women faced some of the same pressure from manufacturing as young, less educated men.

Table 7 DISTRIBUTION OF MEN AND WOMEN ACROSS INDUSTRIAL SECTORS, BY SELECTED AGE AND EDUCATION, 1973, 1979, AND 1986

	Mfg.	Other Goods Industries	Service Sector	Agr.	Persons Who Did Not Work*
Men, 25–34					
H.S. Grad.					
1973	.34	.14	.46	.03	.03
1979	.32	.14	.44	.03	.06
1986	.24	.17	.48	.04	.07
4 yrs. col.					
1973	.20	.06	.68	.02	.04
1979	.20	.07	.66	.03	.04
1986	.20	.06	.70	.02	.02
Men, 35–44					
H.S. Grad.					
1973	.32	.12	.49	.04	.03
1979	.31	.15	.46	.04	.05
1986	.27	.14	.48	.03	.08
4 yrs. col.					
1973	.28	.05	.64	.02	.01
1979	.22	.06	.66	.02	.03
1986	.23	.06	.67	.02	.02
Men, 45–55					
H.S. Grad.					
1973	.29	.10	.50	.05	.06
1979	.28	.13	.48	.04	.06
1986	.28	.13	.48	.04	.07
4 yrs. col.					
1973	.26	.08	.60	.02	.04
1979	.28	.05	.62	.01	.03
1986	.27	.06	.63	.01	.03
Women 25–34					
H.S. Grad					
1973	.23	.02	.72	.03	n/a
1979	.21	.02	.76	.01	n/a
1986	.17	.01	.80	.01	n/a
4 yrs. col.					
1973	.05	.01	.93	.01	n/a
1979	.09	.01	.90	.01	n/a
1986	.11	.02	.86	.01	n/a
Women 35–44					
H.S. Grad					
1973	.18	.01	.79	.02	n/a
1979	.18	.02	.78	.02	n/a
1986	.16	.02	.81	.01	n/a

Table 7   DISTRIBUTION OF MEN AND WOMEN ACROSS INDUSTRIAL
SECTORS, BY SELECTED AGE AND EDUCATION, 1973, 1979,
AND 1986 (CONTINUED)

	Mfg.	Other Goods Industries	Service Sector	Agr.	Persons Who Did Not Work*
4 yrs. col.					
1973	.03	—	.96	.01	n/a
1979	.07	.01	.92	.01	n/a
1986	.07	.01	.91	.01	n/a
Women 45–55					
H.S. Grad.					
1973	.19	.01	.77	.03	n/a
1979	.18	.02	.79	.02	n/a
1986	.17	.01	.79	.03	n/a
4 yrs. col.					
1973	.04	.01	.94	.01	n/a
1979	.05	.02	.92	.02	n/a
1986	.06	—	.93	.01	n/a

Note: Rows may not sum to 1.00 due to rounding.
Source: Author's Tabulations of the March 1974, March 1980, and March 1987 CPS micro data files. CPS public use sample.

continues to grow at recent rates (Levy 1988b), something that is quite new in the American experience.[37]

Finally, the good jobs-bad jobs debate is more a story about men (in particular, young, less educated men) than women. Women's earnings are systematically below those of men but the proportion of women earning more than $20,000 per year rose from 16% in 1973 to 27 percent in 1986. A large part of this increase reflects increased hours of work but at least some part reflects rising real wages. Among younger women there is some evidence of growing inequality between more and less educated workers. But on the whole, women's position in the labor market improved moderately over this period both in absolute terms and relative to men.

4. Income Per Worker and Income Per Capita

In the long view of U.S. economic history, the period from the end of World War II through 1973 was unusual for its relative tranquility and its

37. In similar calculations, I estimate that today's 30-year-old male college educated worker will out-earn his college educated father but only by about 5 percent, much less than the 1950s and 1960s.

sustained income growth. During this time, Americans experienced steadily rising living standards with the benefits described in Section 2: young people's certainty that they would live better than their parents, a "cushion" for shifting employment patterns, and so on. In this context, the post-1973 stagnation of worker's incomes might have come as an enormous shock to the country.

There was a shock,[38] but it was smaller than one might have expected. One data series helps explain the reason. Income per capita, the most widely used measure of living standards, was growing strongly even though individual wage rates were not. The Census reports that between 1973 and 1986, the median income of all men who worked year-round and full-time declined from $27,490 to $26,926 (−2%) while the comparable figure for women rose from $15,533 to $17,147 (+10%). Over the same period, the Census measure of income per capita (i.e., Census defined income per man, woman and child) rose briskly from $9,926 to $12,250, (+22%). As noted in Section 1, the Census measures pre-tax, money receipts (excluding capital gains) but the Department of Commerce measure of disposable income per capita, which corrects for taxes paid, capital gains, and noncash income, also rose by 21% over the period.

The divergent trends in income per worker and income per capita can be reconciled by noting the substantial increase in the proportion of the population who worked. In 1973, the civilian labor force represented 42% of the entire U.S. population. By 1986, the labor force represented 50% of the entire population.[39] This increase in relative labor supply was the result of three factors: increases in women's labor force participation, the entrance of the largest baby-boom cohorts into the work force (as they entered their late teenage years and early 20s), and sustained low birth rates throughout the period.

In microcosm, these changes meant a sharp move away from "1950s families" with one paycheck and two or three children. 1980s families typically had two paychecks and one or two children. In the limit, a sharp rise in the median age at first marriage increased the number of persons who remained outside of families and who had only themselves

38. One can argue, for example, that one cause of the late-1970s taxpayer revolt was the tension between stagnant incomes and growing government expenditures. Idiosyncratic conditions in various states also played important roles (see Levy 1979).
39. See, for example, Council of Economic Advisers (1989), Tables B-31 and B-32. Note that the figures refer to the ratio of the labor force to the entire population rather than the population aged 16 and over which is used in the computation of labor force participation rates.

to support.[40] For the economy as a whole, the changes meant that income per capita (per man, woman, and child) could keep rising despite stagnant income per worker because a growing proportion of the population was at work.[41]

To what extent were smaller families and increased women's labor force participation endogenous responses to stagnant earnings? The answer is far from clear. We know that women's labor force participation had been increasing steadily since the 1950s (Bianchi and Spain 1986), and the baby boom which ended in 1964 (Butz and Ward 1979), both well before the onset of stagnation. At the same time, each trend is consistent with income growth that fails to satisfy consumption aspirations and both trends might have leveled off sooner in an environment of strong wage growth (Elster and Kamlet 1987). Self-reported explanations of behavior are, of course, treacherous because people often see themselves as behaving normally—e.g., having a normal number of children—even while the norms themselves are changing rapidly over time.

What is clear is that demographic shifts are not a mechanism for continued increases in living standards. Today, about two-thirds of young husband-wife couples begin married life with both partners working. At the same time, the birth rate has stopped falling while the median age of first marriage has stopped increasing. Together, these trends place limits on further increases in the proportion of the population at work and they underline what is simply common sense: Whatever their short run divergence, income per capita can ultimately grow no faster than income per worker.[42]

40. In 1970, the median age of first marriage was 21 for women and 23 for men. By 1986, the median age of first marriage had risen by about two years for each group. See U.S. Bureau of the Census, 1987a.

41. During this period, the U.S. also increased its living standards through foreign borrowing, but Census income statistics are not a good device for measuring this increase. As a rough approximation, foreign borrowing permitted the federal government to sharply reduce taxes and run budget deficits without forcing drastic reductions in the rate of gross investment. Because Census incomes statistics are measured on a pre-tax basis, they do not capture the increase in disposable income that comes from reduced taxes. For a discussion of foreign borrowing and living standards, see Litan, Lawrence, and Schultze (1988), Chapters 1 and 2.

42. The stagnation in real incomes has also been questioned on the grounds that we do a poor job of measuring the output of the service sector—particularly convenience aspects—and so understate the growth of output. Recent work by Martin N. Baily and Robert J. Gordon (1988) have examined this question in the context of the productivity slowdown. They find that the probable mismeasurement of output is relatively small.

5. The Family Income Distribution

In casual discussion, inequality in the earnings distribution and inequality in the family income distribution are often treated interchangeably. The two distributions are related, a relationship I begin to explore in the next section, but the distributions also differ in many respects. Put briefly, family incomes depend on trends in individual earnings but they also depend on trends in the number of earners per family as well as trends in incomes from sources other than earnings (interest payments, private pensions, government transfer payments, etc.).

In the years since World War II, Census measures of the U.S. family income distribution have displayed two main characteristics: substantial absolute inequality, and general stability. By Census measures, 1969, a year of extremely tight labor markets, was the year of greatest family income inequality. In that year, however, the poorest quintile of families received 5.6% of all family income while the richest quintile received 40.6%, a ratio of about $1.00 to $7.25. In 1986, the corresponding ratio was $1.00 to $9.50, but as shown in Table 8, a family did not have to be millionaires to be in the top fifth of families.

The best international comparisons of income inequality suggest that U.S. family income inequality is high not only absolutely but also relative to inequality in other countries. For example Sawyer (1976) shows that the poorest quintile of U.S. *households* received 3.8% of pre-tax income in 1972, compared to 5.4% in Germany (1973), 7.6% in Japan (1969), 4.4% in the United Kingdom, 4.3% in Canada (1969), and so on.[43] More recent work by Coder, Rainwater, and Smeeding (1988), using data developed by the Luxembourg Income Study, shows that in the 1979–83 period, the level of disposable income inequality among U.S. families was highest among the ten industrialized countries in their sample (including Germany, the United Kingdom, and Canada).[44]

The relative stability of U.S. family income inequality is displayed in Table 8. Through 39 years, the income share going to the poorest quintile of families has varied between 4.6% and 5.6% while the income share of the top quintile has varied between 40.6% and 43.7%.

The variations in Table 8 are larger than they seem. For example, the income share of the lowest quintile has varied in a range of 1%. But this is a range of 1% of *all family income* for a group that received

43. Households include both families and other living units in which the inhabitants are not related. I have used Sawyer's pre-tax income figures to in order to be consistent with the Census pre-tax income figures used throughout this paper. Sawyer also calculates post-tax distributions and arrives at similar conclusions.
44. This ranking was invariant to three inequality measures: Atkinson's measure (with $e = .5$), the Gini coefficient, and Theil's inequality index.

only about 5% of all family income to begin with. In 1986, for example, an income share of 5.6% rather than 4.6% would have raised mean income in the lowest quintile from $8,363 to $10,181 (in 1987 dollars), no small difference. But over 39 years the size of these swings is relatively moderate.

The stability of the family income distribution over almost four decades raises three quite different questions. First, is the stability real or is it an artifact of Census data definitions and procedures? Second, how is the stability consistent with popular perceptions that the middle class grew dramatically in the 1950s and 1960s (Gans 1967), but is now "in danger of vanishing" (Kuttner 1983; Thurow 1984). Finally, why did inequality remain constant in the face of two developments favoring equality: the declining proportion of families in low wage agriculture, and the improving relative incomes of elderly families. I briefly address each question in turn.

As I noted in Section 1, the Census defines income as pre-tax money receipts excluding capital gains. Moreover, to preserve confidentiality, other income sources are reported with top codes ("caps") that change only infrequently. In 1986, for example, both wages and salaries and self-employment income were not reported in excess of $100,000 for any individual. In the early and mid-1980s, capital gains realizations were high and top salaries in many professions were growing fast. There is little doubt that during this period, income coding limits and the non-reporting of capital gains combined to understate both the level and

Table 8 SHAPE OF THE U.S. FAMILY INCOME DISTRIBUTION

A. *Share of All Family Income Going to Each Fifth of Families*

	1st fifth (poorest)	2nd fifth	3rd fifth	4th fifth	5th fifth (richest)	*Total*
1949	4.5%	11.9%	17.3%	23.5%	42.7%	100%
1959	4.9%	12.3%	17.9%	23.8%	41.1%	100%
1969	5.6%	12.4%	17.7%	23.7%	40.6%	100%
1979	5.2%	11.6%	17.5%	24.1%	41.7%	100%
1986	4.6%	10.8%	16.8%	24.0%	43.7%	100%

B. *1986 Income Upper Limits for Each Quintile (1987 dollars)*

1st Q Ends at	2nd Q Ends at	3rd Q Ends at	4th Q Ends at
$14,500	$25,082	$36,564	$52,597

Note: Percentages may not add up to 100 due to rounding.
Source: U.S. Bureau of the Census (1986b)

growth of income inequality in Census reports.[45] Joseph Pechman, for example, has compiled data from the U.S. Treasury's annual *Statistics of Income* series, which show that the share of gross income received by the top one-fifth of filing units (as distinct from families) rose from 43.1% in 1981 to 52.3% in 1986, a far larger shift than is implied by Census statistics (personal communication). Pechman further estimates that 6.6 percentage points of this 9.2 percentage point gain in share accrued to the top 1% of filing units. A 1987 study by Richard Kasten and Frank Sammartino of the Congressional Budget Office arrives at similar, but less dramatic conclusions for households (as distinct from families) (Congressional Budget Office 1987).[46] Both studies are consistent with recent explorations of CPS data by Gottschalk, Danziger, and Smolensky (1988) who conclude that even among husband-wife families under age 65, property income is important only among the top 1% of the population while the biggest income gains for the rest of this group have come from wives' earnings. In sum, even if one acknowledges the different units of observation used by the Census, Pechman, and the CBO, it is almost certain that Census conventions that exclude capital gains and cap reported incomes have caused understated recent trends in income inequality particularly in the upper ranges of the distribution.

At the same time, reasonable adjustments for this understatement still would leave the inequality figures in Table 8 too uniform to be consistent with a rapidly expanding middle class in the 1950s and 1960s and a middle class under pressure in the 1980s. The issue is further muddled because in 1986, the *top* quintile of the family income distribution began at $52,597 (in 1987 dollars), an income which many families see as squarely in the middle class. The major answer to this paradox, I believe, is the income growth and stagnation described in Section 2. Between 1947 and 1986, median family income rose from $14,830 to $28,890 (36 percent per decade). This growth was accompanied by rapid increases in the proportions of families who owned their own homes, and who owned cars, washing machines, dryers, televisions, air conditioners, and so on. The middle class was growing not because incomes were becoming substantially more equal but because more families could af-

---

45. There is the more general problem of non-response and underreporting of incomes, problems that are not limited to upper income groups. See Levy (1988a) Appendix B, Lillard, Smith, and Welch (1986).

46. Distributional studies based on households can be influenced by such factors as the rising age of first marriage which increases the number of single person households in the sample. The issue has become confused because CBO uses the term "family" to include both families (in the Census definition) and persons who live alone or with other non-relatives.

ford a middle class style of living as we had come to define it (Levy 1988a, Chapter 4). Between 1973 and 1986, median family income grew from $28,890 to $30,670 (5% per decade) and it was this stagnation which helped prompt fears of a vanishing middle class. There is a second element to fears of a vanishing middle class involving changes in the kinds of families that occupy various portions of the distribution. I return to this point shortly.

The relative stability of inequality is also suprising when one considers post-World War II population trends. In the late 1940s, the bottom quintile of the family income distribution was dominated by two kinds of families: elderly families (many of whom still worked) and farm families who comprised about 11% of all families and who typically reported very low money incomes.[47] Since that time, rapid gains in agricultural productivity have reduced the need for agricultural labor and the proportion of families in agriculture has declined from 11% to 2%. At the same time, successive cohorts of elderly families have benefited from greater Social Security coverage, indexed Social Security payments (after 1971) and greater private pension coverage.[48] As a result, incomes of elderly families over the last 15 years have grown more rapidly than the incomes of non-elderly families (Council of Economic Advisors 1985; see also Table 9 below). These events, *cet. par.*, should have increased family income equality particularly after 1971 but, of course, that did not occur.

A partial explanation for the trend in inequality since 1971 is contained in Table 9. These data show that while the incomes of elderly families were rising, the number of families headed by single women was growing rapidly. Among families headed by someone under age 65, the proportion headed by a single woman rose from about one in eight in the early 1970s to one in five today, where in both years, the median incomes of such families were well below the incomes of other families in the population. The result was a kind of "swap" in which elderly families were moving from the bottom of the income distribution to the lower middle while their "vacated places" at the bottom were taken by new female-headed families with children.

I noted above that Census data understate the recent increase in family income inequality. The data in Table 9 suggest that such increased inequality as the Census does report might be driven by changes in family structure: the growing number of families who are *either* headed

47. Money incomes obviously understate the relative well-being of many farm families but the purpose of this discussion is to examine trends in reported Census (i.e., money income) statistics.

48. Peter Diamond reminds me that the incomes of elderly families were further increased because Social Security was not only indexed but over-indexed for much of the 1970s.

by a single woman *or* have two earners. The suggestion, while plausible, is wrong. Recent calculations by Eugene Smolensky suggest that wives' earnings have exerted a moderating influence on increased household income inequality (personal communication). Growing numbers of families headed by single women are clearly important in increased family income inequality but the growing inequality of male earnings is important as well. I return to this point in the next section.

I also noted above that population shifts *within* the income distribution add to perceptions of a vanishing middle class. In particular, the swap of female-headed families for elderly families at the bottom of the distribution has led to a situation in which income inequality among families with children has increased substantially (Figure 7). We saw in Section 4 that part of the post-1973 increase in income per capita reflected low national birth rates. In this context, a growing number of families headed by women led to an even more rapid growth in the proportion of children in female-headed families: .10 of all children in 1973 to .20 of all children in 1986. The result has been to increase the proportion of children in families with income under $10,000 (1987 dollars) from one in nine in the early 1970s to one in six today. The growing number of poor children is highly visible and newsworthy—as it should be. Specifically, poor children are more visible than the improved incomes of the elderly, and this leads to a perception that income inequality is rising faster than the Census statistics report.

The perception, moreover, may contain a kernel of truth. If middle class families no longer drop to the bottom of the income distribution

Table 9   FREQUENCY AND MEDIAN INCOME OF MAJOR FAMILY TYPES, 1973, 1986 (INCOMES IN 1987 DOLLARS)

Family Type	1973		1986	
	Percent of All Families	Median Income	Percent of All Families	Median Income
All	100%	$29,890	100%	$30,670
Family Head ≥ Age 65*	14.3%	$15,956	15.8%	$20,752
Hus.-Wife <65, Wife does not Work	39.7%	$30,218	24.5%	$29,787
Hus.-Wife <65 Wife Works	33.6%	$37,158	42.3%	$38,750
Female Fam. Head <65	10.3%	$13,424	14.4%	$11,308
All other families	2.1%	—	3.0%	—

*Includes both male and female headed families over age 65.
Source: Current Population Reports, various issues. Some medians interpolated from published data.

upon retirement and if low income female-headed families remain female-headed families for long periods of time (Bane and Ellwood 1986), it may be that mobility *within* the income distribution has declined over the last 15 years—that a fairly stable distribution of current family incomes obscures a growing inequality of permanent family incomes. This is a topic for future research.

6. Earnings Inequality and Income Inequality

To this point, I have emphasized inequality that arises from between-group differences: mean differences in earnings between high school and college educated workers, mean income differences between female-headed families and two-earner families, and so on. In this section, I look again at changes in family income inequality from a somewhat broader perspective. I showed in Sections 1 and 3 that earnings of prime age men have also become less equal over 1973–86 and we can reasonably ask to what extent this individual earnings inequality—a growing within-group difference—was translated into family income inequality. In this section, I present some illustrative, incomplete calculations on this question.

I begin by reviewing one version of the steps that link male earnings to family income. For clarity, I focus on men ages 25–34.

Figure 7 DISTRIBUTION OF CHILDREN BY FAMILY INCOME 1973, 1986

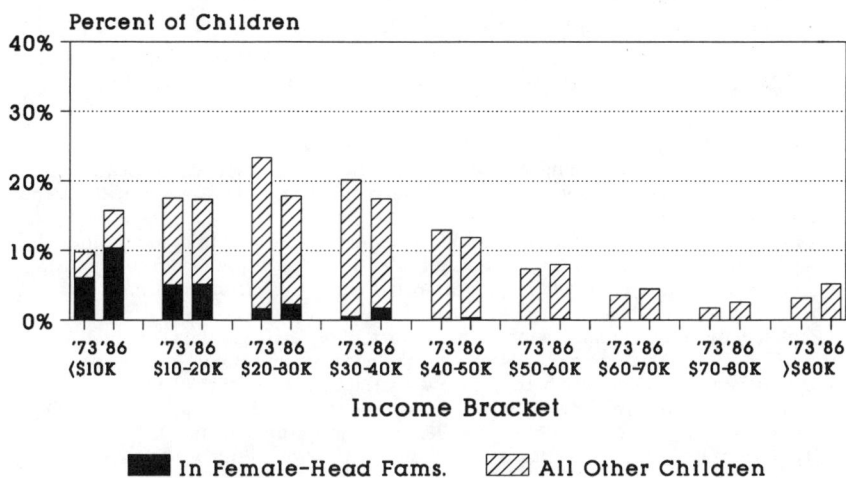

Source: author's tabulations of CPS micro data files.
Income in 1987 dollars. Inflation-adjusted using PCE Index.

The process begins with the distribution of earnings of all men, ages 25–
34, including men who have no earnings whatsoever.[49]

The next step is the move from the distribution of individual earnings to
the distribution of individual incomes including unemployment compensation, rents, dividends, and other income sources as reported by
the Census.

The third step is the move from the distribution of individual incomes of
all 25–34 men to the distribution of individual incomes of 25–34-year-
old husbands.

The final step is the move from the individual incomes of all 25–34-year-
old husbands to the family incomes of all 25–34-year-old husbands.

While earnings inequality among 25–34-year-old men has increased
over time, the last two steps of the sequence have the potential of mut-
ing this inequality. Andrew Sum, among other authors, has shown that
the individual incomes of married men are higher, on average, than the
individual incomes of unmarried men with similar characteristics (Sum's
work appears in Children's Defense Fund 1988).[50] It follows that moving
from the individual incomes of all men to the individual incomes of
married men (step 3) should both raise mean income and lower relative
income inequality.[51]

In a similar fashion, I have shown, as have a number of other authors,
that wives' earnings increase the relative equality of income of husband-
wife families (Levy 1988, Chapter 8).[52] It follows that moving from husbands' individual incomes to the total of their families (step 4) should
produce a distribution with a higher mean and lower relative inequality.

The issue, however, is not just the direction of these effects but the
magnitudes of the effects: to what extent were the effects able to reduce

49. Men without earnings were excluded from Figure 2 and Tables 2 and 3 because my
    focus there was on the changing nature of employment. Men without earnings are
    included here because they are potential husbands who may appear in the family
    income distribution.
50. A priori, these earnings differences could correspond to either unmeasured differences
    in ability or the change in outlook brought about by the responsibilities of marriage.
    Attempts to determine the relative importance of these two factors have been generally
    unsuccessful.
51. By relative income inequality, I mean the coefficient of variation, the Gini index, Atkin-
    son's index, etc. Absolute inequality—e.g., the variance of income—may well increase
    since husbands' incomes are higher, on average, than the incomes of all men.
52. This equality comes from two sources. First, wives' labor force participation falls as
    husbands' earnings rise (though this is becoming less true over time). Second, varia-
    tions in working wives' earnings is less than the variation in husbands' earnings. The
    joint result is that the wives' percentage contribution to family income declines as
    husbands' earnings rise.

the amount of individual earnings inequality that was passed through to the family income distribution.

Some rough calculations on this point appear in Table 10 which track the four steps described above for 25–34-year-old men with four years of high school, 25–34-year-old men with four years of college, and all 25–34-year-old men (including Ph.D.'s, high school dropouts, etc.).

The results in the Table 10 support two general conclusions. First, as we move from individual earnings to family income, the processes described above reduce the coefficient of variation (c.o.v.) by a total of about 20% (e.g., .518 versus .429 for 25–34-year-old high school men in 1974), a result that is consistent across all groups in the table. Second, the magnitudes of these percentage reductions were similar in 1974 and 1986 and so the increased earnings inequality of the period reappeared largely intact in the family income distribution. For all 25–34-year-old men, the c.o.v. for individual earnings rose from .603 in 1973 to .736 in 1986 (+22%) while the c.o.v. for family income rose from .476 to .594 (+.25%). Thus increased earnings inequality among men did have an impact on increased family income inequality.

The stable proportional reductions in inequality are surprising given the way in which marital patterns changed over the period. The rising age of first marriage (noted in Section 4) and related developments sharply reduced the proportion of 25–34-year-old men who were husbands. A priori, marriage might have increasingly acted to screen low income men out of the family income distribution. In practice, declining marriage rates were uniform across educational groups and the screening did not occur. Among 25–34-year-old *husbands* with a high school diploma, mean individual income fell from $26,262 in 1973 to $21,752 (−17%). Among 25–34-year-old husbands with four years of college, mean individual income rose slightly over the period. In both cases, the changes in mean husbands' incomes parallel the changes in mean earnings for all men of similar characteristics (married or not). Thus among families headed by 25–34-year-old high school graduates, increased wives' earnings were needed to maintain 1986 family income at its 1973 level. Among families headed by 25–34-year-old college graduates, increased wives' earnings caused family income to rise by about 14% over the period.

It should be noted that the calculations in Table 10 are only one of two mechanisms in which male earnings trends may have influenced family income inequality. The other mechanism is the postulated relationship between low men's earnings and the formation of female-headed families per se. A chief proponent of this view is William Julius Wilson who

Table 10 THE TRANSLATION OF 25–34-YEAR-OLD MEN'S EARNINGS INTO FAMILY INCOME (1987 DOLLARS)

25–43-Year Old Men with 12 Yrs. of Ed.

	1973				1986			
	Cohort (% chng)	Mean	Coef. of var.	% chng. in c.o.v.	Cohort (%chng.)	Mean	Coef. of var.	%chng. in c.o.v.
All Indiv. Earnings	5.4m (–)	$24,153	.518	—	8.5m. (–)	$18,664	.653	—
All Indiv. Income.	5.4m (–)	$24,729	.503	–2.9%	8.5m. (–)	$19,430	.632	–.9%
Hsbnds' Indiv. Income	4.3m (–20.4%)	$26,262	.457	–9.1%	4.8m. (–43.6%)	$21,752	.574	–9.1
Hsbnds' Family Income	4.3m (–)	$31,376	.429	–6.1%	4.8m. (–)	$31,034	.524	–9.1%

25–34 Year Old Men with 16 Yrs. of Ed.

	1973				1986			
	Cohort (% chng.)	Mean	Coef. of var.	% chng. in c.o.v.	Cohort (%chng.)	Mean	Coef. of var.	%chng. in c.o.v.
All Indiv. Earnings	1.8m (–)	$27,413	.568	—	5.3m. (–)	$28,165	.622	—
All Indiv. Income.	1.8m (–)	$30,357	.569	+.1	5.3m. (–)	$30,299	.612	–1.7%
Hsbnds' Indiv. Income	1.4m (–22.2%)	$32,827	.523	–8.1%	2.7m. (–49.1%)	$33,281	.552	–8.9%
Hsbnds' Family Income	1.4m (–)	$40,763	.455	–13.1%	2.7m. (–)	$46,402	.504	–8.7%

All 25–34 Year Old Men. (includes all educational levels)

	1973				1986			
	Cohort (% chng.)	Mean	Coef. of. var.	% chng. in c.o.v.	Cohort (%chng.)	Mean	Coef. of var.	%chng. in c.o.v.
All Indiv. Earnings	14.2m. (−)	$24,282	.603	—	21.1m. (−)	$20,981	.736	—
All Indiv. Income.	14.2m. (−)	$25,061	.583	−3.4%	21.1m. (−)	$21,905	.710	−3.6%
Hsbnds' Indiv. Income	10.9m. (−23.7%)	$27,038	.522	−10.5%	11.9m. (−43.6%)	$24,620	.643	−9.9%
Hsbnds' Family Income	10.9m. (−)	$33,081	.476	−8.6%	11.9m. (−)	$34,293	.594	−7.7%

Note: % change in cohort refers to the percent reduction from the previous step. Percent in c.o.v. refers to the percent change in the coefficient of variation from the previous step.
Source: Author's tabulations of CPS micro data files

argues that the prominence of female-headed families among blacks reflects a pool of black "marriageable men" that has been sharply limited by unemployment and low earnings (as well as incarceration and homicide). Wilson offers some suggestive evidence on this proposition (Wilson 1988) while other attempts to test the proposition do not reach clear conclusions (e.g., Bassi 1987).

7. Conclusion

It is sometimes argued that the income distribution is the preoccupation of intellectuals: the population at large does not care about it, and if the government cares about it, it should not since it will only make things worse.[53] People can argue about the normative content of this view, but as a description of behavior, it is increasingly incorrect. In recent years, the distributions of U.S. earnings and family incomes have increasingly been the subject of public discussion. There are, I believe, two reasons why this trend will continue. The first reason involves the ramifications of continued slow growth of individual incomes (should growth, in fact, remain slow). With the conspicuous exception of Social Security, the U.S. has not engaged in significant income redistribution to reduce inequality. Rather, we have relied on rapid economic growth to improve living standards across the board. This is a sensible enough strategy when growth is strong but it leaves us vulnerable when growth is weak. Today, for example, something like half of all 25–34-year-old men have a high school diploma or less. If this group has greatly difficulty in buying single family homes—in particular, more difficulty than their fathers had—this economic issue will surely become a political issue as well.

The second reason for predicting continued attention is the growing bi-modality in the distribution of children's families' incomes (Figure 7). Through much of the 1970s, the labor force was growing at 2–2.5% per year and labor with weak skills could simply be disregarded. Over the next decade, the labor force will be growing at 1–1.5% a year and labor will become a relatively scarce commodity. It is very hard to predict the required skill distribution of future occupations, but it is plausible that many occupations will require more skills in the future than they did in the past. A number of recent newspaper articles and anecdotes have described the growth of applicant testing for automobile production workers (particularly at U.S.-Japanese joint ventures), telephone operators, and other "good high school jobs" (Levy and Murnane, forthcom-

---

53. This spirit is captured in Irving Kristol's comment on Alan Blinder's 1980 review of income inequality (Kristol 1980).

ing). In this context, the growing proportion of children in homes with incomes less than $10,000 is not a good sign. Sarah McLanahan (1985), among others, has demonstrated that coming from a low income, female headed family sharply increases the probability of not finishing high school for both whites and blacks. The implications of this situation have already stimulated both substantial public discussion and growing business interest in assisting local school systems.[54] A decade ago, when the labor force was increasing at 2–3% per year, such cooperation was largely unknown.

In sum, issues of inequality are very much today in the public eye. I believe they have reached that position as much from a failure of growth as from increased inequality per se. But whatever their origins, the issues will be with us for the foreseeable future.

REFERENCES

Baily, Martin Neil and Robert J. Gordon. 1988. "The Productivity Slowdown, Measurement Issues, and the Explosion of Computer Power." *Brookings Papers on Economic Activity.* 1988. No. 2., pp. 347–421.

Bane, Mary Jo and David T. Ellwood. 1986. "Slipping In and Out of Poverty: The Dynamics of Spells." *Journal of Human Resources*, 21, No. 1. Winter. pp. 1–23.

Bassi, Lauri, J. 1987. "Family Structure and Poverty Among Women and Children: What Accounts for the Change," Georgetown University. Mimeo. June.

Bianchi, Suzanne M. and Daphne Spain. 1986. *American Women In Transition.* New York: The Russell Sage Foundation.

Blackburn, McKinley, David Bloom, and Richard B. Freeman. 1988. "Why has the Economic Position of Less-Skilled Male Workers Deteriorated in the United States?" Paper presented at the Brookings Institution Conference on Future Job Prospects. March 1989.

Blanchard, Olivier J. and Lawrence H. Summers. 1986. "Hysteresis and the European Unemployment Problem." *National Bureau of Economics Research Macroeconomics Annual.* Cambridge, Mass.: MIT Press. 1986. pp. 15–78.

Bluestone, Barry and Bennett Harrison. 1986. "The Great American Job Machine: The Proliferation of Low-Wage Employment in the U.S. Economy." Study prepared for the Joint Economic Committee of the U.S. Congress. Washington, D.C. December.

Brookes, Warren T. 1987. "Low-Pay Jobs: The Big Lie." *The Wall Street Journal* (op-ed). March 25, 1987.

Butz, William P. and Michel P. Ward. 1979. "The Emergence of CounterCyclical U.S. Fertility." *American Economic Review.* 69 (June), pp. 318–28.

Coder, John, Lee Rainwater, and Timothy Smeeding. 1988. "Inequality Among Children and Elderly in Ten Modern Nations: The U.S. in an International Context." Paper prepared for the American Economic Association Meetings, New York, December.

54. I am thinking here of the Boston Compact and corporate-school ventures in Houston, Cleveland and elsewhere. The Philadelphia firm Public Private Ventures is currently evaluating a number of projects of this kind.

Children's Defense Fund. 1988. *A Call for Action to Make Our Nation Safe For Children: A Briefing Book on the Status of American Children in 1988.* Washington, D.C.

Council of Economic Advisers. 1985. *The Economic Report of the President, 1985.* Washington, D.C.: GPO, January.

Council of Economic Advisers. 1988. *The Economic Report of the President, 1988.* Washington, D.C.: GPO, February.

Council of Economic Advisers. 1989. *Economic Report of the President, 1989.* Washington, D.C.: GPO, January.

Dennison, Edward F. 1985. *Trends in American Economic Growth, 1929–82.* Washington, D.C.: The Brookings Institution.

Easterlin, Richard. 1980. *Birth and Fortune.* New York: Basic Books.

Elster, Susan and Mark S. Kamlet. 1987. "Income Aspirations and Married Women's Labor Force Participation." Pittsburgh: Carnegie Mellon University. Mimeo. September 21, 1987.

Freeman, Richard B. 1976. *The OverEducated American.* New York: Academic Press.

Fuchs, Victor. R. 1968. *The Service Economy,* New York: National Bureau of Economic Research and Columbia University Press.

Fuchs, Victor. R. 1988. *Women's Quest for Economic Equality.* Cambridge, Mass.: Harvard University Press.

Gans, Herbert. 1967. *The Levittowners,* New York: Pantheon Books.

Gottschalk, Peter, Sheldon Danziger, and Eugene Smolensky. 1988. "Recent Developments in the Upper Tail of the Income Distribution." Paper prepared for the Annual Meetings of the American Economic Association. New York City, December.

Horvath, Francis W. 1987. "The Pulse of Economic Change: Displaced Workers 1981–85." *Monthly Labor Review.* July, pp. 3–12.

Katz, Lawrence F. and Lawrence H. Summers. 1988. "Can Inter-Industry Wage Differentials Justify Strategic Trade Policy?" National Bureau of Economic Research. Mimeo. April.

Kendrick, John. 1984. "The Implications of Growth Accounting Models." In *The Legacy of Reaganomics: Prospects for Long Term Growth,* Charles R. Hulten and Isabel V. Sawhill. eds. Washington, D.C.: The Urban Institute Press.

Kosters, Marvin H. and Murray N. Ross. 1988. "A Shrinking Middle Class?" *The Public Interest,* No. 90, Winter 1988, pp. 3–27.

Kristol, Irving, 1980. "Comment" [on Alan Blinder's Chapter] in Martin Feldstein, ed. *The American Economy in Transition,* National Bureau of Economic Research and University of Chicago Press.

Kuttner, Bob. 1983. "The Declining Middle." *Atlantic.* July 1983, pp. 60–72.

Lawrence, Robert Z. 1982. *Can America Compete?* Washington, D.C.: The Brookings Institution.

Lawrence, Robert Z. and Charles L. Schultze, eds. 1987. *Barriers to European Growth: A Transatlantic View.* Washington, D.C.: The Brookings Institution.

Levy, Frank. 1979. "On Understanding Proposition 13." *The Public Interest.* Summer.

Levy, Frank. 1988a. *Dollars and Dreams: The Changing American Income Distribution.* New York: W. W. Norton.

Levy, Frank. 1988b. "Incomes, Families, and Living Standards." Ch. 5 in Robert E. Litan, Robert Z. Lawrence, and Charles L. Schultze, eds. *American Living Standards: Threats and Challenges.* Washington, D.C.: The Brookings Institution.

Levy, Frank and Richard C. Michel. 1987. "Understanding the Low Wage Jobs Debate." The Urban Institute. Mimeo.

Levy, Frank and Richard J. Murnane. 1989 Forthcoming. "Jobs, Demography, and the Mismatch Hypothesis." University of Maryland School of Public Affairs Working Paper.

Lillard, Lee, James P. Smith, and Finis Welch. 1986. "What Do We Really Know about Wages?" *Journal of Political Economy.* 94, No. 3. June, pp. 489–506.

Litan, R.E., Lawrence, R.Z., and Schultz, C.L. (eds.) 1988. *American Living Standards: Challenges and Threats.* Washington, D.C., The Brookings Institution.

Maddison, Angus. 1987. "Growth and Slowdown in Advanced Capitalist Economies: Techniques of Quantitative Assessment." *Journal of Economic Literature* Vol. xxv. June, pp. 649–98.

McClanahan, Sara S. 1985. "Family Structure and the Reproduction of Poverty." *American Journal of Sociology.* 90, No. 4, pp. 873–901.

Murphy, Kevin and Finis Welch. 1988. "Wage Differentials in the 1980s: The Role of International Trade." Paper presented at the Mont Pelerin Society General Meeting, September 9.

Norwood, Janet. 1987. "The Job Machine Has Not Broken Down." *The New York Times,* February 22, Section F, p. 3.

Rosenthal, Neal H. 1985. "The Shrinking Middle Class: Myth or Reality?" *Monthly Labor Review.* March, pp. 3–10.

Samuelson, Robert J. 1987. "The American Job Machine." *Newsweek.* February 23, 1987.

Sawyer, Malcolm. 1976. "Income Distribution in OECD Countries." Paris: *OECD Occasional Studies.* July.

Schumpeter, Joseph. 1942. *Capitalism, Socialism and Democracy.* New York: Harper.

Smith, James P. and Michael P. Ward. 1984. *Women's Wages and Work in the Twentieth Century,* Santa Monica: Rand Corporation.

Sum, Andrew and Neal Fogg. 1987. "Trends in Real Earnings and Incomes of Young Males in the U.S.: 1967–1985." Northeastern University, Center for Labor Market Studies Working Paper. 1987.

U.S. Bureau of the Census. 1987a. "Martial Status and Living Arrangements." March 1986. *Current Population Report,* Series P-20, No. 418, Washington, D.C.: Government Printing Office.

U.S. Bureau of the Census. 1987b. "Money Income of Households, Families and Persons in the United States, 1986." *Current Population Reports,* Series P-60, No. 159, Washington, D.C.: Government Printing Office.

U.S. Congressional Budget Office. 1987. "The Changing Distribution of Federal Taxes: 1975–1990." (authored by Richard Kasten and Frank Sammartino). Washington, D.C.: Government Printing Office.

U.S. Department of Commerce. 1988. *Statistical Abstract of the United States, 1988.* Washington: Government Printing Office.

Thurow, Lester C. 1984. The Disappearance of the Middle Class. *New York Times,* February 5, Section 3, p. 2.

Wilson, William J. 1988. *The Truly Disadvantaged.* Chicago: University of Chicago Press.

Comment

LAWRENCE H. SUMMERS

Frank Levy's impressive paper is largely about the 535 electoral vote question of whether peoples are better off today than they were 16 years ago, or even 8 years ago. Levy's verdict is fairly negative, and is all the more worrisome because it reflects extensive and thorough contact with the data. The American people gave an answer to that question in the November 1988 election—a somewhat more optimistic answer than Levy provides in his paper. Some of my friends and I wish we knew why. I can however offer some observations on Levy's analysis.

First, have living standards really stagnated as badly as the official statistics Levy relies on suggest? There is a kind of disjunction in professional discussions. Had this been a paper called "The Productivity Slowdown" and had it been claimed that productivity had been growing rapidly up until 1973 and stopped growing rapidly thereafter, lengthy discussion of whether the productivity statistics are right would ensue. The issues of whether we measure the quality of goods appropriately and whether we measure improvements in the service sector at an appropriate rate would be debated. Such issues are not usually aired when the subject is the behavior of real wages or family incomes. Yet, they are equally fundamental even when productivity is not the proximate issue. The same price deflators that need to adequately treat quality change in evaluating productivity performance are also crucial components of the price indexes used to study trends in real wages or family incomes. To whatever extent quality measurement issues are important in discussing productivity, they are equally important in discussing stagnation in measured real income growth.

Think of some examples. You can get money from your bank at midnight, when once you could not. You can get a boarding pass before you fly. Perhaps more consequentially, in a world where the average American family has a TV set on for 50 hours each week, you can now choose from 90 TV channels, and you used to be able to choose from only three or four. You can cook in your microwave. Your supermarket has twice as many goods to choose from as it did fifteen years ago. It is probably true that none of those developments are reflected to an appreciable extent in our measure of increases in standard of living, and for that reason, the thesis of stagnation is overstated.

How serious are these biases? It is very hard to get a sense of what their overall magnitude is. Let me suggest one crude criterion. These types of developments that I have been describing have been universal, taking place around the world. If you use the numbers we convention-ally use—the conventional time series numbers of productivity or on quality—and you make international comparisons, what you conclude is that the standard of living in Britain or Japan today is roughly compara-ble to standards of living in the United States at the end of World War II in the case of Britain and in the early 1950s in the case of Japan. If you think this is true, then it follows that you arrive at the conclusion that this quality problem is not serious. If you think that life in Japan is rather better than life in the United States in the early 1950s, you are drawn to conclude that our statistics in the United States have understated the growth in standards of living over time. I think that is almost certainly the case.

Whether or not that any of this explains the productivity slowdown is of course a very different question. While I can not produce as good a list of new innovations that took place between 1960 and 1973 that would have increased standards of living as I can between 1973 and the pres-ent, I suspect that has more to do with the fact that I was six years old in 1960 than it does with those innovations not having taken place. On balance, I think there are strong reasons to believe that real income growth is greater in the United States than official statistics suggest. Whether official statistics correctly portray its deterioration is much less obvious.

Second, I think that the political and the op-ed discussions of stan-dards of living issue have introduced two sets of verbiage into the discus-sion of the change in the distribution of standards of living which are not helpful. I would have liked to see Levy go after these ideas more force-fully. One is the notion of the vanishing middle class. One might think, having heard that the middle class had disappeared or had diminished or was vanishing, that there would be some distribution of something relevant that would be bimodal. But this is not the case. All of the distributions—skill, wages, income, everything under discussion in Levy's paper—are not bimodal. They are single peaked. That single peak is very near their middle. That was true, and continues to be true.

Discussions of the disappearance of the middle class have more to do with the way in which we define the middle than it does with factors that are more economically meaningful. This is not to deny that there have been increases in inequality, but I think discussing them in terms of a declining middle class is unhelpful. It leads to the rather sorry spectacle of debates between *the Wall Street Journal* and *The New York Times* over whether the middle class has diminished because of an increase in the size of the upper class or an increase in the size of the lower class. Given the likelihood that 20 percent of the population will continue to be in the top fifth of income distribution, this type of discussion is less than fruitful.

I am also skeptical, though to a slightly lesser degree, about those discussions of living standards that focus on the "good jobs" versus "bad jobs" distinction. Real wages in all jobs have increased much more slowly since 1973 than they had prior to 1973. There have been movements in the employment structure which have moved to some extent between higher wage jobs and lower wage jobs, but those are very much second order relative to the common movement in all jobs.

Furthermore, there is a minimal need to determine how much of any change that has taken place in the distribution of good and bad jobs, and what this has to do with the change in the distribution of good and bad workers as opposed to good and bad jobs. If, as in recent work on industry wage differentials, an effort is made to control for differences between jobs in worker characteristics and to isolate something that is maybe a pure characteristic of jobs, the significance of the movements in the income distribution that are due to movements between good and bad jobs is substantially reduced.

My third observation is that it is time for the literature on the changing American wage structure to move from description toward explanation. Levy's paper is entirely persuasive (subject to the measurement qualification noted above) on the point that wage growth has slowed and that more skilled workers have gained at the expense of less skilled workers. Forecasts of the future and judgments about policy depend on the explanation of these phenomena.

I would distinguish two hypotheses which I hope will be contrasted in future wage structure research. The *macroeconomic* hypothesis links increasing inequality and to some extent slow wage growth to transitory macroeconomic developments. It is a very optimistic viewpoint. According to the macroeconomic view, macroeconomic policies that have pushed the dollar up in the early 1980s and led to deindustrialization are the culprit. This view paints a bright picture for the 1990s.

It is a near certainty that the rest of the world will not continue loaning us money at current rates, so the trade deficit will have to fall. Since manufacturing accounts for 80 percent of U.S. trade, this portends the reindustrialization of America. Recognizing that our trade deficit is nearly 3 percent of GNP and that some deterioration in our terms of trade is nearly inevitable, it is hard to escape the conclusion that manufacturing as a share of GNP will have to raise by 3 to 4 percent in the 1990s. For this to happen by 1995, manufacturing would have to grow more than twice as rapidly as the aggregate economy over the next five years and the share of manufacturing in the American economy would have to reach a record level.

The reindustrialization of America would create opportunities for the kinds of workers who were displaced during the early 1980s, and would no doubt increase the demand for brawn relative to brains. If the macroeconomic disturbances of the 1980s caused increases in inequality during the last decade, then the 1990s will see inequality come down.

A different macroeconomic determinant of the wage structure is the degree of pressure in labor markets. Observing what we pay our cleaning woman, I cannot help but think that in an economy that has very low unemployment, in an economy where for some set of macroeconomic reasons there is a shortage of labor, the return to unskilled labor increases quite rapidly. The average unemployment rate over the 16 year period since 1973 has been considerably greater than the average unemployment rate in the sixteen years preceding 1973. The post-1973 period has seen two very serious recessions, and I wonder whether that does not have something to do with the change in the return to different types of workers that Levy discusses in his paper.

Some variant on the macroeconomic hypothesis is relatively conventional wisdom. The alternative hypothesis, which is vigorously urged by Robert Reich, Barry Bluestone, Bennett Harrison, and some other progressive critics of mainstream economic thinking, stresses *structural* determinants of the wage structure. This view is less optimistic than the macroeconomic viewpoint since it highlights changes in the world economy that will not be reversed as the U.S. trade deficit diminishes.

Three structural stories can plausibly be linked to the changing wage structure. First, the combination of continuing political harmony and technical change are integrating the world economy at a rapid rate—witness the doubling in the share of trade in the U.S. economy over the last 30 years. Trade theory teaches us that trade in goods and factor mobility are substitutes. The rest of the world is longer on brawn than on brains and longer on unskilled workers than on skilled workers. It stands to reason that increased trade volumes will therefore benefit skilled workers at the expense of unskilled workers. This is not just theory. My recent work with Larry Katz (1989) demonstrates that the workers in U.S. export industries are more skilled and paid more than workers in U.S. import industries.

This story clearly works in the right direction for explaining increased inequality. It also suggests no respite in the years to come. The question is whether it is quantitatively important enough to account for the change in inequality given that trade is still relatively small compared to the entire economy.

A second structural explanation for increasing inequality is that the impact of technological changes such as computerization has been to increase the return to being skillful. A single consultant can visit many more companies in a year than was once the case. Managers can now dispense with support staffs when computers can collate and process data. As product variety increases, the return to a salesman's being smart as well as personable is increased. Such effects are difficult to quantify, but may nonetheless be important to determining the wage structure.

There is a third structural explanation for increasing inequality—one that is very difficult to test. It may be that as the world has become a tougher, more competitive place, horizontal equity norms have given way to more ruthless systems of pay for performance. This may be because relatively egalitarian wage structures are luxuries that can no longer be afforded. Or it may be because the importance of providing workers with incentives to do a good job has increased. Consider some examples. Companies are starting to make much more use of profit-sharing and bonuses. Law firms are increasingly compensating partners on the basis of performance, not seniority. And companies are being much more ruthless about eliminating redundant middle managers. This trend, like the other structural factors I have cited, is unlikely to reverse itself.

Is the macroeconomic or the structural view of increasing inequality correct? I am not sure. The structural arguments strike me as more compelling than the macroeconomic ones. On the other hand, many more structural breaks with our economic past are proclaimed than actually take place. Only time and future research (in that order I fear) will resolve the issue.

Let me turn finally to the two policy inferences that are drawn by Levy in his conclusions. The first is that if we are no longer growing we will have to worry more about redistribution. The exact meaning of the phrase "we will have to" is not clear. I would guess as a predictive theory that if we are not growing it will make us less likely to worry about redistribution rather than more likely. Generosity is almost certainly a luxury good. It is not an accident that the Great Society emerged in the 1960s, at the tail end of a boom, supported by projections of very generous growth that made it look like you could do almost anything and have it cost a relatively modest amount.

If we are to grow slowly, and if it is to be the case that the least skilled one-third of the population will have a difficult time earning a substantial income, redistribution on a scale where it will reach everyone who does not go to college, or will reach half the people who do not go to college, strikes me a being an exceedingly unlikely political and undesirable economic prospect. The more direct and appropriate policy response to tough times and widening inequality would not involve income redistribution so much as it would involve doing things that would affect the distribution of skills and doing things that would prepare a larger share of the population for better jobs.

Levy concludes by talking about what all this means for children, emphasizing the specter of poor children falling further and further behind. He may be right, but I would say the evidentiary content of this part of his paper is rather low. First of all, even granting that children in poor families do worse than children who come from more affluent families, it does not follow that transfering income to the poor families and making them no longer poor will solve whatever is giving rise to that correlation. That does not follow and is not really argued in the paper. Without knowing what it is that has taken place that has caused the changes in the income distribution of children, one cannot really support the conclusion that more income redistribution will equalize the distribution of skills among the nation's children.

Furthermore, I suspect that in order to really understand what has happened to the distribution of income among children, one would have to pay more attention than the paper does to changes in the patterns of fertility across different groups in the population. The fact is that, contrary to myth, the number of children being born under the poverty line or near the poverty line has not increased during the 1970s. A large part of what has happened is that fertility has just collapsed among those far above the poverty line. That is responsible for some significant part of the increase in the fraction of kids below the poverty line.

Frank Levy's paper has done an excellent job of describing the American economy's most serious problems. I hope and trust that his future research and that of others will go further and point toward explanations for the unfortunate trends he describes. Only after sound explanations have been provided will one be in a position to offer convincing policy recommendations.

Discussion

Robert Hall felt that Levy's evidence indicated that the US economy is becoming more meritocratic. Though dropouts are important at the lower end of the income distribution, Hall speculated that the rest of the income distribution was largely determined by ability. Levy responded that it was important to keep in mind the large distributional effects of macroeconomic events such as the large trade deficits. Murphy added that while changes in wages are in part due to changes in the supply of labor, the most important factor in changing wage distributions, particularly among the poor, is changing labor demand. This is reflected particularly in the return to higher education.

Robert Gordon took issue with Summers' skepticism about the degree of nominal wage rigidity. If jobs are changing through time, average wages will change even if no individual wages change. Gordon also wondered whether today's high pressure economy, with its increased demand for high-wage manufacturing goods will help the poor as much as past expansions, based more on low-wage output. Finally, Gordon suggested that income distribution may be determined more by the compensation institutions in a country than by any sense of meritocracy, citing the tighter Japanese distribution over the US one. Hall responded that the United States has a more diverse population than many other countries so that it was not right to compare income distributions.

William Nordhaus found puzzling Murphy's evidence that wages for older workers seem more flexible than wages for younger workers. William Brainard suggested that this may be due to differences in working positions for the two groups. Nordhaus also indicated that college admission was still largely restricted to the upper income distributions, suggesting that family characteristics may be as important as merit in advancement.

Mark Bils suggested that Levy control for cost of living changes in different regions of the country. Levy indicated that this was difficult to do because the cost of living varied even within regions.

Levy concluded by emphasizing that aggregate wage stagnation makes relative income changes more important than they are when wages are growing, and that just as it is difficult to explain the productivity slowdown with changes in the quality of output, it is difficult to believe that people are better off because of an increased quality of the goods they purchase.

Christina D. Romer and David H. Romer
UNIVERSITY OF CALIFORNIA, BERKELEY

Does Monetary Policy Matter? A New Test in the Spirit of Friedman and Schwartz

1. Introduction

This paper investigates whether nominal disturbances have important real effects. What differentiates the paper from the countless others on the same subject is that it focuses not on purely statistical evidence but on evidence derived from the historical record—evidence based on what we call the "narrative approach." This approach was pioneered by Friedman and Schwartz in their *Monetary History of the United States* and has provided the evidence that we suspect has been most important in shaping economists' beliefs about the real effects of monetary shocks. Despite its significance, however, the narrative approach has been largely neglected in formal research in the 25 years since Friedman and Schwartz's work. In this paper we both assess the evidence presented in the *Monetary History* and, more importantly, conduct a test of the link between monetary disturbances and real output for the postwar United States in the spirit of Friedman and Schwartz's approach.

The reason that purely statistical tests, such as regressions of output on money, studies of the effects of "anticipated" and "unanticipated" money, and vector autoregressions, probably have not played a crucial role in forming most economists' views about the real effects of monetary disturbances is that such procedures cannot persuasively identify the direction of causation. On the one hand, if firms that are planning to expand their output first increase their demands for liquid assets (or for loans from commercial banks), money could rise before output rises even though money had no causal role (King and Plosser 1984; Tobin

1965). On the other hand, if the Federal Reserve were actively using monetary policy to offset the effects of other factors acting to change output, there might be no discernible relation between money and output even though money had large real effects (Kareken and Solow 1963).

The Narrative Approach.   The approach that we suspect in fact underlies most economists' beliefs concerning whether nominal disturbances matter is quite different from any purely statistical approach. We call it the narrative approach because its central element is the identification of "monetary shocks" through non-statistical procedures. Whether carried out systematically or casually, the method involves using the historical record, such as the descriptions of the process and reasoning that led to decisions by the monetary authority and accounts of the sources of monetary disturbances, to identify episodes when there were large shifts in monetary policy or in the behavior of the monetary sector that were not driven by developments on the real side of the economy. The test of whether monetary disturbances matter is then simply to see whether output is unusually low following negative shocks of this type and unusually high following positive shocks.

In their *Monetary History*, Friedman and Schwartz argue that the study of U.S. monetary history does indeed provide clear examples of large, independent monetary disturbances. They argue further that economic developments subsequent to the disturbances they identify provide overwhelming evidence that monetary shocks have large real effects. Evidence of the same kind, gathered and analyzed less systematically than that presented by Friedman and Schwartz, is also often cited in support of the view that monetary policy matters. References to the "Volcker deflation" represent a common example of this type of argument. It is frequently argued that the fact that the commitment by the Federal Reserve in 1979 to a highly contractionary monetary policy to reduce inflation was followed by the most severe recession in postwar U.S. history provides powerful evidence of the real effects of monetary policy. Both this casual analysis and the more systematic analysis of Friedman and Schwartz have probably been more persuasive than purely statistical studies because the isolation of shocks from the historical record can overcome the reverse causation problem that plagues any regression of output on money.[1]

While the narrative approach has many virtues, implementing it is not straightforward. There are two specific problems that must be addressed. The first and more important possible difficulty involves the

---

1. Summers (1987) provides a cogent discussion of the persuasiveness of narrative studies.

isolation of monetary shocks. Inherently, there cannot be a completely mechanical rule for determining when the historical record indicates that a shock has occurred. Moreover, the identification of shocks generally occurs retrospectively, and thus the researcher may know the subsequent behavior of money and output. The fact that the selection of disturbances is judgmental and retrospective introduces the possibility that there may be an unconscious bias toward, for example, searching harder for negative monetary shocks in periods preceding sharp declines in money and output than in other periods. Such a bias could cause one to misclassify shocks and to conclude that monetary disturbances had real consequences when they had none.

The second potential difficulty arises in determining whether the shocks that are identified are followed by unusual output movements. Neither Friedman and Schwartz nor those who cite similar informal evidence in support of the importance of monetary disturbances test formally whether the behavior of output in the aftermath of the disturbances that they identify is in fact systematically unusual. Indeed, Friedman and Schwartz explicitly deny that monetary shocks have consistent and precise real consequences, arguing their effects occur with long and variable lags. Carried to an extreme, an absence of statistical tests and a belief in irregular and often quite long lags could render the hypothesis that monetary shocks have important real effects void of testable implications. More moderately, these factors could cause the strength and significance of the effect to be overstated, and could compound the effects of biases in the selection of shocks.

Overview. This discussion of the benefits and dangers of the narrative approach leads us to believe that to answer the question of whether nominal disturbances have real effects, the narrative approach should be used, but that it should be used carefully and systematically. That is the goal of this paper.

We pursue that goal in two ways. The first is by reexamining Friedman and Schwartz's evidence concerning the real effects of monetary policy, particularly their identification of monetary disturbances. Despite the immense importance of their work in forming economists' views concerning the real effects of monetary forces, little research has been devoted to the question of how successful Friedman and Schwartz in fact are in isolating independent monetary disturbances. In Section 2 we therefore investigate whether there appears to be any unintended bias in Friedman and Schwartz's choices of monetary shocks.[2] We also use this

2. Many other authors have explored various aspects of Friedman and Schwartz's work. To cite only a few of the most prominent examples, Temin (1976), Gordon and Wilcox

critical analysis of the *Monetary History* to suggest improvements to Friedman and Schwartz's techniques.

The second and more important way in which we pursue the narrative approach is by proposing and implementing a test using this approach for the postwar United States. Friedman and Schwartz, writing in the early 1960s, necessarily focused on the period before World War II. We argue, however, that the postwar era provides a better setting for employing their approach. In particular, we argue that it is possible to come much closer in the postwar than in the prewar or interwar periods to the ideal of using a precise and unambiguous rule for identifying a central set of major monetary disturbances. Thus we believe that the postwar era provides not just additional, but superior evidence concerning whether nominal shocks matter. This new test is the subject of Section 3. We describe the class of disturbances that we wish to identify, our procedures for identifying them, and our tests of whether the behavior of output in the wake of those disturbances provides evidence for or against the view that nominal disturbances have important real consequences.

Finally, in Section 4 we return to the evidence from the interwar era. Having discussed in Section 2 whether Friedman and Schwartz's identification of monetary disturbances might involve some unintended bias, in this section we propose what we think is a more appropriate list of major independent monetary disturbances for the interwar period. Then, paralleling the test in Section 3, we ask whether real activity responds systematically to those disturbances.

2. *Friedman and Schwartz Challenged*

The purpose of this section is to examine how successful and persuasive Friedman and Schwartz are in isolating independent monetary disturbances. We do this for two reasons. First, because the *Monetary History* has been so influential in shaping economists' beliefs, it is important to approach the work critically and to evaluate anew the quality of the evidence that it presents. Second, because the main purpose of our paper is to extend the narrative approach to the postwar era, it is useful to identify any potential shortcomings in Friedman and Schwartz's classic work so that we can avoid them in our own study of the historical record.

(1981), and Hamilton (1987) study Friedman and Schwartz's analysis of the Great Depression, and Bordo (1988) assesses their contributions to monetary history more generally. Hendry and Ericsson (1987) criticize Friedman and Schwartz's econometric methods, focusing mainly on their later work.

2.1 FRIEDMAN AND SCHWARTZ'S MAJOR MONETARY SHOCKS

To set the stage, we begin by describing the episodes that Friedman and Schwartz identify as the most important monetary shocks during the period covered by their book. In keeping with the view that the most compelling evidence that Friedman and Schwartz provide of the importance of monetary shocks comes from the most dramatic events that they describe, we limit our attention to the episodes they emphasize in summarizing their work (1963a, ch. 13; 1963b, pp. 48–55); we do not consider the various more minor or less clear cut episodes that they cite as providing further evidence of the importance of monetary disturbances. In addition, we limit ourselves to the shocks in the period after 1919. For the period before World War I, all of the shocks that Friedman and Schwartz emphasize are related to financial panics. We do not focus on the panics both because the degree to which panics represent independent monetary disturbances is a particularly complex issue and because Friedman and Schwartz place less emphasis on the panics than on the interwar shocks.[3]

With these restrictions, there remain four episodes that Friedman and Schwartz identify as major monetary shocks. Three of these episodes involve overt actions on the part of the Federal Reserve. In their chapter entitled "A Summing Up," Friedman and Schwartz state:

On three occasions the System deliberately took policy steps of major magnitude which cannot be regarded as necessary or inevitable economic consequences of contemporary changes in money income and prices. Like the crucial experiments of the physical scientist, the results are so consistent and sharp as to leave little doubt about their interpretation. The dates are January–June 1920, October 1931, and June 1936–January 1937 (1963a, p. 688).

The fourth episode that Friedman and Schwartz characterize as a major monetary shock is the Federal Reserve's inaction in the face of the severe economic downturn of 1929–31. They describe the events of this period as representing "a fourth crucial experiment" (1963a, p. 694).

Before we sketch Friedman and Schwartz's interpretations of these

---

3. We also exclude the episodes that Friedman and Schwartz cite as providing evidence of the effects of monetary disturbances on *nominal* income, notably the secular deflation of 1879–1897 and the secular inflation of 1897–1914. In the early 1960s, when Friedman and Schwartz wrote, there was widespread agreement that shifts in aggregate demand had important real effects but not that changes in money had important effects on aggregate demand. Thus to Friedman and Schwartz, evidence that monetary disturbances affected either output or prices was evidence that "money mattered." Today, of course, the central motive for interest in the effects of monetary disturbances is the desire to gain insight into the question of whether aggregate demand shocks have real effects.

four episodes, it is useful to point out that by a monetary shock Friedman and Schwartz do *not* mean a monetary movement entirely unrelated to underlying economic developments. Instead, what they mean by a monetary shock is a movement that is *unusual* given economic developments—that is, a movement that would not have occurred in other periods or other circumstances given the pattern of real activity. For the four critical episodes described below, the unusual movements in money arose, in Friedman and Schwartz's view, from a conjunction of economic events, monetary institutions, and the doctrines and beliefs of the time and of the particular individuals determining policy.

January–June 1920. Despite high output, low unemployment, and considerable inflation, monetary policy remained loose in the aftermath of World War I. The major reasons for this monetary ease included a desire to avoid raising the costs to the Treasury of financing outstanding debt, a desire not to inflict capital losses on the purchasers of the final issue of war bonds, and a belief that persuasion rather than high interest rates should be used to discourage borrowing. Then, in November 1919 the Federal Reserve tightened policy somewhat, raising the discount rate from 4 to 4.75%. In 1920 the Federal Reserve raised the discount rate two additional times, from 4.75 to 6% in January and from 6 to 7% in June. According to Friedman and Schwartz, there were two central reasons for the adoption of this extraordinarily restrictive policy at a time when a downturn was in fact already beginning. The first was a concern with the System's own reserve position rather than with broader economic conditions. The second was the fact—hardly surprising, given the brief history of the System—that the Federal Reserve misunderstood the lags with which monetary policy affected the economy. As a result, the Federal Reserve repeatedly tightened policy before previous restrictions had had a chance to have an impact. (1963a, pp. 221–39.)

October 1931. Britain's departure from the gold standard led to widespread fears that the United States would also leave gold, and thus to a vast gold outflow. The Federal Reserve responded by raising the discount rate from 1.5 to 3.5% in two steps in October 1931. Friedman and Schwartz consider this restrictive policy highly unusual because the economy was so severely depressed in 1931 and its condition was continuing to deteriorate. (1963a, pp. 315–17, 380–84.)

June 1936–January 1937. By 1935 banks had accumulated vast excess reserves. Federal Reserve officials believed that these excess reserves reflected a low demand for loans and that as a result open-market operations would for the most part simply alter the relative shares of excess reserves and government bonds in banks' portfolios. Motivated mainly by a desire to put the System in a position where it could use open-market operations to affect the economy in the future should it wish to do so, and partly by a wish to respond to the inflation and rapid output growth that had occurred since 1933, in 1936 and 1937 the Federal Reserve doubled reserve requirements in three steps. Friedman and Schwartz believe that the excess reserves were in fact a reflection of banks' desire for increased liquidity in the aftermath of the widespread banking panics of 1929–33. As a result, the increase in reserve requirements led to a massive contraction of lending as banks worked to restore their excess reserves. Thus, according to Friedman and Schwartz, the Federal Reserve inadvertently caused a major monetary contraction because it misundertood the motives of bankers. Furthermore, they believe that the unfamiliarity of reserve requirements as a policy instrument (the System had been granted authority to vary reserve requirements only in 1933) led to an unintentionally large shift in policy, and that the discreteness of the policy shift made reversal politically difficult. (1963a, pp. 449–62, 515–45.)

The early stages of the Great Depression.   Friedman and Schwartz argue that, beginning most likely with the evidence of a severe downturn in the spring of 1930 and certainly by the time of the first wave of banking failures in late 1930, similar economic developments would not have led to such large declines in the money stock under the National Banking System, or under the Federal Reserve either in the 1910s and 1920s or in the post-World War II era. They therefore conclude that despite the absence of any acts of commission on the part of the Federal Reserve, the large fall in money during the first year and a half of the Depression— before Britain's departure from the gold standard in September 1931— represents a monetary shock. (1963a, pp. 308–16, 367–80, 691–94.)

2.2 IS THERE BIAS IN FRIEDMAN AND SCHWARTZ'S SELECTION OF MONETARY SHOCKS?

Friedman and Schwartz's definition of what constitutes a monetary shock or a "crucial experiment" is not highly precise: an episode involves a monetary shock if monetary developments were highly unusual given all of the relevant developments on the real side of the economy. As a result, Friedman and Schwartz's judgment is central to their identification of shocks; they must weigh a broad range of factors and decide whether the evidence as a whole indicates that a shock occurred. There is therefore a potential for subtle biasing of the selection of shocks. If, for example, their hope was to find evidence of the importance of monetary forces, they may have had an unintentional tendency to search some-what harder for negative monetary shocks in periods before large declines in economic activity than at other times.

In this section we argue that this danger is genuine. We suggest that there does appear to be some unintended bias in Friedman and Schwartz's choice of shocks. This conclusion is based both on an analysis of episodes that Friedman and Schwartz do not identify as shocks and on the consistent presence of contractionary non-monetary forces in the shocks that they do identify.

2.2.1 Candidate Episodes not Included by Friedman and Schwartz. Suppose that Friedman and Schwartz had a tendency to search more carefully for "exogenous" negative monetary shocks before times of large falls in output than at other times. One would then expect there to be events Friedman and Schwartz did not include in their list of independent negative monetary disturbances that it is reasonable to think they would have included had those events been followed by significant declines in output. We believe that there are two such episodes in the interwar period.

1933. A massive wave of banking failures began in the final months of 1932 and worsened in early 1933. In addition, expectations that Roosevelt might devalue or abandon the gold standard on taking office caused large gold outflows and led to an increase in the discount rate from 2.5 to 3.5% in February to defend gold. By February banking conditions had degenerated into panic, causing widespread bank failures. The failures were in turn followed by the declaration of bank holidays in many states. On his inauguration in March, Roosevelt imposed a nationwide banking holiday—a step that, in Friedman and Schwartz's view, was extraordinarily disruptive of the financial system and much more drastic than was needed. (Friedman and Schwartz 1963a, pp. 324–32, 349–50, 389–91, 421–34.)

The events of these months have the features of what under different circumstances Friedman and Schwartz would be willing to describe as a monetary shock, or indeed as several shocks. At other times widespread banking failures and panic conditions much milder than those of early 1933 are considered to be monetary disturbances. The gold outflow and the increase in the discount rate to defend the gold standard despite the depressed level of real activity clearly represent unusual monetary developments, similar to those of the fall of 1931. And the banking holiday shares with the episodes emphasized by Friedman and Schwartz the feature that it appears to be a major contractionary step arising from an inadequate understanding of the workings of the financial system. In sum, it seems extremely plausible that if the Depression had continued to worsen in 1933, Friedman and Schwartz would have characterized the events of January–March 1933 as a fifth "crucial experiment."[4]

1941. In September 1941 the Federal Reserve announced a decision to raise reserve requirements from 22.5 to 25% in November. The increase was the same size as each of the last two steps of the three-step increase in reserve requirements in 1936–37. This is important because it is these last two increases that Friedman and Schwartz emphasize in analyzing 1937. Furthermore, as Friedman and Schwartz note of the 1937 increases, the open-market operations needed to create a comparable reduction in excess reserves would have been extraordinarily large (1963a, pp. 531–32). But they attach little importance to the 1941 increase. They simply state that:

[banks] made no attempt to rebuild their excess reserves, as they had after the increases of 1936 and 1937, but rather proceeded to continue to reduce their remaining excess reserves. The effect of the reserve requirement increase shows up only in a slackened rate of rise of the deposit-reserve ratio . . . (p. 556).

The striking contrast between Friedman and Schwartz's interpretations of the reserve requirement increases of 1936–37 and 1941 suggests that they commit the natural error of using the subsequent behavior of money as a critical factor in identifying monetary disturbances. This is inappropriate because the central reason for employing the narrative approach is that monetary changes may be partly endogenous. If money is in part governed by output, money could have risen even after a contractionary monetary shock, because non-monetary factors were clearly expansionary in 1941. If the 1941 increase in reserve requirements had been followed by falls in the deposit-reserve ratio and in money, it appears plausible that Friedman and Schwartz would have described the action as a monetary shock. Because the Federal Reserve remained unfamiliar with changes in

---

4. It can be argued that this negative shock was followed by a positive shock from Roosevelt's gold policies. While changes in competitiveness arising from the rise in the dollar price of gold in 1933 could certainly have stimulated the economy through increased net exports, Chandler stresses that Roosevelt's gold policies "did not begin to make additions to the monetary base or bank reserves until after the adoption of the Gold Reserve Act at the end of January 1934" (1970, p. 164). Thus, any monetary component to this positive shock did not occur until nearly a year after the negative monetary shock of early 1933. Furthermore, if one follows the logic of Friedman and Schwartz, there may be no monetary shock at all in 1934 because an expansion of high powered money is the usual and expected reaction to severe depression.

reserve requirements, Friedman and Schwartz could reasonably have argued that the System again committed the error of causing a drastic shift in policy when only a modest one was intended.[5]

2.2.2 The Episodes Included by Friedman and Schwartz. A second argument that Friedman and Schwartz's identification of monetary shocks may be biased focuses on the episodes they do select. If their selections are unbiased, the effects of *non-monetary* factors will not be systematically different following the monetary episodes identified from what they are at other times. If the selections are biased, on the other hand, there will be a tendency for episodes in which other factors were acting to increase output to be excluded from a list of negative monetary disturbances and for episodes in which other forces are acting to reduce output to be included. We argue that in all of the episodes identified by Friedman and Schwartz as involving independent negative monetary shocks (with the possible exception of the period following Britain's departure from gold in 1931), non-monetary forces appear to have been strongly contractionary.

January–June 1920. It is not difficult to find candidate nonmonetary explanations of the decline in output from 1919 to 1921. With the end of World War I and the large-scale immediate postwar relief efforts, government spending fell sharply. In addition, it is often argued that the postponement of purchases of durable goods during the war contributed to the high level of demand in 1919 and the subsequent fall in 1920–21 (Gordon 1974, pp. 19–20, for example). Indeed, Friedman and Schwartz agree that non-monetary forces contributed to the downturn and may have made it inevitable (1963a, p. 237).

Two comparisons suggest that non-monetary forces were important in 1920–21. The first comparison is with other countries. Declining output was not unique to the United States. In 1919–21, there were falls in

5. A final episode that is not identified in the *Monetary History* as a major shock, but that could be considered a change in monetary policy, is the contractionary open market operations and increases in the discount rate that began in January 1928 (see, for example, Hamilton 1987; Schwartz 1981; and Temin 1988). While we agree that money became tighter in this period, it is not clear whether this tightening should be viewed as unusual or simply as a usual reaction to real economic events such as the boom in real output and stock prices. Furthermore, we also agree with Friedman and Schwartz that the tightening in 1928 was fairly small, especially when considered relative to the contractionary shocks in 1920, 1931, and 1937. As they note, the Federal Reserve "followed a policy which was too easy to break the speculative boom, yet too tight to promote healthy economic growth" (1963, p. 291). (Gordon and Wilcox, 1981, and Hamilton, 1987, also provide evidence that the monetary shock in 1928–29 was small relative to the subsequent decline in real output.) Hence, unless one uses a procedure that calibrates shocks according to severity, it is prudent not to identify the 1928 tightening as a monetary shock.

output much larger than that in the United States in the United Kingdom, Italy, Norway, and Canada (Maddison 1982, Table A7). The breadth of the downturn suggests that the contractionary forces were broader than the idiosyncrasies of U.S. monetary policy. The second comparison is with the aftermath of World War II. From 1918 to 1921, government purchases as a fraction of GNP fell by 13 percentage points; real GNP rose 1.1% from 1918 to 1919 and then fell 3.5% between 1919 and 1921.[6] From 1944 to 1947, the share of government purchases in GNP fell by 35 percentage points; real GNP fell by 25.8%. That is, the fall in total output relative to the fall in government purchases was considerably larger after World War II than after World War I.[7] This comparison suggests that in isolation, the decline in government spending between 1919 and 1921 may have been depressing the economy greatly.

October 1931. We view the Federal Reserve's response to Britain's departure from gold as perhaps Friedman and Schwartz's clearest example of a monetary disturbance not obviously complicated by strongly contractionary non-monetary forces. Nonetheless, two non-monetary forces do appear to have been acting to reduce output after October 1931. First, fiscal policy turned contractionary, though less sharply than in 1918–20. The enactment of a massive tax increase in 1932 reduced E. Cary Brown's measure of the full employment deficit from 3.6% of GNP in 1931 to 1.8% in 1932 and then to 0.5% in 1933 (Brown 1956, Table 1, col. 14). Second, it was during the period 1930–32 that the erection of massive tariff barriers and the consequent collapse of world trade reached its height, a development often thought to be central to the deepening of the Depression (Kindleberger 1986, pp. 123–26).

June 1936–January 1937. Two non-monetary forces were acting to decrease output in 1937. The first was fiscal policy. From 1936 to 1937 Brown's measure of the full employment deficit moved toward surplus by 2.4% of GNP, reflecting the end of the 1936 veterans' bonus and the first widespread collection of social security payroll taxes. The second was labor market developments. The enactment of the Wagner Act in 1935 led, in a common interpretation, to large inventory accumulation in anticipation of labor market strife and wage increases; both the end of the inventory accumulation and the appearance of the anticipated strikes and wage increases then contributed to the downturn in 1937 (Kin-

6. Throughout the paper, percentage changes refer to differences in logarithms.
7. For 1918–21, the GNP data are from Romer (1988a, Table 5) and the government purchases data are from Kendrick (1961, Table A-IIa). The data for 1944–47 are from the National Income and Product Accounts.

dleberger, pp. 270–71). Over half of the fall in real GNP from 1936 to 1937 took the form of a sharp reversal of inventory investment.

In addition, it is essential to Friedman and Schwartz's interpretation of economic developments in this period that banks strongly desired to hold large excess reserves and that they therefore responded to the increase in reserve requirements by moving to restore their excess reserves. But the behavior of reserve holdings appears strikingly counter to this interpretation: there was no discernible change in the behavior of reserves as a fraction of deposits until December 1937, seventeen months after the first increase in reserve requirements was announced. By this time the declines in money and industrial production were largely complete.[8]

The early stages of the Great Depression. The issue of whether monetary or non-monetary forces were primarily responsible for the initial two years or so of the collapse of economic activity that began in 1929 has been sufficiently debated that there is no need for us to argue that the case in favor of a monetary interpretation is not clear cut. As in the other episodes we have discussed, non-monetary forces were strongly contractionary during this period (see Temin 1976, and Romer 1988b). Indeed, Friedman and Schwartz do not argue that monetary policy (or some other aspect of monetary developments) was unusually contractionary from the stock market crash in October 1929 through the spring of 1930, a period that saw industrial production fall by 13%. Moreover, from the spring through October 1930, when industrial production fell an additional 16%, according to Friedman and Schwartz monetary developments were unusual in at most a passive sense—monetary authorities failed to intervene in the way they normally would have in such a crisis. This view appears to imply that although monetary forces played a role, the initiating shocks during this period were not monetary. And indeed, as has been extensively discussed, the behavior of interest rates appears more consistent with the non-monetary than the monetary interpretation of the initial downturn (Temin 1976; Hamilton 1987). In addition, by late 1930 there were additional non-monetary forces at work: the collapse of world trade (discussed above) and possible non-monetary effects of bankruptcies and bank failures (Bernanke 1983).

8. As an accounting matter, the swing from rapid growth of the money stock from 1934 to 1937 to a decline in 1937–38 was primarily the result of a sharp decline in the growth rate of high-powered money. This in turn appears to have stemmed largely from a switch by the Treasury to sterilizing gold inflows in the first three quarters of 1937. Friedman and Schwartz do not discuss the reasons for this change in Treasury policy (1963a, pp. 509–511).

2.3 CONCLUSION

This discussion of possible bias in Friedman and Schwartz's identification of shocks is not meant to imply that the evidence from the interwar era is unsupportive of the view that monetary disturbances have important real consequences. It does, however, suggest that their evidence may not be as decisive as it once seemed. The fact that Friedman and Schwartz exclude some apparent negative shocks that were followed by improvements in economic performance, and the fact that the effects of the monetary shocks they identify appear to have been compounded by adverse non-monetary factors, both imply that monetary shocks by themselves may be less potent than Friedman and Schwartz argued.

Our analysis of Friedman and Schwartz's identification of shocks also suggests an important lesson about using the narrative approach. The main reason there is room for unconscious bias in Friedman and Schwartz's identification of shocks is that they use a very broad definition of what constitutes a shock: a shock occurs whenever monetary policy is "unusual" given the state of the real economy. Friedman and Schwartz are forced to adopt this definition because there is so much variation in monetary institutions, in the theoretical framework adhered to by central bankers, and in the particulars of important monetary episodes in the interwar era. Because of this variation, it is impossible to lay out a clear and workable set of criteria that can be used to identify monetary shocks throughout the interwar period. Therefore, a natural way to attempt to improve on what Friedman and Schwartz do is to apply the narrative approach to an era where a more precise definition of a shock can be specified.

3. *Friedman and Schwartz Extended*

As a laboratory for a test of the real effects of monetary disturbances, the postwar era stands in admirable contrast to the interwar years. At least in comparison to the interwar era, the Federal Reserve in the postwar era has had a reasonably stable view of the functioning of the economy and of the role of monetary policy. As a result, there have been important similarities across major monetary episodes. Thus, while judgment still plays a role in the identification of shocks, as it must do when identification is based on the historical record, its role can be much smaller than in the earlier period. In addition, for the postwar period there are extensive contemporary records of the nature and motives of Federal Reserve policy. This is useful because reliance on contemporaneous judgments of the sources and intents of shifts in policy again reduces the scope for judgment and unconscious bias.

In this section we therefore use the narrative approach to study whether monetary policy shocks in the postwar era have had important real effects. The section is divided into two parts. Section 3.1 discusses our procedures for identifying monetary shocks in the postwar era and sketches the evidence underlying our choices of monetary shocks. Section 3.2 presents evidence on whether these monetary shocks affect output. It includes both informal evidence and a statistical test of whether the monetary disturbances we identify are followed by unusual movements in real output.

3.1 THE IDENTIFICATION OF MONETARY SHOCKS

3.1.1 Definition. Like Friedman and Schwartz, we use the historical record to identify monetary shocks. We employ, however, a much narrower definition of what constitutes a shock. In particular, we count as a shock only episodes in which the Federal Reserve attempted to exert a contractionary influence on the economy in order to reduce inflation. That is, we focus on times when the Federal Reserve attempted not to offset perceived or prospective increases in aggregate demand but to actively shift the aggregate demand curve back in response to what it perceived to be "excessive" inflation. Or, to put it another way, we look for times when concern about the current level of inflation led the Federal Reserve to attempt to induce a recession (or at least a "growth recession").

This definition of a monetary shock is clearly very limited. It excludes both monetary contractions that are generated by concerns other than inflation and all monetary expansions. This single-minded focus on negative shocks to counteract inflation has two crucial advantages. Its most obvious advantage is that it defines a shock in narrow and concrete terms. Rather than looking for times when monetary policy was unusual given everything else that was going on in the economy, as Friedman and Schwartz do, we look only for times when the Federal Reserve specifically intended to use the tools it had available to attempt to create a recession to cure inflation. This precise definition greatly limits the role of judgment in identifying monetary shocks.

The second reason for our limited focus is that we believe that policy decisions to attempt to cure inflation come as close as practically possible to being independent of factors that affect real output. In other words, we do not believe that the Federal Reserve states an intent to cause a recession to lower inflation only at times when a recession would occur in any event. This belief rests partly on an assumption that trend inflation by itself does not affect the dynamics of real output. We find this assumption reasonable: there appears to be no plausible channel other than policy through which trend inflation could cause large short-run output swings. By contrast, other factors that are important to the formation of monetary policy are likely to affect real activity directly. For example, because shifts to expansionary monetary policy in the postwar era almost always stem from a desire to halt declines in real output, these policy changes are obviously far from independent of factors that affect the path of output. As a result, it would be difficult to distinguish any real effects of expansionary shifts from whatever natural recovery mechanism the economy may have. It is for exactly this reason that we focus only on negative shocks.

Our belief that anti-inflationary shifts in policy are not simply occurring whenever a recession is about to occur also rests on a belief that the Federal Reserve is not always in fact reacting to some other factor—such as a large adverse supply shock or a temporary output boom—that might by itself lead to a recession. As our descriptions of the specifics of the episodes that we consider will show, this does not appear to be the case. Indeed, as we describe, the inflation to which the Federal Reserve responds often appears to be largely the result of past shocks rather than of current real developments. Furthermore, in our statistical work below we attempt to test both for the possibility that anti-inflationary policy shifts are correlated with other factors that potentially affect real output and for the possibility that inflation directly affects real output. We find no evidence of either of these effects.

To actually discern the intentions of the Federal Reserve, we rely entirely on contemporary Federal Reserve records—the "Record of Policy Actions" of the Board of Governors and the Federal Open Market Committee (FOMC) and, until their discontinuance in 1976, the minutes of FOMC meetings. To identify a shock from these sources we look both for a clear statement of a belief that the current level of inflation needed to be lowered and some indication that output consequences would be sought, or at least tolerated, to bring the reduction about. In this process we only consider contemporaneous (or nearly contemporaneous) statements of the Federal Reserve's intent. We do not consider retrospective discussions of intent because such descriptions could be biased by a knowledge of the subsequent behavior of real activity.

3.1.2 Results. On the basis of Federal Reserve records, we identify six times since World War II when the Federal Reserve moved to attempt to induce a recession to reduce inflation. They are October 1947, September 1955, December 1968, April 1974, August 1978, and October 1979. In each case, the Federal Reserve appears to have made a deliberate decision to sacrifice real output to lower inflation. In this section we describe the evidence from contemporaneous Federal Reserve sources of shifts in the objectives of monetary policy during these episodes. In addition, to provide further information about our selection procedure, we describe two episodes that we do not classify as independent monetary disturbances. One occurred in 1966 when the System shifted to a tighter policy out of a desire to prevent increases in aggregate demand rather than out of a desire to contract demand. The other occurred over the extended period 1975–78 when the Federal Reserve expressed considerable concern about inflation but did not appear to be willing to sacrifice real output to reduce it.

October 1947. With the end of World War II, inflation became the Federal Reserve's central concern. Two factors, however, stopped the Federal Reserve from shifting to a significantly tighter policy in the first few years after the war. The first was the wartime policy of pegging interest rates on both short-term and long-term government bonds. By June 1946 there was considerable sentiment on the FOMC in favor of pursuing policies that would cause short-term interest rates to rise (*Minutes*, 1946, pp. 55–56, for example). But obtaining a consensus in favor of such policies and then reaching an agreement with the Treasury to permit short-term rates to increase was a lengthy process; the pegging of short-term interest rates did not end until July 1947. Second, although inflation was the primary concern, there was also fear that the end of the war would lead to another depression.

In October 1947, with short-term interest rates no longer fixed and fears of depression allayed, the Federal Reserve began a series of contractionary measures. These actions included open-market operations designed to increase short-term interest rates, an increase in the discount rate, and an increase in reserve requirements for banks in central reserve cities. The motive behind these measures was a desire to reduce inflation. At the June 1947 FOMC meeting,

it was [the] opinion [of the chief Federal Reserve economist present] that throughout the war and postwar period there had been too many fears of postwar deflation, with the result that actions which should have been taken to counteract inflation were not taken, because of the fear that they would result in contraction, and that, although any downturn should be taken care of at the proper time, the important thing at the moment was to stop abnormal pressures on the inflationary side. (Minutes, 1947, p. 111.)

He held this view even though he believed that economic conditions were not strengthening. The views of the other Board economist present were summarized succinctly: "He thought that there would and should be a mild recession" (*Minutes*, 1947, p.112). In sum, beginning in late 1947 the Federal Reserve was actively attempting to reduce aggregate demand in order to reduce inflation.

September 1955.   Beginning roughly in June 1954, in response to evidence of the end of the 1953–54 recession, the Federal Reserve ceased pursuing what is perceived to be an active expansionary policy. This change, of course, does not represent a monetary shock. The Federal Reserve was not attempting to reduce aggregate demand; rather, it simply believed that an active stimulus was no longer needed for output to grow.

Beginning in early 1955 considerable concern was expressed by the Federal Reserve about inflation.[9] This concern does not seem to have had an important effect on policy during the first part of the year. But in approximately September 1955 the character of policy appears to have changed. The Federal Reserve actively began to attempt to contract aggregate demand even though members of the FOMC did not believe that output growth, or expected future output growth, was stronger than before. At the FOMC meeting of September 14, for example, despite the fact that "review of the available data suggested that the economy had entered a phase of decelerating advance, . . . it was the judgment of the Committee that [the] situation called at least for the maintenance of, and preferably some slight increase in, the restraining pressure it had been exerting through open market operations." The reason was that "price advances were occurring in considerable numbers, with further widespread increases in prospect" (both quotations are from *1955 Annual Report*, p. 105). In October they suggested that a mild downturn might not be undesirable: "the Committee concluded the situation called for continuing the present policy of restraint" despite the fact that a "tendency toward a downturn in the economy . . . might develop"(*1955 Annual Report*, p. 106). In November the Committee wished to dispel "*any idea* of an easing of System policy" (*1955 Annual Report*, p. 108; emphasis added).

The Federal Reserve's conduct in the first part of 1956 lends additional support to the view that System policy shifted in the fall of 1955. During this period the FOMC felt that no change in policy was called for in the face of evidence of essentially zero output growth. This indicates that

---

9. See, for example, the FOMC meetings of January 11, June 22, and July 12, 1955 (*1955 Annual Report*, pp. 90, 98, 100).

expansion at less than trend rates was what they were seeking.[10] In March the Committee explicitly took the view that it should "combat an inflationary cost-price spiral" despite "the risk of incurring temporary unemployment" (*1956 Annual Report*, p. 26). We conclude that the Federal Reserve shifted to a policy of actively attempting to reduce aggregate demand to combat inflation in late 1955.

1966.   Despite its fame, the "credit crunch" of 1966 does not represent a monetary shock by our criteria. The reason is that the Federal Reserve's stated intent was clearly not to reduce aggregate demand, but rather to prevent outward shifts in aggregate demand that it believed would otherwise have occurred. In December 1965, for example, the System raised the discount rate and acted to increase other interest rates in response to evidence that "economic activity was increasing vigorously and that the outlook appeared more expansive than previously," not out of a desire to induce a contraction (*1965 Annual Report*, p. 150). The perception of the economy's strength was based not just on current data but also on projections of growing military expenditures because of the Vietnam War and survey evidence that consumers and firms were planning to increase their spending. The Federal Reserve stated explicitly that the purpose of the shift in policy "was not to cut back the pace of credit flows but to dampen mounting demands on banks for still further credit extensions" (*1965 Annual Report*, p. 64).

The same pattern continued through August 1966. In February, the Committee's perception was that "business activity continued to advance vigorously—and the outlook was becoming increasingly expansive," and that "recent and prospective economic developments clearly called for added policy measures to dampen the rise in aggregate demands" (*1966 Annual Report*, pp. 127, 129). In August, "the economic outlook remained expansive, and prospects were for continuing high levels of resource use and strong upward pressures on wages and prices." Military, investment, and consumption spending were all viewed as contributing to the expansion (*1966 Annual Report*, p. 171).

Thus the Federal Reserve's shift to a tighter monetary policy in 1965–66 does not belong on a list of episodes in which the Federal Reserve was actively attempting to induce a downturn. By our criteria, it would be no more appropriate to include this episode than to include, for example,

10. See, for example, the Record of Policy Actions for the FOMC meetings of January 10, February 15, March 6, and April 17, 1956.

the shift to a tighter policy in 1950 to counteract the expansion that the Federal Reserve expected because of the outbreak of the Korean War.[11]

December 1968. From mid-1967 to late 1968, the Federal Reserve gradually tried to adopt tighter policies as it became clear that the "minirecession" of 1966–67 would not turn into a full-fledged downturn and as growth became stronger. As before, such a shift in the specifics of monetary policy in response to economic developments does not represent a monetary shock. But at roughly the end of 1968 there appears to have been a change in the goals of policy: the Federal Reserve began to feel that it should act to reduce inflation. There were frequent references to "the prevailing inflationary psychology," to the fact that "inflationary expectations remained widespread," to "expectations of continuing inflation," and so on.[12]

Concern about inflation caused the Federal Reserve to attempt to maintain tight monetary policy despite evidence of considerably weaker real growth. In March 1969, for example, despite reductions in present and

11. On the basis of the Record of Policy Actions, one could argue for a similar interpretation of the shift to tighter policy in October of 1947. The record for the FOMC meeting of October 6–7 states: "In the period since the previous meeting of the Committee conditions affecting the money market had changed considerably. Inflationary pressures had increased and there were indications that they would continue to be strong in the months immediately ahead" (*1947 Annual Report,* p. 95). The interpretation that the Federal Reserve was attempting to do more than offset shocks to aggregate demand appears more compelling, however, for two reasons. First, it is very plausible that the minutes could be much franker than the Record of Policy Actions concerning any desire to cause a recession. Second, inspection of the reasons that the Federal Reserve gave in support of the view that inflationary pressures were increasing strongly suggests that what they meant was simply that in the absence of tighter policy, inflation and high output would continue. For example:

> *Inflationary pressures have been strong in our economy during the past few months, and there is ample indication that these pressures will continue strong, and perhaps be accentuated, in the months immediately ahead. The basic causes of this situation are well known. A vast supply of money and other liquid assets was created during the war and there have been additions to this accumulation of purchasing power since the end of the war. There has also been an inadequate supply of goods and services . . . growing out of the destruction of war and the deferment of civilian demands when a large part of output was destined for military use. . . . The existing situation, therefore, spells continuing pressure toward higher prices. In addition we must take cognizance of the fact that conditions are highly favorable to further credit expansion. . . . (From a letter from the FOMC to the Secretary of the Treasury; Minutes 1947, pp. 183–84).*

Aside from the phrase "and perhaps be accentuated," what was being argued was simply that, in the absence of tighter policy, prices, credit, and money would continue to increase.

12. The quotations are from the Records of Policy Actions of the FOMC meetings of December 17, 1968, January 14, 1969, and March 4, 1969–*1968 Annual Report,* p. 224, and *1969 Annual Report,* pp. 109, 117.

projected growth, "the Committee agreed that, in light of the persistence of inflationary pressures and expectations, the existing degree of monetary restraint should be continued at present" (*1969 Annual Report*, p. 121). In May, "The Committee took note of the signs of some slowing in the economic expansion and of the indications of stringency in financial markets. In view of the persistence of strong inflationary pressures and expectations, however, the members agreed that a relaxation of the existing degree of monetary restraint would not be appropriate at this time" (*1969 Annual Report*, p. 145). In October, faced with projections of essentially no real growth over the coming three quarters, "the Committee decided that a relaxation of monetary restraint would not be appropriate at this time in light of the persistence of inflationary pressures and expectations" (*1969 Annual Report*, pp. 185–86). The considerations guiding monetary policy were similar at most other meetings during the year, and inflation and inflationary expectations received great attention and concern throughout. The intent to do more than offset expected increases in aggregate demand is clear.[13]

April 1974. The Federal Reserve responded to the oil embargo that started in October 1973 with an attempt to loosen policy somewhat to mitigate the contractionary influences and uncertainty generated by the embargo. With the lifting of the embargo in March 1974 and the end of wage and price controls in April, the Federal Reserve was faced with a rate of inflation even higher than one that it had already considered excessive in the fall of 1973. It responded with an active effort at contraction. Throughout the spring and early summer, whenever there was conflict between the System's short-run interest rate and money targets, the FOMC, in contrast to its practice in earlier years, resolved the doubts in whichever way produced the higher interest rate. Indeed, on several occasions the Committee pursued (or accepted) higher interest rates despite the fact that monetary growth was within its target range.[14] This occurred in an environment where little or no real growth was taking place or was expected in the near future. The motive for the attempts at contraction was inflation. There were references to "the persistence of inflation and of inflationary psychology" and "the need for policy ac-

---

13. One can plausibly argue that the shock could be dated a month or two later than December 1968. The tightening that occurred in December was in part a response to evidence of stronger growth. By early 1969, however, it was clear that the change in policy involved more. We choose December 1968 because the Federal Reserve cites this as the time when "the Federal Reserve System embarked on a policy of increased monetary restraint" (*1969 Annual Report*, p. 75). Dating the shock in March 1969 has no important effect on our results.

14. See especially *1974 Annual Report*, pp. 165, 173, 180–81.

tions to counter inflationary expectations." In one typical discussion, the central considerations were described as "the rise in market interest rates, the strong performance of the monetary aggregates, and—more broadly—the rapid advances in prices and costs."[15]

1975–78. At the end of the 1973–75 recession in early 1975, the Federal Reserve faced a rate of inflation that was high by historical standards. Over the next few years, inflation was a constant concern of the System. The level of inflation was often cited as a reason for tight policy, and policy was frequently described as "anti-inflationary" or as based on an underlying objective of a gradual return to stable prices. Thus one can argue that the Federal Reserve was attempting to shift the aggregate demand curve back throughout this period.

In our judgment, however, this interpretation of Federal Reserve objectives would be incorrect. Given the level of inflation, expressions of concern about inflation, and of desires to reduce inflation, were inevitable. But the actual commitment to combat inflation appears to have been weak. It was not until April 1976 that "it was observed that this might be an opportune time for the Committee to take a small step toward its longer-range objective of returning growth in the monetary aggregates toward rates consistent with general price stability" (*1976 Annual Report,* p. 203). Target annual monetary growth rates, which were not the central focus of policy, were lowered only one or two percentage points over the next two years, and little other explicit anti-inflationary action was taken. More important, the few comments that relate to the output or employment goals of policy reveal that the Federal Reserve was not attempting to cause discernible output sacrifices to reduce inflation. In February 1978, one FOMC member expressed the view that "a realistic objective for the unemployment rate now was considerably higher than it used to be, perhaps as high as 5.5 to 6 per cent" (*1978 Annual Report,* p. 132). This suggests that previously policy had been aiming at an even lower rate. In May of that year, when the unemployment rate was 6%, "a few members observed that . . . it would be desirable for growth in real output to diminish in the second half of this year toward a rate that could be sustained for the longer term," again implying that the Federal Reserve had previously been aiming for growth above trend rates (*1978 Annual Report,* p. 176).

August 1978. After several years of expressing concern about inflation but taking little concrete action to combat it, Federal Reserve policy

15. *1974 Annual Report,* pp. 109, 108, and 108, respectively. The statments occur in explanations of decisions by the Board of Governors to deny proposed increases in the discount rate. Nonetheless, they are meant to describe the basic stance of policy.

changed significantly in 1978. In August, the FOMC recognized the "possibility that an appreciable slowing of inflation would prove more difficult to achieve than previously had been anticipated" (*1978 Annual Report*, p. 210). Steps to tighten policy began in August, and in November the government announced a major program to strengthen the weak dollar and combat inflation. The discount rate was raised from 7.25 to 9.5% in four steps from August to November 1978, and reserve requirements were also increased in November. By November the System was fairly explicit that its objective was to cause a growth recession. The tightening of policy was continued despite forecasts of sluggish growth, and despite the fact that "skepticism was expressed [by some members of the FOMC] . . . that growth in output could be tapered down to a relatively slow rate without bringing on a recession" (*1978 Annual Report*, p. 247).

The tightening of policy continued in 1979. The discount rate was raised another 1.5 percentage points in three steps from July to September. During this period almost all questions about the conduct of monetary policy were resolved on the side of tightness. When money growth was high the System acted to raise interest rates and dampen growth; when money growth was low no actions were taken to lower interest rates and spur growth. All of this occurred against a background of a deteriorating forecast for short-run real growth (including a belief in the summer of 1979 that a recession was under way), which would typically have led to efforts to stimulate the economy. This clearly indicates a desire to contract the economy rather than just hold it steady.

October 1979. There was another major anti-inflationary shock to monetary policy on October 6, 1979. In effect, the Federal Reserve decided that its measures over the previous year had been unsuccessful in reducing inflation and that much stronger measures were needed. Although the shift in policy was to some extent presented as a technical change, the fact that it was intended to lead to considerably higher interest rates and lower money growth was clear. For example, "the Committee anticipated that the shift . . . would result in . . . a prompt increase . . . in the federal funds rate" (*1979 Annual Report*, p. 204). The upper end of the short-run target range for the federal funds rate was raised by 3.75 percentage points, while the lower end was essentially unchanged. It was also clear that a central underlying objective of the change in policy was a reduction in inflation. For example: "the purpose of this series of actions [taken on October 6] was to assure better control over the expansion of money and bank credit and to help curb speculative excesses in financial, foreign exchange, and commodity markets, thereby dampening inflationary forces in the economy" (*1979 Annual Report*, p. 109).

Intents versus Actions.   Our definition of a shock and our discussion of particular episodes makes it clear that our central concern has been with the intentions rather than the actions of the Federal Reserve. We do this because the same actions can occur both independent of the real economy and in response to real events. For example, the monetary base could fall because the Federal Reserve wished to cause a recession or because it was attempting to dampen an expansion that it believed would otherwise have occurred. Thus, only a narrative analysis of intentions can identify changes in policy that are independent of the real economy.

At the same time, however, intentions not backed up by actions would not be expected to have large real effects. It is for this reason that we only consider as shocks episodes when the Federal Reserve genuinely appeared willing to accept output losses. We feel that it is only in these instances that the Federal Reserve is likely to actually use the tools it has available to contract the economy. In this regard, it is useful to note that while actions were not explicitly considered in our identification of shocks, financial market conditions did change greatly in each of the episodes in which we identify a shock. In particular, interest rates rose sharply. For example, from three months before our shocks to three months after, the six-month commerical paper rate rose by an average of 29%. The smallest increase was 16% (for the 1968 shock) and the largest 40% (for the 1955 shock). Thus, the Federal Reserve's intentions appear to have been supported by actions.[16]

3.2 DOES REAL ACTIVITY RESPOND TO MONETARY SHOCKS?

Having identified this sequence of six postwar episodes in which the Federal Reserve appears to have deliberately tried to cause a recession to reduce inflation, the natural question to ask is whether recessions in fact followed these disturbances. In this section, we provide both informal evidence and a statistical test of the relationship between our monetary shocks and the subsequent behavior of industrial production and unemployment in the post-World War II period.

3.2.1 Informal Evidence.   We first examine the behavior of output and unemployment after each of the postwar shocks we have identified. The

---

16. Using the federal funds rate for the five episodes that have occurred since the development of the federal funds market does not alter these results. The growth rate of the monetary base also generally slows around the times of the shocks, though its movements across episodes are less consistent than those of the commerical paper rate. The reason for this greater variability is very likely simply that in all of the episodes (including the 1979 one) the Federal Reserve focused to a considerable extent on interest rate movements, while in many of the episodes it was relatively unconcerned with the monetary base.

data used in this analysis are the monthly total industrial production series compiled by the Federal Reserve Board and the monthly unemployment rate of all civilian workers compiled by the Bureau of Labor Statistics.[17] In both cases we use the seasonally unadjusted version of the series and then account for seasonal movements by regressing the series on a set of seasonal dummy variables.

Figure 1 shows the resulting seasonally adjusted industrial production (in logarithms) and unemployment rate series. We have drawn vertical lines in the six months of the postwar era in which we identify monetary shocks. From these graphs it appears that real economic activity decreases substantially after each of our monetary shocks. The results are particularly striking for the unemployment series: the unemployment rate rises sharply after each shock. Industrial production also falls substantially after each shock, although these movements are somewhat obscured by the high monthly variation in the series and the strong upward trend. Another striking characteristic of Figure 1 is that there are only two major decreases in real activity that are not preceded by monetary shocks. Again, this feature is most apparent in the unemployment series. The two significant rises in unemployment that are not preceded by a monetary shock occur in 1954 (at the end of the Korean War) and in 1961.

While these graphs are suggestive, simple plots of the data cannot distinguish between movements in real activity caused by monetary shocks and movements that occur because the economy may naturally tend to cycle up and down. To abstract from the typical cyclical behavior of real activity, we do the following. We first estimate univariate forecasting equations for both industrial production and unemployment, and then examine the difference between the forecasted behavior and the actual behavior of each series following each shock. If actual activity is less than one would expect on the basis of the univariate forecast following monetary shocks, this would suggest that the change in Federal Reserve policy caused real activity to be lower than it otherwise would have been.

The data used in the regressions are the same two seasonally-unadjusted series described above. For industrial production we exam-

---

17. The industrial production series is from *Industrial Production, 1986 Edition*, Table A-11. The unemployment series is from *Labor Force Statistics Derived from the Current Population Survey, 1948–87*, Table A-31. The unemployment series for 1946 and 1947 is taken from various issues of the *Monthly Labor Review*. The data for 1946 and 1947 are based on the same household survey as later estimates, but have not been revised to take into account modern changes in the definition of the labor force. To prevent a spurious jump in the series in January 1948, we splice the old and new series together in this month.

ine the data in percentage changes to account for the non-stationarity of the series. For the unemployment rate, we look at the data in levels and include a simple linear time trend to account for the apparent upward drift of the series over time. For each series, the simple forecasting equation includes a set of monthly dummy variables to account for typical seasonal fluctuations and 24 own lags.

The own lags are included to capture the normal dynamics of the series. Most important, we wish to control for the possibility that Federal Reserve policy tends to turn contractionary after periods of strong growth that might naturally be followed by downturns even in the ab-

Figure 1 ECONOMIC ACTIVITY AND MONETARY SHOCKS.

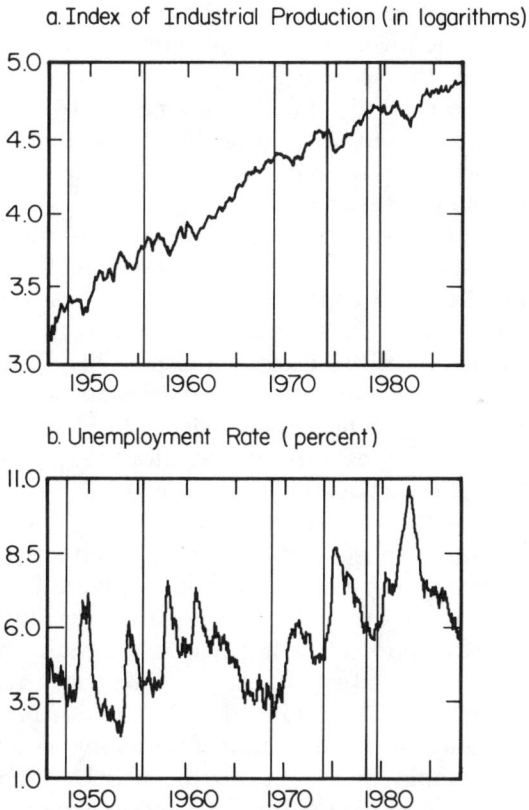

a. Index of Industrial Production (in logarithms)

b. Unemployment Rate (percent)

Notes: Vertical lines are drawn at the dates of monetary shocks. The actual dates are October 1947, September 1955, December 1968, April 1974, August 1978, and October 1979. The sources of the data are described in the text. The data have been seasonally adjusted by a regression on monthly dummy variables.

sence of a shift in monetary policy. The estimation of the unemployment equation in levels with a trend term included is done as an additional precaution in this regard. Because including a trend term can introduce bias toward detecting trend reversion when none is present, by using this procedure we may in fact be introducing some bias against finding real effects of monetary policy.

The results of estimating the equations suggest that our specifications are adequate to capture the typical behavior of the two series. The Q-statistics of the estimated regressions show that no significant serial correlation remains when 24 own lags are included. Furthermore, expanding the regressions to include as many as 48 own lags does not alter any important features of the results.

The forecasting equations are estimated over the period 1948–87. We then do a dynamic forecast of both the percentage change in industrial production and the level of the unemployment rate for the 36 months following each of the six shocks identified above. The differences between these forecasts and actual behavior are shown in Figures 2 and 3. For industrial production, the figure shows the cumulative error at each point so that one can more readily identify the impact of the shock on the level of industrial production.

Consider first industrial production. Figure 2 shows that after each of the six times in the postwar period that the Federal Reserve shifted to a policy of attempting to contract output to reduce inflation, industrial production over the next several years was considerably lower than would be predicted on the basis of the past history of the series. The average maximum departure of industrial production from its forecasted path over the three-year horizon considered in the figure is −14%. The smallest maximum forecast error is −8% (for the August 1978 shock); the largest is −21% (for the October 1979 shock).

Figure 3 shows that the results using unemployment are, with one exception, similar to those using industrial production. The unemployment rate two years after a monetary shock is typically 1.5 to 2.5 percentage points higher than the value predicted from the univariate forecasting regression. The exception is the behavior of unemployment following the policy shift of December 1968. In this episode, though industrial production fell sharply below its predicted path, the unemployment rate rose only slightly more than the univariate forecasting model predicts. Figure 1 shows that unemployment rose sharply after December 1968, but from an extremely low level. Thus, our forecasting equation is implying that the rise in unemployment was largely predictable simply on the basis of normal reversion toward trend. Since, as mentioned above, the inclusion of a trend term in the forecasting equation can cause the amount of trend

Figure 2 CUMULATIVE FORECAST ERRORS OF UNIVARIATE
AUTOREGRESSIVE MODEL FOR LOG INDUSTRIAL PRODUCTION
FOLLOWING MONETARY SHOCKS.

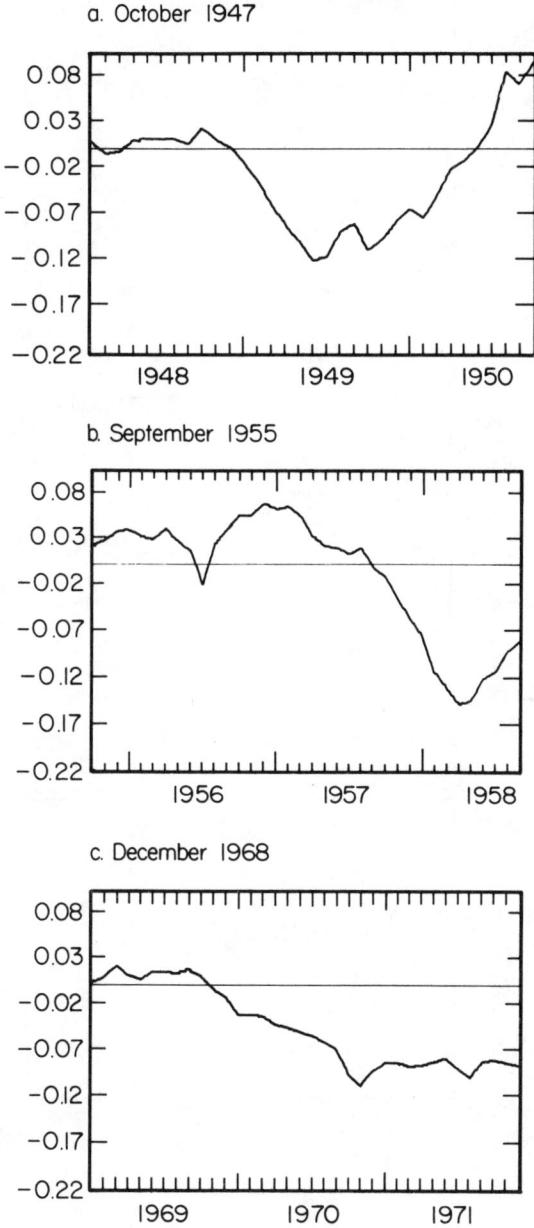

a. October 1947

b. September 1955

c. December 1968

Figure 2 (CONTINUED)

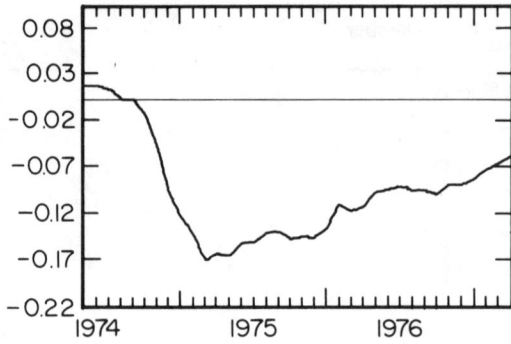

d. April 1974

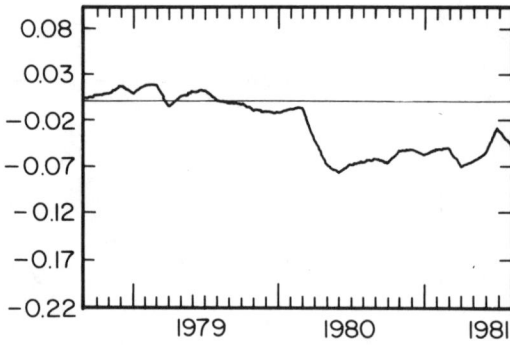

e. August 1978

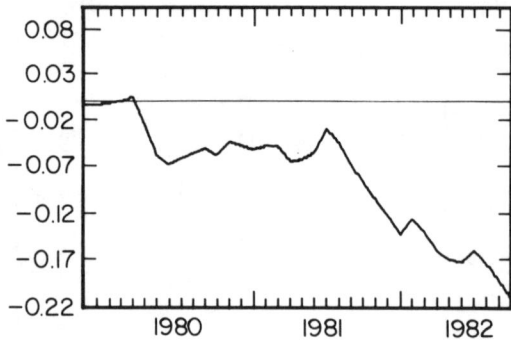

f. October 1979

reversion to be overestimated, Figure 3 may understate the size of the unforecastable increase in unemployment in this episode.

In short, the figures show that the negative monetary shocks that we have identified are followed by marked downturns in real economic activity that cannot be predicted from the past behavior of the economy. Furthermore, the consistency of the results suggests that no one shock will be crucial to any statistical summary of the relationship between monetary disturbances and real output. This finding is important because although one could imagine that in specific episodes some omitted variable (supply shocks in 1974, for example) might be the source of both the real decline and the Federal Reserve's policy shift, it seems unlikely that some omitted factor is present in all six of the episodes.

Another important feature of the results is that the forecast errors typically do not return to zero. For every shock except that in 1947, industrial production is substantially below its forecasted path three years after the shock. On average over the six shocks, industrial production after three years is 7% below the predicted level; that is, only about half of the maximum departure from the forecasted path has been reversed. Carrying the forecasts out further shows only a very gradual return to the predicted path: the average forecast error is 6% after four years and 4% after five. The same pattern is present, though somewhat less strongly, for unemployment; after four of the six shocks, the forecast errors for unemployment remain substantially above zero after three years.

An extreme interpretation of this finding would be that monetary shocks have real effects that are not only substantial but permanent. However, as Cochrane (1988) shows, simple autoregressive procedures such as ours cannot reliably distinguish between permanent effects and very long-lasting but nonetheless transitory ones. Hence, a more moderate interpretation is that our results imply that monetary shocks have very long-lived effects. In either case, since we find that purely nominal disturbances have highly persistent effects, our results cast grave doubt on arguments that the considerable persistence of output movements suggests that demand disturbances cannot be an important source of output fluctuations (Nelson and Plosser 1982; Campbell and Mankiw 1987). Similarly, our results suggest that using the assumption that demand shocks have only temporary effects as an identifying assumption is likely to yield highly misleading results (Blanchard and Quah 1988).

3.2.2 Statistical Test. To test formally whether there is an identifiable statistical relationship between the monetary shocks that we have identified and movements in real output, we employ the following test. To the

Figure 3 FORECAST ERRORS OF UNIVARIATE AUTOREGRESSIVE MODEL
        FOR THE UNEMPLOYMENT RATE FOLLOWING MONETARY
        SHOCKS.

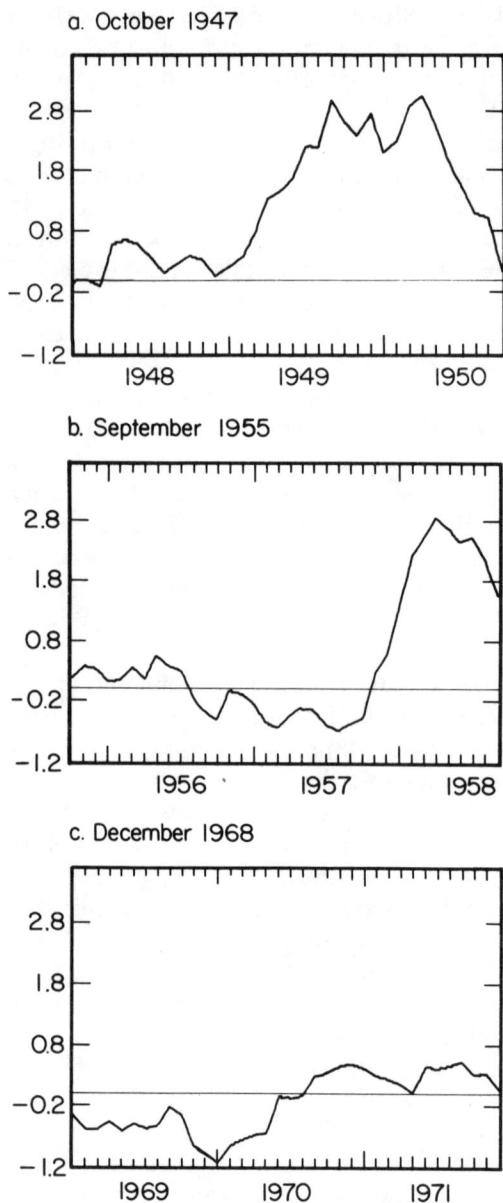

a. October 1947

b. September 1955

c. December 1968

Figure 3 (CONTINUED)

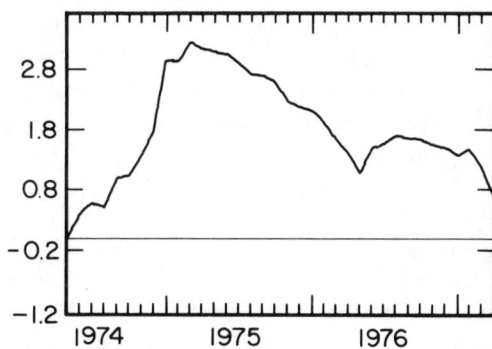

d. April 1974

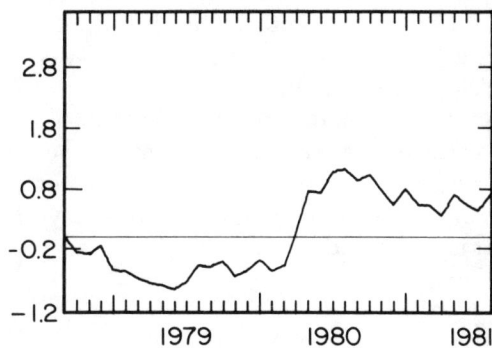

e. August 1978

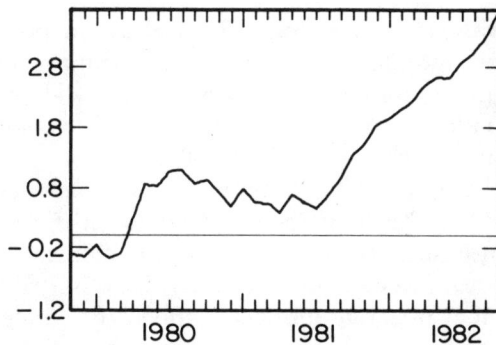

f. October 1979

simple univariate forecasting equations for industrial production and unemployment described above, we add current and lagged values of a dummy variable that is equal to one in each of the six months in which we have identified a change in Federal Reserve policy and zero in all other months. The impulse response function for this expanded forecasting equation provides an estimate of the total effect of a policy change after some horizon. The standard error of the impulse response function provides a way of gauging whether the effects of the nominal disturbances are statistically significant.

Since the dummy variable is the crucial indicator of monetary shocks, it is useful to describe its specification more thoroughly. This variable simply identifies the six months when the Federal Reserve made a decision to try to cause a recession to reduce inflation. The variable does not indicate how long the shocks lasted or attempt to differentiate the shocks by size. The decision not to specify duration was motivated largely by the fact that the ends of these contractionary policies are often much more gradual and difficult to identify than the adoptions of the policies. The decision to give each shock an equal weight was motivated by the fact that our reading of the FOMC minutes and the Record of Policy Actions did not provide evidence of large differences in the severities of the intended downturns or a way of calibrating those intentions.

As before, the equation is estimated for both the percentage change in industrial production and the level of the unemployment rate. The actual equation that is estimated is:

$$y_t = a_0 + \sum_{i=1}^{11} a_i M_{it} + \sum_{j=1}^{24} b_j y_{t-j} + \sum_{k=0}^{36} c_k D_{t-k}, \quad (1)$$

where y is either the change in log industrial production or the level of the unemployment rate, M is a set of monthly dummy variables, and D is the dummy variable for contractionary monetary shocks. For the unemployment equation a simple linear time trend is also included. The regressions are run over the period 1948–87.

The estimation results for the industrial production equation are given in Table 1. Over two-thirds of the coefficients on the monetary shock variable are negative and twelve of them have t-statistics less than -1.0. The predominance of negative coefficients, like the pictures described above, suggests that negative monetary shocks do indeed depress real output. The fact that many of the coefficients have large standard errors indicates that the timing of the response of real output is somewhat variable. This, however, is not surprising given that we are trying to

Table 1 BASIC INDUSTRIAL PRODUCTION REGRESSION
SAMPLE PERIOD: February 1948–December 1987
DEPENDENT VARIABLE: Percentage Change in
Industrial Production

Dummy for Shift in Monetary Policy			Lagged Changes in Industrial Production		
Lag	Coefficient	Standard Error	Lag	Coefficient	Standard Error
0	−.0041	.0062			
1	.0081	.0062	1	.2218	.0492
2	.0014	.0062	2	.0773	.0503
3	.0020	.0062	3	−.0294	.0503
4	−.0004	.0057	4	.0566	.0498
5	−.0061	.0057	5	−.0512	.0496
6	−.0025	.0057	6	−.0937	.0496
7	−.0071	.0057	7	.0504	.0496
8	−.0166	.0057	8	−.0383	.0491
9	.0030	.0057	9	−.0485	.0491
10	−.0067	.0057	10	−.0296	.0489
11	.0020	.0057	11	.0114	.0485
12	.0032	.0057	12	.1497	.0483
13	−.0055	.0057	13	−.1242	.0483
14	−.0001	.0058	14	−.1409	.0487
15	−.0035	.0058	15	−.0810	.0491
16	−.0056	.0058	16	−.0714	.0493
17	−.0025	.0058	17	.1009	.0494
18	−.0105	.0058	18	−.0452	.0494
19	−.0073	.0058	19	−.0085	.0482
20	−.0116	.0058	20	−.0568	.0473
21	.0021	.0058	21	−.0911	.0467
22	.0009	.0058	22	.0222	.0470
23	−.0081	.0058	23	−.0607	.0451
24	−.0100	.0058	24	.1175	.0434
25	.0009	.0058			
26	−.0081	.0058			
27	−.0021	.0058			
28	−.0059	.0058			
29	−.0078	.0058			
30	−.0006	.0058			
31	−.0055	.0058			
32	−.0010	.0058			
33	.0123	.0057			
34	.0079	.0057			
35	−.0024	.0057			
36	−.0034	.0057			

R^2 = .825
S.E.E. = .0132
Q(63) = 53.75
Coefficients and standard errors for the constant term and monthly dummies are not reported.

pinpoint the response at a monthly frequency. Indeed, what is perhaps more surprising is that the response in some of the months is estimated so precisely.

A natural way to summarize the response of industrial production to the monetary shock variable is to examine the impulse response function implied by the estimated equation. In our specification, the impulse response function traces out the effect of a unit shock to the dummy variable (D), including the feedback effect through lagged output. The 36-month impulse response function for the industrial production equation is given in Figure 4.[18] The figure also shows the one standard error bands for the impulse response function.[19]

The impulse response function shows that for the first several months following a monetary shock there is little effect on real output. Output then falls drastically at the ends of both the first and second years, with a slight plateau early in the second year. The maximum impact occurs after 33 months and indicates that a shock causes the level of real industrial production to be approximately 12% lower than it would have been had the shock not occurred.

From the confidence bands, it is clear that this effect is not only large, but also highly statistically significant. For example, the t-statistic for the impulse response function at 33 months is -3.4. The effect of monetary shocks on real production is thus significantly different from zero at the 99% confidence level.

Another way to measure the statistical significance of our results is to ask how likely one would be to obtain estimated effects as strong as those shown in Figure 4 using random dates for shocks. Specifically, we performed 200 trials of an experiment in which we replaced the dummy variable in equation (1) with a dummy set equal to one in six months chosen randomly over the period 1947–85. The estimated maximum depressing effect of the Monte Carlo dummy on industrial production over a 36-month horizon exceeded the 12% figure obtained with our dummy for genuine monetary shocks in just one trial. Thus, it is extremely unlikely that our results could arise by chance.

Figure 4 also confirms the impression gained from Figure 2 that monetary shocks have real effects that are very long-lasting. By the end of 36 months only a quarter of the maximum negative effect of the monetary shock has been undone. Furthermore, if one includes an additional 24

18. As in Figure 2, Figure 4 shows the cumulative sum of the impulse responses so that the effect of the shock on the log level of industrial production can be seen more easily.
19. The standard errors are calculated using the formula for the asymptotic standard error of a non-linear function of the regression paramenters. See Poterba, Rotemberg, and Summers (1986, p. 668) for details.

lags of the monetary shock dummy in the basic regression and then continues the impulse response function out an additional 24 months, the negative effects of a monetary shock still linger. Five years after a monetary shock, industrial production is still 7% lower than it would have been had the Federal Reserve not decided to attempt to cause a recession.

The empirical results for unemployment confirm those for industrial production. Table 2 shows the coefficient estimates for the equation for the unemployment rate. The impulse response function and standard error bands for the unemployment regression are given in Figure 5. The figure shows that unemployment begins to rise sharply 18 months after the shock and reaches its maximum at 34 months. The total impact of the shock after 34 months is that the unemployment rate is 2.1 percentage points higher than it otherwise would have been.

The standard error bands for the impulse response function for unemployment indicate that the depressing effect of a monetary shock is highly statistically significant. The *t*-statistics are over 2.0 for all the impulse responses after month 20 and are often over 3.0. In a Monte Carlo experiment analogous to that for industrial production, the maximum estimated impact of the Monte Carlo dummy on unemployment over a 36-month horizon never exceeded 2.1 percentage points in 200 trials.

The results of the statistical test indicate that monetary policy shocks

Figure 4 IMPULSE RESPONSE FUNCTION FOR BASIC INDUSTRIAL PRODUCTION REGRESSION

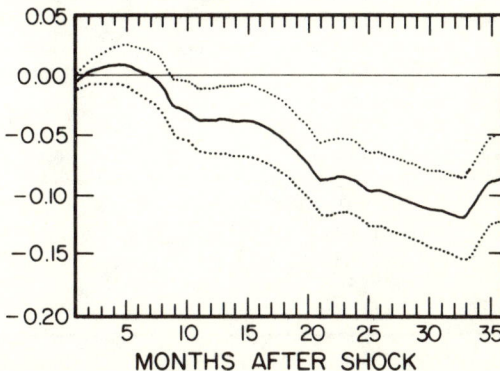

Notes: The impulse response function shows the impact of a unit shock to the monetary dummy variable. The impulse responses for the change in industrial production have been cumulated to reflect the effect on the log level. The coefficient estimates used to generate the impulse response function are given in Table 1. The dashed lines show the one standard error bands.

Table 2   BASIC UNEMPLOYMENT REGRESSION
         SAMPLE PERIOD: January 1948–December 1987
         DEPENDENT VARIABLE: Unemployment Rate

Dummy for Shift in Monetary Policy			*Lagged Unemployment Rates*		
Lag	Coefficient	Standard Error	Lag	Coefficient	Standard Error
0	−.0979	.1272			
1	−.1049	.1272	1	1.0539	.0496
2	.0460	.1274	2	.1091	.0718
3	.0692	.1167	3	−.1685	.0720
4	.0799	.1166	4	.0313	.0724
5	−.0004	.1164	5	−.0140	.0722
6	.1369	.1161	6	−.0659	.0714
7	.0266	.1163	7	−.0371	.0713
8	.0784	.1160	8	.0844	.0712
9	.2989	.1157	9	−.0360	.0704
10	−.0709	.1162	10	−.0389	.0704
11	−.1461	.1162	11	.0881	.0707
12	−.0692	.1165	12	.1659	.0693
13	−.0326	.1162	13	−.2807	.0690
14	.1691	.1179	14	−.0191	.0705
15	.1168	.1181	15	.0113	.0708
16	.0533	.1182	16	.0521	.0704
17	.0162	.1179	17	.0529	.0702
18	.0712	.1176	18	−.0967	.0706
19	.1652	.1175	19	.1399	.0707
20	.1053	.1177	20	−.0852	.0711
21	.2589	.1178	21	.0100	.0708
22	−.0212	.1183	22	.0741	.0702
23	.0320	.1170	23	−.1261	.0702
24	.2330	.1170	24	.0668	.0487
25	−.1101	.1172			
26	.3029	.1173			
27	.2415	.1181			
28	.1263	.1190			
29	.1379	.1190			
30	.0645	.1184			
31	−.0008	.1182			
32	−.0712	.1181			
33	.1046	.1169			
34	−.0071	.1169			
35	−.0202	.1168			
36	−.0824	.1168			

R^2 = .981
S.E.E. = .267
Q(63) = 56.25
Coefficients and standard errors for the constant term, the trend, and monthly dummies are not reported.

have potent real effects. There remains, however, the question of whether the monetary shocks we identify actually account for a large fraction of the total variation in real activity. Figure 1 provides informal evidence that monetary shocks are indeed an important source of real fluctuations. It shows not just that each of our shocks was followed by a sharp rise in unemployment, but also that there have been only two sharp rises in unemployment in the postwar period not preceded by such shocks. In other words, six of the eight postwar recessions have been preceded by decisions by the Federal Reserve to attempt to cause a downturn.

To formalize the impression given by Figure 1, we first regress the monthly level of the unemployment rate on a constant, seasonal dummy variables, and a trend. We then run the same regression including 36 lags of our monetary shock dummy variable. That is, we run the same regression as in (1) above, except that we do not include any of the own lags of the unemployment rate. The equation including the monetary shock variable has a sum of squared residuals that is 21% smaller than that of the simple seasonal regression. This difference is very large. It implies that, by itself, our simple dummy variable for overt Federal Reserve policy decisions to create a recession can account for more than a fifth of the non-seasonal variation in the postwar unemployment rate.

These results strongly suggest that aggregate demand disturbances,

Figure 5 IMPULSE RESPONSE FUNCTION FOR BASIC UNEMPLOYMENT REGRESSION.

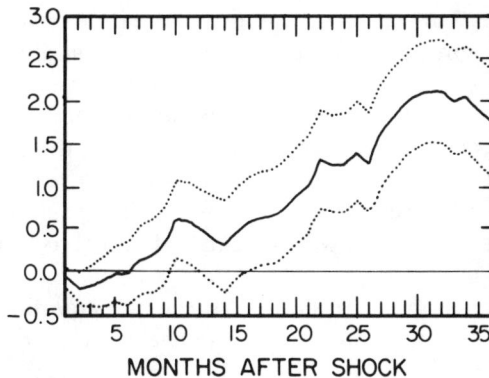

Notes: The impulse response function shows the impact of a unit shock to the monetary dummy variable on the level of the unemployment rate (expressed in percentage points). The coefficient estimates used to generate the impulse response function are given in Table 2. The dashed lines show the one standard error bands.

rather than real shocks, are the predominant source of economic fluctuations. Our simple dummy variable surely captures only a small fraction of demand disturbances. It is a very crude measure of only one aspect of monetary policy, and it neglects all non-monetary demand disturbances, such as changes in fiscal policy and in private demand, entirely. Since the dummy variable alone accounts for a substantial fraction of (non-seasonal) postwar fluctuations, it follows that aggregate demand disturbances as a whole almost surely account for a much larger fraction.

3.2.3 Robustness. While the results appear clear cut, one naturally worries about the robustness of any empirical finding. In the case of this study, the main concern is that the decisions by the Federal Reserve to try to create a recession might be correlated with other factors. If this is true, then these other factors, rather than the monetary shocks we have identified, could be the true source of the movements in real output.

We have already provided several pieces of evidence that indicate that this is not a likely possibility. First, the earlier part of this section discusses the rationale given by the System for its decisions to try to shift back the aggregate demand curve. While inflation was the proximate cause in each case, the perceived cause of the inflation differed across the episodes that we consider. For example, in 1968 it was wartime expenditures, while in 1974 it was earlier oil price shocks and expansionary monetary policy. The fact that there was no consistent source of the inflation that the Federal Reserve wished to cure suggests that there is no consistent alternative factor that was present in each instance of a shift to anti-inflationary monetary policy.

Second, Figures 2 and 3 show that the behavior of real activity relative to predicted following each of our shocks is quite similar. This suggests that even if some other factor were causing inflation and depressing real output in one or two of the periods in which we have identified monetary shocks, this other factor could not be driving the results. We have tested this assertion by eliminating each shock in turn and examining the resulting impulse response functions. After each elimination, the impulse response functions appear nearly identical to those in Figures 4 and 5.[20]

Third, our discussion of the simple forecasting equations stressed that 24 lags of the percentage change in industrial production or the level of

20. Even though it does not represent a monetary shock by our criteria, the "credit crunch" of 1965–66 is often characterized as an important episode of tight monetary policy. We have therefore investigated the effects of adding a shock in December 1965. We find the results are essentially unchanged by this addition.

the unemployment rate are adequate for capturing any natural tendency of real activity to decline after it has been growing briskly for some time. This means that if the Federal Reserve simply said it wished to cause a recession whenever a temporary boom was about to end, these statements would not have any explanatory power once the own lags were included in the regression. The results in Figures 2–5 and Tables 1–2 above clearly show that this is not the case.[21]

In addition to these pieces of evidence, it is possible to control explicitly for other factors that one might fear accounted for our results. We consider three types of other factors. They are supply shocks, fiscal policy, and inflation itself.

Supply shocks are a natural source of concern: it is possible that supply shocks could both generate inflation to which the Federal Reserve wished to respond and directly depress real output. In this regard, it is important to point out that supply shocks that occurred in the past and were accommodated by expansionary aggregate demand policy are of no concern. These shocks would have caused the inflation that the Federal Reserve wished to cure but would no longer be having a depressing effect on real activity.

To ensure that supply shocks do not account for our results, we do two things. First, we try eliminating the two monetary shocks that could plausibly be associated with the oil price rises of the 1970s (1974 and 1979). This change reduces the maximum impact of a shock slightly (the trough of the impulse response function for industrial production is $-.10$ rather than $-.12$), but the results are otherwise unchanged.

Second, we add a measure of supply shocks to our regressions. Following conventional practice, we capture supply conditions by including the current and first 36 lags of the monthly percentage change in the relative price of food and energy in our regressions.[22] We find that accounting for

21. A related point concerns our method for identifying shocks. To identify a change in monetary policy we often use Federal Reserve records for up to six months after the apparent change. We do this because shifts in policy are often not sufficiently sudden or dramatic that they can be identified from, for example, the records of a single meeting. This introduces a slight possibility of bias: if the System has a tendency to state that it was attempting to create a downturn only if evidence that there will be a downturn has appeared, our test will overstate the effects of shifts in policy. To ensure that this possible bias is not affecting our results, we look at the forecast errors of the simple univariate forecasts starting six months after each shock. Even with these six extra months of actual data, however, the declines in output that occur following the monetary shocks cannot be predicted.

22. The relative price of food and energy is measured as the ratio of a weighted average of the producer price indexes for crude foodstuffs and feedstuffs, crude fuel, and crude petroleum to the producer price index for finished products.

supply shocks barely alters the results. For industrial production the cumulative impact of a monetary shock is actually slightly larger when supply shocks are included in the regression than when they are not. For unemployment the maximum impact of a monetary shock is slightly smaller for the expanded regression than for the simple regression. In both cases the supply shock variable has little impact on the timing or the significance of the impulse response functions for the monetary shock variable.[23]

Another factor that one might worry could account for our results is fiscal policy. It could be the case that whenever the Federal Reserve became concerned about inflation and decided to attempt to cause a recession, the fiscal authorities also shifted to a more contractionary policy. This possibility does not appear particularly likely. In the Federal Reserve records there is certainly no mention that the anti-inflationary changes in monetary policy are designed to reinforce shifts in fiscal policy. Furthermore, given the inside lags of fiscal policy, it seems unlikely that the fiscal authorities could change spending and taxes to match the timing of monetary policy very closely.

Nevertheless, it is perhaps useful to test whether a correlation between monetary and fiscal policies could be present and could affect the results. To do this, we add to our regressions the current and first 12 lags of the quarterly change in the ratio of the nominal government budget surplus to nominal GNP.[24] This variable should obviously capture any of the demand side effects of fiscal policy. At the same time, because the deficit is highly correlated with government purchases, this variable should also capture any supply side effects that government purchases might have through the interest rate and labor supply. Thus, it can control for another possible source of supply shocks.

Including the fiscal policy variable lowers the cumulative effect of the monetary shock variable only slightly. For both industrial production and unemployment, a monetary shock still causes a large downturn in economic activity that is statistically significant at at least the 99% confidence level. Thus, the apparent response of the real economy to mone-

---

23. The same results obtain when alternative measures of supply shocks are used. Among the variants we have tried are the percentage change in the relative price of crude petroleum and the percentage change in the relative price of all crude materials for further processing.

24. The budget surplus data are from the National Income and Product Accounts and cover both the federal government and state and local governments. Quarterly observations were included by assuming that the deficit to GNP ratio was constant over a quarter, and then measuring the change in the ratio between the current month and three months ago, between three and six months ago, and so on.

tary shocks cannot be ascribed to possible correlations of monetary disturbances with government spending.[25]

A final additional factor that we consider is inflation. It is difficult to think of a plausible channel through which inflation by itself (independent of supply shocks) might directly depress real output. Nevertheless, since inflation is obviously present during each of our episodes, it may be useful to check whether allowing for a direct effect of inflation on real activity alters our results. To do this, we include the current and first 36 lags of the monthly percentage change in the producer price index for finished goods in our basic regression. For industrial production, including inflation has virtually no effect on the shape, amplitude, or statistical significance of the impulse response function for a monetary shock. For unemployment, including inflation reduces the size of the total real effect of the monetary shock somewhat, but the cumulative impact after 33 months is still large and positive. In sum, in this case, as in the other cases discussed, the result that monetary shocks matter tremendously is robust to the inclusion of additional explanatory variables.

4. Friedman and Schwartz Revisited

A natural next step in our analysis is to return to the interwar period to see what evidence the narrative approach sheds on the effects of monetary shocks in this era. We do this with some trepidation, however, because as we argue in Section 2, we believe that the identification of monetary disturbances in the period before 1947 can never be as clear cut or convincing as it is in the postwar era. Nevertheless, since Section 2 suggests an alternative list of interwar shocks and Section 3 suggests an empirical test for the relationship between monetary shocks and real output, it seems useful to investigate how, if at all, employing a revised version of the narrative approach affects Friedman and Schwartz's conclusion that monetary disturbances had severe real effects in the interwar era.

Specification. In Section 2 we discuss in detail Friedman and Schwartz's identification of monetary shocks in the interwar period. We argue that

25. Using the ratio of the cyclically-adjusted federal budget surplus to nominal GNP rather than the fiscal policy measure employed in the text has essentially no effect on the results. Specifically, we employ the Bureau of Economic Analysis measure of the cyclically-adjusted surplus (from CITIBASE), which is available beginning in 1955. Adding the current and first twelve lags of the quarterly change in the ratio of this measure to nominal GNP to our basic regression estimated over the period 1958–87 has virtually no impact on the estimated impact of the monetary shock dummy.

there may be some bias in their choices, and thus that the list of shocks they focus on may not be the most appropriate one. For our basic inter-war test we therefore consider a list of shocks somewhat different from Friedman and Schwartz's. In particular, we identify monetary shocks in five months of the interwar period: January 1920, October 1931, February 1933, January 1937, and September 1941. This list differs from that considered by Friedman and Schwartz by adding shocks in February 1933 and September 1941 and by not including any shock in the first two years of the Great Depression.

Our reasons for identifying shocks in 1933 and 1941 are described in Section 2. We have two reasons for not including a shock in the early stages of the Great Depression. First, our concern throughout the paper has been with whether Federal Reserve policy actions have real effects. Since whatever monetary disturbance may have occurred in the early part of the Depression involved inaction rather than active changes in monetary policy, it seems reasonable to exclude it. Second, because the interpretation of monetary developments in the early stages of the Great Depression is so controversial, we do not want our results to be driven by the identification of a shock in this period. However, because the most appropriate selection of shocks for the interwar period is not clear cut, below we consider alternatives to our basic list.

Given our list of shocks, it is straightforward to implement the statistical test of the real effects of monetary disturbances that we use in the previous section. As before, we define a monetary shock dummy variable that is equal to one in each of the months in which we identify a shock. The data on real output that we use are the standard Federal Reserve Board monthly index of total industrial production, which begins in 1919.[26] The equation that we estimate is

26. We use the most recent version of this series (given in *Industrial Production*, 1986) and again use seasonally unadjusted data. While the FRB index is the best and most comprehensive monthly index of production avaiable for the interwar period, it is not without problems. Most important, there is a break in the series in 1923. For the period after 1923, the FRB revised its original index to have broader coverage by including data on manhours for those industries where direct measures of physical production were unavailable. This revision was not carried back to the period 1919–23 because the necessary data were unavailable. This difference in procedures is potentially important because the inclusion of the manhours data tends to reduce the volatility of the FRB index after 1923. This means that some of the relatively dramatic movements in the index for 1919–23 would probably disappear if the earlier series were constructed using the same methods as the later index.

Because we want to include the 1920 monetary shock, starting the estimation in 1923 and thus using only the unbroken series is not possible. However, to test whether the inconsistency in the data affects our empirical results, we do the following. Since the revision of the Fed series to include manhour data was not done until 1940, there exists a consistently bad FRB index for 1919 to 1940. We can use this consistent series in the

identical to that given in equation (1) above. The estimation period is 1921–44.

Results. The coefficient estimates of this regression are given in Table 3. Figure 6 shows the corresponding impulse response function, together with the one standard error bands. The point estimates suggest a very potent effect of monetary shocks on real economic activity. The estimated maximum effect of a monetary shock on industrial production is a fall of 20% after 18 months.

While the real effect of a monetary shock in the interwar era appears to be large, it is not estimated precisely. Over months 10 to 18, when the effect is largest, the departure of the impulse response function from zero is 1.5 to 2 times the associated standard error. This implies the hypothesis that the effect is zero is only marginally rejected at conventional significance levels. Thus, while the interwar results are entirely consistent with our finding for the postwar period that monetary disturbances have large real effects, they do not by themselves provide overwhelming evidence of those effects.

At the same time, the timing of the real effects of monetary shocks in the basic interwar regression is quite different from the timing of real effects in the postwar regressions. In both eras the effect over the first six months is small. However, in the next twelve months the response is much more abrupt and severe in the interwar era than in the postwar era. The estimated impact of an interwar monetary shock plummets from essentially zero five months after the shock to −17% after eleven months. Industrial production then falls irregularly to its trough of −20% after 18 months. Then, again in sharp contrast to the results for the postwar period, there is a strong rebound, with the effect rising from −20% to −3% by month 23 and disappearing entirely by month 29.

In short, our results suggest that the effects of demand disturbances were both more rapid and less persistent in the interwar era than in the postwar period. An obvious implication of this finding is that—in contrast to the position taken by De Long and Summers (1988) and others—an explanation of the change in the overall persistence properties of real output after World War II should be sought in changes in the mechanisms that determine the economy's response to a given type of shock, rather than in changes in the nature of the shocks themselves.

---

regressions and see if it yields results that are noticeably different from those based on the inconsistent series. We find that the results are very similar for both the consistent and inconsistent data. We therefore opt for the inconsistent data because they exist after 1940 and thus allow us to examine the real effects of the rise in reserve requirements in late 1941.

Table 3   BASIC INTERWAR INDUSTRIAL PRODUCTION REGRESSION
SAMPLE PERIOD: February 1921–December 1944
DEPENDENT VARIABLE: Percentage Change in
Industrial Production

	Dummy for Change in Monetary Policy			Lagged Changes in Industrial Production	
Lag	Coefficient	Standard Error	Lag	Coefficient	Standard Error
0	−.0294	.0150			
1	−.0017	.0150	1	.5776	.0680
2	.0254	.0150	2	−.0850	.0778
3	.0018	.0151	3	−.1196	.0775
4	.0048	.0151	4	.0110	.0780
5	−.0066	.0150	5	.1157	.0772
6	−.0306	.0150	6	−.1729	.0769
7	−.0183	.0151	7	.1340	.0779
8	−.0186	.0151	8	.0247	.0778
9	−.0209	.0151	9	.0262	.0765
10	−.0010	.0151	10	.0009	.0750
11	.0082	.0151	11	.0481	.0738
12	−.0114	.0151	12	.1407	.0732
13	.0050	.0137	13	−.1474	.0693
14	−.0010	.0136	14	−.0789	.0691
15	.0046	.0135	15	.0734	.0689
16	.0008	.0139	16	−.0281	.0695
17	−.0205	.0139	17	.0333	.0695
18	.0434	.0139	18	−.0282	.0686
19	.0248	.0142	19	−.0500	.0681
20	.0149	.0143	20	.0406	.0661
21	.0213	.0141	21	−.0641	.0658
22	.0156	.0142	22	−.0114	.0645
23	−.0125	.0142	23	−.0381	.0642
24	.0118	.0143	24	.0645	.0584
25	−.0033	.0143			
26	.0171	.0142			
27	−.0264	.0142			
28	.0226	.0144			
29	.0078	.0142			
30	−.0148	.0142			
31	−.0207	.0141			
32	.0349	.0142			
33	.0029	.0143			
34	.0133	.0141			
35	−.0296	.0140			
36	−.0163	.0142			

R^2 = .652
S.E.E. = .0270
Q(48) = 18.08
Coefficients and standard errors for the constant term and monthly dummies are not reported.

Figure 6 IMPULSE RESPONSE FUNCTION FOR BASIC INTERWAR
INDUSTRIAL PRODUCTION REGRESSION

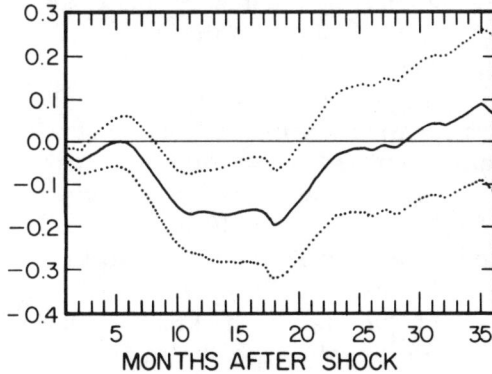

Notes: The impulse response function shows the impact of a unit shock to the monetary dummy variable. The impulse responses for the change in industrial production have been cumulated to reflect the effect on the log level. The coefficient estimates used to generate the impulse response function are given in Table 3. The dashed lines show the one standard error bands.

Robustness. As with our postwar regressions, it is important to investigate whether our results for the interwar era are being driven by the omission of other potentially relevant variables. Because our list of interwar monetary shocks includes one in the aftermath of World War I and another shortly before the outbreak of World War II, the most obvious omitted variable is some measure of fiscal policy.

We attempt to account for the effects of fiscal policy in two ways. Our first approach is to control directly for the effects of fiscal policy. We do this by including in the regression the current and two lagged values of the change since the previous year of the ratio of the federal budget surplus to nominal GNP.[27] Adding this variable has little effect on the results. The coefficients on the fiscal policy variables are of the expected sign (that is, a decrease in the surplus increases output), but they are small and statistically insignificant. The impulse response function for a monetary shock in this expanded regression is virtually identical to that for the basic interwar regression.

The second method that we use to deal with the possible effects of fiscal policy is to exclude the two shocks associated with the World Wars

27. The budget variable used is the nominal administrative budget surplus or deficit given in the statistical appendix of the *Annual Report of the Secretary of the Treasury*, 1980, Table 2. The nominal GNP numbers are from Romer, 1988a, Table 5, and the *National Income and Product Accounts of the U.S.*, Table 1. Both the budget and the GNP data are only available annually. Monthly figures are set equal to the annual value and changes are calculated in multiples of 12.

and shorten the sample period to February 1922–December 1940. These changes greatly strengthen the estimated effect of monetary shocks. The maximum depressing effect of a monetary shock is now a fall in industrial production of 41%. The timing of the effects is essentially the same as for the basic interwar regression.

Finally, it is natural to contrast our results with those that would be obtained using Friedman and Schwartz's list of shocks. To do this, we define an alternative monetary shock dummy variable that is equal to one in the five months in the interwar era when Friedman and Schwartz identify a monetary shock: January 1920, October 1930, March 1931, October 1931, and January 1937. The five shocks include the "three crucial experiments," plus two shocks early in the Great Depression corresponding to the beginnings of the first two waves of banking failures.[28] The specification is otherwise the same as our basic one. The sample period is February 1921–December 1944; no deficit measure is included.

The impulse response function for this regression is given in Figure 7 and shows, not surprisingly, that using Friedman and Schwartz's choices of shocks rather than ours greatly increases the estimated effects of monetary disturbances. The maximum effect of a monetary shock on real output is now a fall of 35% rather than 20% and is overwhelmingly, rather than marginally, significant. The pattern of the responses is similar to that obtained using our preferred list of shocks. The only noteworthy difference is that in Figure 7 output recovers only two-thirds of its maximum loss after 36 months rather than all.

Overall, the results from the interwar regressions support the postwar finding that monetary disturbances have very large effects on real economic activity. They are thus also supportive of Friedman and Schwartz's belief that money mattered tremendously in the interwar period. In fact, they may actually strengthen Friedman and Schwartz's conclusion because they indicate that the lagged effects of monetary shocks are shorter and sharper than informal statistical procedures led Friedman and Schwartz to believe.[29]

---

28. It is difficult to date precisely the monetary shock (or shocks) that Friedman and Schwartz associate with the early stages of the Great Depression. We choose October 1930 and March 1931 because it is in reference to the banking crises that Friedman and Schwartz are most emphatic in arguing that monetary policy was highly unusual. Including only the "three crucial experiments" rather than all five shocks has little effect on the results.

29. An obvious implication of the conclusion that monetary policy had large real effects in the interwar period is that the Great Depression would have been less severe if monetary policy had been less contractionary. In that sense, our results are supportive of Friedman and Schwartz's interpretation of the Depression. But since, as described above, neither we nor Friedman and Schwartz detect an active monetary shock at the

Figure 7 IMPULSE RESPONSE FUNCTION FOR INTERWAR INDUSTRIAL
PRODUCTION REGRESSION USING FRIEDMAN AND
SCHWARTZ'S SHOCKS

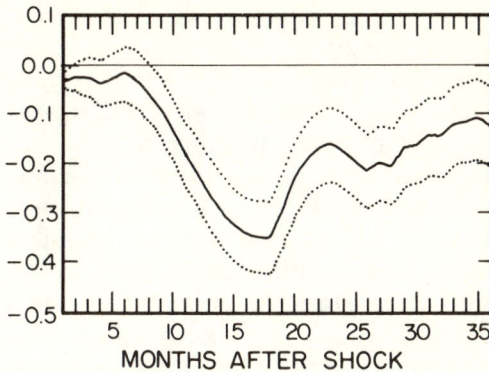

Notes: The impulse response function shows the impact of a unit shock to the monetary dummy variable. The impulse responses for the change in industrial production have been cumulated to reflect the effect on the log level. The dashed lines show the one standard error bands.

5. Conclusion

This paper is based on two premises. The first is that the narrative approach is the method that is most likely to be persuasive in resolving the question of whether monetary disturbances have real effects. The use of the narrative approach allows a vast body of information that cannot be employed in conventional statistical tests to be brought to bear on this question. And it is this additional information that can solve the problem of identifying the direction of causation between monetary factors and real economic developments. The second premise is that employing the narrative approach is difficult. Using it casually, as is typically done, can lead to bias, either in the interpretation of the historical record or in the inference that one draws about the real effects of monetary shocks.

This paper is therefore an attempt to employ the narrative approach carefully and systematically to study the real effects of monetary disturbances. The first and last parts of the paper focus on the interwar era, and are thus largely a reexamination of Friedman and Schwartz's path-breaking work. The middle and more important part considers evidence

onset of the Depression, and since there is strong evidence of non-monetary shocks, the severe initial downturn was most likely largely the result of non-monetary forces. Furthermore, because our results do not provide an estimate of the size of the effect of a given monetary change, we cannot determine how much less severe the subsequent depression might have been under any particular alternative policy.

for the period after World War II. From these two types of analysis we reach five conclusions.

First, in the postwar era there have been a series of episodes in which the Federal Reserve has in effect deliberately attempted to induce a recession to decrease inflation. These episodes are virtually ideal for employing the narrative approach because monetary shocks can be identified using a narrow and concrete set of criteria that are consistent across episodes. Economic developments following these shifts in Federal Reserve policy provide decisive evidence of the importance of monetary policy. In every case, output fell substantially below what one would otherwise have expected. A shift to anti-inflationary monetary policy led, on average, to an ultimate reduction in industrial production of 12% and an ultimate rise in the unemployment rate of two percentage points. These effects are highly statistically significant.

Second, in the postwar era the maximum depressing effect of anti-inflationary shifts in monetary policy occurs after roughly two and one half years, and there appears to be only a limited tendency for real activity to then return toward its pre-shock path. In other words, the real effects of demand disturbances appear to be highly persistent.

Third, our extremely narrowly defined monetary disturbances account for a considerable fraction of fluctuations in postwar economic activity: our dummy variable for negative shifts in policy accounts for more than a fifth of the variation in detrended, deseasonalized unemployment in the postwar period. Because we find that demand disturbances have real effects and because our simple measure of monetary shocks almost surely captures only a small fraction of demand fluctuations, our results strongly suggest that demand disturbances are a primary source of postwar economic fluctuations.

Fourth, the narrative approach is extremely difficult to implement in the interwar period. There is so much variation in monetary institutions and doctrines and in economic events that it is almost impossible to study the historical record of the period systematically. When the set of monetary disturbances for the interwar period that, in our judgment, comes as close as possible to being free of bias is considered, the interwar evidence is also supportive of the view that monetary policy has large real effects. The estimated maximum effect of a monetary disturbance for this period is a reduction in industrial production of 20%.

Fifth and last, the real effects of monetary shocks in the period between World War I and World War II do not appear to be long-lasting. Our estimates imply that by 33 months after a shock, output has essentially returned to the path it would have followed in the absence of the shock. Thus our results imply that demand disturbances have large real effects in both the interwar and postwar eras, but that the persistence properties of those real effects are very different in the two periods.

We have benefited greatly from the excellent comments and suggestions that we have received from numerous colleagues. We wish to thank particularly George Akerlof, Laurence Ball, Ben Bernanke, Olivier Blanchard, Charles Calomiris, Barry Eichengreen, Stanley Fischer, Benjamin Friedman, Milton Friedman, N. Gregory Mankiw, Thomas Mayer, Jeffrey Miron, Anna Schwartz, Richard Sutch, Peter Temin, and Janet Yellen. We are also grateful to the National Science Foundation for financial support and to David Parsley for able research assistance.

REFERENCES

Bernanke, Ben S. 1983. "Nonmonetary Effects of the Financial Crisis in the Propagation of the Great Depression." *American Economic Review* 73:257–76.

Blanchard, Olivier Jean and Danny Quah. 1988. "The Dynamic Effects of Aggregate Demand and Supply Disturbances." NBER Working Paper No. 2737.

Bordo, Michael D. 1988. "The Contribution of *A Monetary History of The United States: 1867 to 1960* to Monetary History." NBER Working Paper No. 2549.

Brown, E. Cary. 1956. "Fiscal Policy in the 'Thirties: A Reappraisal." *American Economic Review* 46:857–79.

Campbell, John Y. and N. Gregory Mankiw. 1987. "Are Output Fluctuations Transitory?" *Quarterly Journal of Economics* 102:857–80.

Chandler, Lester V. 1970. *America's Greatest Depression, 1929–1941.* New York: Harper and Row.

Cochrane, John H. 1988. "How Big Is the Random Walk in GNP?" *Journal of Politial Economy* 96:893–920.

De Long, J. Bradford and Lawrence H. Summers. 1988. "How Does Macroeconomic Policy Affect Output?" *Brookings Papers on Economic Activity:* 433–80.

Friedman, Milton and Anna Jacobson Schwartz. 1963a. *A Monetary History of the United States, 1867–1960.* Princeton: Princeton University Press.

Friedman, Milton and Anna Jacobson Schwartz. 1963b. "Money and Business Cycles." *Review of Economics and Statistics* 45:32–64.

Gordon, Robert Aaron. 1974. *Economic Instability and Growth: The American Record.* New York: Harper & Row.

Gordon, Robert J. and James A. Wilcox. 1981. "Monetarist Interpretations of the Great Depression: An Evaluation and Critique." In *The Great Depression Revisited,* Karl Brunner, ed. 49–107. Hingham, Mass.: Martinus Nijhoff Publishing.

Hamilton, James D. 1987. "Monetary Factors in the Great Depression." *Journal of Monetary Economics* 19:145–69.

Hendry, David F. and Neil R. Ericsson. 1987. "Assertion without Empirical Basis: An Econometric Appraisal of *Monetary Trends . . . in the United Kingdom* by Milton Friedman and Anna J. Schwartz." Oxford University Applied Economics Discussion Paper No. 25.

Kareken, John and Robert M. Solow. 1963. "Lags in Monetary Policy." In Commission on Money and Credit, *Stabilization Policies,* 14–96.

Kendrick, John W. 1961. *Productivity Trends in the United States.* Princeton: Princeton University Press.

Kindleberger, Charles P. 1986. *The World in Depression, 1929–1939.* Berkeley: University of California Press. Revised edition.

King, Robert G. and Charles I. Plosser. 1984. "Money, Credit, and Prices in a Real Business Cycle." *American Economic Review* 74:363–80.

Maddison, Angus. 1982. *Phases of Capitalist Development.* Oxford: Oxford University Press.

Nelson, Charles R., and Charles I. Plosser. 1982. "Trends and Random Walks in Macroeconomic Time Series." *Journal of Monetary Economics* 10:139–62.

Poterba, James M., Julio J. Rotemberg, and Lawrence H. Summers. 1986. "A Tax-Based Test for Nominal Rigidities." *American Economic Review* 76:659–75.

Romer, Christina D. 1988a. "World War I and the Postwar Depression: A Reinterpretation Based on Alternative Estimates of GNP." *Journal of Monetary Economics* 22:91–115.

Romer, Christina D. 1988b. "The Great Crash and the Onset of the Great Depression." NBER Working Paper No. 2639.

Schwartz, Anna J. 1981. "Understanding 1929–1933." In *The Great Depression Revisited*, Karl Brunner, ed. 5–48. Hingham, Mass.: Martinus Nijhoff Publishing.

Summers, Lawrence. 1987. "What is Memorable in Empirical Macroeconomics?" Harvard University, Unpublished manuscript.

Temin, Peter. 1976. *Did Monetary Forces Cause the Great Depression?* New York: W. W. Norton & Company.

Temin, Peter. 1988. "The Cause of the Great Depression." Unpublished manuscript. Cambridge, Mass.: MIT Press, forthcoming.

Tobin, James. 1965. "The Monetary Interpretation of History: A Review Article." *American Economic Review* 55:464–85.

United States Board of Governors of the Federal Reserve System. *Annual Report.* Various years.

United States Board of Governors of the Federal Reserve System. *Federal Reserve Bulletin.* Various years.

United States Board of Governors of the Federal Reserve System. *Industrial Production.* 1986 Edition.

United States Board of Governors of the Federal Reserve System. *Minutes of Federal Open Market Committee.* Various years.

United States Bureau of Economic Analysis. 1986. *National Income and Product Accounts, 1929–82.* Washington, D.C.: U.S. Government Printing Office.

United States Bureau of Labor Statistics. 1988. *Labor Force Statistics Derived from the Current Population Survey, 1948–87.* Washington, D.C.: U.S. Government Printing Office.

United States Bureau of Labor Statistics. *Monthly Labor Review.* Various issues.

United States Bureau of the Census. 1949. *Historical Statistics of the United States, 1789–1945.* Washington, D.C.: U.S. Government Printing Office.

United States Department of the Treasury. 1980. *Annual Report of the Secretary of the Treasury, 1978–79.* Washington, D.C.: U.S. Government Printing Office.

Comment

ANNA J. SCHWARTZ

In times past, when a manuscript was submitted for publication at the NBER, the director of research would appoint a staff and a directors reading committee to vet the study. The Romers' work in essence is a staff reading committee's report even though it comes 25 years after the publication of *A Monetary History*. We had many comments from readers of the manuscript a quarter of a century ago, and the final version reflects additions and revisions we made in response. One director, who had reservations about our criticism of Federal Reserve policy during 1930–33, chose to have his "questioning comment" included in the published volume. That can't be changed now, but we are certainly ready to learn whatever useful lessons the new reading committee can teach us.

The Romers' report reexamines the selection of four episodes, all predating World War II, when in our view actions of the monetary authorities were independent of contemporary changes in output and were associated with subsequent contractions in economic activity. The Romers' verdict, however, is that the evidence for the period before World War II that monetary disturbances had real effects is not conclusive. Their reason is that "there is so much variation in monetary institutions, in the theoretical framework adhered to by central bankers, and in the particulars of important monetary episodes in the interwar period."

For the Romers, the postwar era is a better laboratory for testing the real effects of monetary disturbances. They find "important similarities across major monetary episodes" because "the Federal Reserve in the postwar era has had a reasonably stable view of the functioning of the economy and the role of monetary policy." At a later point I shall question the relevance of the distinction the Romers draw between the supposed constancy of the institutional framework since World War II and the supposed prior instability.

I propose to discuss first the Romers' identification of postwar monetary shocks and then to respond to their challenge to the independence of the monetary shocks we identified in *A Monetary History*. Before doing so, let me record my agreement with them that evidence for a period other than the one we relied on is important. Likewise, evidence from a country other than the United States would be important.

The money-output link that is the focus of the Romers' inquiry is limited to the real effects of contractionary monetary policy. It is not clear, however, why they should not have included shocks when the Fed deliberately adopted expansionary monetary policy in order to increase the growth of output. That money-output link would have increased the sample of shocks they test. They defend their decision to focus only on negative shocks by reason of the difficulty "to distinguish any real effects of expansionary shifts from whatever natural recovery mechanism the economy may have." But as they themselves comment, "the economy may naturally tend to cycle up and down," in which case, why should it be easier to distinguish any real effects of contractionary shifts from whatever natural slump mechanism is inherent in the economy?

To identify monetary shocks in the postwar period, the Romers rely on statements in the "Record of Policy Actions" of the Board of Governors and the Federal Open Market Committee and, until their discontinuance in 1976, the minutes of FOMC meetings, that indicated a degree of concern about inflation sufficient to move the authorities to "attempt to induce a recession (or at least a 'growth recession')." The Romers designate six such episodes between October 1947 and October 1979 as independent monetary disturbances. They exclude the credit crunch of 1966 because their reading of the record is that the Fed was not actively attempting to induce a downturn. Why could the Fed not have produced a downturn even if it was not actively attempting to induce one? Why was the mini-recession of 1966–67 not the work of Fed policy, even if not intended?

The Romers' procedure prompts two questions. Why examine what the Fed said rather than the monetary actions they took? Economists are wary of accepting statements of what agents say they do or will do; revealed preferences are usually regarded as more reliable. The best indicator of the Federal Reserve's actions is the growth of high-powered money. Why in the postwar period should the Romers have eschewed that indicator of independent monetary disturbances? According to them, what they call the "narrative approach" that we used in *A Monetary History* is also their approach. But note that we highlighted *actions* of the monetary authorities that in our view were independent of contemporary changes in output, not statements of intentions or beliefs.

The Romers justify ignoring movements of the monetary base on the ground that "in many of the episodes it [the Federal Reserve] was relatively unconcerned with the monetary base." Whether or not the Fed was concerned, if there were actions to back up its intentions to accept output losses, as the Romers contend, is it conceivable that the monetary base would remain unaffected?

The Romers could have applied one of their statistical tests to judge whether the shocks they selected in fact were matched by a downturn in high-powered money growth: first, a simple univariate forecast equation of high-powered money growth with 24 own lags and a set of seasonal dummy variables, and then a dynamic forecast of high-powered money change for the 36 months following the six shocks. The differences between these forecasts and the actual behavior of high-powered money change would confirm or reject the episodes they chose. They could also have checked their decisions not to classify 1966 and 1975–78 as independent monetary disturbances.

A second question is why, granted that the Fed would like to curb inflation, one should believe that the actions they take are adequate and well-timed? The Romers' discussion of their choice of August 1978 as one of the cases of independent monetary disturbances exposes the reason for doubting the validity of their procedure. They report increases in discount rates from August to November 1978 and from July to September 1979, and increases in reserve requirements and in the Federal funds rate. Their summary is: "During this period almost all questions about the conduct of monetary policy were resolved on the side of tightness." On the contrary, every one of those actions can be regarded as consistent with an easy money policy, since each action was milder than was required to offset other factors making for a higher level of market rates.

The Romers offer two kinds of evidence to support their conclusion that recessions in fact followed the six identified cases of a Fed-engineered monetary disturbance. They deem one kind of evidence to be "informal," the other statistical. To my mind, however, both kinds of evidence the Romers offer is quantitative. The only informal matter in the paper is the narrative evidence for selecting monetary shocks.

The so-called informal evidence is that the downturn in economic activity following each of the six cases cannot be predicted from the past behavior of forecasting equations estimated over the entire postwar period for industrial production and unemployment. As I have already indicated, the forecasting equations include a set of seasonal dummy variables and 24 own lags that are intended to capture the "normal dynamics" of the series. They then construct what they call a "dynamic" forecast of both the percentage change in industrial production and the level of the unemployment rate for the 36 months following each shock. The differences between these forecasts and actual behavior are plotted over the three-year horizon. Except for the industrial production plot following the October 1947 shock, which begins in February 1948, the rest of the plots begin in the month following the shock.

The Romers conclude that on each of the six occasions in the postwar years that the Federal Reserve attempted to cause a recession to lower inflation, it succeeded. The "recessions" that are depicted in the plots, however, are not the recessions that the NBER business cycle chronology defines. Consider the first two shocks the Romers identify: October 1947 and September 1955. The corresponding business cycle peak and trough dates are November 1948–October 1949 and August 1957–April 1958. In the first of these contractions, industrial production reached a peak in July 1948 and a trough in October 1949; in the second, the industrial production peak was in March 1957, the trough in April 1958.

According to the plots, however, the first negative discrepancy between the forecast and actual industrial production, following the October 1947 shock, occurred in January 1949, and the largest negative discrepancy in June 1949. The actual value does not match the forecast until June 1950, although by April 1950, the index exceeded its peak value in July 1948. Similarly, following the September 1955 shock, the first negative discrepancy between the forecast and actual industrial production does not occur until October 1957, and the largest, until April 1958. The actual value never matches the forecast over the horizon of the plot.

One question therefore is, what is the relationship between the recessions the Romers see in their plots and the recessions of common experience? The most troublesome aspect of this part of their work arises in connection with the last two of their shocks, August 1978 and October 1979. The corresponding business cycle peak and trough dates are January 1980–July 1980 and July 1981–November 1982. The index of industrial production reached a peak in March 1979 and a trough in July 1980, and the following peak in July 1981 and trough in November 1982. The plots following the two shocks, however, both begin to record negative discrepancies between the forecast and actual values in April 1980. Are both shocks operating at this date? The consumer credit restraints that the Fed announced in March 1980 is a shock that this work ignores.

The Romers interpret their misnamed informal evidence as indicating that nominal disturbances have highly persistent effects on output. Is such an interpretation consistent with the postwar record of business cycle contractions with an average duration of eleven months? The Romers' response (in a private communication) is that, according to their Figure 1, "the economy often does not return quickly to the path that it appeared to be on prior to the recession"; hence their finding that "the real effects of monetary shocks are highly persistent." Relating the trend rate of growth of the unemployment rate shown in the figure to monetary shocks strikes me as myopic, given conditions in labor markets that are independent of monetary shocks.

The second kind of evidence that the Romers offer to support their conclusion that output declined and unemployment rose following each of their monetary shocks is based on the following test. To the simple univariate forecasting equations for industrial production and unemployment, they add current and 36 lagged values of a dummy variable that is equal to one in each of the six months of a monetary disturbance and zero in all other months. They judge the response of both industrial production and unemployment to the dummy variable by summing the coefficients for various lags. They report that over all 36 lags, the sum is negative for industrial production and positive for unemployment, large, and statistically significant, with the main impact of the dummy at between 12 and 24 lags for industrial production (somewhat later for unemployment). They measure the impulse response function of the estimated equations as the combined effect of a unit shock to the dummy variable and the feedback effect through lagged output and lagged unemployment. They conclude that monetary shocks not only have large real effects, confirming the results of their informal test, but, in addition, the effects are long lasting. My question again is, should not the postwar period have been characterized by long, deep recessions, instead of mild, brief ones, given the number of monetary shocks the Romers have identified? How does one reconcile the statistical results with the facts of cyclical experience?

Nevertheless, even if I do not agree with their procedure for choosing specific dates for anti-inflationary shifts in Fed policy, the exercise in itself is intelligent, and the evidence the Romers have devised is highly imaginative. In particular, they rule out supply shocks, inflation itself, and fiscal policy as driving their results. With respect to fiscal policy, the Romers test whether fiscal policy might have changed to match the timing of monetary policy by adding to their regressions the current and first 12 lags of the quarterly change in the ratio of the nominal government budget surplus to nominal GNP. They find that "the response of the real economy to monetary shocks can not be ascribed to possible correlations of monetary disturbances with government spending." Should this result be seen as a confirmation of the St. Louis equation?

Let me now turn to the challenge the Romers pose to the selection of independent monetary shocks that we cited in *A Monetary History*. At the time *A Monetary History* was published the money-output link was hardly a mainstream doctrine. In a paradox that Axel Leijonhufvud has commented on, those who initially dismissed the notion of a link between monetary change and output change are now its fervent supporters, while many of those who initially upheld the validity of a link now insist on the neutrality of money. The former are keen to offset putative contractionary fiscal policies by expansionary monetary policies; the latter would ignore monetary change altogether.

The possibility of bias in our selection of monetary shocks arises, according to the Romers, because we omitted independent negative monetary disturbances that would have been included had they been followed by significant declines in money and output, such as the banking failures at the end of 1932 and early 1933, and the increase in reserve requirements in 1941, as well as the open market purchases following the stock market crash, which we ordinarily would have associated with positive output effects, but which did not occur.

As for the episodes we selected, only two qualify in the Romers' view as "a monetary disturbance at all"—the discount rate hikes by the Fed in 1920 and 1931 following Britain's departure from gold. The third episode we selected—the 1936–37 increases in reserve requirements—they find ambiguous. The evidence from the early stages of the Great Depression is again not clear cut in their view. Moreover, in all the episodes we selected, they characterize non-monetary forces "to have been strongly contractionary." Hence the Romers' conclusion that the pre-World War II evidence linking money to output at best is weak.

I could dispute each of the allegations by the Romers. For example, they assert that it was only in December 1937, seventeen months after the first increase in reserve requirements was announced, that there was a discernible change in the behavior of reserves as a fraction of deposits. In my reading of the numbers, from a low point in June 1936, two months before the imposition of the first increase in reserve require-ments, the fractions rose thereafter until mid-1940. But I see no point in challenging each of the Romers' doubts about our selection of crucial experiments.

The reason is that when they regress the monthly change in industrial production on 24 own lags, a set of monthly dummy variables, and current and 36 lagged values of a dummy variable showing monetary shocks, whether the shocks are the altered set they prefer or our original set, the results confirm a depressing effect of money on output. They conclude that we may have been biased in our classification of shocks, but bias does not account for the outcome that money matters.

Finally, I am not convinced that the Romers' belief in the institutional stability of the Fed post-World War II and variability earlier is justified. The big changes earlier were the establishment of the Fed itself and the considerable attentuation of gold standard constraints thereafter. In the post-World War II period, the Fed has operated with a succession of techniques and policies: bills only, twisting the yield curve, manipulat-ing the Phillips curve, responding to balance of payments movements, administering credit controls, responding to exchange rate movements, etc. Institutional change during the period *A Monetary History* covers was something we took for granted. What we found invariant was the relationship between money and output. Results are more robust the wider, not the narrower, the range of institutional circumstances on which they are based, contrary to the Romers' view.

Let me conclude by saying that despite my reservations the Romers' report is well worth studying.

Comment

BENJAMIN M. FRIEDMAN
Harvard University

Christina Romer and David Romer's historical investigation of the effect of monetary policy on real economic activity is, in some ways, very much in the spirit of Friedman and Schwartz's classic monetary history. In other ways, both the methodology and the findings of the Romer and Romer paper run counter to the central thrust of Friedman and Schwartz's work.

Methodology: Narrative History and Statistical Apparatus

Romer and Romer address not only a familiar question of economic behavior—do central bank actions affect real output?—but also an important issue of research methodology: How should economists go about answering this question? In particular, is the narrative historical method useful for this line of inquiry? Is it perhaps *superior* to the standard approach based on statistical testing of time series data, which in recent decades has come to dominate research in this area? Indeed, in light of the economics profession's failure to resolve questions about whether and how monetary policy affects real output, despite several decades of ever more sophisticated and more intensive manipulation of the standard macroeconomic time series, is research grounded in historical narrative the *only* methodology likely to provide persuasive answers? Romer and Romer, without explicitly stating that no other methodology can provide convincing answers, argue that the evidence they present stands in sharp contrast to the notoriously flimsy product delivered by statistical exercises relying on time series data alone.

Wholly apart from the merits of Romer and Romer's claim in the context of monetary policy and real output, the renewed interest in historical narrative—motivated in large part by dissatisfaction with the cumulative results of the more statistically oriented research methods that have mostly displaced it from the toolkit of modern scholarship—is not unique to economists. In his 1981 presidential address to the American Historical Association, for example, Bernard Bailyn described the loss due to the passing of the narrative method from vogue in this way: "Narratives that once gave meaning to the details have been undermined and discredited with the advance of technical scholarship, and no new narrative structures have been constructed to replace the old. Few historians even attempt now to incorporate the mass of technical findings and the analytical studies that dominate modern research into historical narratives. . . . Yet the . . . relevance and significance of the technical writings can only be found within and as part of such comprehensive, developmental accounts."[1] Clearly economists are not alone, either in feeling a sense of frustration in the failure of modern statistical technology to provide persuasive answers to long-standing questions, or in the hope that a revival of narrative historical methods may be helpful in this regard. Romer and Romer's reliance on historical narrative constitutes a major similarity between their work and Friedman and Schwartz's.

Nevertheless, it is startling to read Romer and Romer's assertion—in the very first paragraph of their paper—that "This approach was pioneered by Friedman and Schwartz in their *Monetary History of the United States . . .* " The tradition of using historical narratives to draw inferences about how monetary disturbances affect the economy goes back at least as far as the "Digression Concerning the Variations in the Value of Silver During the Course of the Last Four Centuries," which took up a sizable chunk of Adam Smith's *Wealth of Nations* (1776). Early works along these same lines that are more familiar on today's student reading lists include Henry Thornton's *Enquiry into the Nature and Effect of the Paper Credit of Great Britain Together with the Evidence* (1802) and Thomas Tooke's *History of Prices and of the State of Circulation* (1838). Notable British works within the twentieth century but certainly prior to Friedman and Schwartz's contribution include Keynes' *Indian Currency and Finance* (1913), the section on "Historical Illustrations" in Keynes's *Treatise on Money* (1930), Sayers's *Bank of England Operations* (1936), Clapham's classic history of the Bank of England (1945) and Clay's biography of Montagu Norman (1957). American works in this vein that also preceded Friedman and Schwartz include Sprague's *History of Crises Under the National Banking Systems* (1910), Hamilton's *American Treasure and the Price Revolution in Spain* (1934), Schumpeter's *Business Cycles* (1939)—which bore the subtitle "A Theoretical, *Historical* and Statistical Analysis" (emphasis added)—and Chandler's biography of Benjamin Strong (1958).

The methodological innovation introduced by Friedman and Schwartz's *Monetary History* was not its use of historical narrative, which these and other authors had been applying to the analysis of monetary disturbances for nearly 200 years, but its use of that method in conjunction with a formal statistical apparatus—in particular, the NBER reference cycle concept, as initially developed by Wesley Mitchell and subsequently refined by Burns, Moore, Zarnowitz, and others.

1. Bailyn, Bernard. "The Challenge of Modern Historiography." *American Historical Review.* 87. February, 1982. 1–24.

Here too, Romer and Romer's work is similar to that of Friedman and Schwartz, in that the Romer and Romer paper likewise bases its inferences not just on historical narrative but on the narrative used in conjunction with a specific statistical apparatus.

The central intellectual organizing principle of Romer and Romer's paper (although they never acknowledge it as such) is the vector autoregression. The purpose to which they apply their historical narrative is, in their words, "the identification of 'monetary shocks' "—that is, "to identify episodes when there were large shifts in monetary policy or in the behavior of the banking system that were not driven by developments on the real side of the economy." And what do Romer and Romer do with their list of monetary shocks, once they have identified it? "The test of whether monetary disturbances matter is then simply to see whether output is unusually low following negative shocks of this type and unusually high following positive shocks."

If all this sounds like what a vector autoregression is supposed to do, that is because it *is* what a vector autoregression is supposed to do. Indeed, both the graphical evidence and the statistical tests presented by Romer and Romer address precisely the same question that Sims first addressed using a bivariate vector autoregression: In Romer and Romer's words, "If actual activity is less than one would expect on the basis of the univariate forecast following monetary shocks, this would suggest that the change in Federal Reserve policy *caused* real activity to be lower than it otherwise would have been" (emphasis added). Even the regression underlying the formal statistical tests, as specified in equation (1), has the typical form of one element of a vector autoregression—and for just the same reason. The role of the 24 lagged values of the dependent variable is, as usual, to enable the regression to determine whether the independent variable has explanatory power beyond that contained in the prior history of the dependent variable itself. Apart from the somewhat unusual lag structure, the only difference between the Romer-Romer regression and standard bivariate vector autoregressions linking output and money, or unemployment and money, is the use here of the time series that Romer and Romer constructed from their historical narrative, in place of some measure of the quantity of money or its growth rate.

Behavior: Monetary Policy, Monetary Disturbances, and Money

The substitution of a dummy variable, constructed out of historical narrative, for any of the conventional monetary time series is not only central to Romer and Romer's methodological approach; it is fundamental to their substantive findings about economic behavior. And in this important respect, the conclusion offered by Romer and Romer differs sharply from that of Friedman and Schwartz.

Romer and Romer motivate their use of historical narrative, and the constructed time series stemming from it, primarily as a matter of methodology: Vector autoregressions have been unsuccessful in determining whether or not money affects output. A major part of the reason is the old question of "what is driving what" when two economic variables move in conjunction, even when a time lag appears to separate these co-movements.[2] Non-quantitative evidence, like minutes of Federal Open Market Committee discussions, can help resolve this question. And so on.

But surely a further motivation for Romer and Romer's crucial reliance on their constructed dummy variable in place of some standard monetary time series is that—Friedman and Schwartz to the contrary—no single measure of money appears capable of representing the aspects of monetary policy actions that matter for purposes of this inquiry.

No reader of Friedman and Schwartz's book could fail to understand two basic conclusions of their work. First, monetary policy actions taken by the central bank systematically affect real economic activity and prices. And second, money provides a sufficient statistic for the monetary policy actions that the central bank takes, in that fluctuations in the quantity of money (or its growth rate) tell most if not all of what can be told about the effects on output and prices that those monetary policy actions have.

No reader of Romer and Romer's paper could fail to grasp their conclusion that monetary policy actions taken by the central bank systematically affect real output.[3] But an unsuspecting reader might well fail to register the significance of the paper's omission—indeed, the authors' outright eschewal—of any effort to show that the quantity of money or its growth rate captures the aspects of monetary policy that matter in this regard. In fact, Romer and Romer's historical narrative not only does not emphasize measures of money in identifying the episodes that qualify as "monetary shocks" but, in the case of some episodes, fails to mention money at all.[4]

2. An early exposition of these difficulties which is still valuable is James Tobin, "Money and Income: Post Hoc Ergo Propter Hoc." *Quarterly Journal of Economics.* 84. May, 1970. 301–17.
3. Effects on prices are not part of their investigation.
4. Two elements of Romer and Romer's choice of episodes for the postwar period require, at the least, more justification than they provide here. The first is the exclusion of 1966 as a "monetary shock." It is highly likely that President Johnson's harsh reaction to the December 1965 discount rate increase resulted in Federal Reserve System documents that understated the degree to which monetary policy was actively moving to combat price inflation in 1966. The second is the astonishing exclusion of 1981–82.

Unfortunately, Romer and Romer's choice of language—in particular, their repeated use of the ambiguous label "monetary disturbances," or "monetary shocks," to refer to the episodes of central bank action that they single out from their historical narrative—blurs this distinction and therefore increases the likelihood that readers may miss the important contrast between their findings and Friedman and Schwartz's. After all, in much of the literature investigation whether monetary policy affects output, "monetary disturbances" are conventionally measured by some monetary quantity. Here that is simply not the case. As a result, when Romer and Romer report, for example, that "extremely narrowly defined monetary disturbances account for a considerable fraction of fluctuations in postwar economic activity," the reader must be alert to the absence of any demonstrated connection between these "extremely narrowly defined monetary disturbances" and fluctuations in the stock of money or its growth rate.[5]

Further, Romer and Romer's use of the historical narrative to construct their time series to represent the independent movements of monetary policy runs strongly counter to the thrust of Friedman and Schwartz's contribution in yet another way. While there is nothing in Friedman and Schwarz's work to suggest that fluctuations in money growth have asymmetrical effects depending on whether they are positive or negative, Romer and Romer identify only *negative* shocks. The time series that they use in their formal statistical tests correspondingly assumes values limited to zero and *minus* one. It is always possible, of course, to rationalize this representation by arguing that the central bank could have chosen to conduct monetary policy in a way that would have amounted to a positive shock, but—even over a period spanning more than six decades—simply never did so. The net result of this choice, however, is that Romer and Romer's representation of monetary policy has the pre-Friedman-Schwartz character of a string on which the central bank can pull but not push.

Similarity and Contrast

In the end, therefore, whether the Romer and Romer paper reinforces or undercuts the Friedman-Schwartz book is mostly a matter of what is at issue. On the methodological question of what set of tools can best support investigation of the links between monetary policy and economic activity, both works not only begin from a strong presumption

5. Indeed, it is somewhat surprising that Romer and Romer never report even the simple correlation between their time series representing "monetary disturbances" and any familiar measure of money or the monetary base.

favoring the use of narrative history in conjunction with statistical analysis but also go on to demonstrate the validity of that presumption. And on the behavioral question of whether monetary policy systematically affects real output, both works answer a decisive "yes."

But on the question that bears most directly on practical issues of monetary policy—specifically, whether fluctuations in the quantity of money or its growth rate can serve as a reliable center focus of monetary policy making—Romer and Romer not only offer no support for Friedman and Schwartz's "yes" but, indeed, adopt a methodology implicitly motivated by the presumption that the answer is really "no."

Discussion

David Romer responded to Schwartz's discussion by emphasizing that they were interested in the intent of the Fed more than its actual policy outcomes. He noted as well that the recessions identified in the paper correspond well to the NBER dating. Finally, he asserted that the stability of monetary regimes in the postwar period made it a more natural time to test for the effects of monetary policy.

Bennett McCallum questioned whether the shocks identified in the paper were truly exogenous, since they were all intended to reduce inflation. Christina Romer responded that the shocks were exogenous to the state of the real economy, and that one identifying assumption made in the paper is that steady-state changes in the level of inflation have no real effects.

Laurence Ball asked why monetary policy shocks had such long effects on output and unemployment. David Romer indicated that they did not examine the propagation mechanism in this paper, but merely documented the evidence.

Robert Gordon wondered whether the monetary policy shocks just ratified recessions that would already occur. He speculated that the high interest rates associated with high inflation might have caused the recession, independent of the Federal Reserves actions. Robert Hall questioned several aspects of the results. First, he noted that the t-statistic on the difference between output eighteen months after a monetary policy shock and output unconditional on the shocks was only about -2. Second, since the authors knew the path of output and unemployment in the post-war period, it was unlikely that the identification of shocks was truly unbiased. Third, the Federal Reserve is also a regulatory and fiscal policy body, in addition to a monetary authority. Thus, it is difficult to determine what aspect of Federal Reserve behavior affects output. David Romer responded that the common policy response across all the shocks was open market operations, indicating that it may be the money supply that affects output.

Michael Bordo noted that Friedman and Schwartz identified money as an exacerbating factor in business cycle fluctuations, not an exogenous event. He also wondered how the proposed shock in 1933 could be differentiated from the banking holiday and the other policies of the Roosevelt Administration. Christina Romer indicated that measures of fiscal policy could be included in the regressions to control for these aspects.

Olivier Blanchard suggested that the authors use their series of monetary policy surprises as an instrument to determine whether money supply changes lead to changes in output. Christopher Sims agreed with this suggestion. Sims also indicated that he found the identifying assumption that trend inflation has no real effects unconvincing, given the strong predictive power of short term interest rates for output. Christina Romer indicated that they would use the series on monetary shocks as an instrument in future research.

John Y. Campbell and N. Gregory Mankiw
PRINCETON UNIVERSITY AND NBER/HARVARD UNIVERSITY AND NBER

Consumption, Income, and Interest Rates: Reinterpreting the Time Series Evidence

Introduction

The study of aggregate consumption behavior was profoundly altered by the rational expectations revolution in macroeconomics. The first example in Robert Lucas's (1976) influential critique of econometric policy evaluation involved consumption. Lucas argued that traditional consumption functions, no matter how well they fit the data, were not useful for evaluating the effects of alternative policies. Soon thereafter, Robert Hall (1978) proposed a new approach to studying consumption that was firmly founded on the postulate of rational expectations and that was immune to the problems Lucas pointed out. Hall suggested that aggregate consumption should be modeled as obeying the first-order conditions for optimal choice of a single, fully rational, and forward-looking representative consumer. The new style of research based on this assumption—sometimes called the "Euler equation approach"—has dominated work on consumption during the past decade.

In this paper we appraise what has been learned about aggregate consumption from this approach. We propose a simple, alternative characterization of the time series data on consumption, income, and interest rates. We suggest that the data are best viewed as generated not by a single forward-looking consumer but by two types of consumers. Half the consumers are forward-looking and consume their permanent income, but are extremely reluctant to substitute consumption intertemporally in response to interest rate movements. Half the consumers follow the "rule of thumb" of consuming their current income. We document three empirical regularities that, we argue, are best explained by this model.

The first regularity is that expected changes in income are associated with expected changes in consumption. In contrast to the simplest version of the permanent income hypothesis, consumption is not a random walk: when income is expected to rise by 1 percent, consumption should be expected to rise by 0.5 percent. The strong connection between current income and consumption provides at least circumstantial evidence for "rule-of-thumb" behavior on the part of some consumers.

The second empirical regularity is that expected real interest rates are not associated with expected changes in consumption. This means that the predictable movements that we observe in consumption cannot be explained as a rational response to movements in real interest rates. It also means that forward-looking consumers do not adjust their consumption growth in response to interest rates, so their intertemporal elasticity of substitution in consumption must be close to zero. Hall (1988) also argues that the elasticity of substitution of permanent income consumers is small; but since he does not allow for current income consumers, he cannot explain the existence of any predictable movements in aggregate consumption.

The third empirical regularity is that periods in which consumption is high relative to income are typically followed by rapid growth in income. This finding suggests that at least some consumers are forward-looking: their knowledge of future income growth is reflected in current consumption. Yet we show that the magnitude of the association between consumption and future income growth is best explained by a model with both permanent income consumers and current income consumers.

Most of this paper is devoted to analyzing the data and documenting its consistency with the simple model we propose. In the final section, we briefly discuss the broader implications for economic policy and economic research.

1. Is Consumption a Random Walk?

In this section we reexamine the evidence on the simplest version of the permanent income hypothesis, according to which consumption should follow a random walk. We begin by reviewing the basic model and discuss how it can be tested. Our approach differs from the standard one in two ways. First, we emphasize a specific alternative hypothesis under which some consumers follow the "rule of thumb" of consuming their current income rather than their permanent income. Second, we argue that more structural estimation using instrumental variables should be preferred over the standard tests for a random walk using the reduced form of the model. When we look at the data, we find that a substantial fraction of income accrues to rule-of-thumb consumers, indicating an economically important deviation from the permanent income hypothesis.[1]

1.1. THE PERMANENT INCOME HYPOETHESIS AND A RULE-OF-THUMB ALTERNATIVE

The permanent income hypothesis as usually formulated assumes that aggregate consumption can be modeled as the decisions of a representative consumer. The representative consumer maximizes

$$E_t \sum_{s=0}^{\infty} (1+\delta)^{-s} U(C_{t+s}) \qquad U' > 0, \qquad U'' < 0 \quad (1.1)$$

where C is consumption, δ is the subjective rate of discount, and E_t is the expectation conditional on information available at time t. If the representative consumer can borrow and lend at the real interest rate r, then the first-order condition necessary for an optimum is

$$E_t U'(C_{t+1}) = \left(\frac{1+\delta}{1+r}\right) U'(C_t). \quad (1.2)$$

This says that marginal utility today is, up to a constant multiple, the best forecast of marginal utility tomorrow.

If we assume that $r = \delta$ and that marginal utility is linear, then we obtain the random walk result,[1] $E_t C_{t+1} = C_t$. Consumption today is the optimal forecast of consumption tomorrow. This in turn implies

$$\Delta C_t = \epsilon_t \quad (1.3)$$

where ϵ_t is a rational forecast error, the innovation in permanent income. Thus, according to this formulation of the permanent income hypothesis, the change in consumption is unforecastable.

In evaluating how well this model fits the data, it is useful to keep in mind an explicit alternative hypothesis. We nest the permanent income hypothesis in a more general model in which some fraction of income λ

---

1. Obviously, these assumptions can be justified only as an approximation. One can obtain the random walk result with other sorts of approximations as well, e.g., the Taylor approximation in Mankiw (1981) or the log-normality assumption in Hansen and Singleton (1983). These other approximations may imply that the log of consumption, rather than the level, is a random walk—a more appealing specification. They also often introduce other terms, such as the difference between δ and r and the variance of consumption growth; these other terms are usually included as part of the constant drift in consumption.

accrues to individuals to consume their current income, while the remainder $(1-\lambda)$ accrues to individuals who consume their permanent income. If the incomes of the two groups are Y_{1t} and Y_{2t} respectively, then total income is $Y_t = Y_{1t} + Y_{2t}$. Since the first group receives λ of total income, $Y_{1t} = \lambda Y_t$ and $Y_{2t} = (1-\lambda)Y_t$. Agents in the first group consume their current income, so $C_{1t} = Y_{1t}$, implying $\Delta C_{1t} = \Delta Y_{1t} = \lambda \Delta Y_t$. By contrast, agents in the second group obey the permanent income hypothesis, implying $\Delta C_{2t} = (1 - \lambda)\epsilon_t$.

The change in aggregate consumption can now be written as

$$\Delta C_t = \Delta C_{1t} + \Delta C_{2t} = \lambda \Delta Y_t + (1 - \lambda)\epsilon_t. \quad (1.4)$$

Under this alternative hypothesis, the change in consumption is a weighted average of the change in current income and the unforecastable innovation in permanent income. Equation (1.4) reduces to the permanent income hypothesis, equation (1.3), when $\lambda = 0$.[2]

Having set up the permanent income hypothesis as the null hypothesis and the existence of these rule-of-thumb consumers as the alternative hypothesis, there are two approaches to estimation and testing. The approach we advocate is to estimate λ directly and test the hypothesis that $\lambda = 0$. It is important to note, however, that (1.4) cannot be estimated by Ordinary Least Squares, since the error term ϵ_t may be correlated with ΔY_t. The solution is to estimate (1.4) by instrumental variables. Any lagged stationary variables are potentially valid instruments since they are orthogonal to ϵ_t. Of course, good instruments must also be correlated with ΔY_t—therefore, one should choose lagged variables that can predict future income growth. Once such instruments are found, one can easily estimate the fraction of income accruing to the rule-of-thumb consumers.

The second approach to testing the permanent income hypothesis—used by Hall (1978) and in most of the subsequent literature—is to regress the change on consumption on lagged variables to see whether the change in consumption is forecastable. To see the relation between the two approaches, note that equation (1.4), estimated by instrumental variables, can be viewed as a restricted version of a more general two-equation system in which ΔC_t and ΔY_t are regressed directly on the

2. This alternative model with some rule-of-thumb consumers is discussed briefly in Hall (1978). It is also a simpler version of the model proposed in Flavin (1981), in which the change in consumption responds not only to the contemporaneous change in current income, but also to lagged changes in current income. Flavin designs her model so that it is just-identified; by contrast, we view the over-identification of our model as one of its virtues. See also Bean (1986).

instruments. If we have K instruments, X_{1t} through X_{Kt}, then the general system is

$$\Delta C_t = \beta_0 + \beta_1 X_{1t} + \ldots + \beta_K X_{Kt} + \eta_{Ct} = X_t \beta + \eta_{Ct}$$

$$\Delta Y_t = \gamma_0 = \gamma_1 X_{1t} + \ldots + \gamma_K X_{Kt} + \eta_{Yt} = X_t \gamma + \eta_{Yt}. \quad (1.5)$$

The permanent income hypothesis implies that the vector $\beta = 0$ (that is, $\beta_1 = \ldots = \beta_K = 0$). This implication can be tested directly, without any need for considering the ΔY_t equation, by OLS estimation of the ΔC_t equation. When there is more than a single instrument, however, equation (1.4) places over-identifying restrictions on the two equation system (1.5): predictable changes in consumption and income, and therefore the vectors β and γ, are proportional to one another ($\beta = \lambda \gamma$, or $\beta_1 / \gamma_1 = \ldots = \beta_K / \gamma_K = \lambda$). The instrumental variables test that $\lambda = 0$ is in essence a test that $\beta = 0$ under the maintained hypothesis that these over-identifying restrictions are true.

Although estimating the reduced form equation for ΔC_t is more standard, there are compelling reasons to prefer the instrumental variables approach. One reason is power. Since there are many possible instruments, the instrumental variables procedure estimates far fewer parameters than are in the reduced form, thereby conserving on the degrees of freedom and providing a more powerful test of the null hypothesis.

Perhaps more important, estimation of λ provides a useful metric for judging whether an observed deviation from the null hypothesis is economically important. As Franklin Fisher (1961) emphasized long ago, an economic model can be approximately true even if the strict tests of over-identification fail. It is therefore hard to interpret a rejection of the permanent income hypothesis in the reduced form framework. Indeed, Hall (1978) concluded that the evidence favors the permanent income hypothesis even though he reported formal rejections using stock prices. An estimate of λ is more informative about the economic importance of deviations from the theory.[3] For example, if the estimate of λ is close to zero, then one can say the permanent income is approximately true—most income goes to consumers who obey the theory—even if the estimate of λ is statistically significant. Conversely, if the estimate of λ is large, then one must conclude that the evidence points away from the permanent income hypothesis.

One question that arises in interpreting a failure of the permanent

---

3. Flavin (1981) also stresses this point.

income hypothesis is whether our rule-of-thumb alternative adequately captures the reason for the failure. The best way to answer the question is to consider explicitly other alternative hypotheses.[4] Another way— more statistical and less economic—is to test the over-identifying restrictions that equation (1.4) imposes. This test is performed simply by regressing the residual from the instrumental variables regression on the instruments, and then to compare T times the R^2 from this regression, where T is the sample size, with the χ^2 distribution with $(K - 1)$ degrees of freedom. We use this test below.

1.2. TWO SPECIFICATION ISSUES

Before we can estimate the model, we need to address two issues of specification that arise from the nature of the aggregate time series on consumption and income.

Our discussion so far has been couched in terms of levels and differences of the raw series C_t and Y_t. This is appropriate if these series follow homoskedastic linear processes in levels, with or without unit roots. Yet aggregate time series on consumption and income appear to be closer to log-linear than linear: the mean change and the innovation variance both grow with the level of the series. A correction of some sort appears necessary. The approach we take is simply to take logs of all variables. Although the paramenter λ can no longer be precisely interpreted as the fraction of agents who consume their current income, one can view the model we estimate as the log-linear approximation to the true model. Thus, the interpretation of the results is not substantially affected. We use lower-case letters to denote log variables.[5]

A second data problem is that consumption and income are measured as quarterly averages rather than at points in time. If the permanent income hypothesis holds in continuous time, then measured consumption is the time average of a random walk. Therefore, the change in consumption will have a first-order serial correlation of 0.25, which could lead us to reject the model even if it is true.[6] We deal with this problem by lagging the instruments more than one period, so there is at least a two-period time gap between the instruments and the variables in equation (1.4). The time average of a continuous-time random walk is uncorrelated with all variables lagged more than one period, so by using twice-lagged instruments we obtain a test of the model that is valid for time-averaged data.

---

4. For some examples see Campbell and Mankiw (1987).
5. An alternative scaling method is to divide ΔC_t and ΔY_t by the lagged level of income, Y_{t-1}. In practice both scaling methods give very similar results.
6. See Working (1960).

1.3. ANOTHER LOOK AT U.S. DATA

To estimate our model, we use standard U.S. quarterly time series data, obtained from the Data Resources, Inc. data bank. Y_t is measured as disposable personal income per capita, in 1982 dollars. C_t is consumption of non-durables and services per capita, in 1982 dollars. The sample period is 1953:1 to 1986:4.[7]

Table 1, which reports the results, has six columns. The first gives the row number and the second the instruments used.[8] The third and fourth columns give the adjusted R^2 statistics for OLS regressions of Δc_t and Δy_t, respectively, on the instruments. In parentheses we report the p-value for a Wald test of the hypothesis that all coefficients except the intercept are zero. The fifth column gives the instrumental variables estimate of λ, with an asymptotic standard error. The final column gives the adjusted R^2 statistic for an OLS regression of the residual from the instrumental variables regression on the instruments. In parentheses we report the p-value for the corresponding test of the over-identifying restrictions placed by equation (1.4) on the general system (1.5). For reference, the first row of Table 1 shows the coefficient obtained when we estimate equation (1.4) by OLS.

Rows 2 and 3 of the table use lagged income growth rates as instruments. These are not strongly jointly significant in predicting consumption or income growth; in row 3, for example, lags two through six of income growth are jointly significant at the 21% level for consumption growth and at the 14% level for income growth. It appears that the univariate time series process for disposable income is close enough to a random walk that income growth rates are not well forecast by lagged income growth rates. Our instrumental variables procedure estimates λ at 0.506 with an asymptotic standard error of 0.176 in row 3; this rejects the permanent income hypothesis that $\lambda = 0$ at the 0.4% level. Yet instrumental variables procedures can be statistically unreliable when the instruments have only weak forecasting power for the right hand side variable.[9] The rejection of the permanent income hypothesis in rows 2 and 3 should be interpreted cautiously.[10]

7. In Campbell and Mankiw (1987) we discuss the importance of sample period and, in particular, the peculiar behavior of the first quarter of 1950, when there was a one-time National Service Life Insurance dividend payment to World War II veterans. The sample period of Table 1 extends the data used in Campbell and Mankiw (1987) by one year.
8. A constant term is always included as both an instrument and a regressor, but is not reported in the tables.
9. See Nelson and Startz (1988) for an analysis of this issue.
10. These findings confirm the conclusions of Mankiw and Shapiro (1985): since disposable income is so close to a random walk, modelling income as a univariate process (e.g., Flavin (1981) or Bernanke (1985)) leads to tests with little power.

We obtain stronger results in row 4 and 5 of the table, where we use lagged consumption growth rates as instruments. It is striking that lagged consumption forecasts income growth more strongly than lagged income itself does, and this enables us to estimate the parameter λ more precisely. This finding suggests that at least some consumers have better information on future income growth than is summarized in its past history and that they respond to this information by increasing their consumption. At the same time, however, the fraction of rule-of-thumb consumers is estimated at 0.523 in row 5 (and the estimate is significant at better than the 0.01% level). The OLS test also rejects the permanent income model in row 5.

Table 1   UNITED STATES 1953–1986
$$\Delta c_y = \mu + \lambda \Delta y_t$$

		First-stage regressions		λ estimate (s.e.)	Test of restrictions
Row	Instruments	Δc equation	Δy equation		
1	None (OLS)	—	—	0.316 (0.040)	—
2	$\Delta y_{t-2}, \ldots, \Delta y_{t-4}$	−0.005 (0.500)	0.009 (0.239)	0.417 (0.235)	−0.022 (0.944)
3	$\Delta y_{t-2}, \ldots, \Delta y_{t-6}$	0.017 (0.209)	0.026 (0.137)	0.506 (0.176)	−0.034 (0.961)
4	$\Delta c_{t-2}, \ldots, \Delta c_{t-4}$	0.024 (0.101)	0.045 (0.028)	0.419 (0.161)	−0.009 (0.409)
5	$\Delta c_{t-2}, \ldots, \Delta c_{t-6}$	0.081 (0.007)	0.079 (0.007)	0.523 (0.131)	−0.016 (0.572)
6	$\Delta i_{t-2}, \ldots, \Delta i_{t-4}$	0.061 (0.010)	0.028 (0.082)	0.698 (0.235)	−0.016 (0.660)
7	$\Delta i_{t-2}, \ldots, \Delta i_{t-6}$	0.102 (0.002)	0.082 (0.006)	0.584 (0.137)	−0.025 (0.781)
8	$\Delta y_{t-2}, \ldots, \Delta y_{t-4},$ $\Delta c_{t-2}, \ldots, \Delta c_{t-4},$ $c_{t-2} - y_{t-2}$	0.007 (0.341)	0.068 (0.024)	0.351 (0.119)	−0.033 (0.840)
9	$\Delta y_{t-2}, \ldots, \Delta y_{t-4},$ $\Delta c_{t-2}, \ldots, \Delta c_{t-4},$ $\Delta i_{t-2}, \ldots, \Delta i_{t-4},$ $c_{t-2} - y_{t-2}$	0.078 (0.026)	0.093 (0.013)	0.469 (0.106)	−0.029 (0.705)

Note: The columns labeled "First-stage regressions" report the adjusted R^2 for the OLS regressions of the two variables on the instruments; in parentheses is the p-value for the null that all the coefficients except the constant are zero. The column labeled "λ estimate" reports the IV estimate of λ and, in parentheses, its standard error. The column labeled "Test of restrictions" reports the adjusted R^2 of the OLS regression of the residual on the instruments; in parenthesis is the p-value for the null that all the coefficients are zero.

We next consider using some financial variables as instruments. We tried using lagged changes in real stock prices (the quarterly percentage change in the real value of the Dow Jones Industrial Average), but found that this variable had no predictive power for consumption growth or income growth.[11] Results using lagged changes in quarterly average three-month nominal Treasury bill rates (i_t) were more successful, and we report these in rows 6 and 7 of Table 1. The instruments are jointly significant for consumption growth at the 1.0% and 0.2% levels. The parameter λ is estimated at 0.698 in row 6 (significant at the 0.3% level), and at 0.584 in row 7 (significant at better than the 0.01% level).[12]

The final two rows of the table report restricted error-correction models for consumption and income. Row 8 has lags of consumption growth, income growth, and the log consumption-income ratio as instruments; row 9 adds lagged interest rate changes. The results are broadly consistent with those in earlier rows.

Table 1 also tests the over-identifying restrictions of our model (1.4) on the unrestricted system (1.5). The test results are reported in the last column of the table. There is no evidence against our restrictions anywhere in this column.

Figures 1 and 2 illustrate what is going on in these instrumental variables estimates. Figure 1 is a scatterplot of ex post consumption growth against ex post income growth. The figure shows a positive relation, but not a tight one. Figure 2 is a scatterplot of expected consumption growth against expected income growth, where expectations were taken to be the fitted values from the reduced form equations estimated in row 9 of Table 1. Note that these points lie along a distinct line. In contrast to the permanent income hypothesis, expected increases in income are associated with expected increases in consumption.

The two lines shown in the figure are estimated by IV regression of Δc_t on Δy_t, as reported in Table 1, and by the reverse IV regression of Δy_t on Δc_t. It is apparent that the normalization of the IV regression makes little difference to the estimate of the slope λ; this is what we would expect to

11. This finding contrasts with the positive results for stock prices reported by Hall (1978) and others. Yet close inspection of Hall's stock price regression (his equation (8), on p. 984) suggests that almost all the explanatory power comes from the first lagged stock price change. When we include the first lag, we also find strong predictive power from stock price changes; but for the reasons discussed above, we regard this as an illegitimate test of the permanent income model.

12. The spread between the yield on a long-term government bond and that on a three-month Treasury bill also provided a useful instrument. Using only the second lag of the yield spread, we obtained adjusted R^2's of 0.094 for Δc and 0.048 for Δy, and an estimate of λ of 0.741 with a standard error of 0.235.

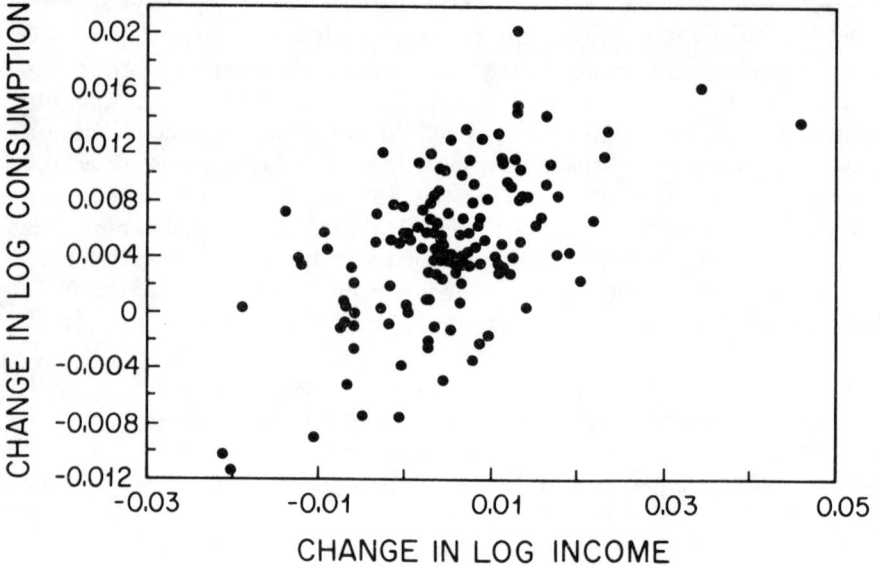

Figure 1 SCATTERPLOT OF CHANGES IN CONSUMPTION AND INCOME

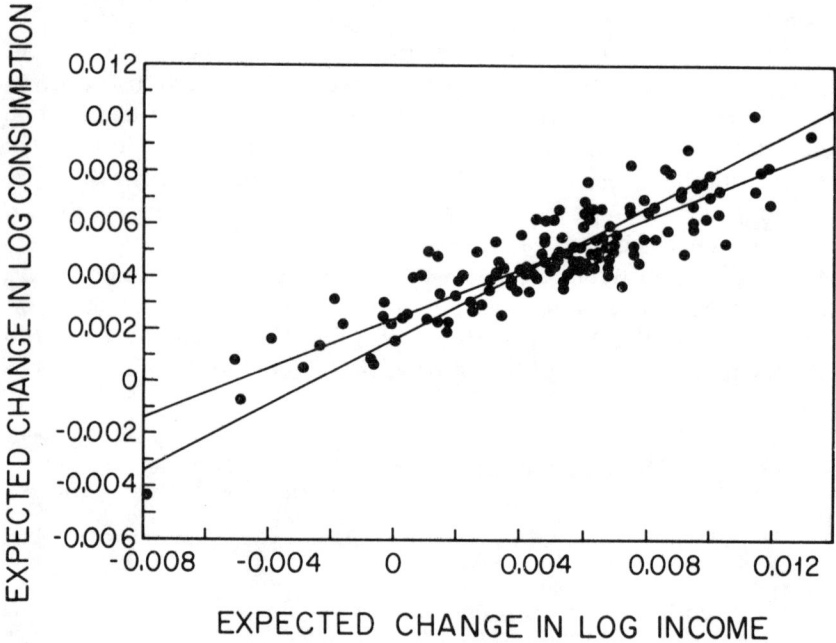

Figure 2 SCATTERPLOT OF EXPECTED CHANGES IN CONSUMPTION AND INCOME

find if our model is correctly specified and the true slope is not zero or infinite.[13]

While the results in Table 1 follow most of the literature by examining consumer spending on non-durables and services, we have also examined two measures of consumption that include consumer durable goods. The results are potentially sensitive to the treatment of durable goods, because spending on them is so volatile. We therefore estimated equation (1.4) both using total consumer spending and using the sum of spending on non-durables and services and the imputed rent on the stock of consumer durables.[14] The results obtained with these two measures turned out to be similar to those reported in Table 1.

In summary, we have found striking evidence against the permanent income hypothesis. The results from our instrumental variables test are particularly unfavorable to the permanent income model. When we use instruments that are jointly significant for predicting income growth at the 5% level or better, we get estimates of λ, the fraction of the population that consumes its current income, of about 0.5. The estimates are always strongly significant even though we have potentially lost some power by lagging the instruments two periods instead of one. The over-identifying restrictions of our model are not rejected at any reasonable significance level.

1.4. EVIDENCE FROM ABROAD

To examine the robustness of our findings for the United States, we now turn to examining data for several other countries. From various DRI data banks, we obtained data on consumption and income to estimate equation (1.4) for the G-7 countries: Canada, France, Germany, Italy, Japan, the United Kingdom, and the United States.[15]

Two data issues arise. First, we found that long time series of quarterly consumption data are often avaiable only for total spending, which includes spending on durables. Assuming exponential depreciation, however, durability should merely lead to the change in consumer spending

13. Nelson and Startz (1988) point out that there are severe problems with the IV regression approach if the instruments do not forecast the right hand side variable. In our framework, this would occur in the IV regression of consumption growth on income growth if λ is infinite, and in the IV regression of income growth on consumption growth if λ is zero.
14. To calculate the stock of durables, we began with the Commerce Department's net stock of consumer durables for 1947 and then accumulated the spending flow assuming a depreciation rate of 5 percent per quarter. To calculate the imputed rent, we assumed a user cost of 6 percent per quarter.
15. Other studies that have used international data to test the permanent income hypothesis include Kormendi and LaHaye (1987) and Jappelli and Pagano (1988).

being a first-order moving average process rather than white noise.[16] Since we are using twice-lagged instruments, the inclusion of spending on durables does not change the implication of the permanent income hypothesis that forecastable changes in income should not lead to fore-castable changes in consumption. We can therefore proceed as before.

The second data issue is that, for Canada, France, Italy, and Japan, we were unable to find a quarterly disposable personal income series and therefore used GDP as a proxy. The use of GDP to measure Y should still provide a valid test of the null hypothesis that the permanent income theory is correct. Yet real GDP is an imperfect proxy: in U.S. data, the correlation of real GDP growth and real disposable personal income growth is only 0.55. The use of this proxy can potentially reduce our test's power. It turns out, however, that loss of power appears not to be a problem.

Table 2 presents the estimates obtained for these seven countries. The results from six of these seven countries tell a simple and consistent story. For Canada, France, Germany, Italy, Japan, and the United States, the estimate of the fraction of income going to rule-of-thumb consumers is significantly different from zero and not significantly different from 0.5. Moreover, the over-identifying restrictions imposed by our model are not rejected. The only exception is the United Kingdom, where nei-ther the permanent income hypothesis nor our more general model appear to describe the data adequately. Taken as a whole, these results confirm the failure of the simple random-walk model for consumption and the apparent rule-of-thumb behavior of many consumers.

2. Consumption and the Real Interest Rate

The "random walk" theorem for consumption rests crucially on the as-sumption that the real interest rate is constant. Here we examine the Euler equation that allows for a varying and uncertain real interest rate.

There are two reasons we look at this extension of the basic model. First, a rejection of the theory might be attributable to the failure of this assumption, rather than to an important deviation from the permanent income hypothesis. In particular, variation through time in the real inter-est rate can make consumption appear excessively sensitive to income, even though individuals intertemporally optimize in the absence of bor-rowing constraints.[17] We show, however, that the departure from the

---

16. See Mankiw (1982). Matters become more complicated, however, if one allows more complicated forms of depreciation or the possibility of adjustment costs; see Heaton (1988).

17. Michener (1984) makes this argument. See also Christiano (1987).

theory documented above—the apparent existence of rule-of-thumb consumers—is not an artifact of the assumed constancy of the real interest rate.

Second, we want to check whether Hall's (1988) conclusion that the intertemporal elasticity of substitution is close to zero is robust to the presence of current-income consumers. Hall assumes that the underlying permanent income theory is correct and uses the absence of a relation between consumption growth and real interest rates as evidence for a small elasticity. In contrast, we argue that the underlying theory is not empirically valid. Unless one is willing to admit that a substantial fraction of income goes to rule-of-thumb consumers, the data cannot yield an answer on the intertemporal elasticity of substitution.

2.1. THE MODEL WITH ONLY PERMANENT INCOME CONSUMERS

We begin our examination of consumption and real interest rates by maintaining the hypothesis that the permanent income theory is correct. We will then go on to consider a more general model with some rule-of-thumb consumers.

The generalization of the consumer's Euler equation to allow for

Table 2   EVIDENCE FROM ABROAD
$$\Delta c_t = \mu + \lambda \Delta y_t$$

Country (sample period)	First-stage regressions		λ estimate (s.e.)	Test of restrictions
	Δc equation	Δy equation		
1 Canada (1963–1986)	0.047 (0.127)	0.090 (0.030)	0.616 (0.215)	0.007 (0.263)
2 France (1970–1986)	0.083 (0.091)	0.166 (0.015)	1.095 (0.341)	−0.055 (0.714)
3 Germany (1962–1986)	0.028 (0.211)	0.086 (0.031)	0.646 (0.182)	−0.030 (0.639)
4 Italy (1973–1986)	0.195 (0.013)	0.356 (0.000)	0.400 (0.094)	−0.034 (0.488)
5 Japan (1959–1986)	0.087 (0.020)	0.205 (0.000)	0.553 (0.096)	0.018 (0.178)
6 United Kingdom (1957–1986)	0.092 (0.012)	0.127 (0.002)	0.221 (0.153)	0.086 (0.010)
7 United States (1953–1986)	0.040 (0.092)	0.079 (0.014)	0.478 (0.158)	0.004 (0.269)

Note: For all countries, the consumption data are total spending. The set of instruments is: $\Delta y_{t-2}, \ldots, \Delta y_{t-4}, \ldots, \Delta c_{t-2}, \ldots, \Delta c_{t-4}. c_{t-2} - y_{t-2}$. Also see note, Table 1.

changes in the real interest rate is now well-known. The log-linear version of the Euler equation is[18]

$$\Delta c_t = \mu + \sigma r_t + \epsilon_t, \quad (2.1)$$

where r_t is the real interest rate contemporaneous with Δc_t, and as before the error term ϵ_t may be correlated with r_t but is uncorrelated with lagged variables. According to (2.1), high ex ante real interest rates should be associated with rapid growth of consumption. The coefficient on the real interest rate, σ, is the intertemporal elasticity of substitution.[19]

Equation (2.1) can be estimated using instrumental variables, just in the way we estimated equation (1.4). The nominal interest rate we use is the average three-month treasury bill rate over the quarter. The price index is the deflator for consumer non-durables and services. We assume a marginal tax rate on interest of 30%.

We obtained the results in Table 3. We find fairly small values for the coefficient on the real interest rate. Hall interprets evidence of this sort as indicating that the intertemporal elasticity of substitution is close to zero—that is, consumers are extremely reluctant to substitute intertemporally.

In our view, however, the equation estimated in Table 3 is misspecified because it does not allow for the presence of rule-of-thumb consumers. This misspecification shows up in several ways in Table 3. First, the hypothesis that consumption growth is unpredictable is rejected at the 1% level or better in five out of eight rows of Table 3, and at the 5% level or better in seven rows. This is inconsistent with Hall's interpretation of the data: if the permanent income theory were true and σ were zero, consumption should be a random walk. Second, the over-identifying restrictions of equation (2.1) are rejected at the 5% level or better whenever lagged real interest rates are included in the set of instruments. Third, the estimates of σ are highly unstable; while they are generally small, they do exceed one when nominal interest rate changes are used as instruments.

Perhaps the most telling check on the specification comes from revers-

18. See, for example, Grossman and Shiller (1981), Mankiw (1981), Hansen and Singleton (1983), and Hall (1988). Note that in the process of log-linearizing the first-order condition, the variance of consumption growth has been included in the constant term. Hence, heteroskedasticity is one possible reason for rejection of the model; see Barsky (1985) for a preliminary exploration of this issue.

19. If the representative agent has power utility, then σ is the reciprocal of the coefficient of relative risk aversion. Epstein and Zin (1987a, 1987b) and Giovannini and Weil (1989) have shown that the same Euler equation can be obtained in a more general model in which risk aversion and the intertemporal elasticity of substitution are decoupled.

Table 3   UNITED STATES, 1953–1986

$$\Delta c_t = \mu + \sigma r_t$$

Row	Instruments	First-stage regressions		σ estimate (s.e.)	Test of restrictions
		Δc equation	r equation		
1	None (OLS)	—	—	0.276 (0.079)	—
2	$r_{t-2}, \ldots, r_{t-4}$	0.063 (0.009)	0.431 (0.000)	0.270 (0.118)	0.031 (0.029)
3	$r_{t-2}, \ldots, r_{t-6}$	0.067 (0.014)	0.426 (0.000)	0.281 (0.118)	0.034 (0.050)
4	$\Delta c_{t-2}, \ldots, \Delta c_{t-4}$	0.024 (0.101)	−0.021 (0.966)	−0.707 (2.586)	0.000 (0.215)
5	$\Delta c_{t-2}, \ldots, \Delta c_{t-6}$	0.018 (0.007)	0.007 (0.316)	0.992 (0.478)	0.008 (0.189)
6	$\Delta i_{t-2}, \ldots, \Delta i_{t-4}$	0.061 (0.010)	0.024 (0.105)	1.263 (0.545)	−0.021 (0.918)
7	$\Delta i_{t-2}, \ldots, \Delta i_{t-6}$	0.102 (0.002)	0.028 (0.119)	1.213 (0.445)	−0.022 (0.700)
8	$r_{t-2}, \ldots, r_{t-4},$ $\Delta c_{t-2}, \ldots, \Delta c_{t+4},$	0.062 (0.026)	0.455 (0.000)	0.204 (0.114)	0.047 (0.033)
9	$r_{t-2}, \ldots, r_{t-4},$ $\Delta c_{t-2}, \ldots, \Delta c_{t-4},$ $\Delta i_{t-2}, \ldots, \Delta i_{t-4}$	0.103 (0.006)	0.476 (0.000)	0.150 (0.111)	0.100 (0.005)

Note: See Table 1.

ing the Hall IV regression. Table 4 shows the IV regression of the real interest rate on the change in consumption. We do not find that the estimates of $1/\sigma$ are extremely large, as would be predicted by the Hall hypothesis; instead, they cluster around one.[20]

Figure 3 shows graphically why the results are so sensitive to normalization. We regressed Δc and r on the instruments in row 9 of Table 3 and then plotted the fitted values as estimates of the expected change in consumption and the real interest rate. The figure shows that there is substantial variation in these two variables over time. Yet contrary to the predictions of the theory, the fitted values do not lie along a line. The two lines in this figure correspond to the two regressions estimated with the two normalizations. Because the fitted values are not highly correlated, the estimated regression is crucially dependent on which variable

20. This cannot be explained by small-sample problems of the Nelson and Startz (1988) variety, since consumption growth is fairly well predicted by the instruments in Table 3.

is on the left-hand side. Hence, this scatterplot does not imply that the elasticity of substitution is small. Instead, it suggests that the model underlying the Euler equation (2.1) should be rejected.

2.2. INCLUDING RULE-OF-THUMB CONSUMERS

We now reintroduce our rule-of-thumb consumers into the model. That is, we consider a more general model in which a fraction λ of income goes to individuals who consume their current income and the remainder goes to individuals who satisfy the general Euler equation (2.1). We estimate by instrumental variables

$$\Delta c_t = \mu + \lambda \Delta y_t + \theta r_t + \epsilon_t, \quad (2.2)$$

where $\theta = (1 - \lambda)\sigma$. We thus include actual income growth and the ex post real interest rate in the equation, but instrument using twice lagged variables. The results are in Table 5.

Table 4   UNITED STATES, 1953–1986
$r_t = \mu + 1/\sigma \, \Delta c_t$

Row	Instruments	First-stage regressions		$1/\sigma$ estimate (s.e.)	Test of restrictions
		Δc equation	r equation		
1	None (OLS)	—	—	0.304 (0.087)	—
2	$r_{t-2}, \ldots, r_{t-4}$	0.063 (0.009)	0.431 (0.000)	1.581 (0.486)	0.086 (0.001)
3	$r_{t-2}, \ldots, r_{t-6}$	0.067 (0.014)	0.426 (0.000)	1.347 (0.390)	0.113 (0.001)
4	$\Delta c_{t-2}, \ldots, \Delta c_{t-4}$	0.024 (0.101)	−0.021 (0.966)	−0.342 (0.428)	−0.021 (0.878)
5	$\Delta c_{t-2}, \ldots, \Delta c_{t-6}$	0.018 (0.007)	0.007 (0.316)	0.419 (0.258)	−0.010 (0.440)
6	$\Delta i_{t-2}, \ldots, \Delta i_{t-4}$	0.061 (0.010)	0.024 (0.105)	0.768 (0.334)	−0.021 (0.919)
7	$\Delta i_{t-2}, \ldots, \Delta i_{t-6}$	0.102 (0.002)	0.028 (0.119)	0.638 (0.249)	−0.024 (0.747)
8	$r_{t-2}, \ldots, r_{t-4}, \Delta c_{t-2}, \ldots, \Delta c_{t-4}$	0.062 (0.026)	0.455 (0.000)	1.034 (0.333)	0.236 (0.000)
9	$r_{t-2}, \ldots, r_{t-4}, \Delta c_{t-2}, \ldots, \Delta c_{t-4}, \Delta i_{t-2}, \ldots, \Delta i_{t-4}$	0.103 (0.006)	0.476 (0.000)	0.521 (0.220)	0.455 (0.000)

Note: See Table 1.

The first implication of the results is that the rule-of-thumb consumers cannot be explained away by allowing for fluctuations in the real interest rate. The coefficient on current income remains substantively and statistically significant.

The second implication of the results in Table 5 is that there is no evidence that the ex ante real interest rate is associated with the growth rate of consumption after allowing for the rule-of-thumb consumers. The coefficient on the real interest rate is consistently less than its standard error. The small estimated coefficients on the real interest rate indicate that the intertemporal elasticity of substitution for the permanent income consumers is very small. In addition, there is no evidence of any misspecification of the sort found when the rule-of-thumb consumers were excluded. The over-identifying restrictions are never close to being rejected.

Figure 4 illustrates the finding of a small elasticity of substitution by plotting the expected real interest rate and the expected change in consumption for the permanent income consumers assuming $\lambda=0.5$. This figure is exactly analogous to Figure 3, except that Δc has been replaced by $\Delta c-0.5\Delta y$. These fitted values lie almost along a horizontal line, as is required for an elasticity near zero. The figure also includes the regres-

Figure 3 SCATTERPLOT OF EXPECTED CHANGE IN CONSUMPTION AND THE EXPECTED REAL INTEREST RATE

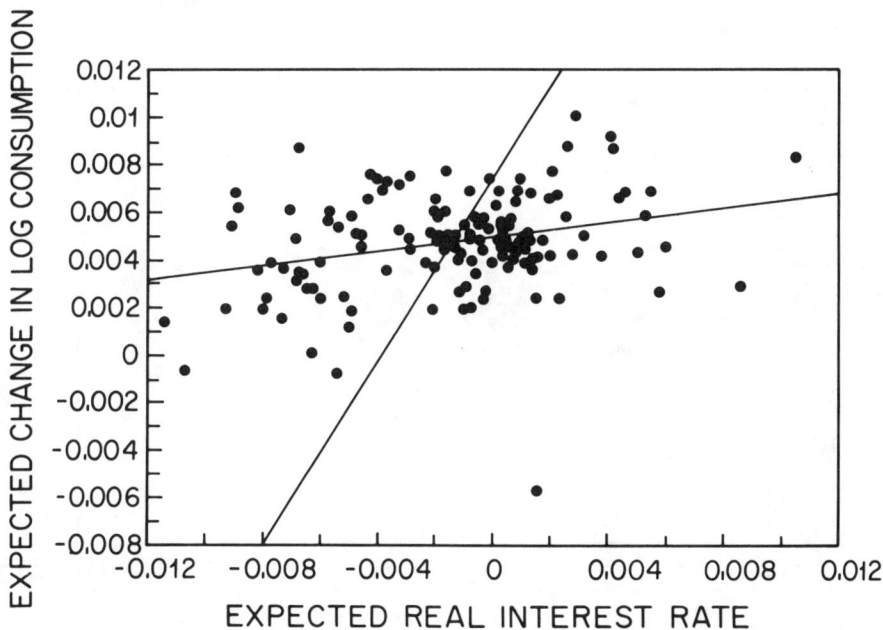

sion line of the expected consumption change on the expected real interest rate, and it is near horizontal. Note that we cannot estimate the
reverse normalization: we have been unable to find any instruments that
forecast $\Delta c - 0.5\Delta y$ (as must be the case if $\lambda = 0.5$ and $\sigma = 0$).

Table 5   UNITED STATES, 1953–1986
   $\Delta c_t = \mu + \lambda \Delta y_t + \theta r_t$

Row	Instruments	First-stage regressions			λ (s.e.)	θ (s.e.)	Test of restrictions
		Δc	Δy	r			
1	None (OLS)	—	—	—	0.294 (0.041)	0.150 (0.070)	—
2	$\Delta y_{t-2}, \ldots, \Delta y_{t-4}$ $r_{t-2}, \ldots, r_{t-4}$	0.045 (0.061)	0.030 (0.125)	0.471 (0.000)	0.438 (0.189)	0.080 (0.123)	−0.010 (0.441)
3	$\Delta c_{t-2}, \ldots, \Delta c_{t-4}$ $r_{t-2}, \ldots, r_{t-4}$	0.062 (0.026)	0.046 (0.060)	0.455 (0.000)	0.467 (0.152)	0.089 (0.110)	−0.006 (0.391)
4	$\Delta i_{t-2}, \ldots, \Delta i_{t-4}$ $r_{t-2}, \ldots, r_{t-4}$	0.092 (0.005)	0.034 (0.106)	0.431 (0.000)	0.657 (0.212)	0.016 (0.146)	−0.022 (0.665)

Note: See Table 1

Figure 4 SCATTERPLOT OF EXPECTED CHANGE IN CONSUMPTION FOR
"PERMANENT INCOME" CONSUMERS AND THE EXPECTED
REAL INTEREST RATE

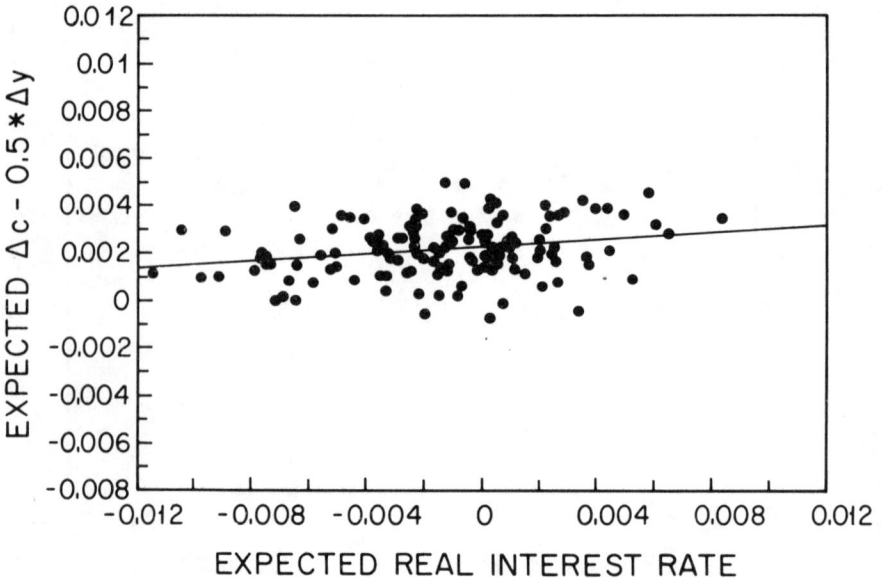

In summary, the data show little or no correlation between expected changes in consumption and ex ante real interest rates. Yet this finding should not be interpreted as implying that the permanent income hypothesis holds with a small intertemporal elasticity of consumption: that hypothesis would require that expected changes in consumption are small and linearly dependent on the ex ante real interest rate. Instead, it seems that expected changes in consumption are dependent on expected changes in income, which can be explained by the existence of some rule-of-thumb consumers. Once these rule-of-thumb consumers are admitted into the model, the data become consistent with an elasticity of substitution near zero for the permanent income consumers.

3. From Euler Equation to Consumption Function

Modern empirical work on consumption behavior has focused almost exclusively on the Euler equations implied by optimizing models of intertemporal choice. Our own work is no exception. Yet is seems that something has been lost in this change of emphasis. The Euler equation determines only the level of consumption today, *relative* to the level of consumption tomorrow. We would like to be able to determine the absolute level of consumption, given either wealth and expected future interest rates, or expected future income flows and interest rates. For this we need a traditional consumption function, that is, a closed-form solution for consumption given exogenous variables.

Of course, there are considerable technical difficulties in deriving a consumption function from an optimizing model. In fact, closed-form solutions are available only in a very few special cases, the best-known being log utility or power utility with independently and identically distributed asset returns.[21] The problem is that a closed-form solution is obtained by combining an Euler equation with the intertemporal budget constraint. But even when the Euler equation is linear or log-linear, the budget constraint is always non-linear when asset returns are random. Consumption is *subtracted* from wealth to give the amount invested, and this amount is then *multiplied* by a random rate of return to give tomorrow's level of wealth.

In this section we explore a class of approximate consumption functions obtained by log-linearizing the intertemporal budget constraint. These approximate consumption functions give considerable insight

---

21. See Samuelson (1969) or Ingersoll (1987).

into the implications of alternative models, and they offer an alternative way to confront the modesl with the data.[22]

3.1. THE INTERTEMPORAL BUDGET CONSTRAINT

To see the way our approach works, consider the budget constraint of a consumer who invests his wealth in a single asset with a time-varying risky return R_t. We do not explicitly model income at this stage; this is legitimate provided that all the consumer's income flows (including his or her labor income) are capitalized into marketable wealth. The period-by-period budget constraint is

$$W_{t+1} = R_{t+1}(W_t - C_t) . \quad (3.1)$$

Solving forward with an infinite horizon and imposing the transversality condition that the limit of discounted future wealth is zero, we obtain

$$W_t = C_t + \sum_{i=1}^{\infty} C_{t+i} / \left(\prod_{j=1}^{i} R_{t+j} \right) . \quad (3.2)$$

This equation says that today's wealth equals the discounted value of all future consumption.

We would like to approximate the non-linear equations (3.1) and (3.2) in such a way that we obtain linear relationships between log wealth, log consumption, and log returns, measured at different points of time. To do this, we first divide equation (3.1) by W_t, take logs and rearrange. The resulting equation expresses the growth rate of wealth as a non-linear function of the log return on wealth and the log consumption-wealth ratio. In the appendix we show how to linearize this equation using a Taylor expansion. We obtain

$$\Delta w_{t+1} \approx k + r_{t+1} + (1 - 1/\rho)(c_t - w_t) . \quad (3.3)$$

In this equation lower-case letters are used to denote the logs of the corresponding upper-case letters. The parameter ρ is a number a little

22. Our log-linearization is similar to the one used by Campbell and Shiller (1988) to study stock prices, dividends, and discount rates. It differs slightly because we define wealth inclusive of today's consumption, which is analogous to a cum-dividend asset price. There is also an interesting parallel between our approach and the continuous-time model of Merton (1971). Merton was able to ignore the product of random returns and consumption flows, since this becomes negligible in continuous time. See also Hayashi (1982), who examines a similar model under the maintained assumption of a constant real interest rate.

less than one, and k is a constant.[23] This equation says that the growth rate of wealth is a constant, plus the log return on wealth, less a small fraction $(1-1/\rho)$ of the log consumption-wealth ratio. In the appendix we solve equation (3.3) forward to obtain

$$c_t - w_t = \sum_{j=1}^{\infty} \rho^j(r_{t+j}-\Delta c_{t+j}) + \rho k/(1-\rho) \, . \quad (3.4)$$

Equation (3.4) is a log-linear version of the infinite-horizon budget constraint (3.2). It states that a high log consumption-wealth ratio today must be associated either with high future rates of return on invested wealth, or with low future consumption growth.

3.2. WEALTH-BASED AND INCOME-BASED CONSUMPTION FUNCTIONS

So far we have merely manipulated a budget constraint, without stating any behavioral restrictions on consumer behavior. We now assume that the consumer satisfies the log-linear Euler equation discussed earlier in Section 2:

$$E_t\Delta c_{t+1} = \mu + \sigma E_t r_{t+1} \, . \quad (3.5)$$

Equation (3.5) can be combined with equation (3.4) to give a consumption function relating consumption, wealth, and expected future returns on wealth. Take conditional expectations of equation (3.4), noting that the left-hand side is unchanged because it is in the consumer's information set at time t. Then substitute in for expected consumption growth from (3.5). The resulting expression is

$$c_t - w_t = (1-\sigma) \, E_t \sum_{j=1}^{\infty} \rho^j r_{t+j} + \rho \, (k-\mu)/(1-\rho) \, . \quad (3.6)$$

This equation generalizes Paul Samuelson's (1969) results for independently and identically distributed asset returns. It says that the log consumption-wealth ratio is a constant, plus $(1-\sigma)$ times the expected present value of future interest rates, discounted at the rate ρ. When $\sigma = 1$, the consumer has log utility and we get the well-known result that consumption is a constant fraction of wealth. When $\sigma > 1$, an increase in

---

23. The parameter ρ can also be interpreted as the average ratio of invested wealth, $W-C$, to total wealth, W.

interest rates lowers the log consumption-wealth ratio because substitution effects outweigh income effects; when $\sigma < 1$, income effects are stronger and high interest rates increase consumption. Whatever the sign of the effect, persistent movements in interest rates have a stronger impact on the level of consumption than transitory movements do.

Traditional macroeconomic consumption functions usually determine consumption in relation to income flows rather than wealth. We can move from the wealth-based consumption function (3.6) to an income-based consumption function by expressing the market value of wealth in terms of future expected returns and the future expected income flows from wealth. A full derivation is given in the appendix. The resulting consumption function is

$$c_t - y_t = E_t \sum_{j=1}^{\infty} \rho^j(\Delta y_{t+j} - \sigma r_{t+j}) - \rho\mu/(1-\rho), \quad (3.7)$$

where y_{t+j} is the income at time $t+j$ generated by the wealth held at time t. The log consumption-income ratio depends on the expected present value of future income growth, less σ times the expected present value of future interest rates. As σ falls towards zero, interest rates have less and less effect on the consumption-income ratio and the model becomes a log-linear version of the standard permanent income model which ignores interest rate variation.

Two aspects of (3.7) are worthy of special mention. First, the interest rate terms in (3.7) capture the effects of changes in interest rates holding future income constant (while the market value of wealth is allowed to vary). By contrast, the interest rate terms in (3.4) capture the effects of changes in interest rates holding wealth constant (while future income is allowed to vary). When one holds future income constant, higher interest rates lower the market value of wealth; when one holds the market value of wealth constant, higher interest rates increase future income flows. As Lawrence Summers (1981) has emphasized, higher interest rates reduce consumption more when income flows are held fixed, since there is no positive income effect to offset the negative substitution effect of interest rates on consumption. With fixed income flows, the impact of interest rates on consumption approaches zero as σ approaches zero.

Second, the income growth terms in (3.7) represent the influence of expected growth in income on current wealth, that is, net of the effects of further wealth accumulation. This complicates the use of (3.7) in empirical work, although the component of measured income growth that is due to wealth accumulation may be small in practice.[24]

The analysis of this section has so far ignored the possibility that some fraction λ of income accrues to individuals who consume their current income rather than obeying the consumption function (3.7). But it is straightforward to generalize (3.7) to allow for these consumers. We obtain

$$c_t - y_t = (1-\lambda) E_t \sum_{j=1}^{\infty} \rho^j (\Delta y_{t+j} - \sigma r_{t+j}) - (1-\lambda)\rho\mu/(1-\rho) . \quad (3.8)$$

The presence of current-income consumers reduces the variability of the log consumption-income ratio. The model of Hall (1988) sets $\sigma = \lambda = 0$ and thus has the consumption-income ratio responding fully to expected income growth but not at all to expected interest rates. By contrast, our model with $\lambda = 0.5$ has a reduced response of the consumption-income ratio to expected future income growth.

3.3. EMPIRICAL IMPLEMENTATION

Since equation (3.8) shows that both the permanent income model and our more general model with rule-of-thumb consumers can be written as a present value relation, all the econometric techniques available for examining present value relations can be used to test and estimate these models. Applying these techniques is beyond the scope of this paper. To see what such exercises are likely to find, however, we take an initial look at the data from the perspective of this present value relation.

If we assume the intertemporal elasticity of substitution is small and set $\sigma = 0$, equation (3.8) says that the log of the average propensity to consume $(c-y)$ is the optimal forecast of the present value of future income growth. To see if in fact there is any relation between these variables, Figure 5 plots the log of the average propensity to consume (computed using spending on non-durables and services) and the present value of realized income growth (computed using personal disposable income per capita). We assume a quarterly discount factor of 0.99, and set the out-of-sample income growth rates at the sample mean. As the theory predicts, the figure shows a clear positive relationship between these variables. When consumption is high relative to current income, income will tend to grow faster than average. When consump-

24. For a discussion of this issue see Flavin (1981).

tion is low relative to current income, income will tend to grow slower than average.[25]

We can obtain an estimate of λ, the fraction of income going to rule-of-thumb consumers, by regressing the present value of realized income growth on the log of the average propensity to consume. Since the error in this relationship is an expectations error, it should be uncorrelated with currently known variables—in particular, $c-y$. The coefficient on $c-y$ is therefore a consistent estimate of $1/(1-\lambda)$. We can see from Figure 5 that the estimate is likely to be greater than one: the present value of future income growth seems to respond more than one-for-one to fluctuations in $c-y$, which suggests that λ is greater than zero.

Table 6 shows the regression results for three measures of consumption: spending on non-durables and services, total consumer spending, and the sum of spending on non-durables and services and the imputed rent on the stock of consumer durables. We present the results with and without a time trend.[26] The implied estimates of λ in Table 6 vary from 0.233 to 0.496, which are similar to those obtained in Table 1.[27] These findings lead us to believe that more sophisticated examinations of the present value relation will likely yield a conclusion similar to the one we reached examining the Euler equation: a model with some permanent income consumers and some rule-of-thumb consumers best fits the data.

4. Conclusions

We have argued that aggregate consumption is best viewed as generated not by a single representative consumer but rather by two groups of consumers—one consuming their permanent income and the other consuming their current income. We have estimated that each group of consumers receives about 50 percent of income and that the intertemporal elasticity of substitution for the permanent income consumers is close to zero. This alternative model can explain why expected growth in consumption accompanies expected growth in income, why expected

25. This figure thus confirms the findings using vector autoregressions in Campbell (1987).
26. We include a time trend to proxy for mismeasurement in the average propensity to consume attributable to the treatment of consumer durables. The ratio of spending on consumer durables to spending on consumer non-durables and services has grown over time. Therefore, a failure to include consumer durables or an incorrect imputation is likely to cause mismeasurement in $c-y$ that is correlated with time. We confess that inclusion of a time trend is a crude correction at best.
27. We have somewhat more confidence in the estimates of λ obtained from Euler equation estimation. In Table 6, measurement error in consumption biases downward the estimate of λ (as does the inability to observe the out-of-sample values of future income growth.) Yet such measurement error does not affect the Euler equation estimates if this measurement error is uncorrelated with the instruments.

Figure 5 THE AVERAGE PROPENSITY TO CONSUME AS A FORECAST OF
FUTURE INCOME GROWTH

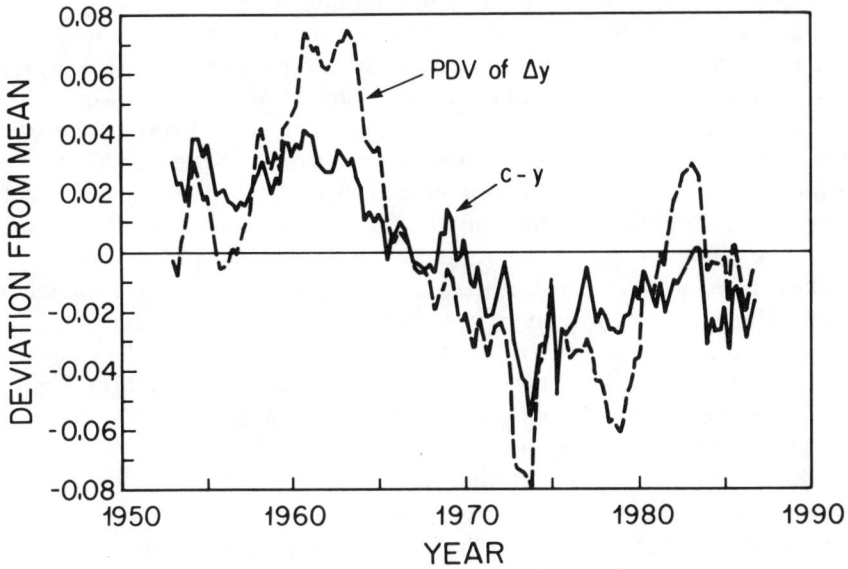

Table 6   UNITED STATES, 1953–1986
$\sum_{j=1}^{\infty} \rho^j \Delta y_{t+j} = \mu + [1/(1-\lambda)](c_t - y_t)$

Consumption Measure	$1/(1-\lambda)$	time	R^{-2}	Implied λ
Non-durables and Services	1.306 (0.223)		0.690	0.234
Non-durables and Services	1.983 (0.221)	0.0005 (0.0001)	0.792	0.496
Total Consumer Spending	1.455 (0.408)		0.302	0.313
Total Consumer Spending	1.303 (0.256)	−0.0004 (0.0002)	0.463	0.233
Non-durables, Services, and Imputed Rent on Durables	1.576 (0.225)		0.740	0.366
Non-durables, Services, and Imputed Rent on Durables	1.937 (0.203)	0.0003 (0.0001)	0.776	0.484

Note: These regressions were estimated using Ordinary Least Squares. The present value of future growth was computed assuming $\rho = .99$; out-of-sample growth rates were set at the sample mean. Standard errors in parentheses were computed using the Newey-West (1987) correction for serial correlation; these standard errors use a lag length of 20, although lag lengths of 10 and 30 yielded similar results.

growth in consumption is unrelated to the expected real interest rate, and why periods in which consumption is high relative to income are typically followed by high growth in income.

Our model also has the potential to explain the "excess smoothness" of aggregate consumption pointed out by Angus Deaton (1987).[28] Deaton shows that if income follows a persistent time series process, then the variance of the innovation in permanent income exceeds the variance of the change in current income. According to the permanent income model, the change in consumption should then be more variable than the change in income; but in fact consumption is considerably smoother than income. Our model can resolve this puzzle because it makes the change in consumption a weighted average of the change in current income and the change in permanent income. If these two income changes are not perfectly correlated, then a weighted average of them can be less variable than either one considered in isolation. Aggregate consumption is smooth in our model because it is a "diversified portfolio" of the consumption of two groups of agents.[29]

Although our emphasis in this paper has been on characterizing the aggregate data rather than on analyzing economic policies, our findings are suggestive regarding the effects of policies. In particular, if current income plays as central a role in consumption as our alternative model suggests, economists should not turn so readily to the permanent income hypothesis for policy analysis. An important application of this conclusion is in the debate over the national debt. Since the Ricardian equivalence proposition relies on the permanent income hypothesis, the failure of the permanent income hypothesis casts doubt on this proposition's empirical validity. Rule-of-thumb consumers are unlikely to increase private saving and bequests in response to government deficits. The old-fashioned Keynesian consumption function may therefore provide a better benchmark for analyzing fiscal policy than does the model with infinitely-lived consumers.

Our alternative model with rule-of-thumb consumers is very different from the alternative models considered in much recent work on Ricardian equivalence.[30] Those alternatives are forward-looking, but in-

28. See also Campbell and Deaton (1989), Christiano (1987), Flavin (1988) and West (1988).
29. As an example, consider the case in which income is a random walk but is known one period in advance Flavin (1988). In this case, since the change in permanent income and the change in current income are contemporaneously uncorrelated, our model implies that the variance of the change in consumption will be one-half the variance of the change in income. For more discussion of excess smoothness in our model, see Flavin (1988) or the 1989 version of Campbell and Mankiw (1987).
30. For example, see Evans (1988), which tests Ricardian equivalence within the framework of Blanchard (1985).

volve finite horizons or wedges between the interest rates that appear in private sector and government budget constraints. We believe that such effects may be present, but are hard to detect because they are much more subtle than the rule-of-thumb behavior we document here. Thus, the tests in the literature may have low power.[31]

The failures of the representative consumer model documented here are in some ways unfortunate. This model held out the promise of an integrated framework for analyzing household behavior in financial markets and in goods markets. Yet the failures we have discussed are not unique. The model is also difficult to reconcile with the large size of the equity premium, the cross-sectional variation in asset returns, and time series fluctuations in the stock market.[32] The great promise of the representative consumer model has not been realized.

One possible response to these findings is that the representative consumer model examined here is too simple. Some researchers have been attempting to model the aggregate time series using a representative consumer model with more complicated preferences. Non-time-separabilities and departures from the von Neumann-Morgenstern axioms are currently receiving much attention.[33] It is also possible that there are non-separabilities between non-durables and services consumption and other contemporaneous variables.[34]

Alternatively, some have argued that random shocks to the representative consumer's utility function may be important.[35] This contrasts with the standard assumption in the consumption literature that fluctuations arise from shocks to other equations, such as productivity shocks or changes in monetary and fiscal policy. If there are shocks to the utility function and if they are serially correlated, then they enter the residual

31. An exception is the study by David Wilcox (1989) which reports that consumer spending rises when Social Security benefits are increased. This finding provides evidence against the infinite-horizon model of the consumer. Moreover, since these benefit increases were announced in advance, this finding also provides evidence against models with forward-looking, finite-horizon consumers.

32. See Mehra and Prescott (1985), Mankiw and Shapiro (1986), and Campbell and Shiller (1988).

33. For models with non-time-separability, see Constantinides (1988) and Heaton (1988). For departures from the von Neumann-Morgenstern axioms, see Epstein and Zin (1987a, 1987b) and Giovannini and Weil (1989).

34. In Campbell and Mankiw (1987), we looked at cross-effects with labor supply, government spending, and durable goods; we found no evidence for these types of non-separabilities. There is perhaps more evidence for non-separability with the stock of real money balances; see Koenig (1989). Nason (1988) proposes a model in which the marginal utility of consumption depends on current income. His model is observationally equivalent to ours, and has the same implications for policy; it is a way to describe the same facts in different terms.

35. See Garber and King (1983) and Hall (1986).

of the Euler equation and may be correlated with lagged instruments, invalidating standard test procedures.[36]

Unlike our model with rule-of-thumb consumers, these approaches remain in the spirit of the permanent income hypothesis by positing forward-looking consumers who do not face borrowing constraints. We believe that such modifications of the standard model are worth exploring, but we doubt that they will ultimately prove successful. We expect that the simple model presented here—half of income going to permanent income consumers and half going to current income consumers—will be hard to beat as a description of the aggregate data on consumption, income, and interest rates.

Appendix: Derivation of Approximate Consumption Functions

We first divide equation (3.1) by W_t and take logs. The resulting equation is

$$w_{t+1} - w_t = r_{t+1} + \log(1-C_t/W_t) = r_{t+1} + \log(1-\exp(c_t-w_t)). \quad (A.1)$$

The last term in equation (A.1) is a non-linear function of the log consumption-wealth ratio, $c_t - w_t = x_t$. The next step is to take a first-order Taylor expansion of this function, $\log(1-\exp(x_t))$, around the point $x_t = x$. The resulting approximation is

$$\log(1-\exp(c_t-w_t)) \approx k + (1-1/\rho)(c_t-w_t), \quad (A.2)$$

where the parameter $\rho \equiv 1-\exp(x)$, a number a little less than one, and the constant $k \equiv \log(\rho) - (1-1/\rho)\log(1-\rho)$. The parameter ρ can also be interpreted as the average ratio of invested wealth, $W -C$, to total wealth, W. Substituting (A.2) into (A.1), we obtain (3.3).

The growth rate of wealth, which appears on the left-hand side of equation (3.3), can be written in terms of the growth rate of consumption and the change in the consumption-wealth ratio:

36. One response to this point is to try to find instruments that are uncorrelated with taste shocks. We have experimented with several instrument sets, including lagged growth of defense spending and political party dummies, but these did not have much predictive power for income. On the other hand, the change in the relative price of oil had significant predictive power two quarters ahead. When we used lags 2 through 6 as instruments, we estimated the fraction of current income consumers to be 0.28 with a standard error of 0.09. These instruments, however, did not have significant predictive power for real interest rates, so we were unable to estimate the more general Euler equation.

$\Delta w_{t+1} = \Delta c_{t+1} + (c_t - w_t) - (c_{t+1} - w_{t+1})$. (A.3)

Substituting (A.3) into (3.3) and rearranging, we get a difference equation relating the log consumption-wealth ratio today to the interest rate, the consumption growth rate, and the log consumption-wealth ratio tomorrow:

$c_t - w_t = \rho(r_{t+1} - \Delta c_{t+1}) + \rho(c_{t+1} - w_{t+1}) + \rho k$. (A.4)

Solving forward, we obtain (3.4).

To obtain an income-based consumption function, we suppose that total wealth W_t consists of N_t shares, each with ex-dividend price P_t and dividend payment Y_t in period t:

$W_t = N_t(P_t + Y_t)$. (A.5)

The return on wealth can be written as

$R_{t+1} = (P_{t+1} + Y_{t+1})/P_t$. (A.6)

Combining (A.5) and (A.6) and rearranging, we get

$W_{t+1}/N_{t+1} = R_{t+1}(W_t/N_t - Y_t)$, (A.7)

where $W_t/N_t = P_t + Y_t$ is the cum-divided share price at time t. This equation is in the same form as (3.1) and can be linearized in the same way. The log-linear model is

$y_t - w_t = -n_t + E_t \sum_{j=1}^{\infty} \rho^j(r_{t+j} - \Delta y_{t+j}) + \rho k/(1-\rho)$. (A.8)

(Implicitly we are assuming that the mean dividend-price ratio equals the mean consumption-wealth ratio since the same parameter ρ appears in (A.8) and in (3.4)). Normalizing $N_t=1$ ($n_t=0$) and substituting (A.8) into (3.6), we obtain (3.7).

An earlier version of this paper was presented at the NBER Macroeconomics Conference, Cambridge, MA, March 10–11, 1989. We are grateful to Karen Dynan for research assistance; Olivier Blanchard, Alan Blinder, and Robert Hall for comments, and to the NBER and the National Science Foundation for financial support.

BIBLIOGRAPHY

Barsky, Robert B. *Three Interest Rate Paradoxes*. MIT. PhD Dissertation. 1985.
Bean, Charles R. "The Estimation of 'Surprise' Models and the 'Surprise' Consumption Function." *Review of Economic Studies* 53:497–516. August 1986.
Bernanke, Ben S. "Adjustment Costs, Durables and Aggregate Consumption." *Journal of Monetary Economics* 15:41–68. January 1985.
Blanchard, Olivier J. "Debt, Deficits, and Finite Horizons." *Journal of Political Economy* 93:223–47. April 1985.
Campbell, John Y. "Does Saving Anticipate Declining Labor Income? An Alternative Test of the Permanent Income Hypothesis." *Econometrica* 55:1249–73. November 1987.
Campbell, John Y. and Angus S. Deaton. "Why is Consumption So Smooth?" *Review of Economic Studies*. April 1989. Forthcoming.
Campbell, John Y. and Richard H. Clarida. "Saving and Permanent Income in Canada and the United Kingdom," in Elhanan Helpman, Assaf Razin, and Efraim Sadka, Eds. *Economic Effects of the Government Budget*, Cambridge, Mass.: MIT Press, 1988.
Campbell, John Y. and N. Gregory Mankiw. "Permanent Income, Current Income, and Consumption." NBER Working Paper No. 2436, November 1987; revised January 1989.
Campbell, John Y. and Robert J. Shiller. "The Dividend-Price Ratio and Expectations of Future Dividends and Discount Factors." *Review of Financial Studies* 1:195–228. Fall 1988.
Christiano, Lawrence J. "Why Is Consumption Less Volatile than Income?" *Federal Reserve Bank of Minneapolis Quarterly Review* 2–20. Fall 1987.
Constantinides, George M. "Habit Formation: A Resolution of the Equity Premium Puzzle." University of Chicago, Graduate School of Business. Unpublished paper. 1988.
Deaton, Angus S. "Life-Cycle Models of Consumption: Is the Evidence Consistent with the Theory?" in T. F. Bewley, ed. *Advances in Econometrics, Fifth World Congress*. Vol. 2, Cambridge: Cambridge University Press. 1987.
Epstein, Larry G. and Stanley E. Zin. (1987a). "Substitution, Risk Aversion, and the Temporal Behavior of Consumption and Asset Prices I: A Theoretical Framework." *Econometrica*. Forthcoming.
Epstein, Larry G. and Stanley E. Zin. (1987b). "Substitution, Risk Aversion, and the Temporal Behavior of Consumption and Asset Prices II: An Empirical Analysis." Unpublished paper. 1987.
Evans, Paul. "Are Consumers Ricardian? Evidence for the United States." *Journal of Political Economy* 96:983–1004. October 1988.
Fisher, Franklin. "On the Cost of Approximate Specification in Simultaneous Equation Estimation." *Econometrica* 29: 139–170. April 1961.
Flavin, Marjorie A. "The Adjustment of Consumption to Changing Expectations about Future Income." *Journal of Political Economy* 89:974–1009. October 1981.
Flavin, Marjorie A., "The Excess Smoothness of Consumption: Identification and Interpretation," NBER Working Paper No. 2807, December 1988.
Garber, Peter M. and Robert G. King. "Deep Structural Excavation? A Critique of Euler Equation Methods." NBER Technical Paper 31. 1983.
Giovannini, Alberto, and Philippe Weil. "Risk Aversion and Intertemporal Substitution in the Capital Asset Pricing Model." NBER Working Paper 2824. 1989.

Grossman, Sanford J. and Robert J. Shiller. "The Determinants of the Variability of Stock Market Prices." *American Economic Review* 71:222–27. May 1981.

Hall, Robert E. "Stochastic Implications of the Life Cycle-Permanent Income Hypothesis: Theory and Evidence." *Journal of Political Economy* 86:971–87. October 1978.

Hall, Robert E. "The Role of Consumption in Economic Fluctuations." *The American Business Cycle: Continuity and Change*, Robert J. Gordon, ed. Chicago: University of Chicago Press. 1986. 237–66.

Hall, Robert E. "Intertemporal Substitution in Consumption." *Journal of Political Economy* 96:339–57. April 1988.

Hansen, Lars P. and Kenneth J. Singleton. "Stochastic Consumption, Risk Aversion, and the Temporal Behavior of Asset Returns." *Journal of Political Economy* 91:249–65. April 1983.

Hayashi, Fumio. "The Permanent Income Hypothesis: Estimation and Testing by Instrumental Variables." *Journal of Political Economy* 90:895–916. October 1982.

Heaton, John. "The Interaction Between Time-Nonseparable Preferences and Time Aggregation." University of Chicago. Unpublished paper. November 1988.

Ingersoll, Jonathan E., Jr. *Theory of Financial Decision Making.* Totowa: Rowman and Littlefield. 1987.

Jappelli, Tullio and Marco Pagano. "Consumption and Capital Market Imperfections: An International Comparison." CEPR Discussion Paper No. 244. June 1988.

Koenig, Evan. "Real Money Balances and the Timing of Consumption: An Empirical Investigation." Federal Reserve Bank of Dallas. Discussion Paper. March 1989.

Kormendi, Roger C. and Laura LaHaye. "Cross-Country Evidence on the Permanent Income Hypothesis." University of Michigan. Unpublished paper. Revised December 1987.

Lucas, Robert E., Jr. "Econometric Policy Evaluation: A Critique." in *Carnegie-Rochester Conference Series on Public Policy* 1:19–46. 1976.

Mankiw, N. Gregory. "The Permanent Income Hypothesis and the Real Interest Rate." *Economics Letters* 7:307–11. 1981.

Mankiw, N. Gregory. "Hall's Consumption Hypothesis and Durable Goods." *Journal of Monetary Economics* 10:417–26. November 1982.

Mankiw, N. Gregory and Matthew D. Shapiro. "Trends, Random Walks and Tests of the Permanent Income Hypothesis." *Journal of Monetary Economics* 16:165–74. 1985.

Mankiw, N. Gregory and Matthew D. Shapiro. "Risk and Return: Consumption Beta versus Market Beta. *Review of Economics and Statistics* 68:452–59. August 1986.

Mehra, Rajnish and Edward C. Prescott. "The Equity Premium: A Puzzle." *Journal of Monetary Economics* 15:145–61. 1985.

Merton, Robert C. "Optimum Consumption and Portfolio Rules in a Continuous-Time Model." *Journal of Economic Theory* 3:373–413. 1971.

Michener, Ron. "Permanent Income in General Equilibrium." *Journal of Monetary Economics* 13:297–306. 1984.

Nason, James M. "Permanent Income, Current Income, Consumption, and Changing Tastes." Board of Governors, Federal Reserve System. Unpublished paper. December 1988.

Nelson, Charles R. and Richard Startz. "The Distribution of the Instrumental Variables Estimator and its *t*-Ratio When the Instrument is a Poor One." University of Washington. Discussion Paper 88–07. May 1988.

Newey, Whitney, and Kenneth West. "A Simple, Positive Definite, Heteroskedasticity and Autocorrelation Consistent Covariance Matrix. *Econometrica* 55:703–708. 1987.

Samuelson, Paul A. "Lifetime Portfolio Selection by Dynamic Stochastic Programming." *Review of Economics and Statistics* 51:239–46. 1969.

Sargan, J.D. "The Estimation of Economic Relationships Using Instrumental Variables." *Econometrica* 26:393–415. 1958.

Summers, Lawrence H. "Capital Taxation and Accumulation in a Life Cycle Growth Model." *American Economic Review* 71:533–44. September 1981.

West, Kenneth D. "The Insensitivity of Consumption to News about Income." *Journal of Monetary Economics* 21:17–33. January 1988.

Wilcox, David. "Social Security Benefits, Consumption Expenditure, and the Life Cycle Hypothesis." *Journal of Political Economy.* April 1989.

Working, Holbrook. "Note on the Correlation of First Differences of Averages in a Random Chain." *Econometrica* 28:916–18. October 1960.

Comment

LAWRENCE J. CHRISTIANO
Federal Reserve Bank of Minneapolis and NBER

Introduction

Campbell and Mankiw report several empirical results that they feel warrant abandoning the representative agent model as an abstraction for thinking about aggregate consumption. The most important of these is that the predictable component of consumption growth is linearly related to the predictable component of income growth and the predictable component of the inflation-adjusted rate of interest. In this linear relation, the coefficient on income growth is around .5, while the coefficient on the interest rate is close to zero. Campbell and Mankiw argue that the most likely explanation of this result is that 50% of income goes to "rule-of-thumb" households who set consumption equal to income, and the other 50% goes to "representative agent" households whose consumption decisions are consistent with the choices of a representative agent with low intertemporal substitution in consumption. They claim that the representative agent model ought to be replaced with this hybrid model, saying that such a model "will be hard to beat as a description of the aggregate data on consumption, income, and interest rates." Unfortunately, it is impossible to evaluate the merits of this claim based on the evidence in the paper.

The reason for this is that their description of the model being criticized and of the model being proposed is not precise enough. The Campbell-Mankiw claim that introducing rule-of-thumb households into the representative agent environment helps it account for the co-movements between predictable components in consumption growth, income growth, and interest rates seems plausible enough. But, without a more detailed description of the economic structure, it is impossible to say what the other empirical implications of introducing rule-of-thumb households might be. That there probably *are* other implications is suggested by the extensive cross-variable restrictions that characterize the typical fully specified representative agent model. To illustrate the possible quantitative significance of this observation, I have taken the liberty of filling in the missing details in both the representative agent model that Campbell and Mankiw criticize and their proposed alternative. I do so by drawing on the model specification in Christiano and Eichenbaum (1988). I find, consistent with the author's claim, that introducing rule-of-thumb households into my prototype representative agent model helps on the empirical dimension on which Campbell and Mankiw focus. At the same time, however, this modified model substantially overstates the volatility of consumption relative to income. Significantly, the representative agent model does very well on this dimension.

The relative smoothness of consumption versus income stands out as one of the most robust and well-documented empirical regularities in macroeconomic time series. Moreover, this fact has played a central role driving theoretical work on consumption. Initially, it inspired the permanent income hypothesis (PIH) and more recently it inspired further work when Deaton (1985) argued that the PIH has a hard time accounting for consumption smoothness when income is modeled as having a unit root.[1] In the light of these considerations, it is not so clear that Campbell and Mankiw's rule-of-thumb household model beats the representative agent model. Conditional on the maintained assumptions of the experiment, the former model cannot account for a traditional concern of the consumption literature—the relative volatility of consumption—but can account for some facts about consumption that have (as yet) attracted relatively less interest. My prototype representative agent model, while not able to account for the Campbell and Mankiw facts, scores a bullseye on consumption smoothing.

Of course, the proposition that rule-of-thumb households *raise* the relative volatility of consumption cannot be general, and probably re-

---

1. For a review of the role of consumption smoothing in the construction of the PIH, see Sargent (Chapter XII, 1987).

flects the structure and parameter values of my prototype representative agent model. A feature of this example that probably is robust is the principle that introducing rule-of-thumb households can be expected to alter a variety of model implications. Any full evaluation of the Campbell-Mankiw recommendation—whether informal or formally, using a likelihood ratio statistic—would take into account an estimate of the quantitative magnitude of these implications.

My comments are divided into three parts. First, I document that the Christiano-Eichenbaum (C/E) version of the representative agent model does indeed have a difficult time accounting for the results in the second sentence. Before accepting the authors' conclusion on this point I first investigate several potential ways that the C/E model could be reconciled with the facts cited in the first sentence. The first is a simple model of measurement error. The second is motivated by the observation, associated with Mankiw and Shapiro (1985), that disposable income (the income measure used by the authors) is a random walk from a univariate perspective. This observation draws attention to the possibility that the forecastable component of income growth is also small in the present multivariate context. If it is too small, then Campbell and Mankiw's estimate that 50% percent of the population follows rule-of-thumb could be a statistical artifact.[2] Several Monte Carlo experiments are reported in this section which suggest that the empirical multivariate predictability in income growth is large enough to ensure the validity of Campbell and Mankiw's instrumental variables method. Since this kind of result may be somewhat model specific, it is comforting that Campbell and Mankiw (1987) reach the same conclusion in an earlier paper based on a Monte Carlo study that uses a different data generating mechanism from mine. Absent these kinds of considerations, it is perhaps not surprising that the C/E model is embarrassed by the Campbell-Mankiw observations, since it satisfies all the assumptions they place on the representative agent model.

Second, I document the claims made about the relative volatility of consumption above. Namely, I show that a version of the C/E model predicts exactly the amount of consumption smoothing observed in the data. However, introducing rule-of-thumb households into the C/E model in the manner advocated by Campbell and Mankiw substantially raises the model's implication for the relative volatility of consumption. I then point out the role played by time aggregation and interest rate movements in the C/E model's account of consumption smoothing. I argue there that it is by no means obvious what the appropriate empirical counterpart to the rate of return in the C/E model is. In any event, it

2. For another analysis of this point, see Nelson and Startz (1988).

seems clear that it is *not* the inflation adjusted return on three-month T-bills, used by Campbell and Mankiw. In all likelihood a more appropriate measure is one which aggregates over the returns on many assets. I examine several such crude measures and find some support for the proposition that the interest rate movements anticipated by the C/E model are present in the data. These calculations are meant to be suggestive only, however. More effort needs to be directed at finding a good empirical counterpart for the rate of return in the C/E model to see whether its account of consumption smoothing is supported. The final part of these comments offers some concluding remarks.

2. The Campbell-Mankiw Empirical Observations Reject the C/E Model

Campbell and Mankiw show that the forecast of consumption two periods ahead is linearly related to the forecast of disposable income growth two periods ahead and the forecast of the real rate of interest two periods ahead. Here, a variable's forecast two periods ahead is the fitted value in its regression on variables lagged two and more periods. In this relation, they show that the coefficient on income growth is around .5 and statistically significantly different from zero based on asymptotic sampling theory. In addition, the coefficient on the rate of interest is positive and close to zero. They argue that this result rejects a version of the representative agent model in which preferences for consumption are separable across time and other commodities. In such a model, one expects the coefficient on income to be zero and the coefficient on the interest rate to be the representative agent's elasticity of intertemporal substitution in consumption. Campbell and Mankiw speculate that this rejection is unlikely to be overturned by considering non-separabilities and other modifications to the utility function. Instead, they conclude that the most likely explanation for the failure is that roughly 50 percent of disposable personal income goes to households who simply set consumption equal to disposable income period by period, and the other 50 percent goes to households whose aggregate consumption decisions look as though they were selected by a representative agent with intertemporal substitution in consumption close to zero.

Before tentatively agreeing with Campbell and Mankiw that their evidence embarrasses their version of the representative agent model, I first carried out two Monte Carlo experiments. First, I investigate the possibility that their results are a statistical artifact and reflect the lack of predictability in disposable income growth. I then investigate the potential for measurement error in the rate of return to account for their results. Neither of these considerations seem to be able to be able to reconcile their results with the particular representative agent model studied in Christiano and Eichenbaum. Before reporting these experiments, I describe the versions of the C/E used to generate the data in the Monte Carlo studies.

FOUR VERSIONS OF THE C/E MODEL

According to the C/E model, a representative agent selects contingency plans for private consumption, c_t, capital, k_{t+1}, and hours worked, n_t, to maximize:

$$E_0\Sigma_{t=0}^{\infty}(1.03)^{-t/4}\{\ell n(c_t) + 6.98\ell n(2190-n_t)\}, \quad (1)$$

subject to the following resource constraint:

$$c_t + g_t + k_{t+1} - 0.9793k_t = (z_t n_t)^{0.65}k_t^{0.35}. \quad (2)$$

The expression to the right of the equality in (2) is gross output, which is a function of n_t, k_t, and a technology shock, z_t. It is assumed to have the following representation:

$$z_t = z_{t-1}\exp(\lambda_t), \lambda_t = .0047(1-\rho_\lambda) + \rho_\lambda\lambda_{t-1} + \epsilon_t, \epsilon_t \sim \text{IIN } (0,.018^2). \quad (3)$$

where, as usual, IIN means independent (over time), identically and normally distributed. In C/E, $\rho_\lambda = 0$, but we shall find it useful to also consider other values of ρ_λ. In (2), g_t is government consumption, and it is assumed to have the following time series representation:

$$g_t = 199z_t\exp(x_t), x_t = 0.97x_{t-1} + \nu_t, \nu_t \sim \text{IIN } (0,.021^2). \quad (4)$$

In addition, I defined disposable labor income as the wage bill (labor's share times gross output) minus government consumption. In defining disposable income as net of government consumption, I am implicitly assuming that the government balances its budget period by period by levying taxes on workers only. Thus, labor income, y_t, is as follows:

$$y_t = 0.65(z_t n_t)^{0.65}k_t^{0.35} - g_t. \quad (5)$$

I define the interest rate, r_t, in this model as the return on investment in capital:

$$1 + r_t = 0.35(z_t n_t/k_t)^{0.65} + .9793 + .003254. \quad (6)$$

Here, .9793 is one minus the rate of depreciation on a unit of capital. Also, .003254 is an estimate of the quarterly growth in population. All variables, including k_t and n_t, are measured in per capita terms so that without this adjustment, r_t would be the additional per capita output associated with a unit of per capita investment in k_t and would therefore not be comparable with empirical measures of returns, which are not in per capita terms. For details about the computation of the decision rules and the choice of parameter values (which have been rounded), see Christiano and Eichenbaum (1988).

The time period in the C/E model is quarterly. Campbell and Mankiw have in mind a situation in which agents' decision rule is finer than the data sampling interval. In order to be consistent with this I work with a time aggregated version of the above model. In that version, the time period is ⅛ of a quarter and all parameters with a time dimension are appropriately adjusted. In particular, the discount rate, one minus the rate of depreciation on capital (i.e., .9793 in [2] and [6]), all auto-regressive coefficients and the discount rate are adjusted by raising them to the power ⅛. In addition, disturbance standard deviations and means (i.e., 199 in [4] and .0047 in [3]) are divided by 8. Finally, the time endowment in a quarter, 2190 in (1), is divided by 8. Prior to statistical analysis of data simulated from this fine time interval model, an 8 period moving sum of the data is taken and every 8th resulting observation is sampled. The resulting simulated "measured" data reflect the time aggregation properties emphasized by Campbell and Mankiw. In what follows I refer to this time aggregated model simply as the C/E model, without further qualification. Throughout, model parameters are always referred to in quarterly units.

Three other versions of the model are also considered. The first is the C/E model with serially correlated technology growth shocks, which is obtained by setting $\rho_\lambda = .2$. The second also adds measurement error to r_t. That is, the observed rate of return is $r_t + \eta_t$, where η_t has mean zero and is independent of all variables in the model. In addition, η_t is a first order autoregressive process with first order autocorrelation .8 and standard deviation .008. I call this the C/E model with serially correlated technology growth shocks and measurement error. This measurement error is assumed to hit r_t prior to summing and sampling the data. The third model introduces Campbell-Mankiw rule-of-thumb households into the second model. In this version of the model, c_t is replaced by $c_t + y_t$ and y_t is replaced by $2y_t$. Thus, one-half of total disposable income goes to households who set consumption optimally while the other half goes to households who simply equate consumption and disposable income.

I call this the CM version of the C/E model with serially correlated technology growth shocks and measurement error.

Each of these four models was used to generate 100 data sets, each of length 136 observations on quarterly measured rates of return, disposable income and consumption. This was done by first generating $8 \times 136 + 100$ observations and then ignoring the first 100 in order to randomize initial conditions. The resulting 8×136 observations were then summed over the quarter and then skip-sampled to generate the 136 observations that were actually used. The results analyzed in this section are reported in Table A.

The first row in Table A reproduces the results in row 3 of Table 6 in Campbell and Mankiw's paper. $R^2_{\Delta y_t}$ is the R-bar square of the regression of Δy_t on the instruments and measures the amount of information in the instruments for Δy_t. (Throughout, Δs_t denotes the first difference of log s_t.) The other rows report results of doing the same calculations on the 100 simulated data sets using the version of C/E model indicated in the first column. In each location, the number not in parentheses is the average, across 100 simulations. The number in ( ) is the standard devia-

Table A[1] $\quad \Delta c_t = \mu + \lambda \Delta y_t + \theta r_t$
INSTRUMENTS: $\Delta c_{t-2}, \ldots, \Delta c_{t-4}, r_{t-2}, \ldots, r_{t-4}$

	λ	θ	$R^2_{\Delta y}{}^2$	Test of Restrictions[3]
CM Point Estimates	.0467	0.089	.046	−0.006
C/E Model	0.449	.972	.0025	−.026
	(.015)	(.046)	(.024)	(.019)
	[.55]	[1.00]	[.07]	[.09]
C/E Model with serially correlated technology growth	−.0093	.820	.098	−.017
	(.136)	(.485)	(.044)	(.022)
	[.00]	[.89]	[.92]	[.15]
C/E Model with serially correlated technology growth and measurement error	.163	.073	.074	−.0028
	(.165)	(.188)	(.052)	(.033)
	[.02]	[.53]	[.64]	[.38]
CM Version of C/E Model with serially correlated technology growth and measurement error	.594	.047	.046	−.0027
	(.114)	(.096)	(.053)	(.031)
	[.90]	[.35]	[.44]	[.40]

[1]Results in the first row taken from row 3 in Campbell and Mankiw's Table 5. Results in subsequent rows based on Monte Carlo simulation of model indicated in left column. Numbers in those rows not in parentheses are averages across 100 simulations. Numbers in ( ) are standard deviations and numbers in [ ] are the frequency of times that simulated results exceed the corresponding parameter value in row 1.
[2]Adjusted R^2 of regression of Δy_t on the instruments and corresponds to Δy column in the "First-Stage Regressions" section of Campbell and Mankiw's Table 5.
[3]Corresponds to the "Test of Restrictions" column in Campbell and Mankiw's Table 5.

tion across 100 simulations. Finally, the number in [ ] is the frequency of times that the simulated number exceeded the corresponding empirical point estimate in the first row. It is the *p*-value of the empirical point estimate under the null hypothesis that the data generating mechanism underlying the simulations is true.

IS THE CAMPBELL-MANKIW ESTIMATE OF THE NUMBER OF RULE-OF-THUMB HOUSEHOLDS A STATISTICAL ARTIFACT? NO.

The second row in Table A reports results of calculations on artificial data generated by the C/E model identical to those performed by Campbell and Mankiw on actual data and reported in the first row of Table A. The surprising feature of those results is that the simulated λ's are very close to the estimated value of λ. Thus, though by construction there are no rule-of-thumb households in the C/E economy, Campbell and Mankiw's estimator would suggest that 44.9 percent of the households are liquidity constrained. The reason for this perverse result lies in the simulated $R^2_{\Delta y}$'s, all but seven of which were less than .046. To see this, consider the results in the third row of Table A. It reports calculations using a modified version of the C/E economy in which Δy_t has been made more predictable by introducing some serial correlation into λ_t. Note that the simulated $R^2_{\Delta y}$'s for this model are much closer to its empirical value. Significantly, the simulated value of λ are now close to what one would expect: zero. This suggests that the C/E model's ability to account for Campbell and Mankiw's estimated number of rule-of-thumb households reflects the implausibly low degree of predictability implied for Δy_t in that model. When the model is modified so that it implies empirically plausible values for $R^2_{\Delta y}$, then it can no longer account for the high estimated value of λ, as asserted by Campbell and Mankiw.[3]

CAN A SIMPLE MEASUREMENT ERROR ARGUMENT BE USED TO DISMISS THE CAMPBELL-MANKIW ESTIMATES? APPARENTLY NOT.

Measurement error is another possible source of distortion to the Campbell-Mankiw estimates. For example, they use the inflation adjusted return on three-month Treasury bills as their measure of r_t. From the perspective of a highly aggregated representative agent model like the C/E model, this seems inappropriate since T-bills are the return on a

---

3. Evidently, the C/E model with serially correlated technology shocks generates $R^2_{\Delta y}$'s which are somewhat *larger* than are observed in the data. I did another Monte Carlo simulation to make sure that the conclusion in the text—that Campbell and Mankiw's estimate of λ is not a statistical artifact—is robust to this. In the simulation I halved ρ_λ, setting it to .1. The results corresponding to λ, θ, $R^2_{\Delta y}$ and "Test of Restrictions" are .091 (.159) [0.0], .790 (.416) [.56], .036 (.037) [.31], and −.01 (.026) [.15], respectively. Evidently, the results are not much different from those reported in the second row of Table A. Moreover, now the simulated $R^2_{\Delta y}$'s are somewhat smaller than the estimated value.

single asset. Presumably, a better measure of r_t would be a weighted average of *all* asset returns. Such a measure would preserve symmetry with the way empirical estimates of other variables in the model are computed. For example, the empirical measure of consumption averages across many heterogeneous consumption goods. In any case, the C/E model has no hope of accounting even for the mean of three-month Treasury bills. Roughly, the average rate of return in the C/E model is 6% annually (3% discount rate + unit risk aversion × 1.88% per capita consumption growth + 1.31% population growth.) This exceeds by far the average return on three-month Treasury bills.

Another source of measurement error in r_t is more conventional, and centers on the calculation of the price index used to deflate r_t. In order to see how measurement error in r_t might affect the results, I simulated the C/E model with serially correlated technology shocks and measurement error. Results appear in the fourth row of Table A. The impact of measurement error can be seen by comparing these results with those in the third row. Doing so, we see that measurement error reduces θ substantially, bringing it close to its estimated value of .089. It also moves the coefficient on disposable income in the right direction. However, that coefficient does not go up by very much, since the *p*-value of the estimated coefficient rises from 0% to only 2%. The other reported characteristics of the Campbell-Mankiw results are well accounted for by the C/E model with serially correlated shocks and measurement error. Apparently it is very hard for the C/E model to account for the high empirical estimate of λ.[4]

Campbell and Mankiw posit the presence of rule-of-thumb households in order to account for the large estimated value of λ. To see why, consider the results based on the CM version of the C/E model with serially correlated technology shocks and measurement errors. These are reported in row five in Table A. There we see that all features,

4. I investigated another possible modification of the C/E model which in principle could account for the large estimate of λ. In this modification the period utility function in (1) is replaced by $\{\ell n(c_t + \alpha g_t) + 6.98\ell n(2190 - n_t)\}$ for $\alpha = \pm .5$. (When $\alpha < 0$, a jump in g_t increases the marginal utility of private consumption, and when $\alpha > 0$, it decreases the marginal utility of private consumption.) Permitting $\alpha \neq 0$ raises the possibility that the statistical role of Δy_t in the Campbell-Mankiw regressions reflects the absence of g_t from the equation. However, it turns out that in practice this omitted variable effect is not quantitatively large. I simulated the C/E model with serially correlated technology shocks with these utility specifications. When $\alpha = .5$, the results corresponding to λ, θ, $R^2_{\Delta y}$ and "Test of Restrictions" were $-.040$ (.134) [0.0], .878 [.92], .103 (.043) [.93], and $-.0175$ (.020) [.16], respectively. When $\alpha = -.5$, the results for λ, θ, $R^2_{\Delta y}$ and "Test of Restrictions" were .020 (.139) [0.0], .767 (.472) [.86], .094 (.451) [.87], $-.016$ (.023) [.13]. Evidently, α negative moves the model in the direction of the empirical results. However, the effect is too small quantitatively to help.

including λ, of the Campbell-Mankiw results are reasonably well accounted for.

In sum, conditional on the model of measurement error, the key problem for the C/E model posed by Campbell and Mankiw's results is the high coefficient on disposable income growth, not the small coefficient on r_t. The measurement error added to r_t is very substantial. In particular, the standard deviation of r_t with and without measurement error is 3.10 (.272) and .665 (.153), respectively (numbers in parentheses are standard deviations across 100 replications.) These numbers—in contrast with all other quantities having a time dimension, which are reported in quarterly terms—are reported in annual terms. Thus the measurement error-ridden rate of return barely resembles r_t, the former having four times the standard deviation of the latter. I do not know whether this is empirically implausible. In any case, the estimated coefficient on Δy_t is too large to be accounted for by the C/E model, and this is enough to reject it.

3. So the C/E Model is False. But is the Campbell-Mankiw Model Any Better?

The first part of this section documents that a version of the C/E model accounts very well for the observed smoothness of consumption, while the introduction of rule-of-thumb households hurts. The second part acknowledges that the C/E's explanation for consumption smoothing rests on certain joint behavior of consumption and asset returns. Although, as suggested in the preceding section, it is by no means obvious how to measure the empirical counterpart of r_t, preliminary calculations reported below suggest the possibility that the joint behavior anticipated by the C/E model is present in the data.

ACCOUNTING FOR LOW ORDER DYNAMICS OF CONSUMPTION OF INCOME DATA

Panel A of Table B reports several characteristics of the low order dynamics of Δc_t and Δy_t as implied by the four versions of the C/E model, as indicated in the first column. Panel B presents the corresponding empirical estimates. There, I use consumption of non-durables and services and disposable labor income. The data are quarterly, real, per capita, and seasonally adjusted, covering the period 1953Q2 to 1984Q4. They are the data used in Blinder and Deaton (1985) and Campbell (1987).[5] In Table B,

5. I am grateful to John Campbell for supplying me with this data.

σ_s, $\rho(\tau)$ denote the standard deviation and τ^{th} order autocorrelation of the variable, s_t, for $\tau = 1,2$.

We evaluate the performance of each model in relation to the empirical results, reported in Panel B of Table B. Note that the C/E model understates the relative volatility of consumption, measured by $\sigma_{\Delta c}/\sigma_{\Delta y}$. In each of the 100 artificial data sets generated by this model, $\sigma_{\Delta c}/\sigma_{\Delta y}$ is less than its empirical counterpart. Also, in view of the discussion about $R^2_{\Delta y}$ in the previous section, it is not surprising thtat the C/E model understates the persistence in Δy_t. Finally, the C/E model overstates the first order autocorrelation in Δc_t.

The second set of three rows shows that the C/E model with persistence in technology growth performs much better empirically. First, this model implies an empirically plausible degree of persistence in Δy_t, as can be seen by inspecting the p-values in the middle set of rows of Panel A, which correspond to $\rho_{\Delta y}(1)$ and $\rho_{\Delta y}(2)$ in Table B. The greater persistence in Δy_t implied by this version of the C/E model reflects the greater persistence in the technology shock in that model. This in turn implies that the wealth effect associated with an innovation in the technology

Table B[1] LOW ORDER DYNAMICS

	$\sigma_{\Delta y}$	$\sigma_{\Delta c}/\sigma_{\Delta y}$	$\rho_{\Delta y}(1)$	$\rho_{\Delta y}(2)$	$\rho_{\Delta c}(1)$	$\rho_{\Delta c}(2)$
Model			Panel A: Simulated Data[2]			
C/E Model with serially correlated technology growth	.0047 (.00031) [0.0]	.500 (.018) [0.0]	.248 (.062) [0.0]	.010 (.101) [.06]	.341 (.075) [.99]	.125 (.119) [.61]
C/E Model with serially correlated technology growth	.013 (.0008) [100.0]	.545 (.026) [.34]	.421 (.063) [.41]	.074 (.108) [.18]	.298 (.099) [.81]	.116 (.130) [.59]
CM Version of C/E Model with serially correlated technology growth	.013 (.0008) [100.0]	.668 (.022) [100.0]	.421 (.063) [.41]	.074 (.108) [.18]	.539 (.060) [100.0]	.161 (.112) [.77]
			Panel B: U.S. Data, 1953Q3–1984Q4			
	.0088	.554	.443	.190	.220	.077

[1]Δs is the first difference of log s. σ_s and $\rho_s(\tau)$ are the standard deviation and τ^{th} order autocorrelation of s, $\tau = 1, 2$. Results are not reported for the C/E model with serially correrlated technology growth *and* measurement error because these coincide with the results in the middle set of rows.
[2]Numbers not in parentheses are averages of the corresponding statistic across 100 artificial data sets generated by the model listed in the first column, while numbers in ( ) are the associated standard deviation. Numbers in [ ] are the frequency of times that simulated results exceed the corresponding empirical parameter value reported in the last row.

shock is greater, thus driving up the relative volatility of consumption. The distribution of $\sigma_{\Delta c}/\sigma_{\Delta y}$ implied by the C/E model contains the empirical value of .554 very close to its central tendency. Inspection of the relevant p-values reveals that the serial persistence pattern for Δc_t implied by this model is also empirically plausible.

Next, we analyze the second moment implications of introducing rule-of-thumb households in the C/E model with serially correlated technology growth. Significantly, one effect is to substantially raise relative consumption volatility. As indicated by the p-value, every simulated value of $\sigma_{\Delta c}/\sigma_{\Delta y}$ exceeds the empirical value of .554. Introduction of rule-of-thumb households also has the effect of driving $\rho_{\Delta c}(1)$ implausibly high. In particular, every simulated value of $\rho_{\Delta c}(1)$ exceeds the empirical value of .220. Of course, in this context rule-of-thumb households have no impact on the dynamics of Δy_t since disposable income is double what it is in the C/E model with serially correlated technology growth. This doubling has no effect after logging and first differencing.[6]

Note from the numbers in the column marked $\sigma_{\Delta y}$ that the amount of volatility in output in each model economy differs substantially from its empirical counterpart. This may reflect problems with my method of parameterizing the time aggregated version of the C/E models. In any event, this should act like a scale effect and probably does not affect the remaining results in Table A and B.

THE ROLE OF ASSET RETURNS AND TIME AGGREGATION IN THE C/E MODEL'S EXPLANATION OF CONSUMPTION SMOOTHING

The fact that the C/E model accounts so well for the observed smoothness of consumption may seem puzzling in light of the analysis of Deaton (1985). This is because the C/E model implies both that consumption is about half as volatile as income and that (the log of) measured income is approximately a first order autoregression in first differ-

---

6. To check the robustness of the result that rule-of-thumb households imply too much consumption volatility, I did one additional Monte Carlo simulation. Here I introduced the rule-of-thumb households into the C/E version of the model, i.e., the one in which ρ_λ = 0. I obtained the following results − $\sigma_{\Delta y}$: .0047 (.0003) [100.0], $\sigma_{\Delta c}/\sigma_{\Delta y}$: .730 (.0085) [100.0], $\rho_{\Delta y}(1)$: .248 (.062) [0.0], $\rho_{\Delta y}(2)$: .010 (.101) [.06], $\rho_{\Delta c}(1)$: .276 (.065) [.79], $\rho_{\Delta c}(2)$: .044 (.106) [.57]. Evidently, this model implies even more volatile consumption. Algebraically, this increased volatility must be due to an increase in $\sigma_{\Delta c}$, since $\sigma_{\Delta y}$ is unaffected by the introduction of rule-of-thumb households. One factor that may account for the increased volatility as ρ_λ falls from .2 to .0 is that the correlation between representative agent households' consumption and disposable income rises with the fall in ρ_λ. In particular, in the C/E model the correlation between Δc_t and Δy_t averages .98 (.0085) across artificial data sets. On the other hand, in the C/E model with serially correlated technology growth the corresponding results are .53 (.069). (Numbers in parentheses are standard deviations.)

ences with autoregressive coefficient roughly .4. Indeed, with this time series representation for income, Deaton would predict that consumption is considerably *more* volatile than income. There are two reasons why consumption is instead predicted to be about half as volatile as income in this model.[7] The first was described in Christiano (1987), and reflects that most of the fluctuations in income in the C/E model reflect the impact of technology shocks. It follows from this and the assumed positive autocorrelation in technology shocks, that jumps in income are typically associated with an increase in the prospective return on investment. The latter factor, which dampens the positive wealth effect of an income shock on consumption, is ignored in Deaton's analysis, which assumes a fixed rate of return on investment. The second reason the C/E model is able to account for the observed smoothness of consumption is that—consistent with Campbell and Mankiw's assumption—the timing interval of the C/E model is assumed to be much finer than the data sampling interval. The measured data simulated from this model, because they have been time averaged, display more persistence than do the data actually observed by the agents in the model.[8]

THERE IS SOME EVIDENCE THAT THE ASSET RETURN MOVEMENTS ANTICIPATED BY THE C/E MODEL ARE PRESENT IN THE DATA

A particular pattern of co-movements between interest rates and consumption and income is at the heart of the C/E model's account of the relative smoothness of consumption. Obviously, the C/E model's explanation for consumption smoothing would be uninteresting if the co-movements it invokes are counterfactual. In addition to Campbell and Mankiw, Hall (1988) and Deaton (1985) argue that there is virtually no association between interest rates and consumption growth. However, each of these authors defines the interest rate as the real return on three-month T-bills. As I have suggested above, this may not be the appropri-

---

7. Deaton measures the relative volatility of consumption as the ratio of the standard deviation of changes in consumption to the standard deviation of the disturbance of a univariate model of income.
8. To see the role of time averaging of data here, consider the simple case in which labor income is a continuous time random walk. Point-in-time samples from this variable will also be a random walk and a Deaton-type analysis will conclude by predicting that consumption ought to be equally volatile as income. On the other hand, if the measured income data are sampled *and* averaged, then Working's (1960) result indicates that measured income changes will be a first order moving average with MA(1) coefficient roughly .265. A Deaton-type calculation based on these data would conclude that consumption ought to be 1.26 times as volatile as income. This reflects that time averaging a continuous time random walk imparts positive slope to the initial part of the impulse response function of the measured data.

ate empirical counterpart for r_t in a highly aggregated model. For this reason I investigated several alternative candidates.

Panel B of Table C reports the correlation between Δc_t and $r_{t-\rho}$ for $\tau = -2, \ldots , 2$ and several empirical measures of r_t, including the three-month T-bill. Apart from the last one, which measures the return on economy-wide capital, each is adjusted for inflation using the CPI. In

Table C   RATE OF RETURN RESULTS

	$Corr(\Delta c_t, r_{t-\tau})^1$						Standard
	$\tau = -2$	$\tau = -1$	$\tau = 0$	$\tau = 1$	$\tau = 2$	Mean, r_t	Deviation, r_t
Model	Panel A: Results Based on Simulated Data						
C/E Model	.524	.563	.533	.262	.185	6.07	.213
	(.064)	(.044)	(.047)	(.115)	(.135)	(.075)	(.047)
C/E Model with ser. corr. tech. growth	.559	.538	.348	.213	.210	5.89	.665
	(.057)	(.057)	(.109)	(.141)	(.135)	(.248)	(.153)
C/E Model with ser. corr. tech. growth and meas. error	.106	.118	.108	.088	.093	5.20	3.10
	(.148)	(.162)	(.177)	(.193)	(.198)	(.494)	(.272)
CM version of C/E Model with ser. corr. tech. and meas. error	.075	.076	.079	.063	.060	5.20	3.10
	(.152)	(.162)	(.176)	(.190)	(.205)	(.494)	(.272)
Return Data	Panel B: Real, Ex Post Returns, U.S. Data, 1953Q3–1984Q4[2]						
S&P 500	−.075	−.010	.262	.244	.099	6.43	25.11
Industrial Bonds	−.046	.052	.177	.175	.151	2.79	3.13
3-Month T-Bills	−.054	.015	.095	.075	.054	1.04	2.55
Corporate Bonds	−.054	.044	.166	.164	.143	2.99	3.19
Economy-wide Capital Stock	.275	.280	.229	.155	.137	5.26	.528

[1]In the simulated data, r_t, is the date t net marginal product of capital, plus measurement error as indicated. In the U.S. data, r_t is the real return on the indicated asset, inclusive of capital gains, adjusted for inflation using the consumer price index. The exception is the return on aggregate capital, which does not include capital gains.
[2]The exception is the return on capital, for which data for the period 1953Q3–1984Q1 were used.

addition, the return on the S&P 500 includes the change in the S&P 500 price index to take into account capital gains. The last yield measure is the most comprehensive in coverage. It is the ratio of a measure of the earnings of capital to the stock of capital. Earnings of capital are measured as GNP minus compensation of employees and proprietor's income, all in real terms. The capital stock covers public and private residential housing, household durables, and public and private plant, equipment, and structures. This measure is documented in Christiano (1988). To place this measure on a net basis, I subtracted, .068, the quarterly measure of capital depreciation estimated in Christiano (1988). I did not adjust this measure of return for capital gains using, say, a measure of the change in the relative price of capital and consumption goods. This would be desirable. Without a doubt, this indicator of the return on capital has severe measurement error. For example, excluding proprietor's income from the numerator surely misses out some earnings to capital. Similarly, measurement problems with the stock of capital have been widely discussed. A measurement problem shared by all five asset returns is that they ignore tax effects. Despite these problems, results based on these measures of r_t are suggestive.

Four things in Panel B of Table C are notable. First, the correlation between Δc_t and $r_{t-\tau}$ is close to zero for all reported values of τ when r_t is measured by the inflation adjusted return on three-month T-bills. At least for $\tau = 0$ the association between Δc_t and r_t is greater for all the other return measures. Second, the correlation between Δc_t and $r_{t-\tau}$ is greater for $\tau > 0$ than for $\tau < 0$ for market measures of return, while the pattern is reversed in the case of the measure of return on capital. Third, the standard deviation of the return on capital is considerably lower than is the standard deviation of the other return measures. This is reported in the last column of Table C, and is expressed in terms of percent per annum. Fourth, it is roughly the case that an asset with a higher correlation with consumption growth also has a higher mean return. Grossman, Melino, and Shiller (1987), who also noted this pattern, interpreted this as qualitative evidence in favor of a representative agent model. This is because the relevant measure of the riskiness of an asset is its correlation with consumption. Greater correlation implies higher riskiness, which therefore requires a higher average return as compensation.

To see how well the four versions of the C/E model account for the empirical relation between Δc_t and r_t, one can compare the results in Panel A with those in Panel B. First note that—not surprisingly—the models with measurement error imply relatively little correlation between Δc_t and $r_{t-\tau}$ for all reported values of τ. They appear consistent with all the results in Panel B. Now consider the first two models in

Panel A, the ones without measurement error in r_t. Of these, it was seen earlier that the second performs better empirically in that it accounts best for the observed relative volatility in consumption and the serial correlation properties of Δc_t and Δy_t. Interestingly, this model also performs better in its implication for the correlation between Δc_t and r_t. For example, the contemporaneous correlation between these two variables is .348 with a large standard deviation: .109. Although all simulated correlations between Δc_t and r_t implied by this model exceed the empirical value of .095 obtained using the three-month T-bill, the other empirical correlations are much closer. In particular, the p-values of the correlation between Δc_t and r_t when the S&P 500, industrial bonds, corporate bonds, and economy-wide capital measures of return are used are .77, .93, .93, and .83, respectively.[9]

Two other interesting features of these results are worth noting. First, the pattern of correlations between Δc_t and $r_{t-\tau}$ follows that exhibited by the results in the last row in Panel B of Table C, with the correlations being larger for $\tau < 0$ than for $\tau > 0$. Second, the standard deviation of the simulated r_t is on the same order of magnitude as that of the empirical return on capital, and much smaller than for the market rates of return.

In sum, the C/E model anticipates a positive association between rates of return and consumption growth. Several (admittedly crude) measures of rates of return suggest that that positive association may also be present in the data. This suggests the possibility that the interest rate argument implicit in the C/E's account for consumption smoothing may be on the mark. These results are obviously only suggestive at best and certainly far from definitive, since they use very crude empirical measures of r_t. Further research to develop better empirical measures of r_t is required. In addition a further study of these issues ought to consider variations in model parameters. For example, simulations in Christiano (Tables 5–7, 1989) suggest that increasing risk aversion reduces the correlation between consumption growth and the interest rate, while not substantially affecting the implications for the relative volatility of consumption.

4. Concluding Remarks

I have made two points. First, it is hard to make the case that the statistical relation between the forecastable components of consump-

9. Hansen and Singleton (1983) also find that a representative agent model with preferences like those used here performs better empirically when r_t is measured by the S&P 500 than by the three-month T-bill.

tion growth, income growth, and interest rates found by Campbell and Mankiw is spurious. I reach this conclusion after ruling out the possibility that the results reflect one kind of measurement error or bias in their econometric technique. Second, Campbell and Mankiw have not yet made a convincing case that this statistical relation warrants the inference that 50% of disposable income goes to rule-of-thumb consumers. One needs to have a sense of what the other implications of this assumption are first. Not enough detail is provided in the paper to make a judgment about this. I report calculations which suggest that the implications on other dimensions may be quantitatively large. I show that a version of the Christiano-Eichenbaum (1988) representative agent model accounts well for the observed smoothness of consumption relative to income. However, introducing rule-of-thumb households into that model raises its implied relative volatility of comsumption to a counterfactually high level.

There is another reason for being cautious about accepting the Campbell-Mankiw rule-of-thumb model. If one accepts their estimate that 50% of disposable income goes to rule-of-thumb consumers, then there is a puzzle as to why time series data imply so many rule-of-thumb households, while micro data studies (e.g., Hall and Mishkin [1982] and Runkle [1983] imply that the number is much smaller, if not zero. One possibility is that the Campbell-Mankiw rule-of-thumb model is misspecified. One particularly suspicious feature of that model is its assumption that the fraction of total disposable income going to rule-of thumb households is constant. An alternative model which does not have this property posits that a fraction of the population has no capital and is shut out of credit markets. Because of this they face a static consumption/leisure choice each period. They are rule-of-thumb households in the sense that they set consumption to disposable income period by period. The other part of the population, which owns the capital, faces a non-trivial dynamic optimization problem. (For details about a model like this, see Danthine and Donaldson [1989]). One expects that in this model the fraction of economy-wide disposable income going to rule-of-thumb households would vary in a systematic way. It would be of interest to see whether such an economy, with a relatively small fraction of rule-of-thumb households and with a reasonable amount of intertemporal substitution in consumption, could account for the Campbell-Mankiw empirical regularity.

Revised version of comments presented to NBER Annual Conference on Macroeconomics. The conference was organized by Olivier J. Blanchard and Stanley S. Fischer, and held on March 10 and 11, in Cambridge, Massachusetts. I gratefully acknowledge helpful conversations with Dave Backus and Fumio Hayashi.

REFERENCES

Blinder, Alan S., and Angus Deaton. 1985. "The Time Series Consumption Function Revisited." Brookings Papers on Economic Activity, 2.

Campbell, John Y. 1987. "Does Saving Anticipate Declining Labor Income? An Alternative Test of the Permanent Income Hypothesis." Econometrica 55:1249–73. November.

Campbell, John Y., and N. Gregory Mankiw. 1987. "Permanent Income, Current Income, and Consumption." Princeton University, Woodrow Wilson School. October.

Christiano, Lawrence J. 1987. "Is Consumption Insufficiently Sensitive to Innovations in Income?" American Economic Review Papers and Proceedings. Vol. 77, No. 2. May.

Christiano, Lawrence J. 1988. "Why Does Inventory Investment Fluctuate So Much?" Journal of Monetary Economics. 21 2/3 (March/May) 247–80.

Christiano, Lawrence J. 1989. "Solving a Particular Growth Model by Linear Quadratic Approximation and by Value Function Iteration." Institute for Empirical Macroeconomics, Federal Reserve Bank of Minneapolis. Discussion Paper 9.

Christiano, Lawrence J. and Martin Eichenbaum. 1988. "Is Theory Really Ahead of Measurement? Current Real Business Cycle Theories and Aggregate Labor Market Fluctuations." NBER Working paper number 2700. September.

Danthine, Jean-Pierre, and John B. Donaldson. 1989. "Risk Sharing Labor Contracts and the Business Cycle." Columbia University. Manuscript.

Deaton, Angus. 1985. "Life-cycle Models of Consumption: Is the Evidence Consistent with the Theory?" presented at the Fifth World Congress of the Econometric Society, Cambridge, Mass. August.

Grossman, S. J., A. Melino, and R. J. Shiller. 1987. "Estimating the Continuous-Time Consumption-Based Asset-Pricing Model. Journal of Business and Economic Statistics. Vol. 5, No. 3. July.

Hall, R. E., and F. S. Mishkin. 1982. "The Sensitivity of Consumption to Transitory Income: Estimates from Panel Data on Households." Econometrica 50: 461–81.

Hansen, Lars Peter and Kenneth J. Singleton. 1983. "Stochastic Consumption, Risk Aversion, and the Temporal Behavior of Asset Returns." Journal of Political Economy. Vol. 91, No. 2.

Mankiw, N. Gregory and Matthew D. Shapiro. 1985. "Trends, Random Walks and Tests of the Permanent Income Hypothesis." Journal of Monetary Economics 16:165–74.

Nelson, Charles R. and Richard Startz. 1988. "The Distribution of the Instrumental Variables Estimator and its t-Ratio When the Instrument is a Poor One." University of Washington. Discussion Paper 88-07. May.

Runkle, David. 1983. "Liquidity Constraints and the Permanent Income Hypothesis: Evidence from Panel Data." Brown University.

Sargent, Thomas J. 1987. Macroeconomic Theory, 2nd edition, Academic Press.

Working, Holbrook. 1960. "Note on the Correlation of First Differences of Averages in a Random Chain." Econometrica 28:916–18. October.

Comment

ALBERT ANDO

1. Lucas's Critique and the Euler Equation Approach

Before I comment on the substantive content of the paper by Campbell and Mankiw directly, I wish to say a few words about the so-called Euler equation approach to the study of savings by households.

As Campbell and Mankiw say in their paper, the development of this approach was in response to Lucas's critique of econometric policy evaluation. Lucas's critique emphasized the point that behavioral equations in most econometric models were decision rules of a group of economic agents, and usually contained explicitly or implicitly a specification of how expectations of future values for some critical variables are generated. Such procedure for the formation of expectations is, however, dependent on the characteristics of the environment, and in particular, it is subject to change when the policy rules of the government, which form a part of the environment in which economic agents must operate, are changed. Hence, any evaluation of the effects of policy changes without allowing for changes in the expectation formation procedures are subject to biases and not to be trusted.

In a narrow sense, the Euler equation approach is a proper response to Lucas's critique, since in this approach the rational expectations hypothesis is explicitly incorporated so that any significant changes in the environment are automatically reflected in the expectations formation procedure. On the other hand, so long as changes in the behavioral equations in question are very small in response to a change in the policy rule, the biases in the evaluation of policies pointed out by Lucas will also remain small (Sims, 1982 and 1986). In order to formulate the Euler equation approach, we must assume that the synthetic optimization behavior of a single, representative agent is a good approximation to the collective behavior of the whole population of households. In particular, we must assume that the collective preference ordering of all households over time can be represented by a time invariant utility function of a single representative agent. This is surely very unlikely to be the case, given the difficulties of aggregating preferences well known in the literature, unless the preference ordering of all households happens to be identical. If preferences are not identical, then the aggregate preference ordering (that is, the preference ordering of the representative agent) either cannot exist, or, if it exists at all, it will be subject to substantial changes over time, and therefore subject to Lucas's critique in the wider sense.

We can obtain some feel of how similar the consumption behavior of various groups is, and hence whether or not all groups can be presumed to be acting according to a common preference ordering. In Table A, I present the pattern of the net worth-permanent income ratio by age of the head of the household and by percentiles on the distribution of permanent income, based on the data from Survey of Consumer Finance conducted by the Board of Governors of the Federal Reserve System in 1983. A number of questions might be raised about the procedure followed in generating this table, especially in estimating "permanent income" for each household, but I do not believe that the basic conclusion for the purposes of the present discussion is dependent on such details. The pattern of savings and asset accumulation varies very significantly among age groups and also depends on the household's position in the distribution of permanent income. Therefore, the presumption of common preference ordering among all households cannot be maintained, and the description of the aggregate data based on a single representative consumer is of doubtful value. As the age structure of the population changes or the distribution of income changes over time, the Euler's equation for the representative agent must also change, and the procedure is subject to Lucas's critique as much as the consumption decision rule involving some fixed expectation formation procedure.

The advocate of the Euler equation approach may appeal to the "as if" methodology of Milton Friedman, and say that the empirical validity of the assumptions does not matter, and the test of the theory must be exclusively based on the empirical validity of its market implications. I do not accept this proposition. If we do not make some mistake in our derivation, the assumptions and the implications of a theory should be logically equivalent, and whichever are easier to check against data must be utilized. In the case under discussion, the assumptions are much easier to test than the implications.

2. Effects of Current Income

I now turn to specific results reported in the paper by Campbell and Mankiw. Given that we are working within the framework of the Euler equation approach, I like the formulation of the authors. The original formulation of Hall and most subsequent implementations do not specify the alternative hypothesis, so that when the simple version of the permanent income hypothesis is rejected, the rejection does not suggest where the difficulties are and what other possibilities should be investigated, while in the Campbell-Mankiw formulation, we have an alternative which can be elaborated and further investigated. Furthermore, I

Table A   NET WORTH—PERMANENT INCOME RATIO'S BY AGE CLASS AND PERMANENT INCOME CLASS [1]

Permanent Income Percentile

Age Group	0 to 5	6 to 10	11 to 25	26 to 50	51 to 75	76 to 90	91 to 95	96 to 99	100	all
0 to 25	0.39	1.57	0.32	0.99	0.44	0.42	0.29	0.59	1.19	0.62
	17	18	55	90	90	53	17	14	4	358
	18.6	19.9	58.3	98.3	97.9	58.4	19.5	15.6	4.5	390.9
26 to 35	3.13	1.59	1.79	1.70	1.60	1.47	1.52	2.18	1.76	1.73
	44	45	132	218	216	126	43	37	14	875
	46.7	46.5	140.9	235.3	234.3	140.4	48.0	37.0	10.0	939.1
36 to 45	5.78	3.05	3.42	2.55	3.45	3.56	3.29	4.97	7.86	3.43
	35	35	104	169	171	102	36	53	40	745
	37.4	38.3	113.8	190.1	187.7	114.0	37.5	31.4	7.6	759.7
46 to 55	16.64	5.07	4.63	5.71	4.05	7.01	7.06	16.81	18.97	6.48
	29	30	88	141	149	86	36	76	40	675
	31.0	32.9	96.0	159.6	160.5	95.4	32.6	26.1	6.5	640.6
56 to 60	15.56	3.33	8.64	6.98	7.25	9.73	10.10	15.33	18.83	8.59
	14	14	41	65	66	42	18	43	24	327
	14.8	14.5	44.8	74.0	74.0	44.3	15.0	12.9	3.2	298.5

Age	Measure										
61 to 65	Wealth/income	52.11	10.68	7.21	7.22	8.20	9.19	14.02	26.38	18.60	11.40
	Sample	15	13	40	67	68	41	18	48	23	333
	Weighted	15.1	14.9	45.3	75.2	75.7	45.1	15.1	12.1	3.2	301.7
66 to 70	Wealth/income	34.42	14.85	7.06	8.43	7.40	9.81	15.27	18.55	30.29	10.71
	Sample	11	11	36	60	59	33	18	34	15	277
	Weighted	12.4	12.2	39.2	63.9	64.9	38.2	13.1	10.6	2.6	257.1
71 to 75	Wealth/income	31.61	17.64	4.36	9.39	9.46	8.63	12.27	5.36	27.96	10.19
	Sample	8	10	25	42	43	26	11	11	15	191
	Weighted	8.6	9.9	27.7	46.8	46.5	27.5	10.1	7.6	1.9	186.7
75 and over	Wealth/income	4.68	26.88	5.34	7.99	6.48	5.61	4.37	10.40	32.33	7.83
	Sample	11	11	33	52	52	32	11	13	19	234
	Weighted	11.4	12.4	36.2	59.4	60.6	36.0	12.8	9.5	2.6	240.8
All	Wealth/income	13.53	6.37	4.00	4.40	4.17	4.95	5.77	9.45	12.87	5.27
	Sample	184	187	554	904	914	541	208	329	194	4015
	Weighted	196.0	201.6	602.3	1003.4	1004.1	599.2	203.7	162.9	42.0	4015.0

Top: Wealth to permanent income ratio.
Middle: Sample size.
Bottom: Weighted sample size.
[a]Data from *Survey of Consumer Finance*, Federal Reserve Board, 1983, and estimates prepared by Scott Hoyt.

find the basic result obtained by Campbell and Mankiw to be broadly consistent with results that some of us often encounter working with micro data; namely, that only one-half to two-thirds of households behave according to the permanent income hypothesis, while the remaining one-third to one-half respond to current income.

We must, however, be cautious in interpreting the results like the ones reported in Table 1 of their paper. The authors are saying that equation (1.4) is obtained by summing (1.3) and the equation given on the second line at the top of page 188 of their paper, and hence the estimated coefficient λ in equation (1.4) must be the properly weighted average of the coefficients applicable to the two groups, namely, zero and unity. There are a number of fairly strict conditions under which the expected value of the estimated parameter using aggregated data would in fact turn out to be such a weighted average, and we must pay careful attention to such conditions (Theil, 1954).

In order to assess how robust the results reported in their Table 1 may be, we may ask ourselves what mechanisms may be present that would make current consumption a function of past events such as ΔC_{t-i}, $i \geq 2$, given C_{t-1}. Any gradual adjustment process may cause such a correlation, and even though the authors are dealing with non-durables and services, there are prime examples of slowly adjusting items among consumption goods. Income contains many different components. When the weight for some income component, such as social security benefits, increases over time during the sample period, some biases in the estimate of λ can easily be introduced, especially if this component behaves differently from the rest.

I wish to deal explicitly with one possible mechanism that may create biases in the estimate of λ. According to the life cycle theory as distinct from the permanent income hypothesis, the consumption needs of families are critically dependent on the age of the family. The earnings pattern over life is also known to be a significantly dependent on age. Therefore, both aggregate consumption and aggregate income are dependent on the age distribution of population, and hence, if the age distribution has been changing over time during the sample period, this may generate the positive correlation between ΔC and ΔY even when the instrumental variables procedure is used.

I have conducted a quick experiment to see if there is any indication suggesting that this consideration is significant. In Table B, I report a slight modification of one of the estimates reported in Table 1 of the Campbell-Mankiw paper. Row 1 of Table B corresponds to Row 8 of Campbell-Mankiw, except that I drop $c_{t-2} - y_{t-2}$ from the list of instruments. Actually, this was an oversight on my part, but it makes little difference to the point that I wish to make. For Row 2 of Table B, I introduce a set of age compositions variables, both as instruments and as regressors. The estimate of the weight λ is reduced substantially, although none of the coefficients for the population composition variables is significant. The lack of significance is not surprising in view of the fact that the linear introduction of the age composition variables is not really appropriate, but the result is suggestive in that the presence of these variables even in this crude form appears to have an important effect in the coefficient of ΔY.

This result is more or less consistent with Table A and suggestive of the significance of the age composition of the population. In order to estimate the effect of age composition, a much more precise formulation must be undertaken.

3. *Consumption Income Ratio and the Expected Growth of Income*

I now turn to the novel attempt by Campbell and Mankiw to look at the consumption decision rule rather than the Euler equation. The basic non-linearity of the budget constraint that they refer to arises because they focus their attention on the random character of the rate of return. There is little question that the rate of return in reality is a random variable. Does a typical consumer, however, really optimize in the context of such a complex formulation of his environment? And, if so, can such a sophisticated consumer really be characterized by an infinite horizon, symmetric and separable utility functions?

Modigliani thought otherwise. He thought that the savings-income ratio was positively related to the rate of growth of income. His reason-

Table B   EFFECTS OF INTRODUCING SHIFTS IN AGE COMPOSITION OF POPULATION ADDENDUM TO CAMPBELL-MANKIW TABLE 1

				Coefficients of		
	Instrument	λ*Estimate*	*N20*	*N25*	*N45*	*N65*
Row 1	$\Delta y_{t-2}, \Delta y_{t-3}, \Delta y_{t-4}$ $\Delta c_{t-2}, \Delta c_{t-3}, \Delta c_{t-4}$	.455 (.123)				
Row 2	$\Delta y_{t-2}, \Delta y_{t-3}, \Delta y_{t-3}, \Delta y_{t-4}$ $\Delta c_{t-2}, \Delta c_{t-3}, \Delta c_{t-4}$ N20, N25, N45, N65	.386 (.131)	.025 (.221)	+.020 (.116)	+.041 (.203)	+.110 (.226)

N20: The ratio of population aged 20–24 to population 16 and over
N25: The ratio of population aged 25–44 to population 16 and over
N45: The ratio of population aged 45–64 to population 16 and over
N65: The ratio of population aged 65 and over to the population 16 and over

ing was based on the assumption that the relative age pattern of consumption observed in the micro data represented, to a large extent, the preferred pattern of consumption, independent of the size or the life pattern of income, including the dissavings by retired families (Modigliani, 1966, 1970, and 1980).

For a few countries for which there are data covering long periods of time, the savings-income ratio tends to be very stable. In one case, Japan, the savings rate during the 1950–85 period when the growth rate was very high was distinctly higher than the years before World War II when Japan's growth rate was lower. The cross country correlation between the savings rate and the rate of growth of output appears to be very strong and positive (Modigliani 1970). Thus, the finding by Campbell and Mankiw that these two ratios are actually negatively correlated in the U.S. came as a surprise to me.

I then realized that they are working with the NIA definition of disposable income during a period when the rate of inflation varied quite significantly. Since the NIA definition of disposable income includes nominal interest flows while it does not adjust for real capital gains or losses in nominally fixed assets and liabilities due to inflation, it contains an inflation bias. One may argue exactly which assets and liabilities may be subject to this bias, but my experience with this subject suggests that the results of the correction do not depend on the choice of assets within reason. I have supposed that corporation and financial institutions are a veil for this purpose, and taken government debt outside the government (alternatively, government debt in private hands plus currency plus reserves at the FRB) as the quantity subject to real capital loss by households, and made a rough correction based on this assumption. The resulting changes in the savings-income ratio is shown in Table C. Column (3) is the savings-income ratio before the correction, and column (7) is the ratio after the correction. We can see that the savings rate during the period between the 1950s and 1980s is virtually constant for the corrected ratio except for the very low rate for the 1980s. It is unlikely that we get any relationship between column (7) and the rate of growth of income.

It is also useful to remember the accounting identity. For the household sector of the economy, we have

$$s \equiv g_a\, a$$

where s is the savings-income ratio, g_a is the rate of growth of net worth, and a is the ratio of net worth to income. For the U.S., a is very stable over time so that, except for very short-run fluctuations, the rate of growth of net worth, g_a, is very close to the rate of growth of income, g. Therefore, in order for s to be negatively related to g, in view of the above identity, the net worth-income ratio must move inversely with the rate of growth of income very sharply. That is, when the growth rate rises by 20% from .015 to .018 per year, the net worth-income ratio must decline much more than 20% in order for the saving-income ratio to decline, except in very short-run fluctuations of one or two years. This seems very implausible to me.

4. Stability of the Relationship Between Consumption and Income

I began this note by suggesting that Lucas's critique should be more broadly understood and that the basic question is how stable and reliable the critical macro relationships are over time, especially when some conditions in the economy including major policy rules of the government change. I suggested that this question must be an empirical one. In the case of consumption-savings behavior of the household, I expressed my skepticism of a single representative agent model on the basis of micro data indicating that the behavior of different groups of households, for example, age groups and groups defined by relative positions in the income distribution, appears to be very different from each other.

In the older literature, a number of investigators found that the relationship between consumption and some combination of income and wealth seemed to be quite stable over time. We have always known that

Table C   AGGREGATE SAVINGS/INCOME RATIO FOR U.S. HOUSEHOLDS NIA DEFINITION AND INFLATION ADJUSTMENTS

	(1) YD$	(2) S$	(3) S$/YD$	(4) Inflation Adjustment	(5) (1)–(4)	(6) (2)–(4)	(7) (6)/(5)
1953	255.1	18.4	7.2	4.4	250.7	14.0	5.6
1954	260.5	16.4	6.3	1.2	259.3	15.2	5.6
1955	278.8	16.0	5.8	4.5	274.3	11.5	4.2
1960	358.9	20.8	5.8	6.7	252.2	14.1	5.6
1965	486.8	34.3	7.0	7.2	479.6	27.1	5.7
1970	715.6	57.7	8.1	16.7	698.9	41.0	5.8
1975	1142.8	104.6	9.2	44.5	1098.3	60.1	5.5
1980	1918.0	136.9	7.1	88.1	1829.9	48.7	2.7
1985	2838.7	125.4	4.4	64.3	2774.4	61.1	2.2

(1): NIA Table 2–1, Line 25
(2): NIA Table 2–1, Line 30
(3): MPS Model Data File, (Government Dept Outside Government and Outside Fed + Currency + Reserves) Inflation Rate (Consumption Component of GNP Deflator).

such an empirical relationship is subject to serious questions, and the causality may be running from consumption to income rather than income to consumption. In recent years, we have not paid attention to this formulation, but I have taken this occasion to quickly review the history of this type of relationship. I am rather impressed that the stability of this relationship appears to persist for a very long time. In Table D, I reproduce some of this history, covering the period from 1900 to 1987 divided into three segments and excluding the major war years.

First, the results of the regression in level form are almost identical for all three sub-periods, in spite of the differences in the quality of the data and the fact that for the two earlier periods, income is represented by labor income after taxes while for the last period it is total income after taxes (the coefficient of Y for the last period is therefore somewhat smaller), and for the earlier two periods annual average data were used

Table D   RELATION BETWEEN CONSUMPTION AND INCOME

1. OLS Estimate of Consumption − Income + Wealth Relation 1953–II—1987–I
   1a. Level Regression
   $$C = .714\ Y + .055\ W - .589$$
   $$\quad\ (.020)\quad\ (.005)\quad\ (.078)$$
   $R^2 = .995 \qquad DW = .25$
   1b. Regression of 1st difference in logs
   $$\Delta ln\ C = .307\ \Delta lnY + .094\ \Delta lnW + .003$$
   $$\qquad\ (.041)\qquad\ (.026)\qquad\ (.0004)$$
   $R^2 = .43 \qquad DW = 1.92$
   $R^2 = .43 \qquad DW = 1.92$

2. Ando-Modigliani Estimates (1963)
   2a. Annual Data for 1929–59 excluding 1941–46
   $$C = .75\ YL + .042\ W + 8.1$$
   $$\quad (.05)\qquad (.009)\qquad (1.0)$$
   $R^2 = .948 \qquad DW = 1.26$
   $$\Delta C = .52\ \Delta YL + .072\Delta W$$
   $$\quad (.16)\qquad (.018)$$
   $R^2 = .929 \qquad DW = 1.85$
   2b. Annual Data for 1900–1928 excluding 1917–19
   $$C = .76\ YL + .073\ W$$
   $$\quad (.13)\qquad (.020)$$
   $R^2 = .995 \qquad DW = 1.63$
   $$\Delta C = .73\Delta YL + .047\Delta W$$
   $$\quad (1.8)\qquad (.037)$$
   $R^2 = .44 \qquad DW = 2.48$

while for the last period quarterly data were used. If annual data were used for the last period, estimates would have been about the same, but the DW statistics would have been considerably larger.

It also turns out that the results using data in first difference form are very similar to the level regression for the first two periods. For the most recent period, I present the result using data in the form of the first difference of logarithms, but if the appropriate transformation is carried out to get an approximate linear form, the result in the level and the result in the first differences are similar.

These results are subject to all the well known objections to the naive formulation and estimation procedure, and hence we must view them as merely suggestive rather than as a strong evidence for any well formulated hypothesis. See, however, the proximity theory of Wold (1953) and Fisher (1961). We can improve the quality of the result and strengthen the stability of the result over time by recognizing that income and wealth both contain a number of different components and they should be treated somewhat differently, by smoothing short-term fluctuations of income by some filtering procedure to approximate a longer-term normal income, and by recognizing that the coefficients are functions of the age distribution of the population and hence they should be allowed to change in response to the changing age distribution over time. The proximity theorem would then apply to these results with even more force.

Some of us thought that the formulation like the one presented in Table D was a unique implication of the life cycle theory. It turns out, however, that they can be derived almost equally well from very different theories, so in this context I am reporting them merely as a surprisingly stable empirical relationship, not as an implication of any particular theory. On the other hand, I should point out that the stability of the result persisted over a long period in which very radical changes in government policies toward households took place. At the beginning of the period, there was no income tax and the Federal Reserve System did not exist. Given that the relationship retained its stability in spite of all these changes, if this relation formed a part of the model used to analyze policy changes that did take place during this period, this relationship would not have caused any apparent bias in the results.

In an ideal world, we should begin with a description of the individual household's behavior based on micro data, allowing for critical and significant differences among various groups, and go through the detailed aggregation process to arrive at aggregate behavioral functions. In the process, we have some knowledge of properties that aggregate relationships must satisfy, such as the one described in this section and perhaps the one Campbell and Mankiw described in their Table 1. We then have a much better understanding of the source of these relationships that persist over time, and we can judge with more confidence under what conditions persistent relationships will remain stable.

In such an effort to understand the behavior of households combining information from the micro and macro data together, on the macro side, we have come to focus our attention completely on the result obtained from the Euler equation approach to the exclusion of the type of information reported in this section, quoting Lucas's critique as the authority. I believe that we have gone too far, and that judicious attention to all information, especially to those relationships that have survived over very long periods of time under a number of different conditions in several countries, would be essential if we are to make really significant progress in our attempt to improve our knowledge of household behavior.

REFERENCES

Ando, A., and F. Modigliani. 1963. "The 'Life Cycle' Hypothesis of Saving: Aggregate Implications and Tests." *American Economic Review.* March 1963. pp. 55–84.

Fisher, F. M. 1961. "On the Cost of Approximate Specification in Simultaneous Equations Estimation." *Econometrica* 29. pp. 139–70.

Modigliani, F. 1966. "The Life Cycle Hypothesis of Saving, the Demand for Wealth and the Supply of Capital." *Social Research*, 3.3, Summer 1966. pp. 160–217; and *Collected Papers of Franco Modigliani.* Vol. 2. Andrew Abel, ed. Cambridge Mass., MIT Press. 1980. pp. 323–81.

Modigliani, F. 1970. "The Life Cycle Hypothesis of Savings and Intercountry Differences in the Savings Ratio." *Induction, Growth & Trade.* Essays in Honor of Sir Roy Harrod. M. FG. Scott, J. M. Wolpe, and W. Eltis, eds. pp. 197–225, Oxford: Clarendon Press. 1970; and *Collected Papers of Franco Modigliani.* Vol. 2, Andrew Abel, ed. Cambridge, Mass. MIT Press, 1980. pp. 382–414.

Modigliani, F. 1980. "Utility Analysis and Aggregate Consumption Function: An Attempt at Integration." An earlier unpublished manuscript in *Collected Papers of Franco Modigliani.* Vol. 2, Andrew Abel, ed. Cambridge Mass. MIT Press, 1980, pp. 128–97.

Sims, C. 1982. "Policy Analysis with Econometric Models." *Brookings Papers on Economic Activity.* 1:1982, pp. 107–64.

Sims, C. 1986. "Are Forecasting Models Usable for Policy Analysis?" Federal Reserve Bank of Minneapolis *Quarterly Review.* Winter 1986. pp. 2–16.

Theil, H. 1954. *Linear Aggregation of Economic Relations.* Amsterdam: North Holland Publishing Co.

Wold, H. 1953. *Demand Analysis: A Study in Econometrics.* New York: John Wiley. In association with L. Jureen.

Discussion

Mankiw noted that Christiano's implied regressions yielded much poorer first stage regressions than those found by the authors and that interest rate mismeasurement does not matter for the results. He also questioned whether "rule-of-thumb" consumers make Ando's inflation-adjustment to income.

Bob Hall objected that Campbell and Mankiw had set up a "straw man" version of the random walk hypothesis by not taking into account the effects of liquidity constraints. He further stated that Campbell and Mankiw had used the identifying restriction that there are no random consumption components. He argued that if such components exists, they cause spontaneous movement in output, which would be correlated with the instruments used by Campbell and Mankiw. They do not, he argued, establish the direction of causation and yet take a strong stand on the results. In addition, Hall suggested that Campbell and Mankiw should use additional measures of rates of return.

Mankiw responded that there is large variation in post-war real interest rates. Further, the authors had tried "truly exogenous" instruments to account for taste shocks, but the results were insignificant. Theory suggests that such instruments may be poor in small samples.

Kevin Murphy asked whether the estimated coefficient of zero on the interest rate was evidence of bad instrumental variables or zero intertemporal substitution. Bill Nordhaus questioned whether there is measurement error in consumption since the theory applies to utility. Consumption ignores durables, such as housing services consumed. Further, lagged variables would not be good instruments if durables are included. Mankiw responded that since durable goods follow a random walk, that would not affect the estimate.

Kevin M. Murphy, Andrei Shleifer, and Robert W. Vishny
UNIVERSITY OF CHICAGO GRADUATE SCHOOL OF BUSINESS

Building Blocks of Market Clearing Business Cycle Models

---

1. Introduction

This paper discusses market clearing real business cycle models. In these models, economic fluctuations are characterized by movements along a stable labor supply curve. As a result, real wages and labor input both move together with output. Although the procyclical behavior of real wages has been debated, the current consensus seems to be that real wages are moderately procyclical (Bils 1985; Kydland and Prescott 1988; Solon and Barsky 1988).

There are four separate classes of explanations of procyclical real wages in a decentralized market clearing framework. In the first three explanations, labor productivity is procyclical, and real wages follow productivity. These three explanations can be summarized by writing the production function:

$$y(t) = \gamma(t)\, F(K(t), L(t)), \quad (1)$$

where γ is the technological shock, K is the capital, L is labor, and y is output at time t. Labor productivity at time t can be high if either (a) the productivity shock γ is high at time t, or (b) the capital stock is high at time t, or (c) the labor input is high at time t, and production function exhibits increasing returns to scale. The first explanation of high productivity in booms drives the real business cycle theories of Kydland and Prescott (1982), Long and Plosser (1983), and Prescott (1986). The second explanation is the basis of models in which booms result from increases in the capital stock. Shleifer (1986) and Kiyotaki (1988) present examples of such models where increasing returns help generate endogenous fluctuations, but the driving force behind output fluctuations over time is really the changes in the capital stock. The third explanation of procyclical productivity is increasing returns in the form of declining marginal cost, either at an industry or an economy-wide level. Murphy, Shleifer, and Vishny (1988) is an example of such a model.

Procyclical productivity is not the only way to generate procyclical real wages; countercyclical markups of price over cost also give this result. In some models (Phelps and Winter 1970; Okun 1981; Stiglitz 1984; Bils 1986), demand becomes less elastic during recessions, perhaps because customers with elastic demand leave the market, and so optimal markups rise. In other models (Weitzman 1982; Solow 1984; Hammour 1988), markets are monopolistically competitive and the price is tied to the average cost which falls in a larger market. As a result, markups fall in the boom and real wages are procyclical. In yet another approach (Rotemberg and Saloner 1986), competition between oligopolists intensifies and markups fall in a boom. In all these models—whether or not they assume increasing returns—procyclical real wages result from countercyclical markups and not from procyclical marginal productivity. These models should be distinguished from those with real wages driven by procyclical productivity.

In this paper, we focus on the comparison of increasing returns (IR) and technological shock (TS) real business cycle models. We spend relatively little time on models driven by changes in the capital stock. Although additions to the capital stock probably raise productivity in the later stages of the boom, capital stock changes cannot explain all of the business cycle, particularly productivity movements during periods and in sectors of no capacity addition. We also do not spend much time on countercyclical markup stories, although we do find them attractive. The main reason for this omission is that our own work has focused on IR models. We also do not deal with models that do not fit into the market clearing framework. Some of the relevant papers (Roberts 1987; Heller 1986) replace perfectly functioning markets with market games; others (Cooper and Haltiwanger 1989) present centrally planned allocations. Finally, we do not focus on models where prices are rigid or costly to change; these models have been surveyed by Rotemberg (1987).

In comparing TS and IR models, we stress that the building blocks that are likely to make these two approaches work are similar, even though the sources of productivity movements are very different. In particular, we identify durable goods, elastic labor supply, specialized labor, and imperfect credit as key assumptions needed to make these models consistent with stylized facts. Although we occasionally criticize existing TS models, our main task is to argue that these models have many implications and require assumptions similar to business cycle models with increasing returns.

To fix ideas, in section 2 we present a simple 1-sector IR model based on Murphy, Shleifer, and Vishny (1988) and describe its similarities to and differences from the standard TS model. The emphasis in that section is on the importance of durable goods for generating large output fluctuations without large changes in productivity. The section also shows that business cycles almost *have to* arise in a model with increasing returns, durable goods, and elastic labor supply. We conclude that the 1-sector IR model can generate the same essential predictions as the TS model, and is consistent with a broader range of evidence.

Although most research on real business cycles has focused on a 1-sector model, one of the crucial empirical challenges is to explain the significant amount of co-movement of labor inputs and outputs in different sectors. In Section 3, we first document this co-movement over the business cycle. We then suggest that the TS literature has not adequately explained co-movement, even though this step is necessary to generate aggregate fluctuations from sectoral productivity shocks. Finally, we show how two assumptions—immobility of labor across sectors and imperfect capital markets—help generate co-movement in both TS and IR models. To stress the similarities between the two approaches, we use a TS model to make many of the arguments we previously made in Murphy, Shleifer, and Vishny (1988). The upshot of Section 3 is that with immobile labor and imperfect capital markets TS and IR models can be extended to many sectors.

In Section 4, we deal with the crucial ingredient of both the IR and the TS models: elastic labor supply. We discuss some plausible and implausible reasons why the assumption of elastic labor supply might be valid and the relevance of micro-econometric evidence for this debate.

In Section 5 we present some evidence on the behavior of relative prices over the business cycle. We find that the relative prices of finished goods are much less procyclical than those of raw materials and intermediate goods. Among finished goods, durables appear to have countercyclical relative prices. Finally, output prices are strongly countercyclical relative to input prices. Our evidence for the postwar period basically replicates the findings of Mills (1936) and Means et al. (1939) for the Great Depression, except that real wages in the postwar period have been procyclical and in the 1930s they were countercyclical. This evidence on relative prices is problematic for the view that recessions result from adverse shocks to production functions or prices of common inputs, such as oil or steel. The evidence favors models based on increasing returns in distribution or on countercyclical markups on finished durables.

Section 6 concludes.

2. A 1-Sector Real Business Cycle Model with Increasing Returns

In this section we outline a 1-sector general equilibrium model of the economy where production is subject to increasing returns to scale. The model is taken from Murphy, Shleifer, and Vishny (1988), hereafter MSV88, which is both more formal and contains considerably more material. After presenting the model, we compare it to the standard TS model.

The model describes fluctuations in a single durable good industry subject to *industry-wide* increasing returns. Because the good is durable, short run demand for it is extremely elastic, since consumers can easily substitute purchases over time. The industry-wide increasing returns assumption amounts to saying that productivity is high at high industry output and low at low industry output, and that no individual firm can by itself energize the industry and move it to high output and low costs.

The combination of flat short-run demand and downward sloping supply naturally leads to instability in the system. It is efficient for this industry to produce at capacity some of the time and to rest other times, rather than to always produce at a constant output level. More interestingly, even though some output fluctuations are efficient, *equilibrium* output fluctuations are not. Because the industry cannot coordinate the end of a slump, firms in equilibrium often get stuck at the low output level for periods of time that are much longer than is necessary to take advantage of increasing returns. The fact that the economy gets stuck at a low output level is the essence of the IR theory of economic fluctuations.

2.1 DEMAND AND SUPPLY

We consider a model with a representative consumer maximizing the utility function given by:

$$\int_0^\infty e^{-rt}(u(S(t)) - L(t))dt, \quad (2)$$

where $S(t)$ is the stock of durables the consumer owns at time t, and $L(t)$ is his labor supply. The assumption that labor is perfectly (or at least highly) substitutable over time is important; we return to it in Section 4.

The evolution of the stock of durable goods is given by

$$S(t) = X(t) - \delta S(t), \quad (3)$$

where $X(t)$ is output at time t and δ is the depreciation rate.

The durability of the good leads to an important distinction between the long-run and the short-run demand curves. The long-run demand curve for the good, $D(X)$, is given by:

$$u'(X/\delta) = (r + \delta)p, \quad (4)$$

where p is the price of the durable in utility units or leisure units. This demand curve is downward sloping. In the long-run, at a lower price the consumer demands a higher constant stock of durables.

In the short-run, in contrast, the stock of durables is essentially fixed, since the supply and depreciation over an instant are trivial relative to the stock. To calculate the short-run demand curve, we assume that consumers take all future purchases as given. The short-run demand curve is then horizontal, at the level of prices $p(S(t))$ given by the present value of future rental rates $u'(S(\tau))$:

$$p(S(t)) = \int_t^\infty e^{-(r+\delta)\tau} u'(S(\tau))d\tau. \quad (5)$$

At any price above $p(S(t))$, the consumer buys nothing at time t and consumes leisure; at any price below $p(S(t))$, his instantaneous demand is infinite. This demand curve relies on perfect intertemporal substitutability of leisure.

For simplicity, we consider an industry subject to Marshallian external economies. Assume that there is a unit interval of competitive firms in this industry, each with a production function:

$$x = l \cdot f(X), \quad (6)$$

where x is firm's output, X is industry output, and l is the firm's labor input. We assume that each firm faces a capacity constraint, so $l \leq \bar{l}$. We also assume that $f(0) > 0$, and $f' > 0$. The latter is the increasing returns assumption that makes the productivity of each firm an increasing function of *industry* output.

The Marshallian externalities formulation enables us to treat firms as price takers while incorporating increasing returns into the model. We use a competitive formulation both because it is relatively simple and because it underscores the fact that movements in productivity are responsible for fluctuations. Several recent papers (Hall 1986, 1988a; Cooper and John 1988; Cooper and Haltiwanger 1989) have stressed empirically and theoretically the importance of imperfect competition for macroeconomic fluctuations. The assumption of imperfect competition seems to us to serve two functions. First, it can be the source of coordination problems that lead to multiple equilibria. Second, it can be the source of countercyclical markups that lead to procyclical behavior of real wages and therefore to procyclical labor input. Since Marshallian externalities themselves generate coordination problems, and since we focus on productivity movements rather than countercyclical markups as the source of real wage changes, we do not need the assumption of imperfect competition in the exposition, although its inclusion might make the model more realistic.

In a competitive equilibrium of our industry, it must be the case that:

$$x = X, \quad (7)$$

$$f(X) = w/p, \quad (8)$$

where w/p is the real wage. These conditions give us the industry supply curve, defined as the locus of price quantity pairs that can arise as an industry equilibrium. The supply curve subsumes the equilibrium wage, given by the current and future stocks of durables the consumer owns that firms today take as givens. At this equilibrium wage, labor supply is perfectly elastic. Accordingly, industry supply at the real wage w/p is given by:

$$X = f^{-1}(w/p), \quad (9)$$

provided that firms are not at the capacity constraint.

Let X_H solve

$$X_H = l\, f(X_H), \quad (10)$$

so X_H is the industry's capacity output. The goods supply curve is then given in Figure 1: it is decreasing from $p = w/f(0)$ at 0 output to $p = w/f(X_H)$ at capacity output, and then has a vertical spike at capacity output. This industry supply curve can be interpreted as the social average cost curve, since:

$$SAC = \frac{wl}{lf(X)} = \frac{pf(X)l}{lf(X)} = p. \quad (11)$$

The combination of this industry supply curve with horizontal short run demand is the source of equilibrium fluctuations in this model.

How do we interpret our downward sloping industry supply curve? We stress that we do not literally believe that technological externalities are an important explanation of cyclical fluctuations. However, the Marshallian externality formulation can be thought of as a reduced form for some things that we do believe to be important, and discuss at some length in MSV88. The most plausible form of industry-wide increasing returns probably has to do with "thick markets" externalities or with the closely related economies of scale in distribution. When the output in the industry is high, there are many customers in the market, and so the probability of a fast match between the seller and the buyer is much higher. Because the selling costs are a significant component of the costs of making the final good, and because these costs plausibly fall when the industry rather than the firm's output rises, we find specification (6) appealing. In this respect, the work most closely related to our specification is Diamond (1982) and Howitt and McAfee (1988).

There are several industry structures that can be thought of in this way. For example, our supply curve can describe an industry such as

Figure 1 SUPPLY

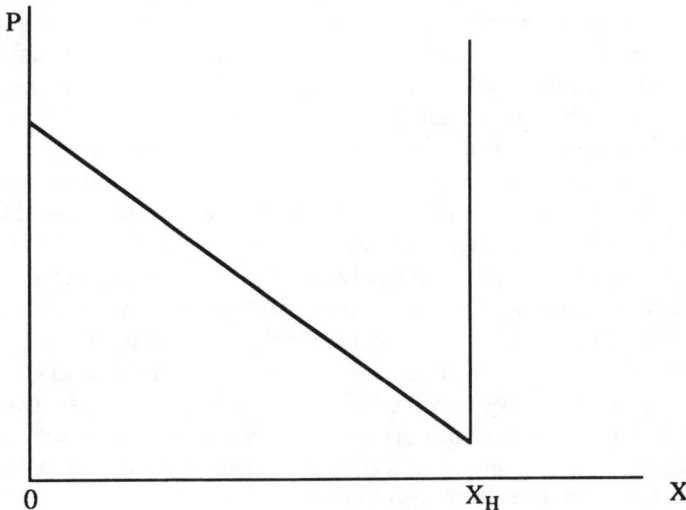

housing in which time to sale falls and therefore productivity rises when there is a lot of construction and many consumers are in the market. Alternatively, our supply curve might be a reduced form description of an industry in which specialized supplies are cheaper when the industry is humming because individual suppliers can take advantage of their increasing returns at the firm level. Our supply curve can also describe an industry in which there are increasing returns in retailing.

An important question is whether our downward sloping supply curve can describe an industry in which markets are perfectly organized, but individual firms face increasing returns in production. Ramey (1987) finds that the industry marginal cost curve for a number of manufacturing industries is declining, suggesting that in fact one can get industry increasing returns purely in production. Ramey also surveys a number of other empirical studies documenting declining industry marginal cost curves. Hall (1988a,c) presents evidence for increasing returns at the industry level, although his evidence pertains to decreasing average rather than marginal cost. As we mentioned in the introduction, the decreasing average cost story typically yields procyclical real wages because of countercyclical markups and not because of procyclical productivity. It is thus a different story from the one we tell.

Despite Ramey's and others' evidence on declining industry marginal cost, there are no good theoretical models of such industries. If an industry where individual firms have increasing returns in production adjusts to declines in demand by shutting down inefficient plants, then even if each plant operates subject to increasing returns, industry returns to scale are decreasing. For increasing returns in production at the plant or firm level to translate into industry increasing returns, an industry must contract in a recession by keeping most plants in operation and reducing the output of each, rather than by shutting down inefficient plants. This would be the case if, for example, products of different plants were geographically or otherwise highly differentiated. Contraction of all plants would also result if different firms in the industry could not, for competitive reasons, share the market in a way that enables a few to produce at capacity and to take advantage of increasing returns. Such firms would rather keep their customers and produce at a high marginal cost. However one thinks of these industries, they must have the property that most firms and indeed most plants are marginal and so increasing returns at the plant level translate into increasing returns at the industry level. Since our paper focuses on the *structure* of increasing returns models, we treat (6) as a primitive assumption and do not pursue a specific model of the market structure.

2.2 EQUILIBRIA

An equilibrium in this model is a path of output $X(t)$, durable stock $S(t)$, wage $w(t)$ and price $p(t)$ such that all markets clear. Note that as long as (5) holds, the consumer is on his labor supply curve.

To make the model interesting, we assume that the long-run demand curve $D(X)$ cuts the downward sloping segment of the supply curve. If $D(X)$ cuts the supply curve at capacity, the equilibrium is the trivial outcome in which all firms produce at capacity all the time. In MSV88 we show that if building capacity is sufficiently cheap relative to the cost saving from operating at a higher output, firms will always build enough capacity so that long run demand curve cuts the downward sloping segment of the supply curve.

This model has a variety of cyclical equilibria, which take the following form. Over some period of time, the economy produces at capacity X_H, the stock of durables grows, and the rental rate on durables falls. During initial stages of this period, people's willingness to work for goods declines since their consumption rises, and so the price of goods falls while real wages rise. Toward the end of the high production period, the price of goods actually rises in the anticipation of lean times and high rental rates in the future. Eventually the boom ends, and the economy switches to zero output, again maintained over some period of time. During this period, the stock of durables depreciates and the rental rate rises. As consumption falls over this period, the willingness of people to work for goods rises, and at least at the initial stages of the recession prices rise and real wages fall. Toward the end of the recession, we again get the effect that prices fall because people know that good times are coming and with them low rental rates.

This business cycle can be easily thought of in terms of Figure 2. During the boom, the economy operates on the vertical segment of the supply curve. As the boom continues, the demand curve essentially slides down the vertical segment of the supply curve, because the willingness to work diminishes (again, the demand curve moves up shortly before the boom ends). At some point, the economy switches to zero output, and at the initial stages of the boom the demand curve is moving up. Eventually, the economy goes back to the high production level. Figure 3 describes the behavior of the capital stock, prices, and real wages over the business cycle.

The period of these cycles can be very short, where the economy "chatters" between high and low output, or much longer. In the longer cycles, the sector gets stuck at a high or low output level because a coordinated change in output by many firms is required to change each firm's productivity and prices. The Marshallian externality in the production function is the source of this coordination failure. The coordination failure is crucial to the model, since without it the economy would fluctu-

Figure 2 EQUILIBRIUM

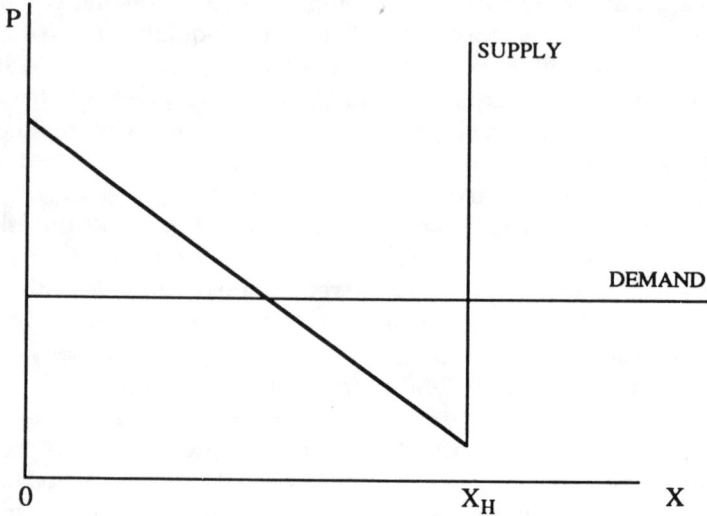

Figure 3 CYCLICAL VARIABLES

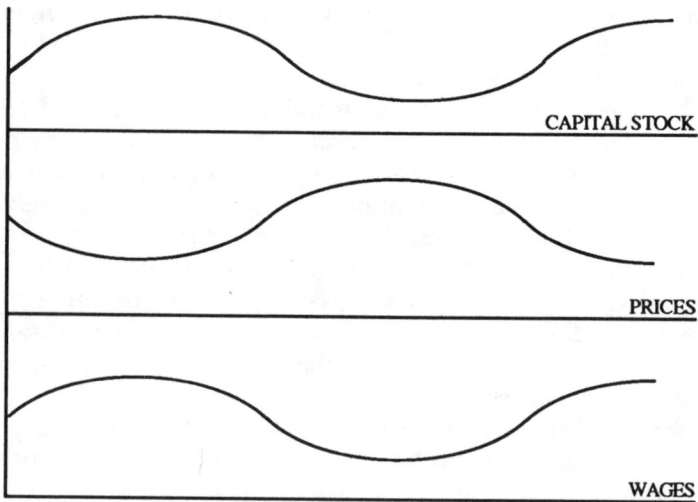

ate at a very high frequency, and there would be no hope of explaining low frequency business cycle fluctuations. Although many cycles are sustainable, constant output is not sustainable as an equilibrium, since in this case any firm raising its output would bring other firms to do likewise and thus destroy the equilibrium.

An interesting property of this model is that it has the cycle of longest possible duration, for reasons detailed by Mitchell (1927). In this cycle, the price of durables reaches its minimum and maximum sustainable values. The longest cycle has the property that both the recession and the boom last as long as they possibly can in a cyclical equilibrium. If the boom were to last any longer, the rental rates would get to be so low that at some point prior to the end of the boom the price of durables would have to fall below production cost even when the sector is operating at maximum efficiency. Because this cannot happen in equilibrium, there is a natural end to the boom, where people get so satiated with durables that they would rather take leisure than work even at a high productivity. In terms of Figure 2, the longest boom can be thought of as the demand curve falling off the cliff at X_H. Similarly, if the recession were to last any longer, at some point prior to its end the prices of durables would get so high that even one firm operating alone at a low productivity can make money by producing. This of course cannot happen in equilibrium. This natural end to the recession means that people eventually want goods so much that they are willing to work at low productivity to get goods rather than consume leisure. The longest cycle is a form of long-run stability in this economy, which arises because the long-run demand curve for goods is steeper than the long-run supply curve.

The welfare properties of the equilibria in this model can be easily summarized. First, at least some output fluctuations are efficient. It is efficient for this sector to take advantage of increasing returns and to produce some of the time and rest the remainder of the time. Second, most equilibrium fluctuations are not efficient. This inefficiency is reflected in the fact that the period of the cycle is too long, which leads to excessive *variability* of consumption. The inefficiency is also reflected in the fact that, for a cycle of a fixed period, recessions last too long relative to booms, leading to too low an *average level* of consumption. The main reason for the latter inefficiency is the Marshallian externality and the resulting coordination problem, that prevents firms from spending more time operating at capacity. The model shows that even in the world where fluctuations of output are efficient, equilibrium business cycles are unlikely to be so.

2.3 A COMPARISON OF THE IR MODEL WITH THE TS MODEL

Similarities: There are a significant number of similarities between the IR model described above and the TS model. Most obviously, fluctuations in both models are driven by productivity movements. In the TS model, such movements result from exogenous technological shocks. In the IR model, they result from endogenous movements along the increasing returns production function. The consequence of either assumption, however, is that business cycles are associated with movements in true, rather than just measured, productivity.

A key feature of our model is durability of the good, that leads to extremely elastic short-run demand and instability. As a result, the model generates large output fluctuations even with small increasing returns. TS models have not stressed durable consumption goods, although they do emphasize the durable nature of capital. The large responsiveness of investment to small changes in productivity is an important element of the Kydland/Prescott and Prescott models as well.

An appealing feature of our model, that can be easily worked into a TS model, is the natural limit on the length of booms and recessions. Proponents of the TS view rarely talk about business cycles per se, and so this issue of mean reversion does not arise. However, the effect we are talking about would appear in a TS model also. Even if the economy is subjected to a sequence of fairly persistent adverse technology shocks, eventually it would pay to work and to produce even if opportunities are poor, provided that people are hungry enough for goods. Such long-run stability would thus appear in a TS model as well.

Differences: Here we note four differences between 1-sector IR and TS models, other than the source of productivity movements. First, the IR model is an *endogenous* business cycle model, and the TS model is an *exogenous* shocks model. To the extent that we have trouble identifying technology shocks, particularly the bad ones that cause recessions, an endogenous business cycle model seems more attractive. Moreover, we find the importance of self-fulfilling expectations an attractive feature of the IR models.

Second, most technology shocks are likely to be persistent, whereas periods of production at high capacity in IR models are temporary. Because Prescott (1986) assumes highly persistent shocks, the ability of agents to engage in intertemporal substitution is limited. Hence, intertemporal substitution must be very high to rationalize the observed movements as an equilibrium response to permanent shocks. In contrast, since in our endogenous model good times are very temporary, we need much less intertemporal substitution to induce agents to respond to periods of high productivity with increased labor supply. Since intertemporal substitutability needed to calibrate TS models is extremely large, the fact that IR models need much less of such substitutability is attractive.

Third, IR and TS models have different implications about the response of labor productivity to demand shocks. Kydland/Prescott predict that, holding technology constant, labor productivity should fall and certainly not rise in response to a demand shock because of diminishing returns. In contrast, our model predicts that a demand shock could switch the economy to a high output level, and so raise productivity because of increasing returns.

Consistent with the last prediction, Hall (1988c), using instruments for demand disturbances, finds that demand shocks positively affect the Solow residual. The appropriateness of Hall's instruments, which include most notably the price of oil, has been questioned. His results can also be explained by unobserved procyclical work effort. If Hall's results stand up to scrutiny, however, they provide strong evidence against TS models. In an observation similar to Hall's, Mankiw (1987) points out that measured labor productivity rose in World War II, at the time of a sharp increase in the government's purchases of durables. One explanation of Mankiw's result is increasing returns, although there are others, including the increased war effort.

A final distinction between the simple IR and the simple TS models is in the treatment of welfare consequences of fluctuations. Our IR model suggests that the efficiency cost of most business cycles is small, since consumption of durables varies a lot less than do purchases. Empirically, we may not be too far from Prescott's (1986) conclusion that business cycles are efficient. Nonetheless, it seems obvious that neither TS nor IR models have yet dealt with important costs of business fluctuations, such as unequal distribution of the burden of the recessions or their excessive duration because of more fundamental problems, such as financial collapse. It is fair to say that neither approach has seriously dealt with policy.

We can summarize this section by stressing that both models are similar in that fluctuations are driven by movements in labor productivity. Both models are significantly more plausible when they stress durability of goods as a way to generate large output responses to small productivity changes. The increasing returns model has the additional advantage of being supported by independent evidence (Ramey 1987; Hall 1988a,c). In the next few sections, we describe in more detail some of the ways to augment both the standard TS model and our IR model to make them match the evidence better.

3. Co-movement of Outputs and Labor Inputs Between Sectors

3.1 THE EVIDENCE AND THE PROBLEM

The previous section has presented a 1-sector IR model of the business cycle and compared it to a 1-sector TS model. One sector models do not, however, address the question of co-movement of outputs and labor inputs across sectors during the business cycle. In this section, we first discuss the fact that such co-movement is extremely pronounced, and is clearly one of the crucial stylized facts that a business cycle model should explain. We then suggest that the Prescott (1986) and Long/Plosser (1983) models do not adequately explain why outputs and labor inputs in different sectors move together. Finally, we present an alternative approach to co-movement, based on immobile (specialized) labor and imperfect credit.

Table 1 presents the evidence on annual correlation of growth rates of different sectors of the economy during 1947–87. Panel A focuses on annual growth rates of real output, and panel B presents data on annual growth rates of employment. Table 1 also includes correlations with changes in detrended employment rate—described in more detail in Section 5—which is our preferred business cycle indicator.

Table 1 shows extremely high correlations of output growth across sectors, as well as high correlations of sectoral growth rates with the business cycle indicator. Most strikingly, the correlation of growth rate of durables with the growth rate of GDP is .95, and with the change in the detrended employment rate it is .92. Growth rates of output in construction, nondurables, and even trade are also extremely highly correlated with the GDP growth rate, the cyclical indicator, and each other. Mining co-moves somewhat less, in part because there is a sharp change in the trend growth rate of mining over this period. Even government and finance seem to move in step with other sectors. In fact, there is not a single negative coefficient in panel A of Table 1. It is very much the case in these data that outputs in broadly defined sectors move together and procyclically.

A similar picture emerges for labor inputs in panel B of Table 1. Growth rates of labor inputs are highly correlated across sectors, and with the cyclical indicator. Durables again lead the pack, showing a .95 correlation with the growth rate of total employment, and a .93 correlation with the changes in the cyclical variable. There are a few negative correlations of employment growth rates, such as between government and trade and government and services, but by and large employment growth rates behave like output growth rates. In fact, the extent of co-movement in labor inputs between durables, non-durables, construc-

Table 1   CORRELATIONS OF GROWTH RATES ACROSS SECTORS ANNUAL 1947–87

	All	Mining	Con-struc-tion	Dur-ables	Non-durables	Trade	Trans-porta-tion	Ser-vices	Gov't	Finance	Detrended Employment Rate
Panel A: Correlations of Output Growth Rates											
All	1.00										
Mining	.32	1.00									
Construction	.76	.05	1.00								
Durables	.95	.27	.69	1.00							
Non-durables	.89	.13	.72	.91	1.00						
Trade	.89	.30	.75	.76	.75	1.00					
Transportation	.92	.51	.67	.83	.73	.84	1.00				
Services	.72	.34	.42	.54	.53	.74	.74	1.00			
Government	.34	.05	.20	.30	.24	.23	.25	.15	1.00		
Finance	.54	.05	.67	.40	.44	.58	.58	.54	.03	1.00	
Detrended Employment Rate	.93	.15	.81	.92	.89	.83	.81	.64	.22	.47	1.00
Panel B: Correlations of Employment Growth Rates											
All	1.00										
Mining	.63	1.00									
Construction	.67	.36	1.00								
Durables	.95	.58	.62	1.00							
Non-durables	.76	.45	.59	.73	1.00						
Trade	.71	.32	.52	.76	.71	1.00					
Transportation	.77	.63	.32	.78	.63	.54	1.00				
Services	.54	.33	.33	.61	.52	.56	.68	1.00			
Government	.48	.28	.20	.28	.08	-.09	.28	-.13	1.00		
Finance	.60	.37	.61	.53	.47	.48	.43	.29	.22	1.00	
Detrended Employment Rate	.89	.59	.58	.93	.64	.65	.81	.68	.33	.52	1.00

tion, and trade is quite remarkable—and those are the sectors across which labor is potentially mobile.

One question Table 1 does not address is whether co-movement between sectors is just a reflection of trend growth rates in the economy, or whether it reflects shorter-run cyclical fluctuation of sectors. To address this issue, Table 2 presents partial correlations of output and employment growth rates controlling for business cycle movements. In these partial correlations, the business cycle control is our detrended employment growth rate. Large residual correlations would be evidence of strong non-cyclical co-movement, which can just reflect the growth rate of the economy.

The partial correlation coefficients in Table 2 are obviously much smaller than those in Table 1, and many of them are negative. For example, the residual correlation of growth rates of durables and non-durables is .50, compared to the correlation of .91 in Table 1, and the residual correlation of durables and construction is .26 to the correlation of .69 in Table 1. Similarly, the residual correlation of growth rates of durable and non-durable employment is .53, compared to the raw correlation of .73, and the residual correlation of growth rates of employment in durables and construction is −.20, compared to the raw correlation of .62. In fact, the average difference between the total correlation of sectoral output growth rates with GDP growth and the residual correlation of these two variables is .28. Similarly, the average difference between the total correlation of sectoral employment growth rates with GDP growth rate and the residual correlation is .24. These results demonstrate quite convincingly that cyclical co-movement of growth rates of output and employment across sectors qualifies as a bona fide stylized fact of business cycle analysis.

Theoretically, generating such strong positive co-movements of outputs and labor inputs from sectoral productivity changes is not easy. To see the problem, suppose that sector A is operating at a high level with an increasing returns technology, or has a good technology shock. Either way, productivity and wages in sector A are high, and so, with a positively sloped labor supply curve, labor input in sector A rises. If other sectors do not also experience a productivity improvement, and if the output of sector A is not complementary in consumption or production with the outputs of these other sectors, labor should move out of these sectors and into sector A, resulting in a negative co-movement of labor inputs across sectors. Unless the good productivity shock is pervasive, so that the only sector that shrinks is leisure, this model has trouble explaining co-movement of labor inputs.

This problem is troubling for both Prescott's (1986) and Long and

Table 2 PARTIAL CORRELATIONS OF OUTPUT AND EMPLOYMENT GROWTH RATES ACROSS INDUSTRIES AFTER CONTROLLING FOR BUSINESS CYCLE VARIATION*

	All	Mining	Construction	Durables	Non-durables	Trade	Transportation	Services	Gov't	Finance
Panel A: Partial Correlations of Output Growth										
All	1.00									
Mining	.28	1.00								
Construction	.42	.03	1.00							
Durables	.69	.10	.26	1.00						
Non-durables	.55	.12	.35	.50	1.00					
Trade	.17	.32	-.32	.10	.26	1.00				
Transportation	.38	-.10	.23	.54	.50	.03	1.00			
Services	-.19	-.11	-.11	-.08	.15	.30	.22	1.00		
Government	.42	.11	.01	-.09	-.19	.01	-.43	-.52	1.00	
Finance	.35	.09	.44	.16	.21	.02	.22	-.10	.06	1.00
Panel B: Partial Correlations of Employment Growth										
All	1.00									
Mining	.49	1.00								
Construction	.05	-.13	1.00							
Durables	.63	.33	-.20	1.00						
Non-durables	.35	.00	.01	.53	1.00					
Trade	.80	.66	.06	.39	.07	1.00				
Transportation	.60	.31	.24	-.01	.06	.51	1.00			
Services	.45	.32	-.21	-.15	-.10	.49	.49	1.00		
Government	.39	.02	.04	.24	.11	.13	.09	.02	1.00	
Finance	.34	-.02	.57	-.07	.08	.40	.38	.35	-.09	1.00

*Partial correlations are conditional on detrended unemployment rate changes as defined in the text.

Plosser's (1983) approaches. As has been pointed out independently by Benhabib, Rogerson, and Wright (1988), Prescott's (1986) model predicts a negative co-movement of labor inputs between consumption and investment sectors. Prescott does not distinguish between consumption and investment sectors, but we in fact can think of the two sectors as separate but having identical production functions. Prescott calibrates his model by noting that, in the long run, labor input does not rise and maybe even declines with increases in productivity. This means that, within the consumption sector, the income effect is at least as strong as the substitution effect. The implication of this assumption is that employment in the consumption sector does not rise, and possibly shrinks, in response to a good productivity shock to that sector. From the point of view of employment in the consumption sector, we can therefore think of shocks in this model as being only to the investment good sector.

Suppose there is a good productivity shock to the investment sector. In response to this attractive temporary opportunity, labor input in the investment sector rises, raising the marginal utility of leisure. Calibration says that holding the labor input in the investment sector constant, labor input in the consumption sector is independent of productivity in the consumption sector. Hence, since labor input in the investment sector rises, we should get a fall in the labor input in the consumption sector. The Prescott (1986) model thus predicts, counterfactually, countercyclical labor input in the consumption sector. This result is much more general than Prescott's (1986) specific model; details are available from us upon request.

A similar problem would arise in Long and Plosser's model, except they assume unit elastic demand for leisure. As a result of this assumption, labor inputs do not change over the cycle in their model: their model generates co-movement in outputs at constant labor inputs. If LP instead assumed a more conventional positively sloped labor supply, they would get a *negative* co-movement of labor inputs between sectors at the time productivity shocks hit. An increase in productivity in one sector raises the real wage and draws labor into that sector out of other sectors as well as out of leisure. Long and Plosser can still get a positive co-movement of final outputs by the time shocks propagate through the input-output matrix. As we show in Section 5, however, this story is inconsistent with relative price evidence.

In the rest of this section, we offer a solution to this problem, based on the idea that, first, labor is specialized and immobile between sectors, and, second, there are borrowing constraints. In practical terms, immobile labor means that people have a strong comparative advantage at working in only one, or a few, sectors, and therefore cannot easily move into whatever sector is productive at the moment. This assumption is perfectly consistent with large gross labor flows in the economy, and with a high level of mobility of some segments of the labor force. It only says that, for many workers, it is better to work in their own sector and to exchange the output for other goods than always to move into the most productive sector. Immobile labor creates a need for people to trade the goods they produce, rather than working in each sector to produce the good for their own consumption.

This need to trade when labor is immobile is an important component of the story explaining co-movement. Consider first the case of mobile labor. When sector A is productive, and labor is mobile, it pays all workers to come work in sector A to buy sector A's good, which is now particularly cheap. Unless some other goods are complements to A— which we assume they are not—the tradeoff between leisure and work in other sectors has not changed. In this case, workers should both consume less leisure and work less in other sectors.

Suppose, in contrast, that outside workers are not trained to work in sector A, so that the increase in sector A's labor input comes entirely from the reduction in leisure of its own workers. Good A is still cheap, and so outside workers want to spend more on it if demand for A is elastic. To do that, they must work more in their own sectors, and then spend more on good A. This leads to increased labor input in other sectors, and a positive co-movement of labor inputs across sectors. Alternatively, workers from outside sector A can borrow and buy more of good A now, working slightly more today and in all the future periods to repay their debts. If workers can easily borrow, there would be some but not much co-movement. Generating significant co-movement between sectors requires both immobile labor and restricted borrowing opportunities.

In the next subsection, we present the immobile labor argument formally using a 1-period TS model. Subsection C summarizes the arguments in MSV88 that use these ideas in an IR model. Our theory of co-movement illustrates the importance of trade, as opposed to Robinson Crusoe, for understanding fluctuations. We show at the end of this section that several earlier papers have made assumptions amounting essentially to immobile labor.

3.2 A FORMAL TS MODEL

This section presents a one-period competitive RBC model with technological shocks. There is a unit interval of small sectors, each producing its own good, s. There is also a unit measure of consumers. The utility function of each consumer is given by

$$\int_0^1 \frac{c(s)^\theta}{\theta} \, ds - \frac{L^\beta}{\beta}, \quad (12)$$

where $c(s)$ is consumption of good s and L is labor. We assume that $\beta \geq 1$ and $\theta \leq 1$. For consistency of the model, we also assume that $\beta - \theta^2 > 0$. In this model, the case of $\theta > 1$ corresponds to elastic demand for goods and upward sloping labor supply. The substitution effect in the demand for goods is stronger than the income effect. In contrast, when $\theta < 0$, the income effect is stronger, the demand for goods is inelastic, and labor supply is backward bending. Naturally, the case of $\theta > 0$ is more plausible for durables. Also note that $\beta = 1$ corresponds to no diminishing marginal utility of leisure and $\theta = 0$ to the Long/Plosser case of unit elastic demand for goods and therefore for leisure.

The production function of good s is given by

$$y(s) = \gamma(s)L(s), \quad (13)$$

where $\gamma(s)$ is technological shock and $L(s)$ is labor input in sector s. Each good is produced competitively in its own sector.

Consider first this model with mobile labor, so there is actually a representative consumer we can talk about. This consumer's budget constraint is given by

$$\int c(s)p(s)ds = Lw. \quad (14)$$

Market clearing requires that $c(s) = y(s)$ for all s, and competition says that $\gamma(s)p(s) = w$. We can let the wage be numeraire: $w = 1$.

This model can be solved for consumption of each good s and labor input in each sector s as a function of technological shocks in all sectors:

$$c(s) = \gamma(s)^{\frac{1}{1-\theta}} \left[\int (s')^{\frac{\theta}{1-\theta}} \, ds' \right]^{\frac{1-\beta}{\beta-\theta}} \quad (15)$$

$$L(s) = \gamma(s)^{\frac{\theta}{1-\theta}} \left[\int \gamma(s')^{\frac{\theta}{1-\theta}} \, ds' \right]^{\frac{1-\beta}{\beta-\theta}} \quad (16)$$

Several observations can be made about these solutions.

First, consumption of good s always increases in $\gamma(s)$. This is because a good productivity shock always reduces the relative price of good s, and since s is normal, its consumption rises. Second, when $\theta > 0$, labor input in sector s rises with the technology shock, and when $\theta < 0$, labor input declines with the shock. The former case corresponds to the elastic demand for good s, so when the price of good s falls, demand for s rises more than the increase in output due to the productivity increase, and so employment rises. Conversely, when $\theta < 0$, the demand for good s is inelastic, and so a rise in productivity leads to a less than proportional increase in the quantity consumed, and so a reduction in the labor input. The case of $\theta > 0$ corresponds to durable goods, and so both labor and output should probably rise when a sector experiences a positive productivity shock.

More interesting results concern co-movement of outputs and labor inputs across sectors. When $\beta = 1$, (15) and (16) show that all sectors move by themselves, without any influence from other sectors, as one would expect in the case of separability of goods and no increasing disutility of work. The same result obtains in the Long/Plosser case of $\theta = 0$, where labor inputs in different sectors are fixed, and outputs move proportionately with productivity because of unit elastic demand. Except for these two cases, however, labor always negatively co-moves between sectors. When $\theta > 0$, a good productivity shock in sector s' raises demand for labor in s', and so, since the tradeoff between employment in sector s and leisure has not changed, there will be a reduction both in leisure and in employment in s. When $\theta < 0$, a good productivity shock to s' reduces labor input in s' because of inelastic demand for this good, and so labor moves both into leisure and into sector s. This case, of course, is blatantly inconsistent with the evidence. In either case, labor inputs in s and in s' move in opposite directions, contrary to what happens over a business cycle.

Furthermore, output negatively co-moves in the plausible case of $\theta > 0$, and positively co-moves with $\theta < 0$. When $\theta > 0$, a good shock in s' raises employment and output in s' but cuts employment in s, as we mentioned earlier. Because productivity in sector s is unchanged, output of good s must also fall. Output in s and s' thus move in opposite directions. When $\theta < 0$, a good shock in s' raises output but reduces employment in s'. Because labor moves into sector s, both employment and output in sector s rise. This leads to co-movement of outputs. In the case of mobile labor, we thus get two unrealistic results: employment co-moves negatively, and output co-moves negatively in the plausible case of upward sloping labor supply. Long and Plosser do not get the latter result because, in their model, shocks are to common intermediate inputs and so are correlated.

Consider next the more interesting case of immobile labor, where a worker can only work in one sector or consume leisure. We assume the same preferences as before, and the same number of workers per sector.

Let $c(s,s')$ be consumption of good s by a worker in sector s'. The budget constraint of worker s' now takes the form:

$$\int c(s,s')p(s)ds = L(s')w(s') \quad (17)$$

for all s'. Competition now does not restrict wages to be the same in all sectors:

$$\gamma(s)p(s) = w(s) \quad (18)$$

for all s. Finally, market clearing takes the form

$$\int c(s,s')ds = \gamma(s)L(s) \quad (19)$$

for all s. For our purposes, we do not need to choose a numeraire.

A considerable amount of grinding leads to the following closed form solution to this model:

$$w(s) = \gamma(s)^{\frac{\theta(\beta-\theta)}{\beta-\theta^2}} \quad (20)$$

$$p(s) = \gamma(s)^{\frac{\beta(\theta-1)}{\beta-\theta^2}} \quad (21)$$

$$c(s,s') = \gamma(s')^{\frac{\theta\beta}{\beta-\theta^2}} \cdot \gamma(s)^{\frac{\beta}{\beta-\theta^2}} [\int \gamma(s^*)^{\frac{\beta\theta}{\beta-\theta^2}} ds^*]^{\frac{\beta-1}{\theta-\beta}} \quad (22)$$

$$L(s') = \gamma(s')^{\frac{\theta^2}{\beta-\theta^2}} [\int \gamma(s^*)^{\frac{\beta\theta}{\beta-\theta^2}} ds^*]^{\frac{1-\theta}{\beta-\theta}}. \quad (23)$$

Using (22)–(23), we can ask the same questions as we did with mobile labor.

Similar to the case with mobile labor, consumption of good s by a worker in sector s' increases both in the shock to sector s and in the shock to sector s'. But there are some crucial differences. First, because of the symmetry assumption, labor input in sectors always rises with productivity in that sector, whether or not θ is positive. When $\theta > 0$, demand for good s is elastic. At the same labor input as before the shock, the price of good s declines less than productivity rises, so that the real wage in sector s rises. Since labor supply is upward sloping for $\theta > 0$, labor input rises in response to the increase in the real wage. In contrast, when $\theta < 0$, demand for good s is inelastic. When $\gamma(s)$ rises, $p(s)$ falls more than the productivity increase, and so the real wage in sector s falls. But labor supply slopes down for $\theta < 0$, and so labor input rises in response to the fall in the real wage. Independent of the value of θ, labor input in sector s always moves in the same direction as productivity in that sector.

The most interesting results again concern co-movement of labor inputs and of consumption. In this model, we get co-movement of labor inputs as long as $\theta > 0$. When productivity $\gamma(s')$ in sector s' rises, $p(s')$ falls, which raises the real wages of workers in all other sectors. With $\theta > 0$, labor supply in these sectors slopes up and so workers there all work more. Conversely, with $\theta < 0$, labor supply slopes down and labor input in sector s falls in response to a rise in $\gamma(s')$. As long as workers want to work more when their real wage rises, they respond to a lower price in another sector by producing more of their own good, and trading it for the productive sector's output.

Co-movement of consumption, like co-movement of labor, depends on the sign of θ. When sector s experiences a good productivity shock, $p(s)$ falls and real wages in all sectors rise. When $\theta > 0$, workers in all sectors want to work more and to buy more of all goods, so consumption of all goods rises. In contrast, when $\theta < 0$, the response to a rise in real wages from a fall in $p(s)$ is to work less, so hours and consumption of all goods other than good s fall. Consumption of different goods co-moves, therefore, as long as labor supply slopes up.

The results for mobile and immobile labor are very different. With mobile labor, employment always co-moves negatively across sectors, and consumption co-moves only if $\theta < 0$. With immobile labor, employment and consumption both co-move for $\theta > 0$ and not otherwise. The reason for the difference is that with mobile labor, one can get more of another good by working in the sector in which it is produced, whereas with immobile labor one has to work in one's own sector and trade. For durables, the case of elastic demand (and therefore positively sloped labor supply) is the empirically correct one. Since in this case the model clearly generates empirically correct predictions about co-movement of labor inputs and consumption over the business cycle, the case for assuming specialization and immobile labor seems to be compelling.

Because our model assumes identical demand elasticities for different goods, it does not deal with Prescott's case. We have looked at a model where $\theta = 0$ for one good, and $\theta > 0$ for another. In such a model, one indeed gets a negative co-movement of labor inputs with mobile labor, and a positive co-movement with immobile labor.

So far we have presented a one period model, and have not addressed the issue of credit. If we think of some of the goods in our model as future consumption goods, the credit point is apparent. Even if labor is immobile, an increase in productivity and the resulting decline in the price of good s is likely to lead to only a small increase in today's labor input in other sectors. Instead of working much harder today, a worker in a sector s' would borrow to take advantage of the low price of good s, and repay the loan by raising his labor supply today and in all the future periods by a small amount. To generate a significant amount of co-movement between sectors, both immobile labor and imperfect credit are required.

The role we have assigned to imperfect credit here is different from—and complementary to—that in other recent models (Bernanke and Gertler 1989; Greenwald and Stiglitz 1987). In those models, a bad shock reduces the internal availability of funds to a firm, which then has to reduce its investment because of the credit constraint. The reduction in investment in turn leads to lower output and therefore a persistently lower availability of funds in the future. Importantly, this is basically a 1-sector (or one-firm) story of the role of credit. In contrast, here and in MSV88 credit serves to facilitate intertemporal trade between sectors. When credit markets are imperfect, such trade is less attractive, leading agents in different sectors of the economy to synchronize their production periods so they can trade instantaneously and economize on credit. In this sense, imperfect credit in our model serves to concentrate the effects of shock at a point in time rather than to spread them over time. We believe that both consequences of imperfect credit are important in practice. In fact, it may be possible to combine the Greenwald-Stiglitz-Bernanke-Gertler view of countercyclical costs of credit with some features of our model, such as immobile labor, durables and elastic labor supply, to generate self-fulfilling fluctuations even in the absence of increasing returns at the sectoral level.

3.3 CO-MOVEMENT IN A MODEL WITH INCREASING RETURNS

So far, we have considered the co-movement issue in a TS model, where it is simpler to see. Identical arguments apply also in a variant of an IR model of Section 2, and are developed in MSV88. The question in the IR model is: why wouldn't different sectors of the economy cycle out of sync with each other, especially if there is an aggregate resource constraint? If they do cycle out of sync, aggregate output would be smooth, and we would not observe aggregate fluctuations.

In MSV88, we show that aggregate fluctuations obtain when labor is immobile and borrowing is constrained. In this case, when a sector is productive and its output is cheap, the only way workers in other sectors can take advantage of low prices is by working themselves and trading their output for the productive sector's output. In equilibrium, all sectors fluctuate together. As in a TS model, aggregate fluctuations obtain with immobile labor and restricted borrowing in an IR model.

The notion of immobile labor has appeared in a number of recent models in somewhat different ways. Diamond (1982), Weitzman (1982), and

Roberts (1987) assume either that workers are specialists in production and generalists in consumption, or that they cannot consume the good that they produce. The power of this assumption is always to make trades necessary for consumption and to preclude the possibility that people, like Robinson Crusoe, simply toil to produce their own consumption good. The point that MSV88 and the current paper emphasize is that these assumptions can be used to explain the observed co-movement of outputs and of labor inputs across sectors in a wide range of models. Specialization does not just generate "Keynesian" results, but also yields empirically correct predictions about co-movement—even in a TS model. There is nothing intrinsically Keynesian about specialization.[1]

4. Elastic Labor Supply

4.1 THE NEED FOR ASSUMING ELASTIC LABOR SUPPLY

Recent empirical research (Bils 1985; Kydland and Prescott 1987; Solon and Barsky 1988) finds that real wages move procyclically over the business cycle, but only mildly so. At the same time, to generate large labor supply movements from small changes in real wages, one needs to assume that the intertemporal or lifetime elasticity of labor supply is much higher. For example, Prescott (1986) takes this elasticity to be 2, and still predicts too-low fluctuations in hours.

Even if one believes that real wages are installment payments that do not reflect underlying productivity, and do not really serve to allocate labor over the business cycle, one still needs a fairly elastic labor supply. The effects of both technology shocks and increasing returns over the business cycle are probably small quantitatively. To get large efficient movements in the labor input in response to such small changes in technology requires easy substitutability of labor over time. That is, for workers and firms to agree to a contract that requires large changes in their labor input in response to small changes in productive opportunities, leisure must be easily substitutable over time. Otherwise, one needs to explain why the worker and the firm do not eliminate inefficient fluctuations in hours that are not justified by fluctuations in productivity.

We have pointed out earlier that TS models with reasonably persistent technology shocks require a greater labor supply elasticity than do IR models to generate the same fluctuations. This is because in an IR model, periods of high productivity are by definition temporary, since it

---

[1] Scheinkman and Weiss (1986) assume immobile labor and imperfect credit to generate a role for money as a store of value. They do not consider the role of immobile labor in generating co-movement of outputs and of labor inputs across sectors.

is not an equilibrium to produce high output all the time. In contrast, in a TS model driven by reasonably permanent shocks, good opportunities to work are equally permanent, and so the instantaneous labor supply response to a shock is small. Because productivity changes are less permanent in an IR model, the labor supply elasticity required by such a model is smaller.

At the same time, whereas a TS model depends on elastic labor supply only quantitatively, an IR model fails to generate fluctuations altogether if labor supply is sufficiently inelastic. In a TS model, less elastic labor supply dampens the effects of technological shocks on output, and consequently reduces output volatility. In our model, in contrast, sufficiently inelastic labor supply can eliminate the possibility of fluctuations altogether. The reason is that when labor supply is sufficiently inelastic, increases in industry output raise costs even if labor productivity rises, and so make the supply curve slope up rather than down. If the supply curve slopes up, the unique stable equilibrium is constant output. In this way, inelastic labor supply completely eliminates the possibility that our model can explain business cycle fluctuations.

As this subsection suggests, even though TS and IR models rely in different ways on the elastic labor supply assumption, they both rely on it strongly. More generally, any model that fits the observed fluctuations of labor input must rely on this assumption. For example, it is needed for countercyclical markup models, since the decline in markups must more than compensate for the rise in costs in a boom. Keynesian rigid wage models also rely on elastic labor supply to the extent that the cost of setting wages flexibly must be large to explain the costly fluctuations in hours. Below we offer a few comments on plausibility of elastic labor supply.

4.2 THE PLAUSIBILITY OF ELASTIC LABOR SUPPLY

Although the macroeconomic models described above require an elasticity of labor supply of at least 1 or 2, the elasticity estimated from micro data is extremely low, perhaps around .3. The reason for this low estimate is that wages and hours for a given individual are both highly variable, and are basically uncorrelated. Put differently, the coefficient of the regression of the change in hours on the change in wages, just as that of the regression of the change in wages on the change in hours, is close to zero. The fact that there are many reasons why measured hours and wages change, unrelated to the labor supply elasticity, is undoubtedly responsible for the low estimate of this elasticity in micro data. This observation has led a number of researchers to try to reconcile the low labor supply elasticity obtained from micro studies with a high elasticity needed to explain the macro evidence.

One recent approach, begun by Rogerson (1988), starts with the observation that there may be important non-convexities in the labor supply decision, such as transportation costs. This model then says that people take leisure in the recession because it is not efficient for everyone to incur these fixed costs of going to work when productivity is low.

We have two reservations about this approach. First, it relies on the assumption that all individuals are identical. If there is heterogeneity of individuals' costs of going to work, then changes in the wage would get a few marginal people to discretely change their labor supply decision, but would not affect hours for inframarginal workers. It is by no means clear that the resulting aggregate labor supply curve is more elastic than it is when fixed costs are absent. For a similar reason, the fact that the decision to eat Chinese food on a particular day is discrete does not mean that the intertemporal elasticity of substitution for Chinese food is infinite. Second, fixed costs of going to work should equally affect both the micro and macro estimates of labor supply elasticity. It is not correct to say that micro evidence yields true preference parameters, since micro estimates are also affected by fixed costs. This approach cannot then explain the inconsistency between micro and macro evidence. Although non-convexities might be part of the explanation of elastic labor supply, they do not reconcile micro and macro evidence.

There seem to be some more plausible ways to explain why hours change a lot over the business cycle when wages change only a little. One obvious possibility in the later period is unemployment insurance with high replacement rates and imperfect experience rating, which should significantly raise the effective elasticity of labor supply. The second possibility is that people with a high intertemporal elasticity of substitution should sort themselves into cyclically sensitive industries. That is, people who like to work hard some of the time and rest other times have a strong comparative advantage at working in durable sectors, where employment volatility is expected. Third, the reason that hours respond strongly to small changes in wages may be that wages are simply installment payments in a long-term relationship and do not serve to allocate labor over the short-run. Finally, it may be the case that the employer gets to choose employment at some fixed wage and so effectively faces an elastic labor supply even though leisure is not easily substitutable over time. On the surface, such a rigid Keynesian wage model looks very similar to a model with a perfectly elastic labor supply (Hall 1988*b*) except with distinctly different welfare implications.

To summarize, market clearing models of economic fluctuations require an intertemporal labor supply elasticity of at least 1 or 2, but micro estimates are much smaller. However, micro evidence is not informative on the intertemporal elasticity of labor supply because it is hard to identify temporary wage changes at the individual level. Trying to reconcile micro and macro evidence may not, therefore, be necessary. A more fruitful approach might be to understand why the true elasticity is high or, alternatively, why wages are rigid.

5. The Behavior of Relative Prices

5.1. OVERVIEW

In this section, we present evidence on the behavior of relative prices of different commodity groups over the business cycle. We then interpret this evidence in light of IR, TS as well as countercyclical markup models of economic fluctuations.

IR and TS models make very strong predictions about the behavior of relative prices. Both models say that goods produced with low productivity are expensive relative to goods produced with high productivity. Since low productivity is associated with recessions, the models say that in the recession the relative price of goods experiencing a productivity decline should rise. This implication leads to a natural question: what are the goods that become relatively more expensive in the recession? By isolating these goods, we can find the nexus of technology shocks or increasing returns.

We consider several commodity groups and ask three questions: (1) What is the cyclical behavior of the prices of finished goods, intermediate goods, and raw materials relative to the GNP deflator and to the private sector wage? (2) What is the difference in the cyclical behavior of the prices of durable and non-durable goods relative to the GNP deflator and to the private sector wage? (3) How do the relative prices of outputs and inputs move over the cycle? Answers to these questions can give us some information about the nexus of increasing returns, technology shocks, and countercyclical markups.

5.2 THE EVIDENCE

This section presents the evidence on the cyclical behavior of relative prices. All the data for this study are annual for 1947–87, taken from the 1988 Economic Report of the President. Our cyclical indicator is constructed from the civilian unemployment rate. To make the regression coefficients interpretable, we rescale this variable before using it in the regression. First, we pass a spline in time through the unemployment rate starting in 1965 to control for changes in the natural rate of unemployment, and then take the residuals. Second, we first difference the resulting series and take the *negative* of such obtained changes. This gives us a *procyclical* measure, equal to detrended changes in the employment rate. In each business cycle, we define a *boom* as the year of the fastest growth rate of (detrended) employment, and a *recession* as the year of the smallest growth rate of (detrended) employment. Finally, we scale these detrended growth rates of employment so that the average over all cycles of the difference of growth rates of employment between boom and recession is equal to .01. That is, in an average cycle, our detrended and normalized employment grows 1% faster in the year defined as a boom than in the year defined as a recession. This cyclical indicator is presented in Figure 4, where vertical lines denote recessions. Importantly, the peaks and troughs of this indicator coincide with peaks and troughs in the growth rate of output.

In addition to using the Normalized Detrended Growth Rate of Employment in the analysis, we also use a dummy equal to 1 in 1974 and 1975, and 0 in all the other years. We do so because the 1974–75 recession has been accompanied by a large and very unusual change in relative prices. In particular, the relative price of oil and derivative products has increased significantly. The 1980 recession also exhibits this pattern of relative

Figure 4

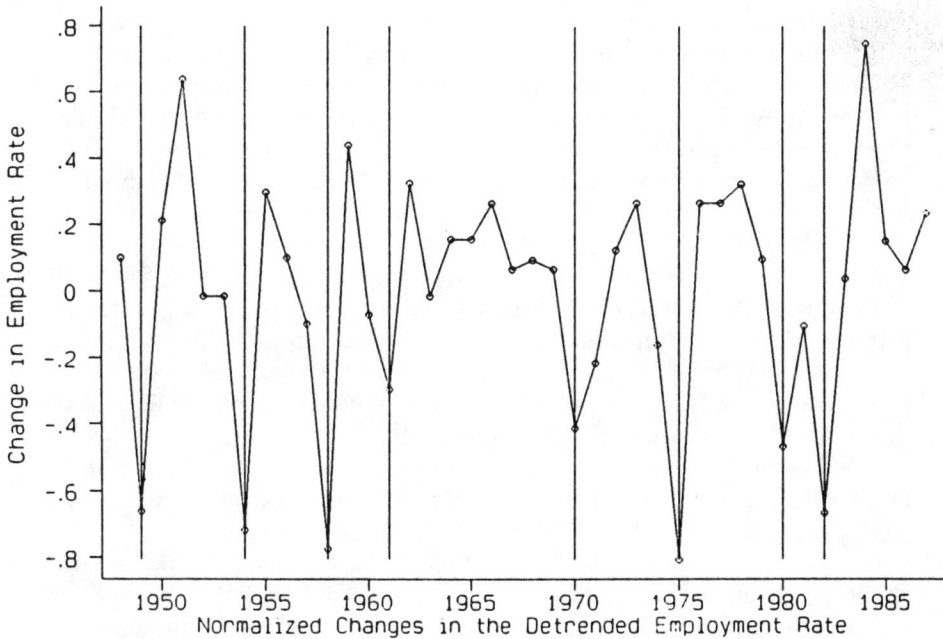

Normalized Changes in the Detrended Employment Rate

prices, but it is not as pronounced. Because the 1974–75 recession looks so different from all the others but one, we did not want to contaminate our inference by this episode. All the regressions we run take the form

Change in relative price = $A + B \times$ (Cyclical Indicator) $+ C \times$ (1974–1975 dummy).

Tables 3–5 present the results. Table 3 presents the evidence on prices relative to the GNP deflator. Table 4 presents the results on prices relative to the average private sector hourly earnings. Table 5 presents the evidence on relative prices. In all tables, panel A deals with broad groups of goods by stage of processing, and panel B deals with individual commodities. Based on the scaling of the cyclical indicator, all the coefficients in the tables are easy to interpret. For example, the coefficient in the finished goods regression in panel A of Table 3 is .79. This means that, relative to the GNP deflator, prices of finished goods on average change .79% more in a boom (the year of the fastest increase in the employment rate for each cycle) than in the recession (the year of the lowest change in the employment rate for each cycle). The coefficient of 4.54 on the 1974–75 dummy in this regression means that the price of finished goods rose 4.54% per year faster relative to GNP deflator in 1974–75 than in other periods.

In interpreting the results of Tables 3–5, we refer to relative prices that yield a positive coefficient on the cyclical indicator as procyclical, and relative prices that yield a negative coefficient as countercyclical. The regression coefficient measures the difference in the growth rate of relative prices between the boom (defined as the year of fastest growth rate of detrended employment in each cycle) and the recession (defined as the year of the lowest growth rate of detrended employment in each cycle). The reason we need such a relative measure is that some prices follow strong trends, and so may, for example, fall relative to the GNP deflator in both booms and recessions. If the relative price does not have a trend, a positive regression coefficient would say that, the relative price rises in a boom and falls in a recession. If, in contrast, the relative price is always falling, a positive coefficient would say that it falls less in the boom than it does in a recession. Either way, the relative price is procyclical in the sense that *relative to how they do in a recession, relative prices rise in a boom*. The same logic explains why negative regression coefficients correspond to countercyclical relative prices.

Two kinds of results emerge from Table 3. First, finished goods do not show much cyclical behavior relative to the GNP deflator, except for slightly countercyclical relative price changes of finished durables. In

Table 3 CYCLICAL BEHAVIOR OF PRICES RELATIVE TO GNP DEFLATOR

Variable	Cyclical Indicator	1974–75 Dummy
Panel A: *Broad Groups by Stage of Processing*		
Finished goods	.79	4.54
	(.92)	(3.20)
Consumer durables	−.77	.78
	(−1.00)	(.61)
Consumer non-durables	.37	7.38
	(.23)	(2.76)
Capital equipment	−.81	4.37
	(−1.00)	(3.26)
Total intermediate	2.69	8.87
	(2.09)	(4.16)
Manufacturing materials	3.32	10.47
	(2.54)	(4.83)
Construction materials	3.05	5.69
	(3.41)	(3.84)
Fuels	1.31	21.4
	(.36)	(3.52)
Crude Materials	9.91	4.59
	(2.44)	(.68)
Panel B: *Commodities*		
Power	.59	22.04
	(.15)	(3.34)
Chemicals	1.78	18.94
	(1.18)	(7.58)
Lumber	10.58	−3.69
	(4.11)	(−.87)
Paper	3.53	10.07
	(2.62)	(4.52)
Metals	3.65	9.70
	(2.39)	(3.83)
Machinery	−.67	4.81
	(−.70)	(3.05)
Household durables	−.20	2.08
	(−.29)	(1.79)
Vehicles	−2.08	.11
	(−2.03)	(.07)
Rubber	4.05	8.89
	(1.67)	(2.22)

Note. *t*-statistics in parentheses.

Table 4   CYCLICAL BEHAVIOR OF PRICES RELATIVE TO AVERAGE
HOURLY EARNINGS OF PRIVATE-SECTOR EMPLOYEES

Variable	Cyclical Indicator	1974–75 Dummy
Panel A: *Broad Groups by Stage of Processing*		
Finished goods	.29	6.35
	(.30)	(3.98)
Consumer durables	−1.27	2.59
	(−1.72)	(2.12)
Consumer nondurables	−.13	9.19
	(−.08)	(3.29)
Capital equipment	−1.31	6.18
	(−1.65)	(4.69)
Total intermediate	2.19	10.68
	(1.63)	(4.80)
Manufacturing materials	2.82	12.28
	(2.08)	(5.47)
Construction materials	2.55	7.50
	(2.99)	(5.30)
Fuels	.82	23.2
	(.22)	(3.76)
Crude Materials	9.41	6.40
	(2.29)	(.94)
Panel B: *Commodities*		
Power	.09	23.85
	(.02)	(3.59)
Chemicals	1.28	20.75
	(.79)	(7.73)
Lumber	10.08	−1.88
	(4.01)	(−.45)
Paper	3.03	11.88
	(2.13)	(5.05)
Metals	3.15	11.52
	(2.07)	(4.57)
Machinery	−1.17	6.62
	(−1.24)	(4.23)
Household durables	−.70	3.90
	(−1.06)	(3.54)
Vehicles	−2.58	1.92
	(−2.55)	(1.15)
Rubber	3.55	10.71
	(1.42)	(2.59)

Note. *t*-statistics in parentheses.

contrast, prices of intermediate goods other than fuels are highly procyclical. For example, in an average cycle manufacturing materials grow 3.32% faster relative to the GNP deflator in a boom than in a recession. One exception to this is capital equipment, which may be thought of as an intermediate good, and which shows mildly countercyclical prices. By far the most procyclical are the prices of crude materials. In an average cycle, crude materials prices rise 9.91% more relative to the GNP deflator in a boom than they do in a recession. The procyclicality of prices clearly declines as one gets further in the production chain.

Similar results come from the more narrowly defined commodities. As is well known, prices of lumber, metals, paper, and rubber are extremely procyclical. In contrast, prices of finished durable goods, including household durables, machinery, and vehicles are countercyclical. Commodities such as power and, surprisingly, chemicals do not show much action over the cycle.

Table 4 confirms the results of Table 3, except that the evidence is a little stronger. Relative to the private sector average hourly earnings, prices of finished goods do not show any cyclical behavior except that durables and capital equipment are more clearly countercyclical. Relative prices of raw materials and intermediate goods are, in contrast, strongly procyclical, except for capital equipment. Durable goods, such as household durables and vehicles, show the opposite pattern. Tables 3 and 4 show very clearly that the place to look for productivity declines in the recession is finished durable goods. Table 4 also suggests that procyclical real wages are most pronounced in terms of durables—a finding common to real wage studies.

Table 5 presents some more novel results, namely those on relative prices. The conclusion of Table 5 is that, in the production chain, the relative price of outputs to inputs is countercyclical. For example, relative to intermediate materials, finished goods grow 1.9% less in the boom than in the recession. Relative to crude materials, this number is 9.1%. Throughout this table, the result is that prices of finished goods are countercyclical relative to intermediate goods and crude materials, and prices of intermediate goods are countercyclical relative to crude materials.

Similar results emerge from panel B of Table 5. Relative to the price of lumber, those of construction materials and household durables move countercyclically. Relative to the price of manufacturing materials, those of vehicles, household durables, and machinery also move countercyclically. Relative to the price of metals, those of vehicles, machinery, household durables are again countercyclical. It is very clear from this table that the price of outputs relative to that of inputs is countercyclical.

We draw three conclusions from Tables 3–5. First, the more finished are the goods, the less procyclical are their relative prices. Second, the goods that exhibit the most countercyclical relative prices are durables. Third, outputs appreciate relative to inputs in the recession. Importantly, these results are very similar to those found for the Great Depression period by Mills (1936) and Means et al. (1939) for a broader range of commodities. However, in the Great Depression, real wages actually increased, and so these findings can be rationalized by the observation that the relative price of goods with a greater labor content should be higher. Our starting point, in contrast, is that in the postwar period real wages have been if anything procyclical. Our next task is to interpret our findings for the postwar period.

Table 5   CYCLICAL BEHAVIOR OF RELATIVE PRICES

Variable	Cyclical Indicator	1974–75 Dummy
Panel A: *Broad Groups by Stage of Processing*		
Finished goods/Total intermediate	−1.90	−4.33
	(−2.96)	(−4.07)
Finished goods/Fuels	−.53	−16.85
	(−.17)	(−3.25)
Finished goods/Crude materials	−9.12	−.052
	(−2.61)	(−.009)
Consumer durables/Total intermediate	−3.46	−8.09
	(−2.77)	(−3.91)
Consumer durables/Manufacturing materials	−4.09	−9.69
	(−3.32)	(−4.74)
Consumer non-durables/Total intermediate	−2.32	−1.49
	(−2.57)	(−.995)
Consumer non-durables/Manufacturing materials	−2.96	−3.09
	(−2.57)	(−1.62)
Capital equipment/Total intermediate	−3.50	−4.50
	(−2.72)	(−2.11)
Capital equipment/Manufacturing materials	−4.13	−6.10
	(−3.24)	(−2.89)
Total intermediate/Crude materials	−7.22	4.28
	(−2.37)	(.850)
Manufacturing materials/Crude materials	−6.59	5.88
	(−2.08)	(1.12)
Construction materials/Crude materials	−6.86	1.10
	(−1.87)	(.181)

5.3 INTERPRETATION

The evidence in Tables 3–5 allows us to discriminate at least partially between various business cycle stories. One story—which we associate with Long and Plosser (1983)—is that technology shocks occur in the production of widely used raw materials or intermediate inputs, and then spread across the economy through the input-output matrix. These shocks need not even be technology shocks; they can simply be price shocks to inputs supplied from outside the economy, like oil. An IR version of this theory says that increasing returns are in the production of raw materials or intermediate goods. As a result, these are the activities experiencing major productivity declines in the recession. Both TS and IR versions of this story predict that the relative price of raw materials and/or intermediate goods is countercyclical.

Table 5 CYCLICAL BEHAVIOR OF RELATIVE PRICES (CONTINUED)

Variable	Cyclical Indicator	1974–75 Dummy
Panel B: *Broad Groups and Commodities*		
Total intermediate/Metals	−.96	−.83
	(−.92)	(−.48)
Manufacturing materials/Metals	−.33	.77
	(−.37)	(.52)
Construction materials/Metals	−.60	−4.01
	(−.58)	(−2.33)
Construction materials/Lumber	−7.53	9.38
	(−3.46)	(2.61)
Vehicles/Manufacturing materials	−5.40	−10.36
	(−3.14)	(−3.63)
Household durables/Manufacturing materials	−3.52	−8.39
	(−3.26)	(−4.68)
Machinery/Manufacturing materials	−3.99	−5.66
	(−3.31)	(−2.83)
Vehicles/Metals	−5.73	−9.59
	(−3.37)	(−3.41)
Machinery/Metals	−4.32	−4.89
	(−3.17)	(−2.17)
Household durables/Metals	−3.85	−7.62
	(−2.92)	(−3.49)
Capital equipment/Metals	−4.46	−5.33
	(−3.27)	(−2.36)
Household durables/Lumber	−10.78	5.77
	(−4.01)	(1.30)

Note. t-statistics in parentheses.

This story is inconsistent with the evidence in Tables 3–5. The tables confirm the standard finding that the relative prices of raw materials are extremely procyclical. An exception might be the case of oil in 1974–75 and 1979–80. However, except in these episodes, it is clear that recessions are not driven by adverse shocks or endogenous productivity declines in raw materials or in intermediate goods. This fact also poses a problem for the Long/Plosser theory of co-movement, which works through shocks to common inputs.

The evidence in Tables 3–5 is much more favorable to the view that productivity changes occur at the latter stages of the production process, particularly in durable goods. The IR version of the story says that increasing returns occur in the final stages of production or distribution of durables or possibly at the stage of producing capital equipment. The productivity of these stages declines in the recessions, and therefore the relative price of durables rises. The reason that relative price movements are so pronounced for wide categories of goods is that the co-movement mechanism outlined in the previous section leads to synchronization of output and productivity movements across sectors.

The TS version of this story is somewhat different, and harder to reconcile with the evidence. In the TS world, the goods that get expensive in the recession are only the goods experiencing adverse technology shocks, and not the goods whose output declines simply because of co-movement. This is an important difference between IR and TS models: even though both generate co-movement with immobile labor and imperfect borrowing, the TS model exhibits countercyclical price movements only in the sectors with bad shocks. In contrast, the IR model yields relative price increases in all increasing returns sectors in response to output declines. To reconcile the TS model with the evidence, to bring on a recession one needs fairly widespread adverse technology shocks in either the finished durable goods sectors or in the capital equipment sector. We leave to the reader to evaluate the plausibility of pervasive adverse technology shocks in durable goods sectors as a cause of recessions.

Before concluding this section, we stress that the evidence in Tables 3–5 is also broadly consistent with countercyclical markups at the later production stages, especially in durables. None of the evidence we have presented bears on the behavior of true productivity; all the action might well be in markups. Hall's (1988a) earlier evidence can be interpreted in terms of countercyclical markups, although his later (1988c) work points to true increasing returns. As we mentioned before, however, Hall finds evidence of declining average costs and firms earning close to zero profits. This finding points to countercyclical markups as a way to generate procyclical real wages. Domowitz, Hubbard, and Petersen (1988) present some evidence bearing on this issue, and conclude that markups are countercyclical. At this point, we are not sure which theory is right and leave this issue to a further investigation.

In summary, the evidence presented in this section enables us to at least partially narrow down the range of theories consistent with the data. If economic fluctuations are driven by technology shocks, these must be pervasive shocks across durable good industries, and not in intermediate input industries. If fluctuations are driven by increasing returns, these must be in the production and distribution of durable goods. Finally, fluctuations could be explained by countercyclical mark-ups in durable good industries, without productivity movements.

6. Conclusion

In this paper we have discussed models of business cycles driven by movements of productivity. In particular, we have compared models in which these productivity movements result from exogenous technology shocks with models in which they result from endogenous movements along an increasing returns production function. We asked what kinds of assumptions these models require to at least roughly fit the data. We have found that although these models have very different sources of productivity changes, the assumptions required to fit the data are very similar. First, to generate large movements in output in response to small changes in productivity, these models rely on durability of goods. Second, to produce co-movement of outputs and labor inputs across various sectors of the economy, these models need to assume specialized (immobile) labor and restricted borrowing. Third, to obtain large movements in labor inputs in response to small changes in real wages or productivity, these models require very elastic labor supply. Although none of these results is completely new, we hope that our emphasis on identifying the critical building blocks of a market clearing model proves useful.

Our paper has also documented the countercyclical behavior of prices of outputs relative to inputs, and of finished durables relative to wages and to the GNP deflator. This evidence suggests that the place to look for technology shocks or increasing returns is at the final stages of produc-tion, or in the distribution of durable goods. In the increasing returns framework, this evidence supports illiquid markets models of reces-sions. In these models, time to sale is long and therefore the marginal cost is high in the recession. The fact that such variable liquidity costs are most plausible for durable goods is evidence favorable to this approach.

There are three topics that are closely related to the issues we have discussed, but that we have not dealt with for lack of space. The first is downward rigid real wages as an alternative to elastic labor supply. Even if one assumes downward rigid real wages, one still needs a source of productivity changes—such as increasing returns or technology shocks—to generate shifts in labor demand. Downward rigid real wages would probably exacerbate the recession in a model of the sort we described, because firms might shut down even when they would not with a flexible real wage. Downward rigid real wages also make the co-movement story look more like an aggregate demand story: instead of changes in relative prices we get changes in income and in demand for individual goods. It remains to be explored what are some of the other consequences of this assumption.

We have also ignored what is perhaps the most natural explanation of our evidence on cyclical behavior of relative prices: countercyclical markups without productivity changes. There are a number of reasons why producers of durables in a recession might not want to cut prices even if marginal costs fall when input prices decline. Most plausibly, we think that the customer mix shifts in the recession away from buyers with elastic demand, and so the profit maximizing markup rises. This change of customer base might occur because most people would require enormous price concessions to buy durables in a recession. The only remaining customers are those who need to replace durables that have fallen apart and so have inelastic demand. The change in the customer base might also occur if people who shop around and therefore have elastic demand are precisely the ones who have very low reservation prices in the recession—they may be individuals who face the risk of unemployment or firms fearing bankruptcy. Such theories of countercyclical markups, developed in particular by Phelps/Winter (1970), Okun (1981), Stiglitz (1984), Bils (1986), Weitzman (1982), and Solow (1984), can probably explain most of our evidence. Not surprisingly, one can build an endogenous business cycle model driven by countercyclical markups without productivity changes.

Finally, all of our discussion has assumed a fixed capital stock in production. In contrast, technology shocks models incorporate capital in the production function. Capital in these models serves in part as a propagation device, whereby today's technology improvements lead to an increase in the capital stock and therefore labor productivity tomorrow. There are also increasing returns models in which a business cycle is generated by movements in the capital stock (Shleifer 1986; Kiyotaki 1988). In these models, waves of investment raise productivity and income, and so lead to increased demand for goods. The higher demand for goods in turn justifies the initial investment outlay. Unifying the increasing returns models discussed in this paper with increasing returns investment models remains a stopic for future work.

We are grateful to Olivier Blanchard, Peter Diamond, and Larry Katz for helpful comments and to the NSF for financial support.

REFERENCES

Bernanke, Ben and Mark Gertler. "Agency Costs, Net Worth, and Business Fluctuations." *American Economic Review.* Forthcoming 1989.

Benhabib, Rogerson, and Wright. "Home Production and Aggregate Models of the Labor Market." November 1988. Mimeo.

Bils, Mark J. "Real Wages over the Business Cycle: Evidence from Panel Data." *Journal of Political Economy* 93: 666–89. August 1985.

Bils, Mark J. "Cyclical Pricing of Durable Luxuries." Mimeo. 1986.

Bils, Mark J. "The Cyclical Behavior of Marginal Cost and Price." *American Economic Review* 77: 838–55. December 1987.

Cooper, Russell and John Haltiwanger. "Macroeconomic Implications of Production Bunching: Factor and Final Demand Linkages," University of Iowa. Mimeo. January 1989.

Cooper, Russell and Andrew John. "Coordinating Coordination Failures in Keynesian Models." *Quarterly Journal of Economics* 103: 441–64. August 1988.

Diamond, Peter A. "Aggregate Demand in Search Equilibrium." *Journal of Political Economy* 90: 881–94. October 1982.

Domowitz, Ian, R. Glenn Hubbard, and Bruce C. Petersen. "Market Structure and Cyclical Fluctuations in U.S. Manufacturing." *Review of Economics and Statistics* 70: 55–66. February 1988.

Greenwald, Bruce and Joseph Stiglitz. "Financial Market Imperfections and Business Cycles." Stanford University. Mimeo. 1987.

Hall, Robert E. "Market Structure and Macroeconomic Fluctuations." *Brookings Papers on Economic Activity:* 285–322. 1986.

Hall, Robert E. "The Relation between Price and Marginal Cost in U.S. Industry." *Journal of Political Economy* 96: 921–47. October 1988a.

Hall, Robert E. "Substitution over Time in Consumption and Work." Stanford University. Mimeo. June 1988b.

Hall, Robert E. "Increasing Returns: Theory and Measurement with Industry Data." Stanford University. Mimeo. September 1988c.

Hammour, Mohamad. "Increasing Returns and Endogenous Business Cycles." Cambridge, Mass.: MIT Press. Mimeo. March 1988a.

Hammour, Mohamad. "Are Business Cycles Endogenous?" Cambridge, Mass.: MIT Press. Mimeo. November 1988b.

Heller, Walter P. "Coordination Failure under Complete Markets with Application to Effective Demand." in *Equilibrium Analysis: Essays in Honor of Kenneth J. Arrow.* vol. 2, W. Heller, R. Starr, and D. Starrett. eds. Cambridge: Cambridge University Press, 1986.

Howitt, P. and R. P. McAfee. "Stability of Equilibria with Externalities." *Quarterly Journal of Economics* 103: 261–277. May 1988.

Kiyotaki, Nobukiro. "Multiple Expectational Equilibria under Monopolistic Competition." *Quarterly Journal of Economics* 103: 695–714. November 1988.

Kydland, Finn and Edward Prescott. "Time to Build and Aggregate Fluctuations," *Econometrica* 50: 1345–700. November 1982.

Kydland, Finn and Edward Prescott. "Cyclical Movements of the Labor Input and Its Real Wage." Federal Reserve Bank of Minneapolis, Mimeo. November 1988.

Long, John and Charles Plosser. "Real Business Cycles." *Journal of Political Economy* 91: 36–39. February 1983.

Mankiw, N. Gregory. "Real Business Cycles: A Neo-Keynesian Perspective." *Journal of Economic Perspectives*. Forthcoming.

Means, Gardiner C., et al. *The Structure of the American Economy.* Washington, D.C.: United States National Resource Committee. 1939.

Mills, Frederick C. *Prices in Recession and Recovery.* New York: NBER. 1936.

Mitchell, Wesley. *Business Cycles: The Problem and Its Setting.* New York: National Bureau of Economic Research. 1927.

Murphy, Kevin M., Andrei Shleifer, and Robert W. Vishny. "Increasing Returns, Durables, and Economic Fluctuations." University of Chicago. Mimeo. October 1988.

Okun, Arthur. *Prices and Quantitites: A Macroeconomic Analysis.* Washington, D.C.: The Brookings Institution. 1981.

Phelps, Edmund and Sidney Winter. "Optimal Price Policy under Atomistic Competition." in *Microeconomic Foundations of Employment and Inflation Theory.* E. Phelps, ed. New York: W. W. Norton, 1970.

Prescott, Edward. "Theory Ahead of Business Cycle Measurements." reprinted in Federal Reserve Bank of Minneapolis, *Quarterly Review.* 9–22. Fall 1986.

Ramey, Valerie. "Non-Convex Costs and the Behavior of Inventories." University of California at San Diego. Mimeo. December 1987.

Roberts, John. "An Equilibrium Model with Involuntary Unemployment at Flexible, Competitive Prices and Wages." *American Economic Review* 77: 856–74. December 1987.

Rogerson, Richard. "Indivisible Labor, Lotteries and Equilibrium." *Journal of Monetary Economics* 21: 3–17. 1988.

Rotemberg, Julio. "The New Keynesian Microfoundations." *NBER Macroeconomics Annual.* 69–104. 1987.

Rotemberg, Julio and Garth Saloner. "A Supergame-Theoretic Model of Price Wars during Booms," *American Economic Review* 76: 390–407. June 1986.

Scheinkman, Jose A. and Laurence Weiss. "Borrowing Constraints and Aggregate Economic Activity." *Econometrica* 54: 23–46. January 1986.

Shleifer, Andrei. "Implementation Cycles." *Journal of Political Economy* 94: 1163–90. December 1986.

Solon, Gary and Robert Barsky. "Real Wages over the Business Cycles." University of Michigan. Mimeo. 1988.

Solow, Robert. "Monopolistic Competition and the Multiplier." Cambridge, Mass.: MIT Press. 1984. Mimeo.

Stiglitz, Joseph. "Price Rigidities and Market Structure." *American Economic Review* 7: 350–55. May 1984.

Summers, Lawrence. "Some Skeptical Observations on Real Business Cycle Theory." Federal Reserve Bank of Minneapolis, *Quarterly Review.* 23–27. 1986.

Weitzman, Martin L. "Increasing Returns and the Foundation of Unemployment Theory." *Economic Journal* 92: 787–804. 1982.

Comment

EDWARD C. PRESCOTT
Federal Reserve Bank of Minneapolis and the University of Minnesota

Over the last two decades much progress has been made in macroeconomics. Using established theory—that is the theory used by leading people in public finance—we have found that variations in the Solow technology parameter are an important source of aggregate fluctuations in the postwar period. Business cycles are not an anomaly for standard neoclassical theory. The methodology employed is quantitative neoclassical theory. The model economies are calibrated to national income and product accounts and household surveys. Equilibrium policy rules for the economic agents are computed and then used to determine the sampling distribution of various statistics.

Subsequent to Kydland and my "Time to Build" paper, a number of issues have been explored with this methodology. For example, Cooley and Hansen (1988) have explored the implications of a cash-in-advance constraint for aggregate fluctuations. They found that they were not very important. Danthine and Donaldson (1989) have come to similar conclusions with regard to the introduction of an efficiency wage construct. Huffman, Greenwald, and Hercowitz (1988) have studied the behavior of economies in which the capital depreciation rate increases with the intensity with which capital is utilized. Again, the consequences for aggregate fluctuations were minor. Hansen and Sargent (1988) found that introducing both a straight time and overtime work options significantly enriches the theory but does not alter the finding that the Solow technology shocks are an important source of fluctuations.

What Does Matter?

Hansen (1985) introduced the Rogerson (1988) labor indivisibilities and found it did matter and did matter a lot for business cycle accounting. It also mattered for assessing the importance of public finance shocks which recently have been explored by Christiano and Eichenbaum (1988), Chang (1988), Braun (1988), and McGratten (1988) using this methodology. If both the hours a plant is operated and the number of workers that operate a plant are choice variables, the results are essentially the same as for the Hansen economy with the labor indivisibility. Most the variation in aggregate hours is accounted for by changes in the number employed. Changes in the hours worked per employed person accounts for the rest of the variation in the aggregate labor input. Hall (1988) surveys the evidence on the intertemporal substitution of leisure and comes to the conclusion that in the aggregate leisure is highly intertemporally substitutable. Given this property, any relatively permanent change in a factor that affects the steady state of the deterministic growth model will contribute to aggregate fluctuations. The question is how much each contributes.

What are the Justifications for Static Marshallian Increasing Returns?

The key feature of the Murphy-Shleifer-Vishny paper is their introduction of a production externality. The authors assume it and refer to a more rigorous paper in which the underlying micro foundations of such a structure are developed. I examined the cited paper and found the argument heuristic and incomplete, and not yet up to the standards of modern general equilibrium theory. What are the theoretical justifications for these static increasing returns at the industry level but not at the firm level? One justification for Marshallian increasing industry returns is Arrow's learning-by-doing. But, this is a dynamic relation. It is not temporary increases in the average product of labor at the firm level that are associated with temporary increases in industry output as in the Murphy-Shleifer-Vishny model. Another justification for industry increasing returns is induced technological change. Jacob Schmookler (1966) has presented evidence for demand induced technological change. But that also is a dynamic story. Changes are permanent. What is the empirical evidence for static industry increasing returns to scale? How big are they? Where are the measurements? Do Chrysler's costs decline when Ford is producing more automobiles? Maybe, but I want to see some evidence before taking the assumption seriously.

One question that has not yet been addressed within the quantitative theoretical framework is whether the findings are sensitive to the assumption of price-taking behavior. Does abstracting from the fact that the corner drugstore has some monopoly power significantly bias the estimate of the importance of Solow technology shocks—or for that matter the importance of public finance shocks, terms of trade shocks, etc.? This is an interesting question. I do not know how to answer it, and it is not an easy question to answer. The theory of monopolistic competition in dynamic stochastic environments is not well developed. In the growth literature there are a couple of deterministic models, but typically they are steady-state or balanced growth models. I, however, would be surprised if a little ex post monopoly power necessitated a significant revision in the estimate of the importance of Solow technology shocks as a source of aggregate fluctuations.

One empirical embarrassment for increasing returns stories is that hours of employment and productivity should move together. They do not. At the business cycle frequencies, the correlation is about −0.2 (see Christiano and Eichenbaum 1988). There surely are errors in measuring the labor input and as a result the correlation is larger than −0.2, but it is a lot less than one. If technology shocks were the only source of fluctuations, standard theory implies that this correlation would be near 1.0. But we do not claim that these shocks are the only source. All that Finn Kydland and I argue is that they are a major source and that the economy would be almost as volatile if they were the only source. Incidentally, when defense expenditure went from 5 to 13 percent of GNP at the beginning of the Korean War, productivity did not jump. It fell.

The authors claim that an implication of standard theory is that employment in the consumption-good producing and investment-good producing sectors should move in opposite directions if technology shocks are the only source of fluctuations. For the Hansen economy (1985) this is not the case. Employment in the consumption-good industry stays constant given that in the aggregate leisure is infinitely substitutable (as it is in the Murphy-Shleifer-Vishny economy). If leisure is durable, as it is in Kydland and my models (1982 and 1988), employment can be procyclical. It is for the Kydland and Prescott (1988) model economy. The authors say Kydland and I assume the shocks are persistent. That is wrong. I, and Nelson and Plosser earlier (1982), found that they were highly persistent. It is an empirical finding—not an assumption.

Why did productivity fall in coal mining in the Seventies if there were increasing industry returns? There was an increase in output in that industry during that period. People in that industry did not know why productivity fell. One coal mining company funded a study at Carnegie-Mellon (Goodman and Leyden (1985)) to find out the reason for the decline—a decline associated with an increase in output. There are random, that is, currently unpredictable, changes in production functions. This is a fact.

The authors report the finding that output and employment changes are correlated across industries. This was known—see Burns and Mitchell (1947). Is there a close association between quarterly changes in employment and output per workers? I doubt it. Determining industry output and inputs on a quarterly basis is fraught with problems. Even at the annual level it is not easy. Jorgenson, Gallop, and Fraumeni (1987) find that productivity changes are correlated and do not average out. If they did average out, there would not be any aggregate shocks and an implication of standard theory would be that Solow technology shocks are not an important source of fluctuations.

At the low frequencies Bailey and Gordon (1988) have concluded that a productivity slowdown has indeed occurred. They point out that the slowdown is across most of the industries. With increasing returns why did productivity growth slow even though output growth did not slow? The reason that output growth did not decline, even though productivity growth did, is that the growth rate of employment increased. This observation matches poorly with the implication of the Murphy-Shleifer-Vishny model with its implication that employment and productivity move together. To summarize, the static increasing returns has not been justified. Economics has come a long way since the Thirties when business cycle stories were a dime a dozen—see Godfrey Haberler's (1937) book, *Prosperity and Depression*, for a plethora of them. I hope we do not go back to the Thirties when theory had no quantitative discipline.

The final point of these comments is that standard theory should be used to address specific questions. In challenging Kydland and my finding, the authors are challenging the findings of Jorgenson and Yun (1988) concerning the 1986 tax reform and a lot of other findings that use established theory. I do not think that the authors have made much of a case for using production functions that display static increasing returns. I will stick with Solow's (1957) neoclassical theory for studying business cycle fluctuations until someone develops a better alternative. What determines the rate of technology change is another matter. There I conjecture increasing returns are important.

Prepared for NBER Annual Conference on Macroeconomics. Organized by Olivier Jean Blanchard and Stanley S. Fischer, held March 10 and 11, 1989 Cambridge, Massachusetts.

REFERENCES

Bailey, M. W. and R. J. Gordon. 1988. "The Productivity Slowdown, Measurement Issues, and the Explosion of Computer Power." *Brookings Papers on Economic Activity* 2, 347–420.
Boldrin, M. and L. Montrucchio. 1985. "On the Indeterminacy of Capital Accumulation Paths." University of Rochester Working Paper.
Braun, R.A. 1988. "The Dynamic Interaction of Distortionary Taxes aand Aggregate Variables in Postwar U. S. Data." Northwestern University Working Paper.
Burns, A. F. and W. C. Mitchell. 1947. *Measuring Business Cycles*. New York: NBER.

Chang, L. J. 1988. "Corporate Taxes, Disaggregated Capital Markets and Business Cycles." Carnegie-Mellon University Working Paper.

Christiano, L. J. and M. Eichenbaum. 1988. "Is Theory Really Ahead of Measurement? Current Real Business Cycle Theory and Aggregate Labor Market Fluctuations." Federal Reserve Bank of Minneapolis Working Paper 412.

Cooley, T. F. and G. D. Hansen. 1988. "The Inflation Tax and the Business Cycle." UCLA Working Paper.

Danthine, J. P. and J. B. Donaldson. 1989. "Efficiency Wages and the Business Cycle Puzzle." Columbia Graduate School of Business Working Paper.

Goodman, P. S. and D. P. Leyden. 1985. *Human Resource Management Skill and Coal Mine Productivity—Final Repoort.* Vol. 2. Pittsburgh: U.S. Bureau of Mines.

Greenwald, J., Z. Hercowitz, and G. W. Huffman. 1988. "Investment, Capacity Utilization and the Business Cycle." *American Economic Review* 78: 402–18.

Haberler, G. 1937. *Prosperity and Depression.* Geneva: League of Nations.

Hall, R. E. 1988. "Substitution over Time in Work and Consumption." NBER Working Paper.

Hansen, G. D. 1985. "Indivisible Labor and the Business Cycle." *Journal of Monetary Economics* 16: 309–28.

Hansen, G. D. and T. J. Sargent. 1988. "Straight Time and Overtime in Equilibrium." *Journal of Monetary Economics* 21: 281–308.

Jorgenson, D. W., F. M. Gallop, and B. M. Fraumeni. 1987. *Productivity and U. S Economic Growth.* Cambridge, Mass.: Harvard University Press.

Jorgenson, D. W. and K. Y. Yun. 1988. "Tax Policies and U.S Economic Growth." Harvard University Working Paper.

Kydland, F. E. and E. C. Prescott. 1982. "Time to Build and Aggregate Fluctuations." *Econometrica* 50: 1345–70.

Kydland, F. E. and E. C. Prescott. 1988. "The Workweeks of Capital and its Cyclical Implications." *Journal of Monetary Economics* 21: 343–60.

McGratten, E. R. 1988. "The Macroeconomic Effects of Tax Policy in an Equilibrium Model." Stanford University Working Paper.

Nelson, C. and C. Plosser. 1982. "Trends and Random Walks in Macroeconomic Time Series: Some Evidence and Implications." *Journal of Monetary Economics* 10: 139–62.

Rogerson, R. E. 1988. "Indivisible Labor, Lotteries and Equilibrium." *Journal of Monetary Economics* 21: 3–16.

Schmookler, J. 1966. *Invention and Economic Growth.* Cambridge, Mass.: Harvard University Press.

Solow, R. M. 1957. "Technical Change and the Aggregate Production Function." *Review of Economics and Statistics* 39: 312–20.

Comment

PETER DIAMOND

I want to begin by introducing a simple one-sector model with the same characteristics as the basic model used by the authors. I found this alternate presentation helpful in understanding their model. Then I want to discuss the issue of co-movements across different industries and the relationship between co-movements and budget constraints. Third, I want to relate the model to the large gross flows of jobs and workers which exist in the U.S. economy.

1. Basic Model

Consider a static model with a continuum of identical agents. Each agent can work zero or one. Without work, there is no output. With work, output is either x or y, $x<y$, depending on whether everyone else works or not. I will not worry about circumstances where only some of the population works, since this will not happen in the equilibria considered. I assume there are no other possible contacts between individuals except through the increasing returns to scale production externality. Utility is separable. With a suitable normalization, utility is equal to $U(0)$, $U(x) - 1$, or $U(y) - 1$, depending on the possible circumstances. We now assume that these values satisfy

$$U(x) - 1 < U(0) < U(y) - 1 \quad (1)$$

Then there are two equilibria, with everyone working and no one working. The two inequalities in (1) assure the presence of each of the equilibria.

Now consider stringing together a continuum of these static models. We have a dynamic rational expectations path with any time structure we would like for the choice between the two static equilibrium positions.

To get a little more structure on the range of possible outcomes, the next step is to modify preferences. (For an argument that the continuous time additive utility function does not have appealing properties, see Huang and Kreps 1987.) Following the authors' description of durables (which also can be interpreted as applying to non-durables), we write instantaneous utility as a function of a stock variable, $U(k)$, and have k deteriorate at the exponential rate d and grow at the rates 0, x, or y according to the level of output. We now let lifetime utility be the present discounted value of U, with utility discount rate r. Putting this structure into preferences rather than durability of the good avoids the embarrassment of having durability but not storability since inventories certainly complicate and may alter the equilibrium.

If the economy is always at the high output level, the consumption stock variable will converge to y/d. We assume that preferences are such that this is not an equilibrium. That is, we assume that someone with consumption stock y/d and marginal product y would choose not to work (for some interval of time) even if everyone else were continuing to work. In order to derive this condition, we need to derive the shadow value of y units of output. The shadow value is equal to the present discounted value of the marginal utility of depreciated output given the time path of future production. Thus, we can rule out this steady state by assuming that the marginal utility of continued production, assuming indefinitely continued production, is less than the marginal disutility of work:

$$yU'(y/d)/r+d) < 1 \quad (2)$$

Similarly, we can rule out convergence to the origin by assuming that it is worth producing at zero stock even if no one else produces:

$$xU'(0)/(r + d) > 1 \quad (3)$$

Thus this economy does not have a steady state with everyone behaving the same.

Considering only uniform behavior, the alternative equilibrium configuration has output alternately produced and not. As set up, there are many such paths as coordinated behavior among producers switches production on and off. These include what the authors call chattering paths with output switching on and off to keep the consumption stock constant. To cut down on the number of such paths, we could assume a fixed cost to beginning a production run. This would require modification of the conditions above to preserve the results. Someone contemplating the start of production at the origin would have to overcome the setup cost; someone considering a temporary stop to production at the high output steady state would have to save enough while stopped to overcome the fixed cost of starting up again. Similarly, equilibrium cycles would have to last long enough to justify the setup cost. These are technicalities, so I will not alter the assumptions.

Following the authors, let us focus on the cycle with the longest phases. To consider rational expectations paths, we shall consider the shadow price of a unit of output, which is denoted p. On a rational expectations path the value of a unit of consumption stock is the present discounted value of the marginal utility of the remaining (i.e., depreciated) stock. Differentiating this equation we have the familiar asset value differential equation.

$$dp/dt = (r + d)p - U'(k) \quad (4)$$

This equation holds whether the good is being produced or not.

In Figures 1a and b, we consider the phase diagrams with the shadow price of a unit of output on the vertical axis and the stock of consumer goods on the horizontal axis. We have two possible uniform behavior regimes. If everyone is producing, we have

$$dk/dt = y - dk \quad (5)$$

Alternatively, if no one is producing, we have

$$dk/dt = -dk \quad (6)$$

In both figures, I have drawn the stationary locus $dp/dt = 0$. It is drawn to satisfy the two conditions, (2) and (3), that guarantee that there is not a steady state equilibrium. Thus the stationary locus is below $1/y$ where it crosses $k = y/d$ and it is above $1/x$ where it reaches the axis. Also drawn in are the directions of motion.

A rational expectations path satisfies the differential equations above, satisfying the appropriate equation for dk/dt as production is or is not profitable given the behavior of other producers. It also satisfies the initial condition on the consumption stock variable, and a transversality condition on the shadow price.

In Figure 1a, we cannot go below the line $p = 1/y$, since that would contradict the profitability of production that makes Figure 1a the appropriate figure. In Figure 1b, we cannot go above the line $p = 1/x$. A rational expectations path spends some of its time in Figure 1a, and some of its time in Figure 1b. We consider only cycles that have precisely two phases, although one could construct more complicated paths with many different alternatively expanding and contracting phases before returning to the initial position, if ever. Since the rate of horizontal movement is independent of p in each diagram, we will find the equilibrium cycle with the longest phases by looking for the one with the greatest width. This cycle has the two phases drawn in Figures 1a and 1b, where trajectories cross the stationary locus (and so are horizontal) as low and as high as possible. The entire cycle is shown in Figure 2.

To see that this is the cycle with the longest phases, let us first note that if production ceases to the left of the stationary locus, movement in Figure 1b is then to the southwest. Second, we note that on any trajectory in Figure 1a which is to the left of the trajectory drawn, we cannot move to the right of the stationary locus since production must stop when the path crosses the horizontal line at $1/y$. Thus, any point to the left of the trajectory drawn is not part of an equilibrium cycle. Similarly,

Figure 1a: $dp/dt = (r + d)p - U'(k)$
$dk/dt = y - dk$

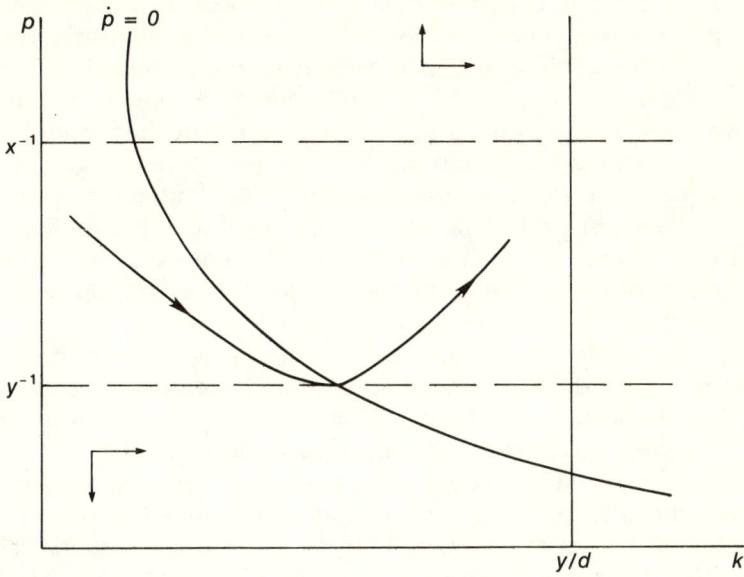

Figure 1b: $dp/dt = (r + d)p - U'(k)$
$dk/dt = -dk$

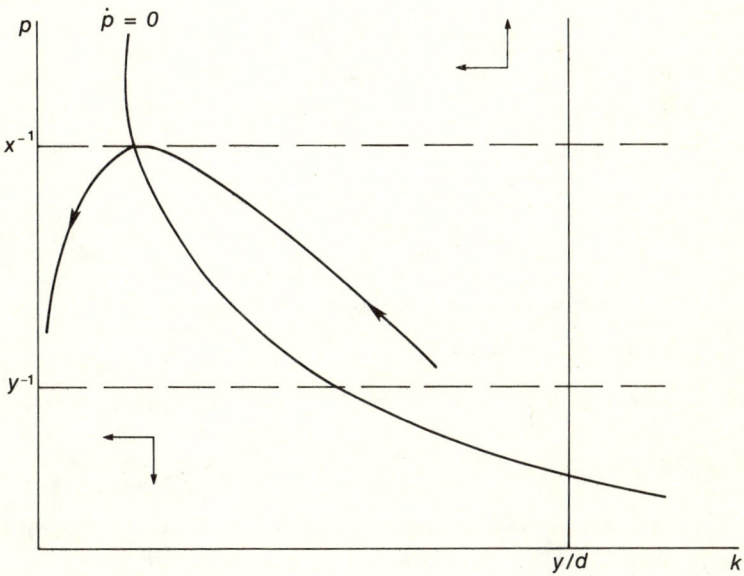

we note that movement in Figure 1a to the right of the stationary locus is to the northeast and that any path in Figure 1b to the right of the drawn path cannot move to the left of the stationary locus. In Figure 2, we have concluded that some of the points outside the closed curve can not be part of a cyclic equilibrium. The remaining points outside the closed curve could be initial points for an equilibrium path, but are not points to which a rational expectations path could return. Thus the candidates for recurrent equilibria are on and inside the closed curve in Figure 2. Since the width of a path relates monotonically to the time on the path (over the same k values), paths inside the cycle have shorter phases than those on the closed curve drawn. Inside the closed curve, every point is part of a continuum of equilibrium paths. All the chattering paths on the stationary locus inside the cycle are also equilibria.

What should we learn from this exercise? It is certainly possible to construct equilibrium cycles from increasing returns in production. Moreover, in such an exercise, the rational expectations paths are not unique, leaving an unreasonable scope for coordinated beliefs.

We have modeled this equilibrium as a non-market equilibrium with no interactions except for the production externality. It is interesting to ask whether there is a market economy with the same equilibria. That is, if we allow trading in consumer goods and labor, do there exist vectors

Figure 2

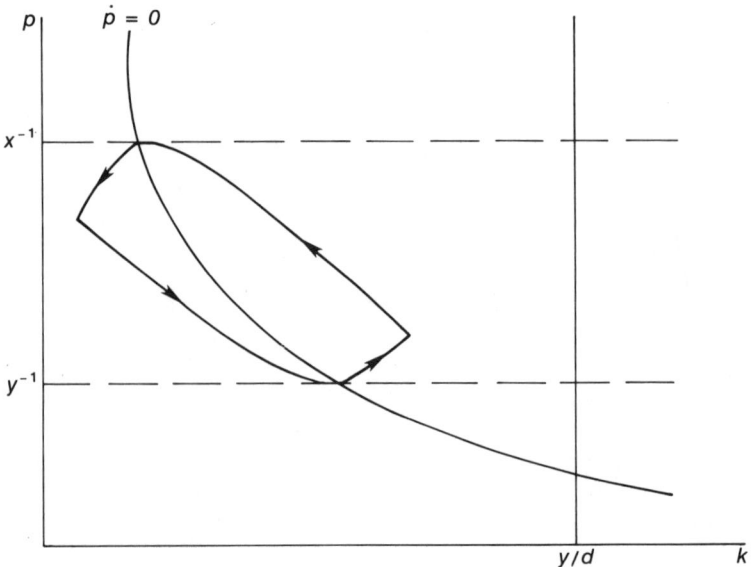

of consumer prices, wages, and interest rates such that there is no trade when everyone optimizes subject to a lifetime budget constraint? It appears that the answer is yes, with the wage as numeraire each moment of time, the price equal to the shadow price, and the interest rate equal to the utility discount rate. We need to assume a continuum of identical firms, each capable of hiring one worker, with more jobs than workers. Competition in the labor market then determines the real wage as the value of the marginal product of labor. Zero profits imply that firms are willing to produce or not, as desired, provided that they are coordinated. Workers want to provide labor when the wage is high and not otherwise. Consumers are content with the pattern of consumption by construction of the shadow price of a consumer good. Thus we have an equilibrium with lifetime budget constraints. The equilibrium has procyclical real wages.

2. Co-movements

Now let us consider two identical sectors, each as described above. If there is no connection between the sectors, there is no reason for the cycles to be the same in the two sectors. If we want to consider co-movements, we need to link the sectors. The natural candidate for linkage is through demand. Let each consumer demand both goods (with additive utility from the two stocks), although production continues to be specialized. For now, assume that labor is immobile between sectors, so that demand is the only linkage. We continue to assume lifetime budget constraints. The equations above need to be changed slightly. Let us consider equilibria where consumption stocks of the two goods are the same vector for consumers working in the two sectors. Then, the pricing equation is unchanged. However, one's stock of one's own good only grows at the rate $y/2 - dk$ when production is positive. We assume that the figures are the same as drawn above after this change. Now, a perfectly coordinated cycle is an equilibrium with consumer goods trading one-for-one.

However, this is not the only equilibrium. Having each sector traverse the maximal cycle with any phasing between the two sectors is also an equilibrium. Relative consumer good prices are set by the stocks of the two consumer goods and would change over the cycle, but each consumer would be content to acquire half of whatever is being produced. (I assume that consumers in the two sectors have the same lifetime incomes even though they are out of phase.) Labor supply and production decisions satisfy the same condition as before. I have not considered whether the different sectors can traverse different cycles. Presumably they can under suitable conditions. It is clear that they can both be in the same cycle even if it is not the maximal cycle.

Now let us consider the implications of allowing perfectly mobile labor. First note that in the perfectly coordinated cycle, there is no reason to trade labor since the wage is the same in both sectors. However, increasing returns with greater labor inputs would tend to desynchronize production, because of the efficiency gains. Thus, labor mobility will tend to generate out-of-phase cycles as productivity shows even larger swings along with the larger swings in labor input. Labor mobility costs would work against desynchronization. So too would capacity constraints in the two sectors. However, capacity constraints are endogenous variables. I suspect that in many equilibria, aggregate capacity would exceed aggregate labor supply, permitting asynchronous movements. Thus, we must turn to limits on intertemporal budget constraints to make a stronger case for coordinated cycles. Thus this production-based cycle theory needs demand conditions.

Again assuming immobile labor, let us turn to the other budgetary extreme, allowing only barter trade in newly produced consumer goods. (Thus consumers can not trade out of stocks.) Note that this is not only a limitation on borrowing, but also on saving. It is clear that the perfectly coordinated cycle remains an equilibrium. When both sectors are producing, the goods trade one for one. If only one sector were producing, there could be no trade. Thus it is clear that this budgetary assumption limits the extent to which the two markets can be out of phase. For example, we can no longer have the two sectors perfectly out of phase. To see this consider the case where the two phases have the same length. If the two sectors were perfectly out of phase, there could be no barter trade. Thus the stock of the "other" consumer good would be going to zero. At some point, this justifies production and trade even if no one else in your sector is producing (i.e., at productivity x).

It is natural to ask how much out of phase the two sectors can be. I have not considered this in detail. There is the complication of the terms of trade when there is a corner solution, with one of the sectors giving up all its current production in trade. I do want to describe one equilibrium cycle, assuming that trade is one for one. This will imply that when both sectors are producing, both will give up all their output for all the output of the other sector unless the marginal rates of substitution are the same in both sectors. In the example I will consider, positions will be symmetric during trade, so there is no problem with the assumption of one for one trade. We start with both sectors having the same equal stocks of both goods. At this point one of the sectors stops producing, with the other continuing to produce and adding its entire output to its stock of its own durable. After some time, the two sectors reverse positions. (Presumably, there could also be a time with both sectors shut down.) After some more time the sectors have equal levels of their own durables (and the sectors have equal levels of each other's durables). At this time both sectors produce, with all production going to the stocks of the other sector. This phase continues until we return to the initial point where all four stocks are equal. Pricing conditions will limit the lengths of the different portions of this cycle. On this equilibrium cycle, the correlation in production is approximately zero. It is precisely increasing returns which appears to make this cycle possible. With constant returns and barter, the sectors would both be on or both be off in this symmetric structure. Thus locating increasing returns in consumer trade, rather than just in production, appears to be an attractive part of this sort of model.

3. Labor market flows

In this model all firms behave the same. However, the labor market is marked by huge gross flows of labor (Abowd and Zellner 1985; Poterba and Summers 1986). Moreover there are huge gross flows of job creation and job destruction (Leonard 1988, Davis and Haltiwanger 1989). These facts raise two questions—the appropriateness of the labor immobility assumption which is critical for preventing the efficiency gains from desynchronization and the appropriateness of the real business cycle assumption that equilibrium is on the labor supply curve.

It is natural to ask whether one thinks that the basic increasing returns model could be fitted up to accommodate the facts of large gross flows. There would be no difficulty superimposing on the structure of this model a pattern of individual, idiosyncratic productivity shocks that generated a pattern of production starts and stops on an individual basis on top of the economy-wide moves (see, e.g., Blanchard and Diamond 1989). This would allow a diverse pattern of job creation and destruction. However, this modification implies a large available labor supply which makes the assumption of labor immobility very uncomfortable. The advantage of the increasing returns story is that demand swings will naturally move productivity together in all sectors. Thus some increasing returns in production are a plausible part of a cycle model. Such increasing returns alone are inadequate.

The model assumes that the economy is always on the labor supply curve. There are two ways to view this assumption. One is that the assumption is convenient, though unrealistic, while studying the workings of the other parts of the model. The alternative is to consider the assumption to be a plausible approximation to the workings of the labor market. The large gross flows imply that some people are working and some are not at all times. In order to induce the fluctuations in labor supply, the model needs (and has) procyclical real wage movements. Yet those who are unemployed at good times are choosing to take their time out of work at a time of high real wages. Of course, this can be partially rescued by a Lucas-Prescott (1974) unemployment while moving between jobs. However that model is not consistent with the widely varying durations of unemployment across individuals. Thus, I feel that the assumption that equilibrium occurs on the labor supply curve is an inaccurate interim assumption until we know how to build better models.

The bottom line is that we have one more way of consistently modeling cyclically varying profitability of production, if only we could explain why the labor market works as it does. That remains a basic puzzle.

REFERENCES

Abowd, John and Arnold Zellner. "Estimating the Gross Labor-Force Flows." *Journal of Business and Economic Statistics* 3–3, 254–283. July 1985.
Blanchard, Olivier Jean and Peter Diamond. "The Beveridge Curve." Brookings Papers on Economic Activity. Forthcoming.
Davis, Steve and John Haltiwanger. "Gross Job Creation, Gross Job Destruction, and Intrasectoral Labor Reallocation." Unpublished. 1989.
Huang, Chi-fu and David Kreps. "On Intertemporal Preferences with a Continuous Time Dimension, I: The Case of Certainty." MIT, Sloan School of Management Working Paper 1882, 1987.
Leonard, Jonathan S. "In the Wrong Place at the Wrong Time: The Extent of Frictional and Structural Unemployment." in Kevin Lang and Jonathan S. Leonard (eds.), *Unemployment and the Structure of Labor Markets*. London: Basil Blackwell, 1988.
Lucas Jr., Robert E. and Edward C. Prescott. "Equilibrium Search and Unemployment." *Journal of Economic Theory* 7: 188–209. 1974.
Poterba, James M. and Lawrence H. Summers. "Reporting Errors and Labor Force Dynamics." *Econometrica* 54-6: 1319–8. 1986.

Discussion

Kevin Murphy pointed out that heterogeneity of individuals suggests an upward sloping labor supply even in the Prescott model.

Valerie Ramey noted that the industrial organization and cost function literature tends to reject constant returns in favor of increasing returns to scale, with evidence of decreasing marginal cost. Bob Hall added that inventory data tends to suggest decreasing marginal cost. Ed Prescott stated that in real business cycle models inventory investment is not the problem, but that rather firm size and growth data tend to favor constant returns.

David Romer asked whether this model should be taken literally or metaphorically in light of the 1982 recession. Shleifer said that this is a model of propagation and dynamics, not shocks. Romer responded that the model predicts that the stock of durables would explain the duration of business cycles and asked if this was the case. Vishny said that it is hard to interpret the time series evidence on duration dependence.

Julio Rotemberg noted that if there were external economies, there would be no co-movement at the aggregate level. Murphy responded that there would be co-movement if specific sectors have varying amounts of external economies. Nobuhiro Kiyotaki stated that the authors should specify their matching and transactions technologies since the form of increasing returns has implications for persistence.

Stephen D. Williamson

FEDERAL RESERVE BANK OF MINNEAPOLIS

Restrictions on Financial Intermediaries and Implications for Aggregate Fluctuations: Canada and the United States 1870–1913

1. Introduction

Advances in the economics of information have permitted recent progress in modeling financial intermediaries. This new financial intermediation literature is somewhat diverse, but the models generally follow the approach of specifying an economic environment in terms of primitives—preferences, endowments, and technology—and analyzing how that environment generates financial intermediation as an endogenous phenomenon. Several things are gained from this type of approach: a deeper understanding of the role of financial intermediaries as institutions that diversify, transform assets, and process information; explanations for bank runs; insights into the role of financial intermediaries in aggregate fluctuations; and implications for the effects of financial regulations.

One branch of this financial intermediation literature, following on the work of Diamond and Dybvig (1983), focuses on deposit contracts, bank runs, and bank failures. In the Diamond-Dybvig model, the banking system has an inherent instability. Banks provide a form of insurance through the withdrawal provision in deposit contracts, but this leaves banks open to runs, during which the expectation of the failure of an otherwise safe bank is self-fulfilling. (This branch of the literature includes Postlewaite and Vives 1987; Wallace 1988; and Williamson 1988.)

Another branch of the financial intermediation literature, which includes work by Diamond (1984), Boyd and Prescott (1986), and Williamson (1986), is concerned with financial intermediation in general (rather than banking in particular) and with the features of economic environments (moral hazard, adverse selection, and monitoring and evaluation costs) that can lead to intermediary structures. Models of this type have been integrated into macroeconomic frameworks by Williamson (1987b), Greenwood and Williamson (1988), and Bernanke and Gertler (1989) to study the implications of financial intermediation for aggregate fluctuations. A general conclusion of this work is that the financial intermediation sector tends to amplify fluctuations. Bernanke and Gertler (1989) show how a redistribution of wealth from borrowers to lenders increases the agency costs associated with lending, causing a decrease in the quantity of intermediation and in real output. Such a wealth redistribution might be associated with debt deflations. Williamson (1987b) shows how some kinds of aggregate technology shocks, which produce no fluctuations in an environment without the information costs that generate an intermediate structure, do cause fluctuations when these costs are present. (See Gertler 1988 for a survey of other related work.)

This paper has two purposes. First, for those unfamiliar with the recent literature on financial intermediation, it shows how an explicit general equilibrium model with endogenous financial intermediation can illuminate some central issues in banking and macroeconomics and can put order on some historical experience and empirical evidence. Second, for those familiar with the intermediation literature, this paper shows how a model related to models in Williamson (1987b) and Greenwood and Williamson (1988) can be used to study bank failures and banking panics. The model here has some novel implications for the role of financial regulations and bank failures in aggregate fluctuations, and I find some (qualified) empirical support for its predictions.

The approach I take is the following. First, I study a historical period when monetary and banking arrangements were strikingly different in two countries. In terms of what has a hearing on aggregate fluctuations, other than financial arrangements, the two countries were quite similar in this period. Next, I construct a general equilibrium model with endogenous financial intermediation which can incorporate the financial arrangements in either country as special cases. Then I study the implications of the differences in banking and monetary arrangements for aggregate fluctuations in the two countries. Last, I go to the data and judge whether the theory fits the evidence.

The period I focus on is the 44 years from 1870 to 1913, and the two countries are Canada and the United States. Over this period, Canada had a branch banking system with, at most, 41 chartered banks, while (in 1890) the United States had more than 8,000 banks, and most were unit banks. Numerous restrictions on branching, along with other constraints absent in Canada, tended to keep U.S. banks small. Canadian banks were free to issue private circulating notes with few restrictions on their backing, but all circulating currency in the United States was effectively an obligation of the U.S. government. In addition to these differences in banking and monetary arrangements, the countries had different records of bank failures and panics. Average bank depositor losses as a fraction of deposits were roughly 60 percent larger in the United States than in Canada. Also, cooperative behavior among the Canadian banks acted to virtually preempt any widespread banking panics, so that disruption from financial crises was considerably smaller in Canada. The history of widespread bank runs and failures in the United States during the National Banking Era (1863–1914) is documented in Sprague (1910).

The model presented here captures the important features of Canadian and U.S. monetary and banking arrangements during 1870–1913. This model is related to others constructed in Williamson (1987b) and Greenwood and Williamson (1988), in that it has costly state verification (Townsend 1979) which provides a delegated monitoring role for financial intermediaries (Diamond 1984; Williamson 1986). When the model includes a restriction on diversification by financial intermediaries, interpreted as a unit banking restriction, banks fail with positive probability. When they fail, banks experience a phenomenon which can be interpreted as a bank run. Banks not subject to the unit banking restriction diversify perfectly, and they never fail.

When subjected to aggregate technological shocks, the model yields patterns of co-movement in the data that are qualitatively similar whether or not there is a diversification restriction or a constraint that banks cannot issue circulating notes. The price level, bank liabilities, and output are mutually positively correlated. Two important results:

- Despite the fact that aggregate bank failures are negatively correlated with output when there is unit banking, the unit banking restriction actually reduces the unconditional variance of output.
- Introducing a restriction that prohibits the issue of private bank notes decreases the unconditional variance of output.

These two results are consistent with the view that intermediation amplifies fluctuations. That is, both restrictions inhibit intermediation, and both reduce the magnitude of fluctuations.

Banks fail for a quite different reason in my model than in Diamond and Dybvig's (1983). Here, the unit banking restriction results in a banking system in which banks are less diversified than they would be otherwise. These banks are therefore more sensitive to idiosyncratic shocks, and they fail and experience runs with higher probability. In Diamond and Dybvig's model, bank failures and runs occur because of an inherent instability associated with the structure of deposit contracts. The Diamond-Dybvig model cannot confront the Canadian/U.S. differences during 1870–1913. It also has difficulty with the Great Depression, when Canada experienced no bank failures while U.S. banks were failing in very large numbers. During the Great Depression, deposit contracts in the United States and Canada were similar, Canada had no deposit insurance, and no Canadian banks suspended convertibility. (For a study of Canadian banking in the Great Depression, see Haubrich 1987.)

The model's implication that the unit banking restriction reduces fluctuations contradicts conventional wisdom about the role of bank failures in the business cycle. Several studies have argued that bank failures propagated negative aggregate shocks during the Great Depression. Friedman and Schwartz (1963) see the propagation mechanism as acting through measured monetary aggregates, while Bernanke (1983) and Hamilton (1987) argue that there are additional, non-monetary effects of intermediation on real activity.

In the model, government deposit insurance in the unit banking system acts to eliminate bank runs, but banks still fail. This arrangement is equivalent to one where banks diversify perfectly and never fail. Therefore, after World War II, when U.S. and Canadian banks face the same restrictions on private note issue and U.S. deposits are insured, the two countries should experience similar macroeconomic behavior, other things held constant.

To test this theory, I examine detrended aggregate annual data for Canada and the United States during 1870–1913 and 1954–87. For the 1870–1913 period, new gross national product (GNP) data have recently been constructed for the United States by Romer (1989) and Balke and Gordon (1989) and for Canada by Urquhart (1986). This makes the study of this period of particular current interest. Of the aggregate data I examine, the GNP data provide the strongest support for the theory. The volatility of Canadian GNP is higher than that of U.S. GNP according to both the Romer data (56 percent) and the Balke and Gordon data (11 percent). For 1954–87, GNP volatility in the two countries is approximately equal. Price level volatility is higher in Canada for the 1870–1913 period, but in the 1954–87 data there are some inconsistencies with the theory in regard to price level volatility and co-movements of prices with output. In apparent contradiction to the theory, bank liabilities are less volatile in Canada than in the United States during 1870–1913. However, there are good reasons to believe that this volatility difference reflects measurement error in the U.S. data.

The paper is organized as follows. In Section 2 I review Canadian and U.S. monetary and banking arrangements in 1870–1913. In Section 3 I construct the model and describe its implications. In Section 4 I discuss the empirical evidence. The final section is a summary and conclusion.

2. Monetary and Banking Arrangements in the United States and Canada 1870–1913

During the 1870–1913 period, the United States had a unit banking system, as it still does today. There were few barriers to entry in the banking industry, but banks faced numerous restrictions which tended to keep them small and to limit diversification. In 1890, the United States had 8,201 banks, including 3,484 national banks (U.S. Department of Commerce 1975). Circulating paper currency consisted mainly of national bank notes (in denominations of $1 and more) and notes issued directly by the U.S. Treasury. National bank notes were more than fully backed by federal government bonds at the time of issue and were guaranteed by the federal government. All banks were subject to reserve requirements.

During the National Banking Era (1863–1914), the U.S. banking system was subject to recurrent periods of widespread panic and bank failure, as is well known. Pervasive financial crises occurred in 1873, 1884, 1890, 1893, and 1907 (Sprague 1910). Figure 1 plots percentage deviations from trend (computed with a Hodrick-Prescott filter; see Prescott 1983) in GNP and in bank suspensions in the United States between 1870 and 1913. There is clearly negative co-movement between the series, with a correlation coefficient of −0.25. Friedman and Schwartz (1963) and Cagan (1965) also find that panic periods tended to be associated with declines in real output growth and with increases in the currency/deposit ratio.

At the same time, Canada's branch banking system, patterned after Scottish arrangements, consisted of, at most, 41 chartered banks. In 1890, when Canada's population was slightly less than one-tenth of the United States', Canada's 38 chartered banks had 426 branches nationwide. The granting of a bank charter required federal legislation, which created a significant barrier to entry. However, once given a charter, a bank faced few restrictions, at least compared to U.S. banks. Canadian banks could issue notes in denominations of $4 and more (raised to $5 in 1880). A bank's note issue was limited by its capital, but this constraint

Figure 1 PERCENTAGE DEVIATIONS FROM TREND OF U.S. OUTPUT AND
BANK FAILURES IN 1870–1913*

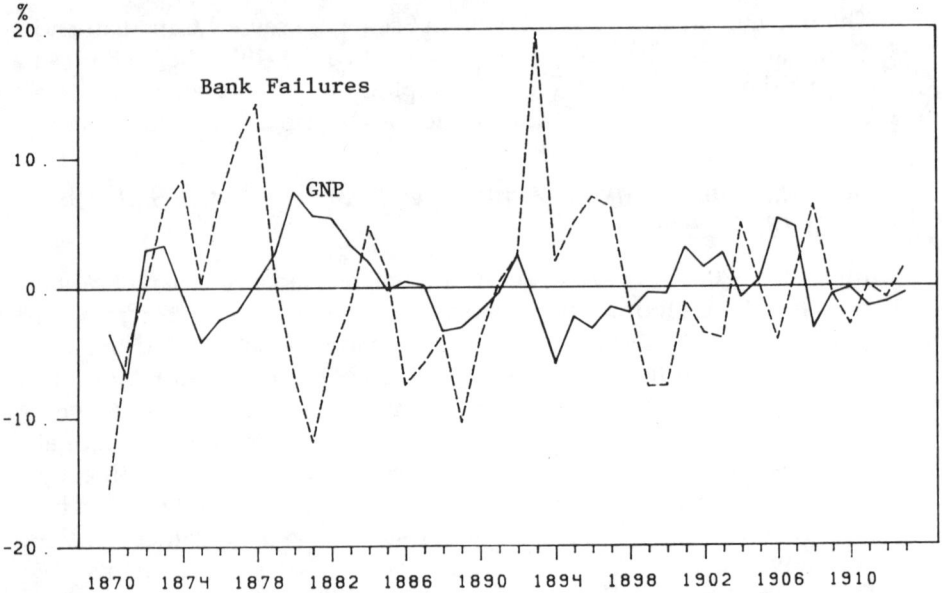

*For bank failures, divided by 10.
Sources: U.S. Department of Commerce (1975); Romer (1989)

does not seem to have been binding on the system as a whole through
most of the period.[1] There were no reserve requirements,[2] but after 1890,
5 percent of note circulation was held on deposit in a central bank circulation redemption fund. This added insurance was essentially redundant,
since notes were made senior claims on a bank's assets in 1880. Most
bank notes appear to have circulated at par, especially after 1890 legislation that required redemption of notes in particular cities throughout
Canada.

The striking difference in the incidence of bank failure in Canada and
the United States during the Great Depression has been noted by Friedman and Schwartz (1963) and Bernanke (1983) and studied by Haubrich
(1987). From 1930 to 1933, more than 9,000 U.S. banks suspended opera-

1. In 1907, the constraint on note issue appears to have become binding during the crop-
   moving season. At that time, the federal government instituted a temporary redis-
   counting arrangement with the banks. It was made permanent with the passing of the
   Finance Act of 1914.
2. If reserves were held, one-third (40 percent after 1880) had to be held in the form of
   Dominion notes.

tions (Friedman and Schwartz 1963), but no banks failed in Canada between 1923 and 1985. The record of bank failures in the two countries during 1870–1913, while showing less striking differences than that, also indicates that the incidence of bank failure was lower and the disruptive effects of these failures were considerably smaller in Canada than in the United States.

Table 1 displays statistics on bank liquidations in Canada during 1870–1913. In total, Canada had 23 bank liquidations while, at the same time, the United States had 3,208. This evidence clearly overstates the difference between Canadian and U.S. bank failure rates, since Canadian banks were larger than U.S. banks and Canadian GNP and population were less than one-tenth of the corresponding quantities in the United States during that period. Thus, the failure of an average-sized Canadian bank would potentially have had a much larger effect on the Canadian

Table 1   THE 23 CHARTERED BANK LIQUIDATIONS IN CANADA IN 1870–1913

Year of Suspension	Bank Liabilities at Suspension ($)	% of Face Value of Bank Liabilities Paid to	
		Note holders	Depositors
1873	106,914	.00	.00
1876	293,379	100.00	100.00
1879	547,238	57.50	57.50
	136,480	100.00	96.35
	1,794,249	100.00	100.00
	340,500	100.00	100.00
1881	1,108,000	59.50	59.50
1883	2,868,884	100.00	66.38
1887	1,409,482	100.00	10.66
	74,364	100.00	100.00
	1,031,280	100.00	100.00
	2,631,378	100.00	99.66
1888	3,449,499	100.00	100.00
1893	1,341,251	100.00	100.00
1895	7,761,209	100.00	75.25
1899	1,766,841	100.00	17.50
1905	388,660	100.00	100.00
1906	15,272,271	100.00	100.00
1908	16,174,408	100.00	100.00
	560,781	100.00	30.27
	1,172,630	100.00	100.00
1910	549,830	100.00	100.00
	1,314,016	100.00	.00

Source: Beckhart (1929, pp. 480–81)

economy than the failure of an average-sized U.S. bank would have had on the U.S. economy.

According to Table 1, noteholders of failed banks received 100 percent of the face value of their liabilities in 21 of the 23 Canadian bank liquidations, and depositors received 100 percent in 12 of the 23. This might indicate relatively little economic disruption from Canadian bank failures, but that conclusion requires comparable statistics for the United States. Table 2 displays some data on bank depositor losses in the United States. These are 16- and 20-year averages of annual losses to depositors as a percentage of total deposits. For the years in which bank failures occurred in Canada, similar Canadian statistics are also provided in Table 2. Thus, on average in the years under study, losses to depositors were 0.11 percent of total deposits in the United States and 0.07 percent in Canada. By this measure, the disruption from bank failures appears to have been significantly smaller—57 percent smaller—in Canada than in the United States.

Further, Canadian chartered banks had cooperative arrangements that tended to mitigate the adverse effects of bank failures. Canadian banks were mainly self-regulated, with a formal organization, the Canadian Bankers' Association, established in 1891 and given special powers through legislation in 1900. The largest banks, particularly the Bank of

Table 2 BANK DEPOSITOR LOSSES AS A PERCENTAGE OF TOTAL DEPOSITS

Country	Year	Annual Percentage*
United States	1865–1890	.19%
	1881–1900	.12
	1901–1920	.04
	1865–1920	.11%
Canada**	1873	.03%
	1879	.15
	1881	.20
	1883	.69
	1887	.87
	1895	.89
	1899	.47
	1908	.04
	1910	.14
	1914	.05
	1867–1920	.07%

*For multi-year spans, average annual percentages.
**For years not included, the annual percentage was zero.
Sources: FDIC (1941), Beckhart (1929)

Montreal, appear to have been willing to act as informal lenders of last resort and to step in to help reorganize troubled banks. This excerpt from Johnson (1910, pp. 124–125) is illustrative:

On the evening of October 12 [1906] the bankers in Toronto and Montreal heard with surprise that the Bank of Ontario had got beyond its depth and would not open its doors the next morning. . . . The leading bankers in the Dominion dreaded the effect which the failure of such a bank might have. The Bank of Montreal agreed to take over the assets and pay all the liabilities, provided a number of other banks would agree to share with it any losses. Its offer was accepted and a representative of the Bank of Montreal took the night train for Toronto. Going breakfastless to the office of the Bank of Ontario he found the directors at the end of an all-night session and laid before them resolutions officially transferring the business and accounts of the bank to the Bank of Montreal. They adopted the resolution before 9 a.m. and the bank opened business for the day with the following notice over the door: "This is the Bank of Montreal."

Before 1 o'clock the same notice, painted on a board or penciled on brown wrapping paper, was over the door of the 31 branches in different parts of the Dominion. Its customers were astonished that day when they went to the bank, but none of them took alarm and many of them were well pleased with the change.

The collective behavior of Canadian banks not only served to minimize the costs of liquidating insolvent institutions; it also appears to have prevented widespread banking panics. Any bank runs seem to have been confined to individual banks or branches (U.S. Congress 1910). While U.S. banks had cooperative arrangements during the National Banking Era, particularly clearinghouses (Gorton 1985), the ability of U.S. banks to act as a single coalition could not approach that of their Canadian counterparts.

The government of Canada had a monopoly on the issue of small-denomination notes during 1870–1913, but circulating currency in large denominations consisted mostly of bank notes (Johnson 1910). There was a limited issue of Dominion notes, backed 25 percent by gold and 75 percent by government securities, with additional issues backed 100 percent by gold. Legislation periodically increased the limit on the fractionally gold-backed component of government-issued currency.

3. The Theory

The purpose of this section is two-fold. First I will construct a model which captures the essential features of the banking and monetary structures of Canada and the United States during the period of interest. Then I will explore the implications of this theory for the interaction between financial structure and macroeconomic fluctuations.

Secton 2 described two important differences between Canadian and U.S. banking and monetary arrangements in 1870–1913. One is that Canadian bank liabilities were much less subject to idiosyncratic risk than were U.S. bank liabilities. The Canadian system let Canadian banks become larger than U.S. banks, and branch banking allowed greater geographical diversification. Further, the cooperative behavior among Canadian banks helped to insure depositors against losses. The other important difference is related to the fact that Canadian banks could issue circulating notes in large denominations and back them with private assets. In the United States, only national banks could issue notes, and these notes had to be backed 111 percent by U.S. government bonds. Thus, Canadian bank notes could perform an intermediation function while U.S. bank notes could not (to the extent that breaking up government bonds into small denominations is an insignificant function compared to the intermediation normally done by banks).

The model should be able to replicate the differences in the U.S. and Canadian experiences with regard to bank failures. That is, bank failures should be negatively correlated with aggregate activity, and the incidence of bank failure should be higher in the model U.S. economy than in the model Canadian economy.

The model constructed here is related to the models in Williamson (1987b) and Greenwood and Williamson (1988), with some differences designed to capture the problem at hand. This model abstracts from reserve requirements, interest-bearing government debt, and the operation of the gold standard monetary regime.

3.1 THE MODEL CANADIAN ECONOMY

3.1.1. Environment This is a model of a closed economy which has a continuum of two-period-lived agents born in each period $t = 1, 2, 3, \ldots$. The measure of a generation is N. Each generation has two types of economic agents, *lenders* and *entrepreneurs*. Lenders each receive an indivisible endowment of one unit of time when young and maximize $E_t(\delta \ell_t - e_t - e_{t+1} + c_{t+1})$, where E_t is the expectation operator conditional on period t information, δ is an individual-specific parameter denoting the value to a lender of consuming leisure, ℓ_t is leisure, e_t is effort expended, and c_t is consumption. Lenders can use their single unit of time in period t either to produce one unit of the period t consumption good or to consume one unit of leisure. Entrepreneurs have no endowments of time, the consumption good, or effort in either period of life. A generation t entrepreneur has access at time t to an investment project which requires K units of the time t consumption good as input in order to operate, where K is an integer greater than 1. If funded, the project yields a random return $\tilde{w}$, for which $Pr[\tilde{w} \leq w] = H(w,\theta,\phi_t)$; here, $H(\cdot,\cdot,\cdot)$ is differentiable in all its arguments and is twice differentiable in its first argument. Let $h(w,\theta,\phi) \equiv D_1H(w,\theta,\phi)$ denote the probability density function, which is positive on $[0,w]$. The variable ϕ_t affects the investment projects of all entrepreneurs, and θ is an entrepreneur-specific parameter which orders probability distributions according to first-order stochastic dominance. That is, $D_2H(w,\theta,\phi_t) < 0$ for $0 < w < \overline{w}$. Project quality strictly improves as θ increases. For fixed θ, an increase in ϕ produces an increase in the riskiness of the project return without changing its expected value. That is, an increase in ϕ is a mean-preserving spread (Rothschild and Stiglitz 1970), though this is carried out in such a way that probability mass is shifted only for lower values of w. Specifically, $\int_0^{\overline{w}} D_3H(x,\theta,\phi)\, dx < 0$ for $0 < w < \overline{w}$, $D_3H(x,\theta,\phi) = 0$ for $w > K$, and $\int_0^{\overline{w}} x D_3h(x,\theta,\phi)\, dx = 0$.

Assume that the aggregate shock ϕ_t follows a two-state Markov process. That is, $\phi_t = \phi_i$ for $i = 1, 2$, and $Pr[\phi_{t+1} = \phi_1|\phi_t = \phi_i] = q_i$ for $i = 1, 2$, where $0 < q_i < 1$ and $\phi_2 > \phi_1$ for $i = 1, 2$ and $q_1 \geq q_2$. Aggregate shocks are therefore non-negatively serially correlated, and all project returns are riskier in state 2 than in state 1.

Project returns are independently distributed across entrepreneurs. As in Townsend (1979, 1988), there is costly state verification. That is, entrepreneurs can observe the return on their own project, w, but any other agent expends γ units of effort to observe w.

Lenders who choose to produce the consumption good in period t save the entire amount, by acquiring fiat money or investing (directly or indirectly) in an entrepreneur's project. There is a fixed quantity of M_0 units of perfectly divisible fiat money which is in the hands of a group of old agents at $t = 1$. These agents supply fiat money inelastically so as to maximize consumption. Claims on period $t + 1$ consumption exchanged for the period t consumption good can take one of two forms: they are either *deposit claims* or *notes*. Deposits and notes are identical from the point of view of the issuer, but a lender who holds a deposit incurs a cost of β units of effort and a note holder, a cost of α units of effort. There are no costs associated with holding fiat money. The parameters α and β are lender-specific, as is δ.

The fact that asset claims are named *deposits* and *notes* at this stage in the analysis is premature, since I have not yet established that arrangements corresponding to real-world banking institutions might arise here. However, to look ahead, my aim is to generate demand functions for two types of intermediary liabilities, deposits and notes, which are both backed by the same portfolio of loans to entrepreneurs. With costs of holding the two liabilities and the costs differing among lenders, it is simple to obtain well-defined demand functions for intermediary liabilities, without having to explicitly specify the spatial and informational features that cause some agents to prefer one type of intermediary liability to another, even if their returns are identical. In terms of the ultimate optimal financial arrangement, the cost α can be interpreted as the cost in inconvenience associated with holding a large-denomination bank note as opposed to perfectly divisible fiat money. Similarly, β can be interpreted as the cost of carrying out an exchange using a check-writing technology rather than fiat currency. These costs might plausibly be thought to differ among individuals or types of transactions.

To obtain simple demand functions for intermediary liabilities, assume there are three types of lenders. *Type 1* lenders have $\alpha = \beta = \infty$, *type 2* lenders have $\delta = 0$ and $\beta = \infty$, and *type 3* lenders have $\delta = 0$ and $\alpha = \infty$. The fraction of agents in any generation who are type i lenders is η_i. The measure of agents in a generation with $\delta \leq \delta'$ is $\eta_1 A(\delta')$, the measure with $\alpha \leq \alpha'$ is $\eta_2 B(\alpha')$, and the measure with $\beta \leq \beta'$ is $\eta_3 F(\beta')$. Here, $A(\cdot)$, $B(\cdot)$, and $F(\cdot)$ are distribution functions which give the distribution of parameter values across each lender type. Let $a(\delta) \equiv DA(\delta)$, $b(\alpha) \equiv DB(\alpha)$, and $f(\beta) = DF(\beta)$, where $a(\cdot)$, $b(\cdot)$, and $f(\cdot)$ are positive on R_+. In equilibrium, type 1 lenders will substitute as a group between consuming leisure and holding fiat money, type 2 lenders will substitute between fiat money and notes, and type 3 lenders will substitute between fiat money and deposits.

Let η_4 denote the fraction of agents who are entrepreneurs, with $\eta_4 G(\theta')$ being the fraction of agents who are entrepreneurs with $\theta \leq \theta'$. Let $g(\theta) \equiv DG(\theta)$, with $g(\cdot)$ positive on $[\underline{\theta}, \overline{\theta}]$ for $\overline{\theta} > \underline{\theta}$. Assume that

$$\int_0^{\overline{w}} xh(x, \overline{\theta}, \phi_1)\, dx > K$$

$$\int_0^{\overline{w}} xh(x, \underline{\theta}, \phi_1)\, dx < K$$

and $\eta_4 K < \eta_2 + \eta_3$. Therefore, for the equilibrium to be examined, there will always be some projects funded, some projects not funded, and some lenders of each type holding fiat money.

3.1.2. Financial Arrangements For investment projects to be financed, lenders and entrepreneurs need to make contractual arrangements. As in the costly state verification setups of Townsend (1979), Gale and Hellwig (1985), and Williamson (1986) and (1987a), assume the following commitment technology and sequence of moves by the contracting parties. In any period t, the lenders jointly funding investment projects agree among themselves on rules for dividing the period $t + 1$ payments from entrepreneurs. No lender can observe payments made to other lenders by the entrepreneur. Lenders make commitments in period t about how they will respond to declarations by an entrepreneur at $t + 1$ about the project outcome, and payment schedules are set. In period $t + 1$, an entrepreneur declares a particular project outcome, w^d, and a lender then incurs the verification cost if $w^d \in S$ or does not incur the cost if $w^d \notin S$, where S is the verification set. Note that stochastic verification is ruled out.[3] Payments from the entrepreneur to lenders depend on the entrepreneur's declaration and on the results of the lenders' state verification, if it occurs.

Let r_t denote the market expected return per unit of the consumption good invested by lenders in entrepreneurs' projects, and let $R_t(w)$ denote the payment to the lenders in a given project by an entrepreneur. Then, from Williamson (1987b) and Greenwood and Williamson (1988), the following is an *optimal arrangement*. Lenders delegate monitoring to a financial intermediary (as in Diamond 1984 and Williamson 1986). The entrepreneur makes a non-contingent payment of x_t to the intermediary if $w \geq x_t$ and pays the intermediary w if $w < x_t$. The expected return to the intermediary is then

$$\pi(x_t,\theta,\phi_t) = \int_0^{x_t} (w-\gamma)h(w,\theta,\phi_t)\,dw + x_t[1-H(x_t,\theta,\phi_t)] \quad (1)$$

or, integrating by parts,

$$\pi(x_t,\theta,\phi_t) = x_t - \int_0^{x_t} H(w,\theta,\phi_t)\,dw - \gamma H(x_t,\theta,\phi_t). \quad (2)$$

---

3. As Townsend (1988) shows, allowing for stochastic verification in more general setups yields an optimal arrangement which in general bears little resemblance to a simple debt contract. Restricting attention to non-stochastic monitoring in my context lends considerable tractability to the analysis. Bernanke and Gertler (1989), in a model with some similar features, show how some of their results remain intact with stochastic verification. This suggests that the operating characteristics of this model may not change if the restriction on verification was relaxed.

The optimal contract between an intermediary and an entrepreneur is a *debt contract,* as in Gale and Hellwig (1985) and Williamson (1987a). That is, there is a fixed promised payment, and if the entrepreneur cannot meet it, then bankruptcy occurs and the entrepreneur consumes zero. The verification cost, γ, can be interpreted as a cost of bankruptcy.

Intuitively, this contract is optimal since, first, incentive compatibility requires that the payment be non-contingent in the event that verification does not occur. Second, since risk sharing is not a factor here, with risk-neutral agents, maximizing the payment in verification states minimizes the probability of verification and therefore minimizes expected verification costs.

Assume that $\pi(x,\theta,\phi_t)$ is strictly concave in its first argument for $\theta \in [\underline{\theta},\bar{\theta}]$ and $\phi_t = \phi_i$ for $i = 1, 2$. Then there is a unique $\hat{x}(\theta,\phi_t)$ such that $\pi(x,\theta,\phi_t)$ reaches a maximum for $x = \hat{x}(\theta,\phi_t)$ with fixed θ and ϕ_t and $\hat{x}(\theta,\phi_t) \in (0,\bar{w})$. Entrepreneurs for whom $\pi(\hat{x}(\theta,\phi_t),\theta,\phi_t) \geq r_t K$ receive loans, while those with $\pi(\hat{x}(\theta,\phi_t),\theta,\phi_t) < r_t K$ do not. For the entrepreneurs receiving loans, the promised payment x_t satisfies

$$\pi(x_t,\theta,\phi_t) = r_t K. \quad (3)$$

Note that x_t decreases with θ; that is, the loan interest rate is lower for higher-quality projects.

Financial intermediaries are those type 3 lenders with $\beta = 0$. These intermediaries are able to commit to making non-contingent payments of r_t to each of their depositors and note holders by holding large portfolios and achieving perfect diversification.[4] Since each of an intermediary's depositors and note holders receives r_t with certainty, the liability holders need never monitor the intermediary.

This optimal arrangement captures some important features of financial intermediation arrangements observed in the real world, including asset transformation, diversification, information processing, and the fact that intermediaries hold debt in their portfolios.

3.1.3. Equilibrium In equilibrium, there is some θ_t' such that entrepreneurs with $\theta \geq \theta_t'$ receive loans while those with $\theta < \theta_t'$ do not. Let x_t' denote the promised payment for the marginal borrower; that is, $x_t' = \hat{x}(\theta_t',\phi_t)$. Then

$$\pi(x_t',\theta_t',\phi_t) = r_t K \quad (4)$$

---

4. Formal arguments rely on the law of large numbers (Williamson 1986, 1987b), although there are some subtleties here because of the continuum of agents.

and

$$D_1\pi(x_t',\theta_t',\phi_t) = 0. \quad (5)$$

Since $\pi(\cdot,\cdot,\cdot)$ is concave in its first argument, equations (4) and (5) solve for x_t' and θ_t' given r_t. Using (2) to substitute in (4) and (5) gives (6) and (7):

$$x_t' - \int_0^{x_t'} H(w,\theta_t',\phi_t)\, dw - \gamma H(x_t',\theta_t',\phi_t) = r_t K \quad (6)$$

$$1 - H(x_t',\theta_t',\phi_t) = \gamma h(x_t',\theta_t',\phi_t) = 0. \quad (7)$$

Given the market expected return r_t, (6) and (7) determine x_t' and θ_t'.

Let p_t denote the price of fiat money in period t, in terms of the consumption good. The expected return on fiat money in period t is then $E_t p_{t+1}/p_t$. The type 1 lender who is indifferent between consuming leisure and producing the consumption good to exchange for fiat money has $\delta = E_t p_{t+1}/p_t$. Similarly, the type 2 lender who is indifferent between holding intermediary notes and holding fiat money has $r_t - \alpha = E_t p_{t+1}/p_t$. And the type 3 lender who is indifferent between holding intermediary deposits and holding fiat money has $r_t - \beta = E_t p_{t+1}/p_t$. Equilibrium in the market for fiat money therefore implies that

$$\eta_1 A(E_t p_{t+1}/p_t) + \eta_2[1-B(r_t-E_t p_{t+1}/p_t)] + \eta_3[1-F(r_t-E_t p_{t+1}/p_t)] = p_t M_0 \quad (8)$$

where the left side of (8) is the demand for fiat money (with the three terms representing the demand for fiat money by type 1, type 2, and type 3 lenders, respectively) and the right side of (8) is the supply of fiat money. In the credit market, equilibrium implies that

$$\eta_2 B(r_t-E_t p_{t+1}/p_t) + \eta_3 F(r_t-E_t p_{t+1}/p_t) = \eta_4 K[1-G(\theta_t')] \quad (9)$$

where the first term on the left side of (9) is credit supplied (through financial intermediaries) by note holders, the second term on the left side is credit supplied by intermediary depositors, and the right side is credit demanded by entrepreneurs.

Now restrict attention to the stationary monetary equilibrium, where $p_t > 0$ for all t and quantities and prices depend only on the state, ϕ_t. Let subscripts denote the state. Then

$$E_t p_{t+1} = q_i p_1 + (1-q_i)p_2, \qquad \phi_t = \phi_i, \qquad i = 1, 2. \quad (10)$$

Let $\hat{p} \equiv p_1/p_2$. Then from (8), (9), and (10) come (11), (12), and (13):

$$\eta_1 A(q_1+(1-q_1)/\hat{p}) + \eta_2[1-B(r_1-q_1-(1-q_1)/\hat{p})] + \eta_3[1-F(r_1-q_1-(1-q_1)/\hat{p})]$$
$$- \hat{p}\{\eta_1 A(q_2\hat{p}+1-q_2) + \eta_2[1-B(r_2-q_2\hat{p}-1+q_2)] + \eta_3[1-F(r_2-q_2\hat{p}-1+q_2)]\} =$$
$$0 \quad (11)$$

$$\eta_2 B(r_1-q_1-(1-q_1)/\hat{p}) + \eta_3 F(r_1-q_1-(1-q_1)/\hat{p}) = \eta_4 K[1-G(\theta_1')] \quad (12)$$

$$\eta_2 B(r_2-q_2\hat{p}-1+q_2) + \eta_3 F(r_2-q_2\hat{p}-1+q_2) = \eta_4 K[1-G(\theta_2')]. \quad (13)$$

Also, from (6) and (7), for $i = 1, 2$,

$$x_i' - \int_0^{x_i'} H(w,\theta_i',\phi_i)\, dw - \gamma H(x_i',\theta_i',\phi_i) = r_i K \quad (14)$$

$$1 - H(x_i',\theta_i',\phi_i) - \gamma h(x_i',\theta_i',\phi_i) = 0. \quad (15)$$

Equations (11)–(15) solve for $\hat{p}$, r_i, θ_i', and x_i' for $i = 1, 2$.

3.2. THE MODEL U.S. ECONOMY

Here I will treat the U.S. economy as simply a scaled-up version of the Canadian economy. Note that in the model summarized by (11)–(15) the measure of the Canadian population, N, is irrelevant for the determination of equilibrium interest rates and prices. Let N^* denote the measure of the U.S. population, which is on the order of 10N for the period under study.

Recall that two important differences between U.S. and Canadian monetary and banking arrangements during 1870–1913 are that (1) restrictions on private note issue in the United States implied that bank notes could not be backed by private assets, and (2) U.S. banks were for the most part unit banks, which could not diversify to the extent that their Canadian counterparts could.

The first restriction can be captured in the model by simply closing off the issue of notes by private agents. Type 2 lenders are then forced to hold fiat money, just as U.S. residents who wished to hold circulating notes could either hold U.S. Treasury notes or national bank notes backed by U.S. government bonds, while Canadian residents had the option of holding large-denomination private circulating notes backed by private loans.

An extreme version of the second restriction, unit banking, is a prohibition on all diversification. Assume that no agent can hold claims on

more than one investment project. With this restriction, financial intermediaries have no role in the model; all lending and borrowing is done
directly between type 3 lenders and entrepreneurs. However, this outcome can be intepreted as a banking arrangement where, for every
funded project, there is one bank with K depositors. Optimal contracts
with entrepreneurs are debt contracts, as in the case without the unit
banking restriction (Williamson 1986), but there is now no delegated
monitoring. If the entrepreneur (bank) defaults, all K depositors incur
the verification costs; that is, the depositors incur collective verification
costs of $K\gamma$ with unit banking and γ with perfect diversification. Therefore, for the unit banking system, the expected return to a bank's depositors is

$$\pi^*(x_t^*,\theta,\phi_t) = x_t^* - \int_0^{x_t^*} H(w,\theta,\phi_t)\,dw - \gamma KH(x_t^*,\theta,\phi_t) \quad (16)$$

where the asterisk (*) superscripts denote variables and functions for the
U.S. economy. Given (16), (14) and (15) become, for the U.S. economy,
(17) and (18): For $i = 1, 2,$

$$x_i'^* - \int_0^{x_i'^*} H(w,\theta_i'^*,\phi_i)\,dw - \gamma KH(x_i'^*,\theta_i'^*,\phi_i) = r_i^*K \quad (17)$$

$$1 - H(x_i'^*,\theta_i'^*,\phi_i) - \gamma Kh(x_i'^*,\theta_i'^*,\phi_i) = 0. \quad (18)$$

Given the restriction on private note issue, instead of (11), (12), and (13)
the U.S. economy has (19), (20), and (21):

$$\eta_1 A(q_1+(1-q_1)/\hat{p}^*) + \eta_2 + \eta_3[1-F(r_1^*-q_1-(1-q_1))/\hat{p}^*]$$
$$- \hat{p}^*\{\eta_1 A(q_2\hat{p}^*+1-q_2) + \eta_2 + \eta_3[1-F(r_2^*-q_2\hat{p}^*-1+q_2)]\} = 0 \quad (19)$$

$$\eta_3 F(r_1^*-q_1-(1-q_1)/\hat{p}^*) = \eta_4[1-G(\theta_1'^*)] \quad (20)$$

$$\eta_3 F(r_2^*-q_2\hat{p}^*-1+q_2) = \eta_4[1-G(\theta_2'^*)]. \quad (21)$$

The differences between (11), (12), and (13), on the one hand, and (19),
(20), and (21), on the other, arise because under the U.S. regime all type
2 lenders hold fiat money and none of them contribute to the supply of
credit to entrepreneurs.

For the U.S. economy, (16)–(21) determine $\hat{p}^*$ and $x_i'^*$, $\theta_i'^*$, r_i^* for $i = 1, 2$.
Note that with the unit banking system banks fail with positive probabil-

ity. For a bank that lends to an entrepreneur with parameter θ in period t, the probability of failure is $Pr[w < x_t^*(\theta)]$, where $x_t^*(\theta)$ is the promised payment by the entrepreneur which satisfies

$$\Pi^*(x_t^*(\theta), \theta, \phi_t) = r_t^* K. \quad (22)$$

The number of banks that fail in period $t + 1$ is, then,

$$\Psi_{t+1}^* = N^* \int_{\theta_t'^*}^{\bar{\theta}} H(x_t^*(\theta), \theta, \phi_t) g(\theta) \, d\theta. \quad (23)$$

The contractual arrangement with unit banking can be interpreted as involving a bank run when a bank failure occurs. That is, the verification cost, γ, could represent the cost to a depositor of getting to the bank early to withdraw her deposit. On receiving a signal at the beginning of period $t + 1$ that failure is imminent, each depositor incurs the cost of running to the bank, each receives less than the promised return, and the bank fails. Runs are never observed with perfect diversification by banks, since depositors would never need to verify the return on the bank's portfolio.

With this interpretation of bank failures and runs, this model seems better able to confront U.S. and Canadian experience than the bank runs model of Diamond and Dybvig (1983) or the related model of Postlewaite and Vives (1987). These other models rely on inherent features of the deposit contract to explain runs, which leaves the very different behavior of U.S. and Canadian banking systems unexplained.

3.3 AGGREGATE FLUCTUATIONS

To analyze fluctuations in the two model economies summarized by (11)–(15) and (16)–(21), I take as a benchmark a stationary monetary equilibrium with no fluctuations. That is, let $\phi_t = \phi$ for all t. Then, for the Canadian economy, $\hat{p} = 1$, $r_1 = r_2 = r$, and $\theta_1' = \theta_2' = \theta'$. Similarly, for the U.S. economy, $\hat{p}^* = 1$, $r_1^* = r_2^* = r^*$, and $\theta_1'^* = \theta_2'^* = \theta'^*$.

The two parallel economies are subjected to the same shocks, with $\phi_1 = \phi$ and $\phi_2 > \phi$. I study the behavior of the two economies for small perturbations; that is, I totally differentiate (11)–(15) and (16)–(21) around the benchmark equilibrium. In particular, I am interested in deriving expressions for unconditional variances and covariances of key variables. As in Greenwood and Williamson (1988), for two time series z_t^1 and z_t^2, for which $z_t^i = z_i^j$ when $\phi_t = \phi_i$ for $i, j = 1, 2$, to find the covariance for a small perturbation to the benchmark equilibrium, a second-order Taylor expansion of the standard covariance formula gives

$$\text{cov}(a_t, b_t) \approx [(1-q_1)q_2/2(1-q_1+q_2)^2][\partial z_1^1/\partial \phi_2 - \partial z_2^1/\partial \phi_2] \ [\partial z_1^2/\partial \phi_2 - \partial z_2^2/\phi_2]. \quad (24)$$

Matters are somewhat more complicated for covariances of output with other key variables. Output, y_t, for the Canadian economy consists of two components. The first component, denoted y_t^1, consists of output produced in period t by lenders:

$$y_t^1 = N[\eta_1 A(E_t p_{t+1}/p_t) + \eta_2 + \eta_3]. \quad (25)$$

The second component, y_{t-1}^2, is the output produced in period t from investment projects funded in period $t - 1$. Let μ denote the expected return on these projects (which is invariant to changes in ϕ). Then

$$y_{t-1}^2 = N\mu\{\eta_2 B(r_t - E_t p_{t+1}/p_t) + \eta_3 F(r_t - E_t p_{t+1}/p_t)\}. \quad (26)$$

Then, for some variable z_t for which $z_t = z_i$ when $\phi_t = \phi_i$,

$$\text{cov}(z_t, y_t) \approx [(1-q_1)q_2/2(1-q_1+q_2)^2][\partial z_1/\partial \phi_2 - \partial z_2/\partial \phi_2]$$
$$\times [\partial y_1^1/\partial \phi_2 - \partial y_2^1/\partial \phi_2 + (q_1-q_2)(\partial y_1^2/\partial \phi_2 - \partial y_2^2/\partial \phi_2)]. \quad (27)$$

The unconditional variance of output is

$$\text{var}(y_t) \approx [(1-q_1)q_2/2(1-q_1+q_2)^2]$$
$$\times [(\partial y_1^1/\partial \phi_2 - \partial y_2^1/\partial \phi_2)^2 + 2(q_1-q_2)(\partial y_1^1/\partial \phi_2 - \partial y_2^1/\partial \phi_2)$$
$$\times (\partial y_1^2/\partial \phi_2 - \partial y_2^2/\partial \phi_2) + (\partial y_1^2/\partial \phi_2 - \partial y_2^2/\partial \phi_2)^2]. \quad (28).$$

The U.S. economy has similar expressions corresponding to (25), (26), (27), and (28).

For the Canadian economy, I totally differentiate (11)–(15) and solve to get the following, where d_t denotes bank deposits and n_t the stock of private bank notes.

$$\partial d_1/\partial \phi_2 - \partial d_2/\partial \phi_2 > 0$$

$$\partial n_1/\partial \phi_2 - \partial n_2/\partial \phi_2 > 0$$

$$\partial \hat{p}/\partial \phi_2 < 0$$

$$\partial y_1^1/\partial \phi_2 - \partial y_2^1/\partial \phi_2 > 0$$

$$\partial y_1^2/\partial \phi_2 - \partial y_2^2/\partial \phi_2 > 0.$$

Similarly, for the U.S. economy:

$$\partial d_1^* / \partial \phi_2 - \partial d_2^* / \partial \phi_2 > 0$$

$$\partial p^* / \partial \phi_2 < 0$$

$$\partial y_1^{1*} / \partial \phi_1 - \partial y_2^{1*} / \partial \phi_2 > 0$$

$$\partial y_1^{2*} / \partial \phi_2 - \partial y_2^{2*} / \partial \phi_2 > 0.$$

(For the details of these derivations, see Appendix A.)

Fluctuations in the two economies are, therefore, qualitatively similar. In both countries, bank liabilities (bank notes plus deposits) and the price level (the inverse of the price of fiat money) are procyclical. Thus, if both economies are subjected to the same real disturbances, they experience business cycles that move in phase. The mean-preserving spread in the distribution of returns on investment projects that occurs in state 2 can be thought of as a decrease in the demand for credit. This disturbance causes the real interest rate, r, and the quantity of credit extended by intermediaries to fall in state 2 relative to state 1. This credit decrease is matched by a decrease in the quantity of bank liabilities, so that the demand for fiat money rises and the price level falls. Output tends to be higher in state 1 than in state 2 for two reasons. One is that the expected real rate of return on fiat money is higher in state 1, so lenders work more and consume less leisure. The other reason for higher output in state 1 is that, since the shock ϕ_t is positively serially correlated, a period with a high quantity of credit extended is followed by state 1 with higher probability than by state 2. Thus, output from the previous period's investment, y_{t-1}^2, tends to be higher in state 1 than in state 2.

From (23), there are two effects on fluctuations in bank failures. First, the number of failures tends to be larger in state 2 because entrepreneurs with the same characteristics (the same θ) who receive loans in state 1 and state 2 face a higher promised payment, $x_t^*(\theta)$, in state 2, the state where investment projects are riskier. Therefore, the probability of failure for banks funding projects of the same quality is higher in state 2. Second, since $\theta_t'^*$ is higher in state 1 than in state 2, the average quality of projects (without taking account of the change in riskiness) is lower in state 1. This tends to make the number of failures larger in state 1 than in state 2. The first effect tends to induce countercyclical bank failures; the second effect, procyclical bank failures. It seems reasonable to assume that the first effect dominates, so that bank failures are countercyclical, as is true in the U.S. data for this period.

The next step is to make a quantitative comparison of fluctuations in the two economies. For this purpose, consider economies where $\gamma = 0$ and $\eta_2 = 0$, that is, where verification is costless, making intermediation irrelevant, and where there is zero demand for private bank notes. Therefore, the two restrictions that make the two economies different are not binding. The two economies then produce the same benchmark steady-state equilibrium and the same unconditional variances and covariances of key variables (in per capita terms). In Appendix A, let $a = a^*$, $b = b^*$, $f = f^*$, $g = g^*$, $A = A^*$, $B = B^*$, $F = F^*$, $\Sigma_\theta = \Sigma_\theta^*$, and $\Sigma_\phi = \Sigma_\phi^*$. Further, assume that $B(r-1) = 0$ in the steady-state equilibrium with $\gamma = 0$ and $\eta_2 = 0$.

Now, to see what effects the unit banking restriction and the prohibition of private bank notes have on unconditional variances and covariances, differentiate equations (A1)–(A9) in Appendix A with respect to K and η_2 and evaluate at $\gamma = 0$ and $\eta_2 = 0$. This results in the following (which is detailed in Appendix B):

$$\frac{\partial}{\partial K} [(\partial d_1/\partial \phi_2)/N - (\partial d_2/\partial \phi_2)/N - (\partial d_1^*/\partial \phi_2)/N^* + (\partial d_2^*/\partial \phi_2)/N^*] > 0$$

$$\frac{\partial}{\partial \eta_2} [(\partial d_1/\partial \phi_2)/N - (\partial d_2/\partial \phi_2)/N - (\partial d_1^*/\partial \phi_2)/N^* + (\partial d_2^*/\partial \phi_2)/N^*] < 0$$

$$\frac{\partial}{\partial K} [(\partial d_1/\partial \phi_2)/N - (\partial d_2/\partial \phi_2)/N + (\partial n_1/\partial \phi_2)/N - (\partial n_2/\partial \phi_2)/N \\ - (\partial d_1^*/\partial \phi_2)/N^* + (\partial d_2^*/\partial \phi_2)/N^*] > 0$$

$$\frac{\partial}{\partial \eta_2} [(\partial d_1/\partial \phi_2)/N - (\partial d_2/\partial \phi_2)/N + (\partial n_1/\partial \phi_2)/N - (\partial n_2/\partial \phi_2)/N \\ - (\partial d_1^*/\partial \phi_2)/N^* + (\partial d_2^*/\partial \phi_2)/N^*] > 0$$

$$\frac{\partial}{\partial K}[(\partial y_1^2/\partial \phi_2)/N - (\partial y_2^2/\partial \phi_2)/N - (\partial y_1^{2*}/\partial \phi_2)/N^* + (\partial y_2^{2*}/\partial \phi_2)/N^*] > 0$$

$$\frac{\partial}{\partial \eta_2}[(\partial y_1^2/\partial \phi_2)/N - (\partial y_2^2/\partial \phi_2)/N - (\partial y_1^{2*}/\partial \phi_2)/N^* + (\partial y_2^{2*}/\partial \phi_2)/N^*] > 0$$

$$\frac{\partial}{\partial K} (|\partial \hat{p}/\partial \phi_2| - |\partial \hat{p}^*/\partial \phi_2|) > 0$$

$$\frac{\partial}{\partial \eta_2}(|\partial \hat{p}/\partial \phi_2| - |\partial \hat{p}^*/\partial \phi_2|) > 0$$

$$\frac{\partial}{\partial K}[(\partial y_1^1/\partial \phi_2)/N - (\partial y_2^1/\partial \phi_2)/N - (\partial y_1^{1*}/\partial \phi_2)/N^* + (\partial y_2^{1*}/\partial \phi_2)/N^*] > 0$$

$$\frac{\partial}{\partial \eta_2}[(\partial y_1^1/\partial \phi_2)/N - (\partial y_2^1/\partial \phi_2)/N - (\partial y_1^{1*}/\partial \phi_2)/N^* + (\partial y_2^{1*}/\partial \phi_2)/N^*] > 0.$$

Therefore, the effect of each restriction (considered separately) is to make per capita bank liabilities, per capita output, and the price level less variable. Though the unit banking restriction makes bank deposits less variable, deposits become more variable with a prohibition on private note issue.

Some partial equilibrium intuition may clarify the forces that produce these results. Ignoring the dynamic effects from movements in the price level, think of the model in terms of credit supply and demand, where the competitively determined price is the interest rate r. In Figure 2, the credit demand curve, D_0, is determined by the number of investment projects which, if funded, will yield a return per lender of at least r. Credit supply is determined by the number of lenders who hold intermediary liabilities for each r. With perfectly diversified banks and no prohibition on bank note issue, an increase in the riskiness of investment projects shifts the demand curve to D_0', since fewer projects are now creditworthy for each r. As a result, r, the quantity of projects financed, and output (in the subsequent period) fall. With the imposition of a unit banking system, the credit demand curve becomes less elastic. That is, in the event of default by an entrepreneur, verification costs incurred by lenders are now γK rather than K, so that expected verification costs increase more rapidly as the quality of investment projects (θ) decreases. An increase in riskiness for all projects thus shifts D_1 to D_1', and the change in quantity and price is smaller than with perfect diversification.

Figure 3 shows the effect of a prohibition on private bank notes. The supply of credit becomes less elastic, and S_0 shifts to S_1, since agents who would otherwise be holding intermediated assets instead hold unproductive fiat currency. When risk increases for all projects, shifting D_0 to D_0', the quantity of credit falls less than it would have otherwise. Thus, credit, bank liabilities, and output are more volatile when bank note issue is permitted.

In the model, disturbances that make credit more volatile also tend to make prices more volatile since, with a fixed nominal stock of currency,

Figures 2 and 3 THE EFFECTS OF TWO RESTRICTIONS ON PROJECT RISK-
INDUCED FLUCTUATIONS IN THE CREDIT MARKET

Figure 2 UNIT BANKING RESTRICTION

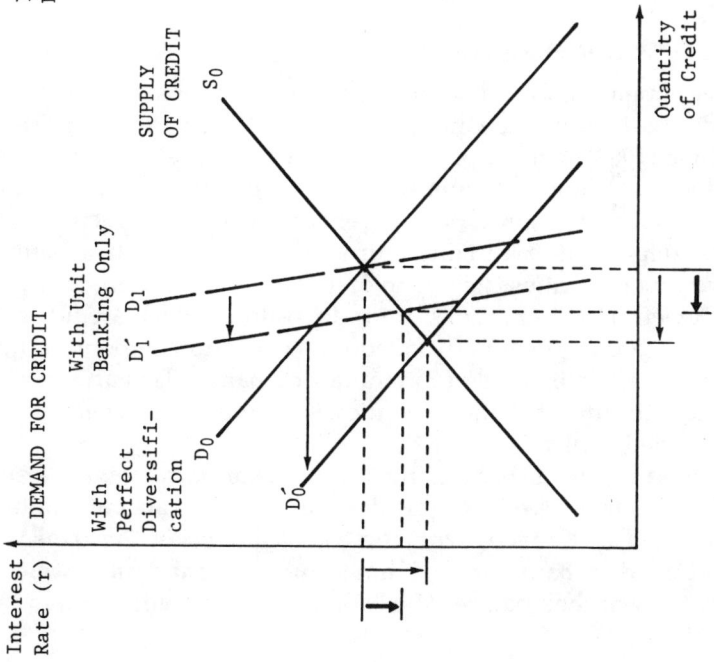

Figure 3 PROHIBITION ON PRIVATE BANK NOTES

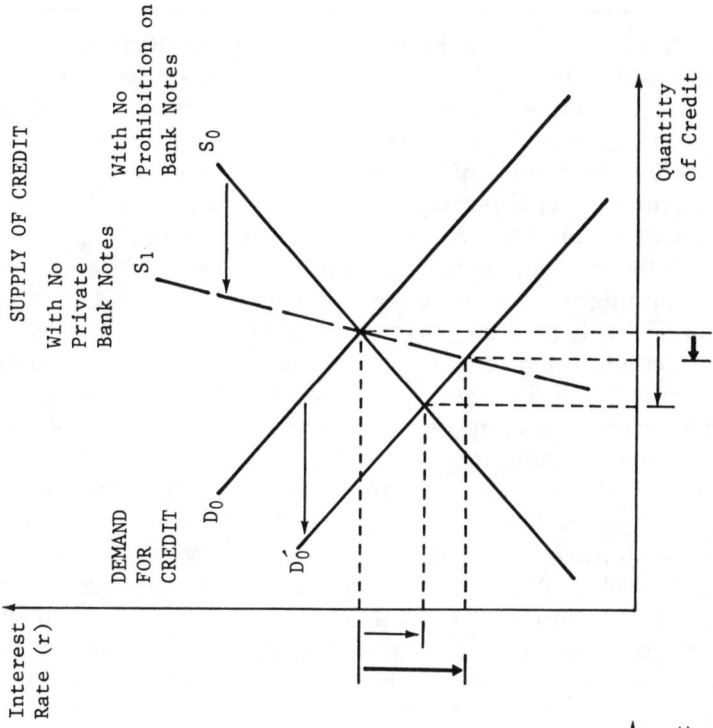

the price level equates the supply of and the demand for fiat money. When bank note issue is permitted, bank deposits tend to be less volatile because the interest rate is less volatile and because price movements induce more substitution into fiat currency from deposits.

The fact that the unit banking restriction induces less volatility in aggregate activity is perhaps surprising. In the model U.S. unit banking economy, we observe countercyclical bank failures. Relaxing this restriction in the model makes bank failures a constant (that is, zero). Thus, intuition might tell us that aggregate volatility should be smaller in the economy with perfectly diversified banks. The model contradicts this intuition and seems also to be at odds with the views of Friedman and Schwartz (1963), Bernanke (1983), and Hamilton (1987). Friedman and Schwartz assign an important macroeconomic role to bank failures in the United States during the Great Depression, a role they think operated through reductions in measured monetary aggregates. Bernanke and Hamilton argue that bank failures in the Great Depression had effects other than those reflected in monetary aggregates. However, note that both Bernanke (1983, pp. 266–67) and Friedman and Schwartz (1963, pp. 352–53) have difficulty reconciling their views with the Canadian experience in the Great Depression. During this time, Canada and the United States experienced comparable declines in output, but no Canadian banks failed (Haubrich 1987).

3.4. DEPOSIT INSURANCE

Government deposit insurance programs have played an important role in discussions of banking instability, as for example, in Diamond and Dybvig (1983). Such a program can be introduced into the unit banking system as follows. Assume that the government is an agent that can supply effort to monitor entrepreneurs. The government guarantees all bank depositors a certain return in each period. If a bank fails, the government verifies the return on the bank's portfolio. Lump-sum taxes are levied, either on banks or on depositors, which are just sufficient to compensate depositors in failed banks and to compensate the government for effort expended in monitoring banks. This arrangement yields an equilibrium allocation identical to the one achieved with perfectly diversified banks.

Canadian and U.S. banking and monetary arrangements since World War II can be viewed as equivalent. In 1935, private bank note issue was prohibited in Canada, with the establishment of the Bank of Canada, and Canadian banks were, if anything, larger and more well-diversified after the war than before. The U.S. deposit insurance system can be seen as accomplishing a function similar to that of a well-diversified banking system; the only difference is that in the U.S. system monitoring is delegated partly to the government rather than entirely to private financial intermediaries. The model constructed here, then, predicts that, other things held constant, aggregate fluctuations should have similar properties across the two countries in the postwar period.

4. The Evidence

4.1. COMPARISON OF CANADIAN AND U.S. AGGREGATE DATA

Now let us examine annual aggregate data for Canada and the United States for the periods 1870–1913 and 1954–87 and look for evidence consistent or inconsistent with the theory in Section 3.

The aggregate data come from several sources. Urquhart (1986) constructed constant dollar Canadian GNP and implicit price deflator series for 1870–1913. Urquhart used a value-added method to assemble the GNP data, and the resulting series seems to be of considerably better quality than anything available for the United States for this period. For U.S. constant dollar GNP in 1870–1913, I use two alternative series, constructed by Romer (1989) and Balke and Gordon (1989) using similar regression methods, but different underlying data. These series seem to be the best existing measures of U.S. GNP for this period. The two series have similar low frequency properties, but their cyclical properties are different. For implicit price deflators for 1870–1913, I use a standard historical series from Balke and Gordon (1986) and an updated series from Balke and Gordon (1989). Data on chartered bank deposits and bank notes in circulation in Canada in 1870–1913 come from monthly statements by the chartered banks, published in the *Canada Year Book* (1915). U.S. commercial bank deposit data are from Friedman and Schwartz (1970). The U.S. banking data are also inferior to the Canadian data, since the U.S. series was constructed from national banks' infrequent call reports and from very poor state bank data. For 1954–87, data come from the CANSIM data base, the Federal Reserve Board data base, and the FDIC *Annual Report* (various issues).

All time series were subjected to a log transformation and were detrended using a Hodrick-Prescott filter (Prescott 1983), which essentially fits a smooth, time-varying trend to the data.[5] Multiplying the resulting series by 100 gives time series which are percentage deviations

---

5. Here I set λ, the parameter which governs the smoothness in the trend, to 400. An increase in λ makes the trend smoother. Prescott (1983) uses $\lambda = 1600$ for quarterly data.

from trend. The theory yields predictions about unconditional variances and covariances of per capita aggregates in economies that do not grow. Thus, the data transformations account as well as seems possible for differences between the two countries in long-run growth, scale, and population.

Tables 3 and 4 show correlation matrices for percentage deviations from the trend of the Canadian and U.S. data in 1870–1913. Table 5

Tables 3–5   CORRELATIONS OF PERCENTAGE DEVIATIONS FROM TREND IN 1870–1913 DATA

Table 3   CANADIAN MATRIX

	(1) Gross National Product	(2) Implicit Price Deflator	(3) Bank Deposits (deflated)	(4) Bank Notes (deflated)	(3)+(4) Bank Liabilities (deflated)
(1)	1.000	.475	.433	.717	.588
(2)		1.000	−.026	.522	.182
(3)			1.000	.491	.941
(4)				1.000	.748
(3)+(4)					1.000

Table 4   U.S. MATRIX

	(1) GNP (Romer)	(2) GNP (Balke & Gordon)	(3) Implicit Price Deflator (standard)	(4) Bank Deposits (deflated)
(1)	1.000	.691	.183	.217
(2)		1.000	.502	.523
(3)			1.000	.494
(4)				1.000

Table 5   CROSS-COUNTRY CORRELATIONS

Indicator	U.S./Canada Correlation
GNP With Romer's Data	.395
With Balke & Gordon's Data	.678
Implicit Price Deflator	.677
U.S. Bank Deposits/Canadian Bank Notes + Deposits (all deflated)	.518

shows cross-country correlations. See also Figure 4. Tables 3 and 4 are generally consistent with the theory in that all but one of the series are mutually positively correlated in both countries. In addition, Table 5 shows a high degree of correlation between corresponding variables in the two countries. This is consistent with the assumption that real disturbances common to both countries dominate over this period.

Tables 6, 7, and 8 show correlations for the period 1954–87 and correspond to Tables 3, 4, and 5. See also Figure 5. Tables 6 and 7 indicate some inconsistencies with the model: in the Canadian data, there is essentially no correlation between GNP and the price level, and in the U.S. data, the GNP/price level and price level/bank deposit correlations are negative. Also, in Table 8, U.S. and Canadian bank deposits are negatively correlated. There thus appear to be important factors affecting aggregate fluctuations in Canada and the United States in the later period that are not captured in the model. Care is needed, therefore, in interpreting the 1954–87 data and in comparing the later period with the earlier one.

Table 9 shows standard deviations of the transformed series for each

Figure 4 PERCENTAGE DEVIATIONS FROM TREND OF U.S. AND CANADIAN GNP IN 1870–1913

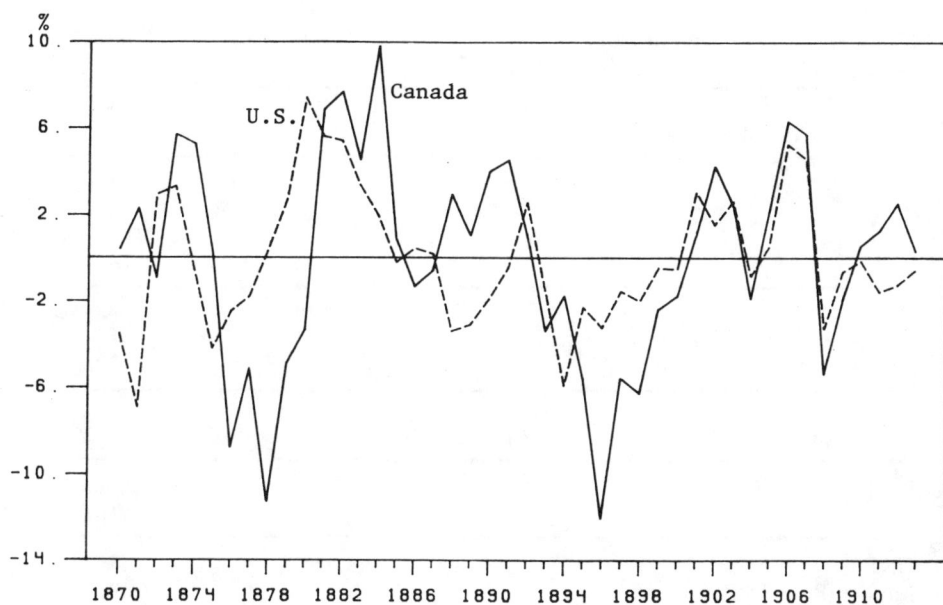

Sources: Urquhart (1986); Romer (1989)

time period, ratios of these volatility measures for Canada and the United States for each period, and volatility ratios for the two periods. Perhaps the strongest evidence supporting the predictions of the model is in the volatility measures for the GNP data from both periods. From column (1), Canadian GNP is considerably more volatile than U.S. GNP for the period 1870–1913. Volatility is 56 percent greater using Romer's GNP data, and 11 percent greater using Balke and Gordon's. For 1954–87, GNP volatility is virtually identical in the two countries, as the theory predicts. See also Figures 4 and 5 for a visual representation.

In column (1) of Table 9, as is consistent with the model, Canadian prices are more volatile than U.S. prices for 1870–1913, by 9 percent

Tables 6–8   CORRELATIONS OF PERCENTAGE DEVIATIONS FROM TREND IN 1954–1987 DATA

Table 6   CANADIAN MATRIX

	(1) GNP	(2) Implicit Price Deflator	(3) Bank Deposits (deflated)
(1) GNP	·1.000	−.023	.320
(2) Implicit Price Deflator		1.000	.594
(3) Bank Deposits (deflated)			1.000

Table 7   U.S. MATRIX

	(1) GNP	(2) Implicit Price Deflator	(3) Bank Deposits (Deflated)
(1) GNP	1.000	−.528	.483
(2) Implicit Price Deflator		1.000	−.588
(3) Bank Deposits (deflated)			1.000

Table 8   CROSS-COUNTRY CORRELATIONS

Indicator	U.S./Canada Correlation
GNP	.607
Implicit Price Deflator	.935
Bank Deposits (deflated)	−.133

using the standard U.S. GNP deflator and by 54 percent using Balke and Gordon's. However, in column (2) of Table 9, the Canadian GNP deflator is 21 percent more volatile than the U.S. GNP deflator in 1954–87, which is inconsistent with the theory.

Returning again to column (1), note that in the early period Canadian bank deposits are less volatile than U.S. bank deposits (deflated using either the standard GNP deflator or Balke and Gordon's). This is not inconsistent with the theory since the prohibition of bank notes makes deposits more volatile in the model. Canada's bank note circulation is considerably more volatile than its bank deposits. But bank note and deposit liabilities in Canada are less volatile than bank deposits in the United States—by approximately 12 percent using the standard U.S. GNP deflator and by 21 percent using Balke and Gordon's deflator. In the 1870–1913 period, this is where the theory has the most trouble explaining the data. However, note that, in column (2), U.S. bank deposits are also more volatile than Canadian bank deposits in the 1954–87 period. Column (3) shows ratios for the two periods of the Canadian/ U.S. bank liability volatility ratios, that is, the relative volatility between

Figure 5 PERCENTAGE DEVIATIONS FROM TREND OF U.S. AND CANADIAN GNP IN 1954–1987

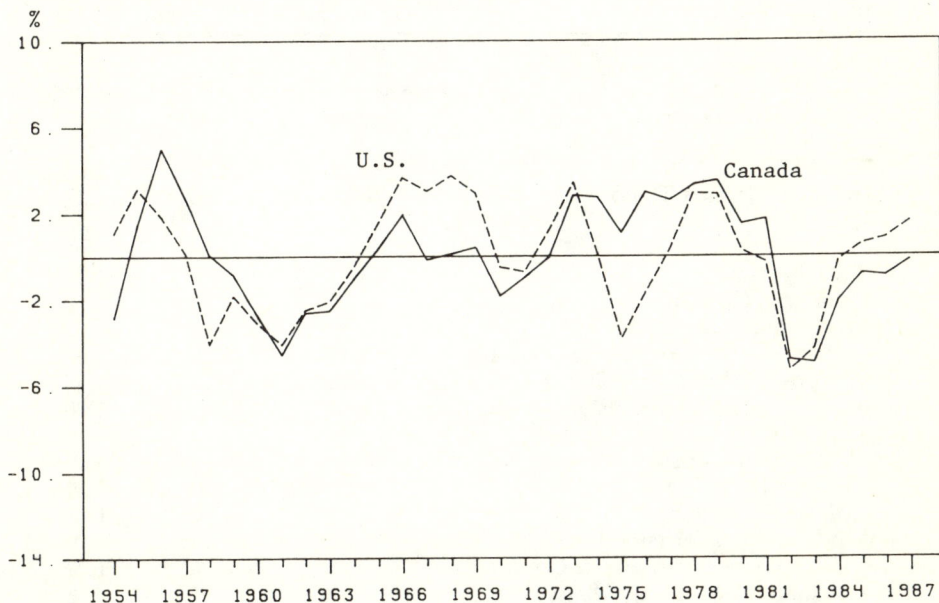

Sources: Federal Reserve Board data base, CANSIM data base

the two periods. This relative volatility measure is higher for U.S. bank liabilities, approximately 2 percent using the standard GNP deflator or 12 percent using Balke and Gordon's deflator. Additionally, the theory could be reconciled with the data if the U.S. bank deposit data for 1870–1913 contained considerably more measurement error than the corresponding Canadian data. As noted earlier, this seems a good possibility.

4.2. INDUSTRIAL COMPOSITION OF CANADIAN AND U.S. OUTPUT FOR 1870–1913

A possible alternative explanation for the difference in the volatility of GNP in Canada and the United States in 1870–1913 is that production in Canada was more concentrated in industries which had high volatility. For example, one might suppose that a larger fraction of Canadian GNP consisted of production of primary commodities which would tend to be more cyclically sensitive than production in other industries. To see whether the empirical evidence supports this alternative hypothesis,

Table 9   VOLATILITY OF PERCENTAGE DEVIATIONS FROM TREND IN TWO COUNTRIES AND TWO PERIODS

	Standard Deviation		
Country and Indicator	(1) 1870–1913	(2) 1954–1987	(1)÷(2)
Canada			
GNP	4.87	2.51	1.94
Implicit Price Deflator	3.84	4.42	.87
Bank Notes	9.22	—	—
Deposits	4.96	4.69	1.06
Liabilities (Notes + Deposits)	5.26	4.69	1.12
United States			
GNP (Romer)	3.13	2.57	1.22
(Balke & Gordon)	4.37	2.57	1.70
Implicit Price Deflator (standard)	3.53	3.66	.96
(Balke & Gordon)	2.49	3.66	.68
Bank Deposits (standard deflator)	5.96	5.20	1.15
(Balke & Gordon deflator)	6.64	5.20	1.28
Canada ÷ United States			
GNP (Romer)	1.56	.98	1.59
(Balke & Gordon)	1.11	.98	1.13
Implicit Price Deflator (standard)	1.09	1.21	.90
(Balke & Gordon)	1.54	1.21	1.27
Bank Liabilities (standard deflator)	.88	.90	.98
(Balke & Gordon deflator)	.79	.90	.88

let's examine comparable value-added data for selected U.S. and Canadian industries.

Gallman (1960) has constructed value-added measures for four U.S. industries, at five-year intervals, which overlap with our sample for the years 1874, 1879, . . . , 1899. Urquhart (1986) provides comparable annual data for Canada. The four industries are agriculture, mining, manufacturing, and construction, and the value-added measures are in current Canadian dollars. For Canada, these four industries accounted for 60 percent of gross domestic product in 1889. Table 10 shows the percentage of value added in each of the four industries in Canada and the United States for the selected years. As anticipated, Canada had a larger portion of output in agriculture and a smaller portion in manufacturing than the United States did, and this difference persists through the sample. The portion of value added in mining was smaller in Canada than in the United States through most of the period, but Canada's portion was slightly larger than the United States' in 1894 and much larger in 1899. However, this 1899 number was temporarily enlarged by the Klondike gold rush (Urquhart 1986). The portion of value added in construction was consistently much smaller in Canada than in the United States.

Using the same detrending method as described above, I computed standard deviations of percentage deviations from trend for current dollar value-added measures for the four Canadian industries in 1870–1913. These statistics are displayed in Table 11. Surprisingly, volatility was lowest in agriculture, followed by manufacturing and mining, with the

Table 10   PERCENTAGE OF VALUE ADDED IN FOUR CANADIAN AND
U.S. INDUSTRIES
(Based on current Canadian dollar data)

	Industry and Country							
	Agriculture		Mining		Manufactur-ing		Construction	
Year	*Canada*	*U.S.*	*Canada*	*U.S.*	*Canada*	*U.S.*	*Canada*	*U.S.*
1874	51.6	46.9	1.6	2.8	36.1	38.4	10.7	12.0
1879	59.1	49.0	2.0	2.9	32.4	37.0	6.5	11.1
1884	49.5	40.0	1.7	2.8	37.9	43.0	10.9	14.2
1889	46.8	35.1	2.7	3.6	41.5	47.4	9.0	13.9
1894	48.9	33.8	4.1	3.7	41.1	46.0	6.0	16.6
1899	44.9	33.3	8.2	4.6	40.2	49.5	6.8	12.6

Note: Percentages may not add up to 100 due to rounding.
Sources: Urquhart (1986); Gallman (1960)

highest volatility in construction. Given the evidence from Table 10, the differences in the composition of output in Canada and the United States would tend to make Canadian output less volatile in the 1870–1913 period. As an additional check, a counterfactual nominal GNP series for Canada for 1870–1913 was constructed. This was done as follows. Let Y_t denote nominal GNP, y_{it} nominal value added in industry i, where $i = 1$, 2, 3, 4 for agriculture, mining, manufacturing, and construction, respectively. An asterisk (*) superscript denotes a U.S. variable. Then, counterfactual Canadian nominal GNP, $\hat{Y}_t$ (what Canadian GNP would have been if Canada had had the same relative composition of output as the United States in agriculture, mining, manufacturing, and construction), is computed as

$$\hat{Y}_t = Y_t - \sum_{i=1}^{4} y_{it} + \sum_{i=1}^{4} \alpha_{it} y_{it}.$$

The weights, α_i for $i = 1, 2, 3, 4$ were constructed as follows:

$$\alpha_{it} = (y_{is}^* / \sum_{i=1}^{4} y_{is}^*)/(y_{is} / \sum_{i=1}^{4} y_{is})$$

where $s = 1874$ for $t = 1870, \ldots, 1876$; $s = 1879$ for $t = 1877, \ldots, 1881$; $s = 1884$ for $t = 1882, \ldots, 1886$; $s = 1889$ for $t = 1887, \ldots, 1891$; $s = 1894$ for $t = 1892, \ldots, 1896$; and $s = 1899$ for $t = 1897, \ldots, 1913$. The standard deviation of percentage deviations from trend in Y_t is 7.53, and for $\hat{Y}_t$ it is 7.54. This evidence provides no support for the alternative hypothesis that historical cross-country differences in volatility can be explained by differences in the composition of output.

The relative industry volatilities in Table 11 would probably not be very different if the value-added measures were based on constant dol-

Table 11   VOLATILITY OF PERCENTAGE DEVIATIONS FROM TREND OF VALUE ADDED IN FOUR CANADIAN INDUSTRIES 1870–1913 (Based on Current Canadian dollar data)

Industry	Standard Deviation
Agriculture	8.2
Mining	13.8
Manufacturing	11.7
Construction	18.4
Sum of Above Four Industries	9.0

Source of raw data: Urquhart (1986)

lar data. (Urquhart 1986 uses an aggregate price index to deflate his aggregate current dollar GNP measures.) For example, if agricultural prices were more volatile than other prices, and if these prices were procyclical, as was true for aggregate price indices over this period, then agricultural output would tend to be relatively less volatile than in Table 11.

5. Summary and Conclusions

The aim of this paper was to adapt a macroeconomic model with an explicit financial intermediation structure to capture financial and monetary arrangements in the United States and Canada in the period 1870–1913, to analyze the model's implications for aggregate fluctuations in the two countries, and to see whether these implications appear to fit the facts. Over this period, Canada had a branch banking system, with few banks compared to the U.S. unit banking system. Canadian banks could issue circulating notes with no restrictions on their backing, while U.S. banks could not issue notes backed by private assets. Canada also experienced considerably less disruption due to bank failures than the United States did, and banking panics were virtually nonexistent in Canada.

The model predicts that, with a unit banking restriction, output, price level, and bank liabilities become less volatile than they would be otherwise, because the restriction causes the demand for credit to become less elastic in the face of technological shocks affecting credit demand. This occurs despite the fact that bank failures and bank runs are countercyclical in the unit banking economy, and the fact that there would be no such failures and runs in an economy where banks could diversify perfectly, as in a branch banking system in a large economy. The model also predicts that a prohibition on circulating bank notes reduces volatility in bank liabilities, output, and prices. Deposit insurance in the unit banking system is an equivalent arrangement to a perfectly diversified banking system, so that Canada and the United States should experience similar fluctuations after World War II, everything else held constant.

With regard to its qualitative predictions for co-movements, the model is consistent with aggregate annual data for the 1870–1913 period for Canada and the United States. However, the model runs into some problems in 1954–87: U.S. and Canadian prices are countercyclical rather than procyclical as the model predicts.

Relative volatilities in U.S. and Canadian GNP in the two periods are most supportive of the model. Depending on the U.S. GNP measure used, Canadian GNP is 56 percent or 11 percent more volatile than U.S. GNP in 1870–1913. Volatility is virtually equal in the two countries in

1954–87. Also consistent with the model is the greater volatility in Canadian prices for 1870–1913. However, for 1870–1913, Canadian bank liabilities are less volatile than U.S. bank liabilities, in contrast to what the model predicts. This result is consistent with greater volatility in true Canadian bank liabilities coupled with greater measurement error in measured U.S. bank liabilities. This possibility seems likely, since Canadian bank liabilities were measured with greater frequency and accuracy for the 1870–1913 period.

APPENDIX A

DERIVATION OF VARIANCES AND COVARIANCES WITH FLUCTUATIONS

For the Canadian economy, totally differentiate (11)–(15) and solve to get

$$\partial d_1/\partial \phi_2 - \partial d_2/\partial \theta_2 = N\eta_3 f \eta_4 Kg\Sigma_\phi[(1-q_1+q_2)\eta_1 a + \eta_1 A + \eta_2(1-B)$$
$$+ \eta_3(1-F)]/\nabla \quad \text{(A1)}$$

$$\partial n_1/\partial \phi_2 - \partial n_2/\partial \phi_2 = \eta_2 b(\partial d_1/\partial \phi_2 - \partial d_2/\partial \phi_2)/\eta_3 f \quad \text{(A2)}$$

$$\partial \hat{p}/\partial \phi_2 = -(\eta_2 b + \eta_3 f)\eta_4 Kg\Sigma_\phi/\nabla \quad \text{(A3)}$$

$$\partial y_1^1/\partial \phi_2 - \partial y_2^1/\partial \phi_2 = -N\eta_1 a(1-q_1+q_2)\partial \hat{p}/\partial \phi_2 \quad \text{(A4)}$$

$$\partial y_1^2/\partial \phi_2 - \partial y_2^2/\partial \phi_2 = N\mu(\partial d_1/\partial \phi_2 - \partial d_2/\partial \phi_2 + \partial n_1/\partial \phi_2 - \partial n_2/\partial \phi_2) \quad \text{(A5)}$$

$$\nabla \equiv \Sigma_\phi(\eta_2 b - \eta_3 f)[(1-q_1+q_2)\eta_1 a + \eta_1 A + \eta_2(1-B) + \eta_3(1-F)]$$
$$+ \eta_4 K^2 g[(1-q_1+q_2)(\eta_1 a + \eta_2 b + \eta_3 f) + \eta_1 A + \eta_2(1-B) + \eta_3(1-F)] > 0$$

$$\Sigma_\theta = -\int_0^{x'} D_2 H(\phi, \theta', \phi)\, dw - \gamma D_2 H(x', \theta', \phi) > 0$$

$$\Sigma_\phi \equiv \int_0^{x'} D_3 H(w, \theta', \phi)\, dw > 0$$

$$g \equiv g(\theta'),\ a \equiv a(1),\ b \equiv b(r-1),\ f \equiv f(r-1),$$

$$A \equiv A(1),\ B \equiv B(r-1),\ F \equiv F(r-1).$$

Similarly, for the U.S. economy:

$$\partial d_1^*/\partial\phi_2 - \partial d_2^*/\partial\phi_2 = N^*\eta_3 f^*\eta_4 Kg^*\Sigma_\phi^*[(1-q_1+q_2)\eta_1 a^* + \eta_1 A + \eta_2 + \eta_3$$
$$(1-F)]/\nabla^* \quad (A6)$$

$$\partial\hat{p}^*/\partial\phi_2 = -\eta_3 f^*\eta_4 Kg^*\Sigma_\phi^*/\nabla^* \quad (A7)$$

$$\partial y_1^{1*}/\partial\phi_2 - \partial y_2^{1*}/\partial\phi_2 = -N^*\eta_1 a^*(1-q_1+q_2)\partial\hat{p}^*/\partial\phi_2 \quad (A8)$$

$$\partial y_1^{2*}/\partial\phi_2 - \partial y_2^{2*}/\partial\phi_2 = N^*\mu[\partial d_1^*/\partial\phi_2 - \partial d_2^*/\partial\phi_2] \quad (A9)$$

$$\nabla^* \equiv \Sigma_\phi^*\eta_3 f^*[(1-q_1-q_2)\eta_1 a^* + \eta_1 A^* + \eta_{/2} + \eta_3(1-F^*)]$$
$$+ \eta_4 K^2 g^*[(1-q_1+q_2)(\eta_1 a^* + \eta_3 f^*) + \eta_1 A^* + \eta_2 + \eta_3(1-F^*)] > 0$$

$$\Sigma_\theta^* \equiv -\int_0^{x'} D_2 H(w,\theta'^*,\phi)\,dw - \gamma K D_2 H(x'^*,\theta'^*,\phi) > 0$$

$$\Sigma_\phi^* \equiv \int_0^{x'^*} D_3 H(w_1,\theta'^*,\phi)\,dw > 0.$$

APPENDIX B

COMPARISON OF VARIANCES AND COVARIANCES ACROSS COUNTRIES

Differentiating (A1)–(A9) with respect to γ and η_2 and evaluating at $\gamma = 0$, $\eta_2 = 0$ gives

$$\frac{\partial}{\partial K}[(\partial d_1/\partial\phi_2)/N - (\partial d_2/\partial\phi_2)/N - (\partial d_1^*/\partial\phi_2)/N^* + (\partial d_2^*/\partial\phi_2)/N^*]$$
$$= \eta_3 f\eta_4 Kg\Sigma_\phi D_2 H(x',\theta',\phi)(1-K)[\eta_1 a(1-q_1+q_2) + \eta_1 A + \eta_3(1-F)]^2/\nabla^2 >$$
$$0 \quad (B1)$$

$$\frac{\partial}{\partial\eta_2}[(\partial d_1/\partial\phi_2)/N - (\partial d_2/\partial\phi_2)/N - (\partial d_1^*/\partial\phi_2)/N^* - (\partial d_2^*/\partial\phi_2)/N^*]$$
$$= -\eta_3 f\eta_4 Kg\Sigma_\phi b\{[(1-q_1+q_2)\eta_1 a + \eta_1 A + \eta_3(1-F)]\Sigma_\phi + \eta_4 K^2 g(1-q_1+q_2)\}/\nabla^2$$
$$< 0 \quad (B2)$$

$$\frac{\partial}{\partial K}[(\partial d_1/\partial\phi_2)/N - (\partial d_2/\partial\phi_2)/N + (\partial n_1/\partial\phi_2)/N - (\partial\eta_2/\partial\phi_2)/N$$
$$- (\partial d_1^*/\partial\phi_2)/N^* + (\partial d_2^*/\partial\phi_2)/N^*]$$
$$= \eta_3 f\eta_4 Kg\Sigma_\phi D_2 H(x',\theta',\phi)(1-K)[\eta_1 a(1-q_1+q_2) + \eta_2 A + \eta_3(1-F)]^2/\nabla^2 >$$
$$0 \quad (B3)$$

$$\frac{\partial}{\partial\eta_2}[(\partial d_1/\partial\phi_2)/N - (\partial d_2/\partial\phi_2)/N + (\partial\eta_1/\partial\phi_2)/N - (\partial n_2/\partial\phi_2)/N$$
$$- (\partial d_1^*/\partial\phi_2)/N^* + (\partial d_2^*/\partial\phi_2)/N^*]$$
$$= \eta_4 K^3 g^2\Sigma_\phi b\eta_1 a(1-q_1+q_2)[\eta_1 a(1-q_1+q_2) + \eta_1 A + \eta_3(1-F)] > 0 \quad (B4)$$

$\frac{\partial}{\partial K}\left[(\partial y_1^2/\partial\phi_2)/N-(\partial y_2^2/\partial\phi_2)/N-(\partial y_1^{2*}/\partial\phi_2)/N^*+(\partial y_2^{2*}/\partial\phi_2)/N^*\right]$
$= \mu\eta_3 f\eta_4 K g\Sigma_\phi D_2 H(x',\theta',\phi)(1-K)[\eta_1 a(1-q_1+q_2)+\eta_1 A+\eta_3(1-F)]^2/\nabla^2 >$
0 (B5)

$\frac{\partial}{\partial\eta_2}\left[(\partial y_1^2/\partial\phi_2)/N-(\partial y_2^2/\partial\phi_2)/N-(\partial y_1^{2*}/\partial\phi_2)/N^*+(\partial y_2^{2*}/\partial\phi_2)/N^*\right]$
$= \mu\eta_4^2 K^3 g^2\Sigma_\phi b\eta_1 a(1-q_1+q_2)[\eta_1 a(1-q_1+q_2)+\eta_1 A+\eta_3(1-F)] > 0$ (B6)

$\frac{\partial}{\partial K}\left(|\partial\hat{p}/\partial\phi_2|-|\partial\hat{p}^*/P\phi_2|\right)$
$= \eta_4 K g\Sigma_\phi(\eta_3 f)^2 D_2 H(x',\theta',\phi)(1-K)[\eta_1 a(1-q_1+q_2)+\eta_1 A+\eta_3(1-F)]/\nabla^2 >$
0 (B7)

$\frac{\partial}{\partial\eta_2}\left(|\partial\hat{p}/\partial\phi_2|-|\partial\hat{p}^*/\partial\phi_2|\right)$
$= \eta_4 K g\Sigma_\phi b[\eta_1 a(1-q_1-q_2)+\eta_1 A+\eta_3(1-F)]/\nabla^2 > 0$ (B8)

$\frac{\partial}{\partial K}\left[(\partial y_1^1/\{\partial\phi_2)/N-(\partial y_2^1/\partial\phi_2)/N-(\partial y_1^{1*}/\partial\phi_2)/N^*+(\partial y_2^{1*}/\partial\phi_2)/N^*\right]$
$= \eta_1 a(1-q_1+q_2)\eta_4 K g\Sigma_\phi(\eta_3 f)^2 D_2 H(x',\theta',\phi)(1-K)$
$\times [\eta_1 a(1-q_1+q_2)+\eta_1 A+\eta_3(1-F)]/\nabla^2 > 0$ (B9)

$\frac{\partial}{\partial\eta_2}\left[(\partial y_1^1/\partial\phi_2)/N-(\partial y_2^1/\partial\phi_2)/N-(\partial y_1^{1*}/\partial\phi_2)/N^*+(\partial y_2^{1*}/\partial\phi_2)/N^*\right]$
$= \eta_1 a(1-q_1+q_2)\eta_4 K g\Sigma_\phi b[\eta_1 a(1-i^2 tq_1+q_2)+\eta_1 A+\eta_3(1-F)]/\nabla^2 > 0.$ (B10)

I thank David Backus for the use of a program for computing Hodrick-Prescott filters and Frank Lewis for assistance with historical sources. The comments of Olivier Blanchard, Mark Gertler, David Laidler, Julio Rotemberg, Lawrence White, seminar participants at the Federal Reserve Bank of Minneapolis, and conference participants at the National Bureau of Economic Research were all helpful. The views expressed here are mine and not necessarily those of the Federal Reserve Bank of Minneapolis or the Federal Reserve System.

REFERENCES

Balke, N. S., and R. J. Gordon. 1986. Appendix B: Historical data. In *The American Business Cycle: Continuity and Change*, R. J. Gordon, ed. Chicago: University of Chicago Press.

Balke, N. S., and R. J. Gordon. 1989. "The Estimation of Prewar Gross National Product: Methodology and New Evidence." *Journal of Political Economy* 97:38–92.

Beckhart, B. H. 1929. *The Banking System of Canada*. New York: Henry Holt.

Bernanke, B. S. 1983. "Nonmonetary Effects of the Financial Crisis in the Propagation of the Great Depression." *American Economic Review* 73:257–276.

Bernanke, B. S., and M. Gertler. 1989. "Agency Costs, Net Worth, and Business Fluctuations." *American Economic Review* 79:14–31.

Boyd, J. H., and E. C. Prescott. 1986. "Financial Intermediary-Coalitions." *Journal of Economic Theory* 38:211–232.

Cagan, P. 1965. *Determinants and Effects of Changes in the Stock of Money, 1875–1960*. New York: Columbia University Press (for NBER).

Canada Year Book, 1914. 1915. Ottawa: J.D. LeTache, Printer to the King's Most Excellent Majesty.

Diamond, D. W. 1984. "Financial Intermediation and Delegated Monitoring." *Review of Economic Studies* 51:393–414.

Diamond, D. W., and P. H. Dybvig. 1983. "Bank Runs, Deposit Insurance, and Liquidity." *Journal of Political Economy* 91:401–419.

FDIC. 1941. *Annual Report of the Federal Deposit Insurance Corporation for the Year Ended December 31, 1940*. Washington, D.C.

FDIC. Various issues. *Annual Report of the Federal Deposit Insurance Corporation*. Washington, D.C.

Friedman, M., and A. J. Schwartz. 1963. *A Monetary History of the United States, 1867–1960*. Princeton: Princeton University Press (for NBER).

Friedman, M., and A. J. Schwartz. 1970. *Monetary Statistics of the United States: Estimates, Sources, Methods*. New York: Columbia University Press (for NBER).

Gale, D., and M. Hellwig. 1985. "Incentive-Compatible Debt Contracts: The One-Period Problem." *Review of Economic Studies* 52:647–663.

Gallman, R. E. 1960. "Commodity output, 1939–99." In *Trends in the American Economy in the Nineteenth Century*. Princeton: Princeton University Press (for NBER).

Gertler, M. 1988. "Financial Structure and Aggregate Economic Activity: An Overview." *Journal of Money, Credit, and Banking* 20:559–88.

Gorton, G. 1985. "Clearinghouses and the Origin of Central Banking in the United States." *Journal of Economic History* 45:277–83.

Greenwood, J., and S. D. Williamson. 1988. "International Financial Intermediation and Aggregate Fluctuations under Alternative Exchange Rate Regimes." Federal Reserve Bank of Minneapolis. Research Department Staff Report 112. Also forthcoming, *Journal of Monetary Economics*.

Hamilton, J. D. 1987. "Monetary Factors in the Great Depression." *Journal of Monetary Economics* 19:145–69.

Haubrich, J. G. 1987. "Money Supply, Bank Failures, and Credit Crunches: Lessons from the Great Depression in Canada." University of Pennsylvania, Wharton School Working Paper.

Johnson, J. F. 1910. *The Canadian Banking System*. Report prepared by the National Monetary Commission for the U.S. Senate. 61st Congress, 2nd sess., S. Doc. 583. Washington, D.C.: Government Printing Office.

Postlewaite, A., and X. Vives. 1987. "Bank Runs as an Equilibrium Phenomenon." *Journal of Political Economy* 95:485–91.

Prescott, E. C. 1983. "Can the Cycle be Reconciled with a Consistent Theory of Expectations? or a Progress Report on Business Cycle Theory." Federal Reserve Bank of Minneapolis Research Department Working Paper 239.

Romer, C. D. 1989. "The Prewar Business Cycle Reconsidered: New Estimates of Gross National Product, 1869–1908." *Journal of Political Economy* 97:1–37.

Rothschild, M., and J. E. Stiglitz. 1970. "Increasing risk: I. A Definition." *Journal of Economic Theory* 2:225–43.

Sprague, O. M. W. 1910. *History of Crises under the National Banking System*. Report by the National Monetary Commission to the U.S. Senate. 61st Congress, 2nd sess., S. Doc. 538. Washington, D.C.: Government Printing Office.

Townsend, R. M. 1979. "Optimal Contracts and Competitive Markets with Costly State Verification." *Journal of Economic Theory* 21:265–93.

Townsend, R. M. 1988. "Information Constrained Insurance: The Revelation Principle Extended." *Journal of Monetary Econonmics* 21:411–50.

Urquhart, M. C. 1986. "New Estimates of Gross National Product, Canada,

1870–1926: Some Implications for Canadian Development." In *Long-Term Factors in American Economic Growth*, S. L. Engerman and R. E. Gallman, eds. Chicago: University of Chicago Press (for NBER).

U.S. Congress, National Monetary Commission Subcommittee. 1910. *Interviews on the Banking and Currency Systems of Canada*. 61st Congress, 2nd sess., S. Doc. 584. Washington, D.C.: Government Printing Office.

U.S. Department of Commerce, Bureau of the Census. 1975. *Historical Statistics of the United States: Colonial Times to 1970*. 93rd Congress, 1st sess., H. Doc. 93–78 (Part 2).

Wallace, N. 1988. "Another Attempt to Explain an Illiquid Banking System: The Diamond and Dybvig Model with Sequential Service Taken Seriously." *Federal Reserve Bank of Minneapolis Quarterly Review* 12:3–16.

Williamson, S. D. 1986. "Costly Monitoring, Financial Intermediation, and Equilibrium Credit Rationing." *Journal of Monetary Economics* 18:159–79.

Williamson, S. D. 1987a. "Costly Monitoring, Loan Contracts, and Equilibrium Credit Rationing." *Quarterly Journal of Economics* 102:135–46.

Williamson, S. D. 1987b. "Financial Intermediation, Business Failures, and Real Business Cycles." *Journal of Political Economy* 95:1196–1216.

Williamson, S. D. 1988. "Liquidity, Banking, and Bank Failures." *International Economic Review* 29:25–43.

Comment

MARK GERTLER
University of Wisconsin and NBER

This paper nicely and elegantly illustrates several basic points regarding the relation between financial structure and real activity. First, it emphasizes the simultaneous nature of this relation. Second, it provides another example of how financial factors can propagate business fluctuations. And third, it demonstrates how the regulation of financial markets can have important real consequences.

The macroeconomic model presented here evolves explicitly from first principles. What makes financial structure determinant and relevant is the presence of informational asymmetries between borrowers and lenders. As the finance literature suggests, these asymmetries introduce agency problems which ultimately add costs to borrowing. A determinant financial pattern emerges because it is optimal to structure financial contracts and institutions to minimize these costs. One may view this paper and other related work in macroeconomics as fleshing out the general equilibrium consequences of having these kinds of agency costs present.

The specific agency framework at the core of the analysis is Townsend's (1979) costly state verification model. Lenders cannot freely observe a borrower's project returns. To do so, they must pay fixed cost.

This creates a problem: If lenders do not audit, the borrower has the incentive to underreport her earnings, but it is inefficient for lenders to audit all the time. Under a certain set of restrictions, the optimal financial contract assumes the following form: Whenever project output w is greater than or equal to a value x, lenders receive x and the borrower gets $w - x$. When w is below x, the borrower declares default and lenders audit. Lenders get $w - \gamma$, where γ is the verification cost, and the borrower gets nothing. The non-default payment x is chosen to guarantee that lenders receive an expected return equal to the opportunity cost of their funds.

The optimal arrangement is interpretable as a risky debt contract, with γ being the cost of default. Intuitively, the contract is structured to minimize the expected default costs, which are the agency costs of borrowing in this example. Making the borrower the residual claimant accomplishes this goal.[1]

A key point is that the default costs make credit rationing possible, as illustrated in Figure 1. θ is an index of project quality; and projects are ordered on the horizontal axis from high quality to low quality, where low quality ones have less favorable return distributions. The solid curve reflects combinations of x and θ which permit lenders to receive a competitive return. The curve bends backward because after a point further increases in x lower lenders' expected return; the rise in expected default costs (due to the rise in the default probability) begins to outweigh the gain from a higher non-default payment. As a result, projects of quality less than θ', the value of θ at which the curve bends backward, will not receive funding even though some of them would be profitable in the absence of informational problems.

Another important insight is that financial intermediation emerges endogenously. In order to avoid the waste incurred in having lenders independently audit a borrower in default, the optimal arrangement has lenders delegate the auditing responsibility to an intermediary. That is, lenders deposit their funds with an intermediary who then channels the funds to the borrower under a bilateral contractual arrangement. The incentive problem between the intermediary and its depositors (depositors cannot observe the intermediary's returns) is overcome by having the intermediary hold a perfectly diversified portfolio, guaranteeing depositors a sure return.

A substantial part of the paper explores how a unit banking regulation

---

1. Making the borrower the residual claimant as a device to solve an incentive problem with lenders is another example of what Hall (1989) terms the "back-to-the-wall" theory of finance.

could influence real activity. It is now easy to see the basic reasoning. Unit banking restricts the ability of an intermediary to diversify. This implies intermediaries can fail (not be able to offer depositors the safe rate of return in all states of nature). Since diversification is no longer available as a device to solve the incentive problem, individual depositors must audit intermediaries in default. The net effect is to increase the average agency costs involved in lending to any given borrower. The dotted line in Figure 1 portrays the combinations of the non-default payment x and project quality θ needed to guarantee lenders a competitive return under unit banking. The curve bends backward before the corresponding curve for laissez-faire banking (the solid line). This is because total default costs are larger under unit banking, making expected default costs rise at a faster rate. As a result the reservation level of project quality under unit banking, θ'_u is higher, implying a lower market equilibrium level of investment.

Figure 1

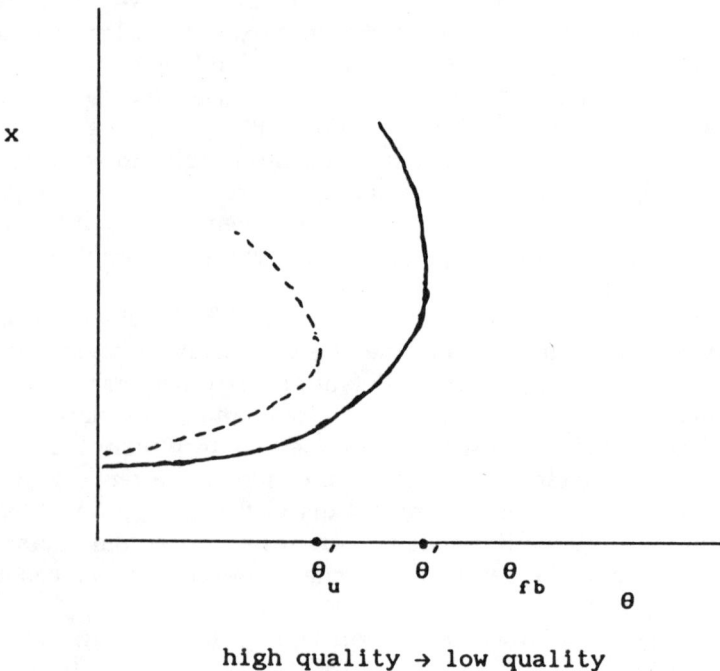

high quality → low quality

θ_{fb}: reservation value of θ under perfect information
θ': reservation value of θ under laissez-faire (branch) banking
θ'_u: reservation value of θ under unit banking

The main point of the paper is to examine the effects of two restrictions on intermediation for aggregate fluctuations. One is the unit banking regulation described above and the other is a limitation on the kinds of liabilities banks can offer. The restrictions are chosen because they applied in the U.S. at the turn of the century but not in Canada, permitting an informal way to test the predictions of the analysis.

In the theoretical model, mean preserving spreads in project return distributions propagate fluctuations by inducing countercyclical movements in the degree of credit rationing. In periods of high risk, expected default costs rise (shifting in the curve in Figure 1), lowering the market level of investment; vice-versa in periods of low risk. The model predicts further that fluctuations are greater under laissez-faire than under legally restricted intermediation. The result arises, roughly speaking, because the credit demand and supply functions are more elastic under laissez-faire: elimination of the high agency costs associated with unit bank makes credit demand more elastic, while elimination of the restriction on the kinds of liabilities intermediaries can offer does the same for credit supply. The result seems more straightforward (at least to me) if one recognizes that not only is the variance of output higher under laissez-faire, so is the mean. The lower agency costs under laissez-faire permit a higher average level of investment, as can be inferred from Figure 1.

Overall, the theoretical model is rich, and cleverly constructed. The descriptive comparison of the U.S. and Canadian financial systems is very interesting; this kind of historical evidence provides a useful background for thinking about the best way to regulate (or deregulate) financial markets. In this regard, I would be interested in seeing more evidence bearing on the relative efficiencies of the two financial systems. For example, one possible disadvantage of the "laissez-faire" Canadian system was the emergence of a heavily concentrated banking industry, suggesting possible inefficiencies in intermediation because of imperfect competition. If data on spreads between deposit and loan rates are available, it may be possible to empirically ascertain whether the Canadian or U.S. system is more efficient.[2]

The main difficulty with the paper is that the evidence used to support the theory is at best suggestive. Because the number of data points is so limited, any kind of formal analysis is impossible. It is indeed an interesting puzzle that the Canadian economy at the turn of the century was so much more volatile than the U.S. economy, particularly given that the

---

2. Depositor losses may not be a totally accurate measure of efficiency since it does not account for the time taken to compensate depositors.

ratio of agricultural to industrial production was higher in Canada. However, more knowledge about the two economies would be desirable before arriving at the conclusion that differences in financial market regulations could largely explain the differences in output fluctuations. In this vein, it would be useful to know whether the theoretical model is capable of explaining the quantitative differences involved. What kinds of parameter restrictions are necessary? Exploring this avenue might provide another way to check the plausibility of the story. Qualitative predictions alone do not seem sufficient here.

It is also fair to ask whether Steve's framework adequately captures the impact of widespread bank failures. I think he is right to insist that previous literature ignores some parallels between bank failures and the failures of non-financial corporations. However, the costs of bank failures in his framework are limited to depositors auditing expenses. There is no suspension of lending owing to previous bank failures; new intermediaries crop up immediately in the subsequent period to facilitate lending. This is distinct from Bernanke (1983) who emphasizes that systematic bank failures can lead to a loss of intermediary services for an indefinite period, implying a prolonged period of disruption because of credit being choked off partly or completely to certain sectors of the economy. It is also distinct from Friedman and Schwartz who emphasize the impact on the money supply.

Who is right is an empirical question. However, it seems to me that the various theories are more compatible than the paper implies, since the version of Steve's model with bank failures predicts not only a lower variance of output, but a lower mean as well. Further, the model economy with bank failures is (roughly speaking) less efficient than the one where failures are absent.

In the end, this paper raises many interesting questions. Perhaps the most compelling involve issues of financial market regulation. In Steve's model, laissez-faire is optimal; the government is no more efficient than private lenders in dealing with the agency problems. Similar results arise in other papers (though not exclusively). Most countries, however, regulate banking and financial markets. More generally, safeguarding the financial system is considered an important task of government policy. One possibility for this discrepancy between theory and practice is that policy makers have been misinformed. Another is that something important has been left out of the theoretical models. My own view is that the frontier of this theoretical research, well reflected in this paper, is providing useful qualitative insights into how the financial sector interacts with the macroeconomy. For the time being, though, any policy conclusions must be regarded as highly tentative.

REFERENCES

Bernanke, Ben. 1983. "Nonmonetary Effects of the Financial Crisis in the Propagation of the Great Depression." *American Economic Review* 79:14–31.
Friedman, Milton and Anna Schwartz. 1963. *A Monetary History of the United States, 1867–1960*. Princeton: Princeton University Press (for NBER).
Hall, Robert. 1989. "Comment on Gertler and Hubbard." In *Financial Market Volatility*. Federal Reserve Bank of Kansas City Symposium.
Townsend, Robert. 1979. "Optimal Contracts and Competitive Markets with Costly State Verification." *Journal of Economic Theory* 21:265–93.

Comment

LAWRENCE J. WHITE
Federal Home Loan Bank Board and New York University

1. Introduction

Stephen Williamson's paper investigates the consequences for macroeconomic fluctuations of two types of restrictions on financial intermediaries: geographic limitations and limitations on the issuance of specific types of liabilities. He constructs a two-period model to examine these effects and then tests the model with data for the U.S. and Canada covering 1870–1913 and 1954–87.

These comments will address both Williamson's theory and his empirical application.

2. Theory

Williamson's major theoretical results are that both types of restrictions tend to dampen macroeconomic fluctuations. The intuition underlying these results are as follows: Geographic limitations on depositories' activities mean that banks cannot diversify their loan portfolios over more regions and are therefore more likely to fail than are banks that are not so limited. Consequently, depositors and other creditors of banks find it worthwhile to engage in more monitoring of the former class of banks; this is especially true when banks' loans are of lower quality (i.e., when the funded projects have lower internal rates of return). This extra monitoring means extra frictions and costs for loans when interests rates are low, which causes the effective demand curve for loans facing the bank to become less elastic. Any exogenous shock that causes a shift in this less elastic demand curve will consequently have a lesser effect on the aggregate quantity of loans; hence, aggregate economic activity will tend to be more stable.

Further, limitations on the issuance of some types of liabilities mean that, *ceteris paribus*, some potential providers of funds to banks choose to hold their assets in currency instead. With a less elastic supply of funds to banks, shifts in the demand curve for loans again have a lesser effect on the aggregate quantity of loans.

I have no quarrel with the basic construction of the model. But I do question the likely quantitative importance of the effects that Williamson has isolated; other effects may well overshadow Williamson's phenomena. For example, with respect to geographic limitations, the greater likelihood of bank failure that is associated with greater limitations tends to be countercyclical. In addition, as a number of authors have noted,[1] these bank failures can have significant direct macroeconomic consequences that exacerbate macroeconomic instability. Thus, geographic limitations on intermediaries have consequences that can both exacerbate (the direct effect) and moderate (the Williamson effect) macroeconomic stability. Williamson does not offer a more general model that would encompass both effects and compare their likely importance. I strongly suspect that Williamson's effect is likely to be less important.

3. Empirical Tests

Williamson tests his model by comparing macroeconomic fluctuations in the U.S. and Canada during the years 1870–1913 and 1954–87. During 1870–1913, Canadian banks were more free to issue private bank notes and to establish branches throughout Canada; U.S. national banks were more restricted in their ability to issue bank notes (the notes had to be backed directly by U.S. government bonds) and were restricted to local areas within states. Williamson's model predicts that macroeconomic fluctuations should have been dampened more in the U.S. than in Canada, and he finds this to have been the case. During 1954–87, neither banking system could issue private bank notes, and deposit insurance in the U.S. smoothed the instabilities that localized banking might otherwise have created. Williamson's model predicts that macroeconomic fluctuations in the two countries should have been more similar in this later period than in the earlier period; again, he finds this to have been so.

Before commenting on these empirical findings, I believe it is worth noting the historical link between the U.S. bank note policy, which insisted that nationally chartered banks back their notes with U.S. bonds, and the tradition of local geographic restrictions. The period of the 1840s

1. See for example, Friedman and Schwartz (1963) and Bernanke (1983).

and 1850s were a period of "wildcat banking" in the U.S. Many states freely issued charters to banks, but restricted them to local geographic areas. These state-chartered banks freely issued bank notes that were backed by the banks' normal portfolios of loans and investments. Some of these banks failed, at least partially because they were restricted geographically, causing losses for the holders of their notes.[2] As a consequence, the National Currency Act of 1863 and the National Bank Act of 1864 established a system of nationally chartered banks (and established the federal Office of the Comptroller of the Currency to charter and regulate them). To ensure a more stable currency, these national banks were allowed only to issue notes that were backed by U.S. government bonds. (At the same time, a 10 percent tax was levied on the notes issued by state chartered banks, in an effort to tax them out of existence. This effort almost succeeded, but the state banks developed checking accounts as an alternative form of liability and thereby managed to survive and prosper.)

An interesting historical footnote to this episode should be added: One hundred twenty-five years later we have come full circle. In the wake of concerns about the current problems with federal deposit insurance, some current observers[3] have suggested that "narrow banks" are the only type of depository that should be backed by federal deposit insurance. What is a "narrow bank"? A bank that has its liabilities backed solely by short-term U.S. debt!

Let me now return to Williamson's empirical results. First, I question whether the differences in the U.S. and Canadian bank note restrictions in the 1870–1913 period are adequately represented in Williamson's model. The U.S. national banks were not forbidden from issuing notes, as is represented in Wiliamson's model; however, they did have to back them with U.S. bonds. How much of a difference did this make? I am not entirely sure. Williamson does not address the point. Also, as was mentioned above, state-chartered banks continued in existence and could offer yet a different kind of liability, checking accounts. The presence of these state-chartered banks—by 1890 they constituted over half of the total number of banks in the U.S. and also more than half of the total assets of banks in the U.S.—surely influenced macroeconomic stability or instability in the U.S. Also, as early as 1870, the value of the deposits in just the national banks alone was more than twice the value of their bank notes, and by 1896 the ratio was more than ten to one. However, Williamson proceeds as if the national banks were the only

2. A discussion of these losses is found in Rolnick and Weber (1983).
3. See, for example, Litan (1987). For a discussion of Litan's proposal, see White (1988).

depositories and their bank notes were the only form of bank liability that could affect macroeconomic stability in the U.S.

Second, and more important, there are other, more plausible explanations for Williamson's empirical results. During the 1870–1913 period the Canadian economy was more oriented toward natural resource production than was true of the U.S. economy, and the two economies were less linked then than they were in the later period. This greater emphasis on natural resources is surely the major reason for the greater macroeconomic fluctuations in the Canadian economy during the earlier period.

Further, during the 1954–87 period the two economies were more similar in structure and were more closely linked: lower import tariffs, a free trade pact in automotive production that started in 1965, and easier transborder capital flows. These phenomena are the most likely reasons for the greater similarity in macroeconomic fluctuations during this period.

If my explanations are correct, then data on *cross-country* correlations of GNP and prices should show a higher correlation in the latter period than in the earlier period. Unfortunately, the results of this test are mixed. Tables 5 and 8 of Williamson's paper show different results with respect to cross-country correlations of GNP, depending on which of two series on U.S. GNP is used. The same two tables do, however, show a much higher cross-country correlation of prices[4] in the second period than in the first period, which is consistent with my explanation.

4. Conclusion

In sum, though Williamson's model is clearly of theoretical interest, its results are likely to involve second-order effects with respect to real-world macroeconomic stability. His empirical findings, though consistent with his model's predictions, are, I believe, better explained by first-order features of the U.S. and Canadian economies. Future research in this vein, then, would require a more complete model and a more sophisticated set of empirical tests that would better allow Williamson to sort out his theoretical effects from the first-order phenomena that are clearly also present.

REFERENCES

Bernanke, B. S. 1983. "Nonmonetary Effects of the Financial Crisis in the Propagation of the Great Depression." *American Economic Review* 73:257–76.
Friedman, M. and A. J. Schwartz. 1963. *A Monetary History of the United States, 1867–1960.* Princeton: Princeton University Press.

4. Technically, these are the correlations of deviations from trend of the GNP deflators of the two countries.

Litan, R. E. 1987. *What Should Banks Do?* Washington, D.C.: The Brookings Institution.

Rolnick, A. J. and W. E. Weber. 1983. "New Evidence on the Free Banking Era. *American Economic Review* 73:1080–91.

White, L. J. 1988. "What Should Banks Do? A Review Essay." *Rand Journal of Economics* 19:305–15.

Discussion

Michael Bordo said that Canada is a more resource-based economy than the U.S., and also that demand in Canada is sensitive to that in the U.S., making Canadian output more volatile than U.S. output. He further noted that branch closings may have effects, such as loss of customer relations, even if deposits are not lost. David Romer questioned the magnitude of the effects captured by the model, in particular how big the difference in the elasticity of demand would have to be between the U.S. and Canada.

Julio Rotemberg asked whether banks saved each other because there were monopoly rents. Williamson responded that banks might save each other to prevent more regulation. White added that an increase in rents would create more implicit capital and make firms less likely to engage in risky behavior.

Allan Drazen asked how bank runs would be interpreted in this model. Williamson stated that this is not really a model of runs but should be interpreted only as a model of bank failures.

Ben Bernanke noted that in this model the real economy causes failures, but failures do not feed back to the real economy. In higher frequency data, he argued, the latter feedback can be identified. Jeff Miron noted that the Canadian bank cooperation suggests implicit deposit insurance. Williamson responded that this is consistent with his results and acts as if Canada had one large intermediary.

James H. Stock

KENNEDY SCHOOL OF GOVERNMENT
HARVARD UNIVERSITY
CAMBRIDGE, MASSACHUSETTS

Mark W. Watson

DEPARTMENT OF ECONOMICS
NORTHWESTERN UNIVERSITY
EVANSTON, ILLINOIS

New Indexes of Coincident and Leading Economic Indicators

1. Introduction

During six weeks in late 1937, Wesley Mitchell, Arthur Burns, and their colleagues at the National Bureau of Economic Research developed a list of leading, coincident, and lagging indicators of economic activity in the United States as part of the NBER research program on business cycles. Since their development, these indicators, in particular the leading and coincident indexes constructed from these indicators, have played an important role in summarizing and forecasting the state of macro-economic activity.

This paper reports the results of a project to revise the indexes of leading and coincident economic indicators using the tools of modern time series econometrics. This project addresses three central questions. The first is conceptual: is it possible to develop a formal probability model that gives rise to the indexes of leading and coincident variables? Such a model would provide a concrete mathematical framework within which alternative variables and indexes could be evaluated. Second, given this conceptual framework, what are the best variables to use as components of the leading index? Third, given these variables, what is the best way to combine them to produce useful and reliable indexes?

The results of this project are three experimental monthly indexes: an index of coincident economic indicators (CEI), an index of leading economic indicators (LEI), and a Recession Index. The experimental CEI closely tracks the coincident index currently produced by the Department of Commerce (DOC), although the methodology used to produce the two series differs substantially. The growth of the experimental CEI is also highly correlated with the growth of real GNP at business cycle frequencies. The proposed LEI is a forecast of the growth of the proposed CEI over the next six months constructed using a set of leading variables or indicators. The Recession Index, a new series, is the probability that the economy will be in a recession six months hence, given data available through the month of its construction.

This article is organized as follows. Section 2 contains a discussion of the indexes and a framework for their interpretation. Section 3 presents the experimental indexes, discusses their construction, and examines their within-sample performance. In Section 4, the indexes are considered from the perspective of macroeconomic theory, focusing in particular on several salient series that are not included in the proposed leading index. Section 5 concludes.

2. Making Sense of the Coincident and Leading Indexes

2.1 THE COINCIDENT INDEX

The coincident and leading economic indexes have been widely followed in business and government for decades, yet have received surprisingly little attention from academic economists.[1] We suggest that one important reason for this neglect is that it is unclear what the existing CEI and LEI measure. That is, with what are the coincident indicators coincident? What do the leading indicators lead? Burns and Mitchell's (1938, 1946) answer was that the coincident indicators are coincident with the "reference cycle," that is, with the broad-based swings in economic activity known as the business cycle. This definition has intuitive appeal but, as Burns and Mitchell (1946, p. 76) recognized, lacks precise mathematical content. It is therefore unclear what conclusions one should draw from swings in the index.

To clarify the issues concerning the reference cycle, it is useful to consider how one might construct a monthly coincident index were real GNP data available accurately on a monthly basis. Would it be appropriate simply to let swings in GNP *define* the reference cycle? The "business

1. Exceptions include Auerbach (1982), Diebold and Rudebusch (1987), Hymans (1973), Kling (1987), Koch and Raasche (1988), the papers in Moore (1983), Neftci (1982), Stekler and Schepsman (1973), Vaccara and Zarnowitz (1978), Wecker (1979), Zarnowitz and Moore (1982), and Zellner, Hong, and Gulati (1987). One of Koopmans' (1947) criticisms of Burns and Mitchell (1946) is their lack of a formal statistical framework in which to interpret their results.

cycle" commonly refers to co-movements in different forms of economic activity, not just fluctuations in GNP; see Lucas (1977) for a discussion of this point. This suggests taking as primitive Burns and Mitchell's (1946, p. 3) definition that a business cycle "consists of expansions occurring at about the same time in many economic activities, followed by similarly general recessions, contractions, and revivals. . . ." If so, it would be incorrect to define a recession solely in terms of monthly GNP. For example, suppose that a drought dramatically reduces agricultural output but that output in other sectors remains stable, so that aggregate unemployment remains steady. This scenario does not fit Burns and Mitchell's definition of a recession even if the decline in GNP is sustained. Rather, the reference cycle reflects co-movements in a broad range of macroeconomic aggregates such as output, employment, and sales.

The model adopted in this research formalizes the idea that the reference cycle is best measured by looking at co-movements across several aggregate time series. The experimental CEI is an estimate of the value of a single unobserved variable, "the state of the economy," denoted by C_t. This unobserved variable is defined by assuming that the co-movements of observed coincident time series at all leads and lags arise solely from movements in C_t. Of course, any particular coincident series, such as industrial production, might move in ways that are not associated with this unobserved variable. Thus each roughly coincident series is thought of as having a component attributable to the single unobserved variable, plus a unique (or "idiosyncratic") component. Each idiosyncratic component is assumed to be uncorrelated with the other idiosyncratic components and with the unobserved common "state of the economy" at all leads and lags.

Technically, this amounts to specifying an "unobserved single index" or "dynamic factor" model for the coincident variables of the type considered by, for example, Geweke (1977), Sargent and Sims (1977), and Engle and Watson (1981). The major features of the model and estimation procedure are summarized here, and the details are given in Stock and Watson (1988a). Let X_t denote an $n \times 1$ vector of the logarithms of macroeconomic variables that are hypothesized to move contemporaneously with overall economic conditions. In the single-index model, X_t consists of two stochastic components: the common unobserved scalar variable, or "index," C_t, and an n-dimensional component, u_t, that represents idiosyncratic movements in the series and measurement error. Both the unobserved index and the idiosyncratic component are modeled as having linear stochastic structures. Looking ahead to the empirical results, the coincident variables used in the analysis appear to be integrated but not cointegrated, so that model is specified in terms of ΔX_t and ΔC_t.[2] This suggests the formulation:

$$\Delta X_t = \beta + \gamma(L)\Delta C_t + u_t \quad (1)$$

$$D(L)u_t = \epsilon_t \quad (2)$$

$$\phi(L)\Delta C_t = \delta + \eta_t, \quad (3)$$

where L denotes the lag operator, and $\phi(L)$, $\gamma(L)$ and $D(L)$ are respectively scalar, vector, and matrix lag polynomials.

The main identifying assumption expresses the core notion of the dynamic factor model that the co-movements of the multiple time series arise from the single source ΔC_t. This is made precise by assuming that $(u_{1t}, \ldots, u_{nt}, \Delta C_t)$ are mutually uncorrelated at all leads and lags, which is achieved by making $D(L)$ diagonal and the $n + 1$ disturbances $(\epsilon_{1t}, \ldots, \epsilon_{nt}, \eta_t)$ mutually and serially uncorrelated. In addition, ΔC_t is assumed to enter at least one of the variables in (1) only contemporaneously. The system is estimated by maximum likelihood using the Kalman filter. The proposed CEI is computed as the minimum mean square error linear estimate of this single common factor, $C_{t|t}$, produced by applying the Kalman filter to the estimated system. Thus $C_{t|t}$ is a linear combination of current and past logarithms of the coincident variables.

It is tempting to interpret the single index specification as implying that there is a single causal source of common variation (or shock) among the real variables X_t (theoretical models can be developed in which this is the case; see Altug (1984) or Sargent and Sims (1977) for discussions). But one ought not read too much into the factor formulation. With three serially uncorrelated variables (the time series analog of a factor model of cross-sectional variables), the model lacks empirical content: Its parameters are exactly identified, so the various shocks that comprise the errors can always be recast in a single index form, and the factor merely summarizes the covariance among the three series. When there are more than three observable series or when the variables are serially correlated, the dynamic factor model is overidentified. Imposing $\gamma(L) = \gamma_0$ (as is done below for all but one of the coincident variables) further restricts the impulse

2. As an empirical matter, many macroeconomic time series are well characterized as containing stochastic trends; see, for example, Nelson and Plosser (1982). Were these stochastic trends to enter only through C_t, then X_t would contain a single common stochastic trend. Thus X_t would be cointegrated of order $n-1$ as defined by Engle and Granger (1987). For the coincident series considered here, however, this appears not to be the case: the hypothesis that the coincident series individually contain a stochastic trend cannot be rejected, but neither can the hypothesis that there is no cointegration among these variables.

response from η_t to ΔX_t to be proportional across the observable series. One interpretation of these restrictions is that there are multiple sources of economic fluctuations, but that they have proportional dynamic effects on the real variables. That is, the combination of shocks that induce business cycles might vary from one cycle to the next, but to a statistically good approximation, the relative movements of the components of ΔX_t in response to these shocks is the same.[3]

2.2 THE LEADING INDEX

Given this definition of the CEI, the next question is how to construct a leading index. The proposed LEI is the estimate of the growth of this unobserved factor over the next six months, computed using a set of leading variables; in the notation of (1)–(3), this is $C_{t+6|t} - C_{t|t}$. This represents a conceptual break with the existing DOC leading index. The objective of the historical NBER approach was to produce a series in *levels*, with turning points that preceded the reference cycle by several months. Thus the original NBER and the current DOC leading indexes can be thought of as forecasts of the level of the CEI several months hence. To the extent that one is interested in the relative growth rather than the absolute level of economic activity, however, it is more useful to forecast the growth of C_t. Forecasts of growth and future levels are, of course, closely linked: because the LEI is $C_{t+6|t} - C_{t|t}$, and the CEI is $C_{t|t}$, the sum of the CI and the LEI is $C_{t+6|t}$, which is a forecast of the (log) level of the CEI six months hence.

The LEI is constructed by modeling the leading variables (Y_t) and the unobserved state of the economy (C_t) as a vector autoregressive system with two modifications. First, the formulation recognizes C_t is unobserved. Second, the number of parameters to be estimated has been reduced by eliminating higher lags of the variables in all equations of the system except the equation for the coincident variable. The specific model estimated is the reduced form simultaneous equation system,

$$\Delta C_t = \mu_c + \lambda_{CC}(L)\Delta C_{t-1} + \lambda_{CY}(L)Y_{t-1} + \nu_{Ct} \quad (4)$$

$$Y_t = \mu_Y + \lambda_{YC}(L)\Delta C_{t-1} + \lambda_{YY}(L)Y_{t-1} + \nu_{Yt}, \quad (5)$$

where (ν_{Ct}, ν_{Yt}) are serially uncorrelated error terms. The orders of the lag polynomials $\lambda_{CC}(L)$, $\lambda_{CY}(L)$, $\lambda_{YC}(L)$, and $\lambda_{YY}(L)$ were determined empirically using statistical criteria; the details are discussed in the next section. The leading variables Y_t were transformed as necessary to appear stationary.

3. More than one factor is typically used to fit models containing both real and nominal variables. For example, Singleton (1980) finds that two factors are necessary in a system containing yields on three-month, six-month, one-year, and five-year government securities, the unemployment rate, and manufacturers' shipments.

The parameters of the coincident and leading models are estimated in two steps. In the first step, the parameters of the coincident model (1)–(3) are estimated by maximum likelihood, where the Kalman filter is used to evaluate the likelihood function. In the second step, the leading model is estimated conditional on the estimated parameters of the coincident model. Technically, (1), (2), (4), and (5) are combined to form a state space model, with ΔC_t and its lags being unobserved elements of the state vector. The parameters of (4) and (5) are then estimated by maximum likelihood (using the EM algorithm), conditional on the estimates of the parameters of (1) and (2). A desirable consequence of this two-step procedure is that the coincident index ($C_{t|t}$), constructed as a weighted average of ΔX_t using (1)–(3), is consistent with the implicit definition of C_t in the full model (1), (2), (4), and (5). The main benefit of this approach is that it prevents potential misspecification in (4) and (5) from inducing inconsistency in the parameters of (1) and (2). The cost of this benefit is potential inefficiency: if the full system is correctly specified, the two-step procedure will produce consistent but inefficient estimators relative to the M.L.E. for the complete system (1), (2), (4), and (5). Thus the simplest way to think of the leading model is as a projection of $\Delta C_{t|t}$ onto leading variables in vector autoregressive (VAR) framework, except that the lack of observability of $\Delta C_{t|t}$ is handled explicitly. Finally, the LEI is computed as $C_{t+6|t} - C_{t|t}$ from the estimated model (1), (2), (4), and (5). Movements in the LEI arising from X_t are negligibly small and will be ignored to simplify the discussion below.

2.3 PREDICTIONS OF RECESSIONS AND EXPANSIONS

A traditional role of the LEI has been to signal future recessions and recoveries; indeed, it was to provide such signals that Mitchell and Burns (1938) developed their original list of indicators.[4] The value of identifying and forecasting cyclical turning points has been a matter of controversy among academic economists. One interpretation of this controversy is that the concepts of expansion and recession are incorrectly perceived to embody a view of the dynamic evolution of the economy that is at odds with the probabilistic foundations of formal macroeconomic models.

In forecasting turning points, recessions and expansions are treated as conceptually distinct objects, perhaps associated with fundamentally different behavior of the economy. In contrast, the structure of standard macroeconomic models does not change from an expansion to a contraction: in terms of the underlying theory of behavior, a month that falls in a

---

4. Moore (1979) recounts how the list was developed at the request of Treasury Secretary Morgenthau and evaluates the out-of-sample performance of the original series.

recession does not differ fundamentally from a month that falls in an expansion. To simplify the argument only slightly, traditional business cycle analysis is associated with treating recessions and expansions as periods of distinctly different economic behavior, defined by intrinsic shifts (essential nonlinearities) in the macroeconomic process by which the data are generated. The alternative view is that expansions and recessions have no intrinsic content, in the sense that they are not associated with fundamental shifts in the behavior of the economy, but rather are the results of a stable structure adapting to random shocks. According to this latter view, recessions and expansions are extrinsic patterns, not intrinsic macroeconomic shifts.[5]

The model described in the previous subsection is consistent with the "extrinsic" view: recessions and expansions are generated by certain configurations of random shocks to a linear time series model. Yet this does not invalidate the concept or the importance of forecasting business cycles. Recessions are important political, social, and economic events. Periods of prolonged, widespread expansion provide opportunities to workers and bounty to consumers; the most severe periods of contraction threaten governments and even forms of government. Thus the question becomes: is it possible to forecast those politically and socially important events that will come to be termed expansions and contractions? Can these patterns be recognized in advance?

The Recession Index is an estimate of the probability that the economy will be in a recession six months hence. This probability is computed using the same time series model used to calculate the proposed LEI, and is based on a definition (in terms of the sample path of ΔC_t) of what constitutes a recession and an expansion. Unfortunately, it is difficult to quantify precisely those patterns that will be recognized as expansions or contractions. Burns and Mitchell (1946, p. 3) considered the minimum period for a full business (reference) cycle to be one year; in practice, the shortest expansions and contractions they identified were six months. The Recession Index is computed by approximating a recessionary (expansionary) period in terms of negative (positive) growth of the CEI that lasts at least six months.[6]

5. Slutzky (1937) and Adelman and Adelman (1959) can be interpreted as arguing for the "extrinsic" view; Neftci (1982) and Hamilton (1987) develop techniques consistent with the "intrinsic" view. This debate is related to the distinction between exogenous shocks and endogenous instability being the source of aggregate fluctuations. The extrinsic/intrinsic terminology focuses on the identification and interpretation of recessions and expansions.

6. More precisely, a recession and an expansion are determined by partitioning future ΔC_t into three regions, or patterns. We define a month to be in a recessionary pattern if that month is either in a sequence of six consecutive declines of C_t below some boundary b_{rt}, or

3. The Revised Indexes

The proposed CEI is plotted in Figure 1, the proposed LEI is plotted in Figure 2, and the proposed Recession Index is plotted in Figure 3. The vertical lines in these and subsequent figures represent the official *ex post* NBER-dated cyclical turning points.

3.1 THE INDEX OF COINCIDENT ECONOMIC INDICATORS

Data and Empirical Results.   The variables entering the proposed CEI and LEI, as well as the variables entering the current DOC coincident and leading indexes, are listed in Table 1. The proposed CEI is based on four series: industrial production, real personal income less transfer payments, real manufacturing and trade sales, and employee-hours in nonagricultural establishments. These are the series currently used by the DOC to construct its coincident index, except that the total number of employees (rather than employee-hours) is used in the Commerce series.[7] The data were obtained from the January 31, 1989 release of CITIBASE. Empirical results are computed using data starting in 1959:1.

The empirical results for the single-index model, specified with employment rather than employee-hours, are discussed in detail in Stock and Watson (1988b); the results for the model estimated with employee-hours are summarized here. Preliminary data analysis suggested modeling the logarithms of these four series as being individually integrated but not cointegrated. Dickey-Fuller (1979) tests were unable to reject the null hypothesis that each of the series are individually integrated. The Stock-Watson (1988a) q_f^τ test of the null hypothesis that the four series are not cointegrated against the alternative that there is at least one cointegrating vector (computed using four lags of the series and a linear time trend) yielded a statistic of -25.25, with a p-value of 60%. Similar evi-

---

is in a sequence of nine declines below the boundary with no more than one increase during the middle seven months. Thus a recessionary pattern is the union of 15 sets contained in $\mathcal{R}^{17}$. An expansionary pattern is defined analogously, with "increases" replacing "declines" and b_{et} replacing b_{rt}. This does not exhaust all possible patterns, and the remaining patterns are said to be indeterminate. Reasonable people might disagree on these boundaries: these regions might constitute fuzzy sets. This "fuzziness" is quantified by making b_{rt} and b_{et} normally distributed random variables. After ruling out the possibility that a given month falls in neither region, the NBER Recession Index is computed as the probability (given currently available data) that, six months hence, the time path of C_t will fall in a recession region. This entails integrating a 17-dimensional normal density conditional on (b_{rt}, b_{et}), which in turn have independent normal distributions.

7. We follow Moore's (1988) recommendation and use employee-hours rather than the number of employees in constructing the CEI. Because of overtime and part-time work, employee-hours measures more directly fluctuations in labor input than does the number of employees.

dence of non-cointegration was obtained from pairwise residual-based tests for cointegration as proposed by Engle and Granger (1987). The subsequent analysis therefore uses first differences of the logarithms of these series (ΔX_t).

Geweke (1977) and Sargent and Sims (1977) point out that the single index model (1)–(3) imposes testable restrictions on the spectral density matrix of the vector time series. Because ΔC_t and u_t are by assumption uncorrelated at all leads and lags, (1) implies that $S_{\Delta X}(\omega) = \gamma(e^{-i\omega})S_{\Delta C}(\omega)\gamma(e^{i\omega})$, $+ S_u(\omega)$, where $S_{\Delta X}(\omega)$ denotes the spectral density matrix of ΔX_t at frequency ω, etc. Because $S_{\Delta C}(\omega)$ is a scalar and $S_u(\omega)$ is diagonal, this provides testable restrictions on $S_{\Delta X}(\omega)$. Performing this test for the coincident indicator model over six equally-spaced bands constructed using ΔX_t (the unconstrained estimate of the spectrum is the averaged matrix periodogram) provides little evidence against the restrictions imposed by the dynamic single-index structure: the x^2_{30} test statistic is 19.8, having a p-value of 92%.

Figure 1 THE PROPOSED INDEX OF COINCIDENT ECONOMIC INDICATORS

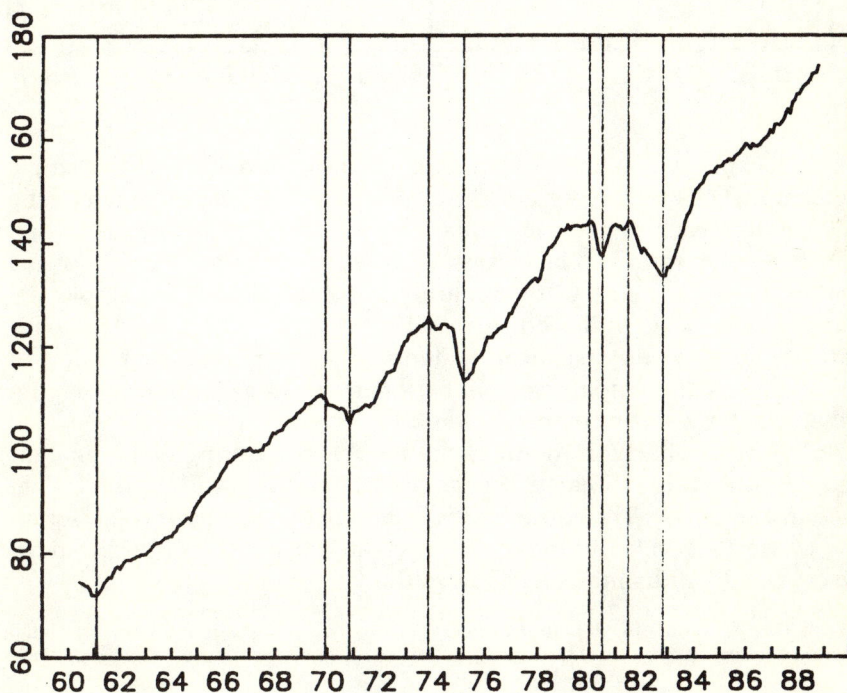

Figure 2 THE PROPOSED INDEX OF LEADING ECONOMIC INDICATORS

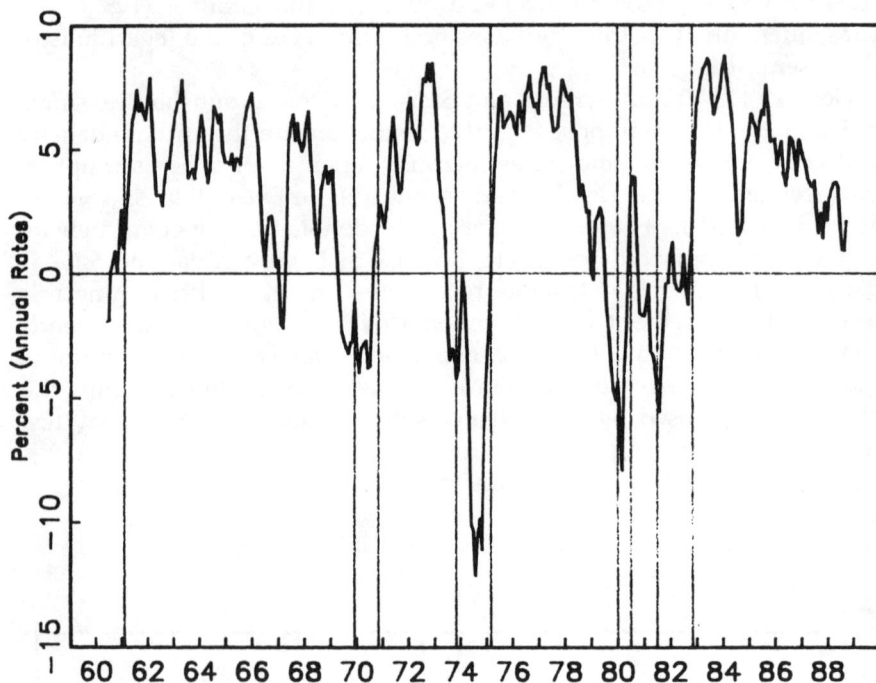

The maximum likelihood estimates of the parameters of the single index model (1)–(3) are presented in Table 2. A specification in which the factor enters each of the four equations only contemporaneously (i.e., $\gamma(L) = \gamma_0$) was found to be inconsistent with the data.[8] This is not the case, however, when lags of ΔC_t are permitted to enter the employee-hours equation: as indicated in panel B of Table 2, various diagnostic statistics provide no statistical evidence of (linear) misspecification of this model. Thus employment is better modeled as a slightly lagging rather than an exactly coincident variable.

As a further check on the fit of the model, several highly parameterized versions were estimated; the results for one specification are summarized in Table 2(D). The additional parameters are not statistically significant at the 5% level, and the $C_{t|t}$ series created using these specifications are essentially indistinguishable from the CEI reported above.

8. With $\gamma(L) = \gamma_0$, the one-step ahead forecast errors for employee-hours were correlated with past observations on ΔX_t.

Figure 3 THE PROPOSED RECESSION INDEX

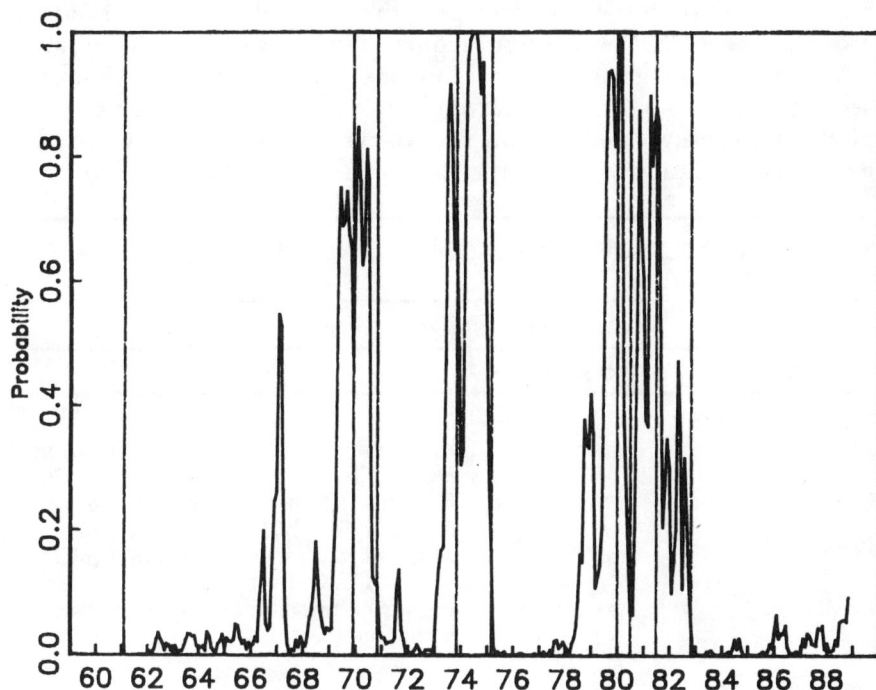

The proposed CEI, the DOC coincident index, and real GNP growth. The proposed CEI is graphed in Figure 1. The figure portrays $C_{t|t}$ computed using the empirical model in Table 2, then exponentiated and scaled to equal 100 in July 1967. Visual inspection indicates that the cyclical peaks and troughs of the CEI coincide with the official NBER-dated turning points, with the exception of 1969, when the peak in the proposed series occurs two months prior to the official NBER turning point.

The proposed CEI is quantitatively similar to the existing DOC coincident index; both are graphed in Figure 4(a). The main differences are the slightly greater trend growth and cyclical volatility of the DOC series. The correlation between the growth rates of the proposed and DOC series is .95, and the average coherence for periods exceeding eight months is .97.[9]

9. This high coherence at low frequencies suggests that the population joint spectral density matrix of the proposed CEI and the DOC index might be singular at frequency zero, i.e., the two series might be cointegrated; but the series are constructed using different implicit weights on ΔX_t, and there is no statistical evidence against non-cointegration.

The growth in the experimental CEI closely tracks the growth in GNP. Figure 4(b) presents the six-month growth of the CEI ($C_{t+6|t+6} - C_{t|t}$) and the growth of real GNP over the subsequent two quarters, at annual rates. (The plotted GNP growth rate for January is the growth in GNP for the second and third quarters, relative to the first quarter; this same rate is plotted for February and March.) The six-month growth in the CEI exhibits greater cyclical swings, particularly in 1974, but the two series are

Table 1   VARIABLES CURRENTLY COMPRISING THE NBER AND DOC CEI AND LEI

A. Current NBER Base Variable List

Mnemonic	Transformation	Description
Coincident Variables		
IP	growth rates	Industrial production, total (BCD 47; in DOC CEI)
GMYXP8	growth rates	Personal Income, total less transfer payments, 1982$ (BCD 51; in DOC CEI)
MT82	growth rates	Mfg and trade sales, total, 1982$ (BCD 57; in DOC CEI)
LPMHU	growth rates	Employee-hours in non-agricultural establishments
Leading Variables		
HSBP	levels	New private housing authorized, index (Building Permits)
MDU82S	growth rates	Manufacturers' unfilled orders: durable goods industries, 1982$, smoothed
EXNWT2S	growth rates	Trade-weighted nominal exchange rate between the U.S. and the U.K., West Germany, France, Italy, and Japan, smoothed.
LHNAPSS	growth rates	Part-time work in non-agricultural industries because of slack work (U.S. Department of Labor, The Employment Situation, Household Survey), smoothed
FYGT10S	differences	Yield on constant-maturity portfolio of 10-yr U.S. Treasury bonds, smoothed
CP6 _ GM6	levels	Spread between interest rate on 6-mo. corporate paper and the interest rate on 6 mo. U.S. Treasury bills (Federal Reserve Board)
G10 _ G1	levels	Spread between the yield on constant-maturity portfolio of 10-yr U.S. T-bonds and the yield on 1-yr U.S. T-bonds. (Federal Reserve Board)

highly correlated (r = .86) and have a coherence in excess of .9 for periods over two years.

3.2. THE INDEX OF LEADING ECONOMIC INDICATORS

Variable Selection and Model Specification.   The experimental LEI is a forecast of the six-month growth (on an annual percentage basis) of the CEI. In a break with tradition, the proposed LEI uses the most recently available data, rather than using only data for the month for which the coincident series are available. For example, the LEI released at the end of October is constructed using unfilled orders data for September, but interest rate and exchange rate data for October. This results in a more timely measure of future economic activity.

The development of the empirical LEI model required making three important sets of judgments: the choice of variables to include in the leading index, whether to transform or smooth some variables, and the number of lags of these variables to use in the ΔC_t equation.

Table 1   VARIABLES CURRENTLY COMPRISING THE NBER AND DOC CEI
AND LEI (CONTINUED)

B. DOC Variable List (December 1988)

CEI
Industrial Production (BCD 47)
Personal income less transfer payments, 1982$s (BCD 51)
Index of Manufacturing and trade sales in 1982 dollars (BCD 57)
Employees on nonagricultural payrolls (BCD 41)

LEI
Average weekly hours of production or non-supervisory workers, mfg (BCD 1)
Avg weekly initial claims for State unempl. insurance (BCD 3)
Mrf's new orders, 1982$s, consumer goods and mat'ls industries (BCD 8)
S&P 500 (BCD 19)
Contracts and orders for plant and eqpt, 1982$s (BCD 20)
New private housing authorized index (Building Permits) (BCD 29)
Vendor Performance, percent of companies receiving slower deliveries (BCD 32)
Change in sensitive mat'ls prices, smoothed (BCD 99)
Money supply M2, 1982$s (BCD 106)
Change in business and consumer credit outstanding (BCD 111)
Change in mfging and trade inventories on hand and on order, 1982$s (BCD 36)

Note: The DOC leading index was revised beginning with the January 1989 data. The final two series in the index (BCD 111 and BCD 36) were dropped from the composite index, and two series were added: the change in manufacturers' unfilled orders in 1982 dollars, durable goods industries, smoothed; and an index of consumer expectations. No revisions were made to the DOC coincident index.

TABLE 2   MAXIMUM LIKELIHOOD ESTIMATES OF THE FACTOR
MODEL (1)-(3) USING THE COINCIDENT INDICATORS

A. Measurement Equations:

$$\Delta IP_t = .708 \; \Delta C_t + u_t^{ip}$$
$$(.044)$$

$$\Delta GMYXP8_t = .500 \; \Delta C_t + u_t^{gmyxp8}$$
$$(.045)$$

$$\Delta MT82_t = .452 \; \Delta C_t + u_t^{mt82}$$
$$(.033)$$

$$\Delta LPMHU_t = .527 \; \Delta C_t - .031 \; \Delta C_{t-1} - .142\Delta C_{t-2} + .235\Delta C_{t-3} + u_t^{lpmhu}$$
$$(.058) \qquad\quad (.078) \qquad\qquad (.080) \qquad\qquad (.054)$$

B. Transition Equations:

$$\Delta C_t = .616 \; \Delta C_{t-1} - .037 \; \Delta C_{t-2} + v_t; \; \sigma_v = 1.0 \text{ (Normalized)}$$
$$(.076) \qquad\qquad (.074)$$

$$u_t^{ip} = -.079 \; u_{t-2}^{ip} + \epsilon_t^{IP}; \; \sigma_{\epsilon_{ip}} = .470$$
$$(.103) \qquad\qquad\qquad (.041)$$

$$u_t^{gmyxp8} = -.068 \; u_{t-1}^{gmyxp8} + .143 \; u_{t-2}^{gmyxp8} + \epsilon_t^{gmyxp8} \sigma_{\epsilon_{gmyxp8}} = .776$$
$$(.042) \qquad\qquad (.048) \qquad\qquad\qquad\qquad (.027)$$

$$u_t^{mt82} = -.436 \; u_{t-1}^{mt82} - .246 \; u_{t-2}^{mt82} + \epsilon_t^{mt82}; \; \sigma_{\epsilon_{mt82}} = .744$$
$$(.053) \qquad\qquad (.057) \qquad\qquad\qquad\qquad (.033)$$

$$u_t^{lpmhu} = -.487 \; u_{t-1}^{lpmhu} - .128 \; u_{t-2}^{lpmhu} + \epsilon_t^{lpmhu}; \sigma_{\epsilon_{lpmhu}} = .662$$
$$(.050) \qquad\qquad (.064) \qquad\qquad\qquad\qquad (.027)$$

C. Marginal Significance Levels of Diagnostic Tests for Single-Index Model

p-values of whether the dep. variable is predictable by lags of:

Dep. Vble.	e_{IP}	e_{GMYXP8}	e_{MT82}	e_{LPMHU}	IP	GMYXP8	MT82	LPMHU
e_{IP}	0.905	0.804	0.296	0.910	0.892	0.796	0.383	0.962
e_{GMYXP8}	0.860	0.994	0.927	0.137	0.671	0.893	0.820	0.060
e_{MT82}	0.256	0.852	0.800	0.590	0.392	0.969	0.798	0.820
e_{LPMHU}	0.875	0.825	0.137	0.716	0.774	0.625	0.162	0.592

D. Comparison with a highly parameterized single index model (Model A)
Orders of lag polynomials: $\Delta(L)$, 5; $\gamma_{LPMHU}(L)$, 6; $\phi(L)$, 8
Likelihood ratio statistic (χ_{21}^2): 27.57, p-value = .153
$Corr(\Delta C_{t|t}^{base}, \Delta C_{t|t}^{model\,A}) = .995$.

Notes: Panel A and B: The parameters were estimated using data from 1959:1–1987:12. Logarithms of variables were used, each series was standardized to growth rates with mean zero and unit variance prior to estimation. The sample means and standard deviations of the growth rates of the original series are: ΔIP: 0.0031, 0.0100; $\Delta GMYXP8$: 0.0027, 0.0047; $\Delta MT82$: 0.0028, 0.0110; $\Delta LPMHU$: 0.0017, 0.0049. *Panel C:* The entries are p-values from the regression of e_y against a constant and six lags of the indicated regressor; the p-values correspond to the usual F-test of the hypothesis that the coefficients on these six lags are zero (with only the usual corrections for degrees of freedom). The series e_y denotes the one-step ahead forecast errors from the single-index model, and growth rates of the original data are used.

The leading variables were chosen from an initial list of approximately 280 series (Mitchell and Burns (1938) started with 487 series). This list included series from ten groups: measures of output and capacity utilization; consumption and sales; inventories and orders; money and credit quantity variables; interest rates and asset prices; exchange rates and foreign trade; employment, earnings, and measures of the labor force; wages and prices; measures of government fiscal activity; and other variables, primarily prominent leading indicators from the *Business Conditions Digest*. An important consideration in developing this list was to include series that have expectational components, that would (under some economic theory) respond rapidly to some shocks to the economy, or that would reflect policy actions. These variables were then screened by examining their bivariate relation to the growth of the DOC coincident index using the coherence and phase lead between each series and the growth of the DOC series, the ability of each series to Granger-cause the DOC series, and the marginal predictive content of each series for the growth of the DOC coincident index beyond that of the current DOC leading index. Several series that performed poorly according to these criteria were nevertheless retained because economic theory suggested that they should have some predictive content, or because they are currently included in the DOC leading index. This procedure resulted in a reduced list of approximately 55 time series. Of these 55 series, many measured closely related concepts.

A critical question is how to construct the LEI from this base list of 55 variables. The approach used here is similar to the traditional NBER approach in the sense that it results in a relatively short list of series, of which the LEI is a weighted average; a key methodological difference between the two approaches is our emphasis on multivariate rather than bivariate predictive content. Selecting the few "best" variables from this list is a daunting task: in theory over 200 million seven-variable indexes could be formed from these 55 series. We simplified this problem by adopting a modified stepwise regression procedure for constructing an LEI based on a relatively few series.[10]

Because the signal extraction error in the proposed CEI from the one-

10. Another strategy rejected at an early stage of this project would be to construct a broad-based index that included many or all of these 55 series. Strong restrictions on how these series entered would need to be imposed. Because the formulation and implementation of these restrictions would require considerable research judgment, one would need to be particularly cautious about out-of-sample performance. In addition, this approach would be less informative about which variables have important predictive content and would result in an index which is more difficult to interpret. Still, this would constitute an interesting and complementary research project.

Figure 4 A. THE PROPOSED INDEX OF COINCIDENT INDICATORS (SOLID
LINE) AND THE CURRENT DOC INDEX OF COINCIDENT
ECONOMIC INDICATORS (DASHED LINE)

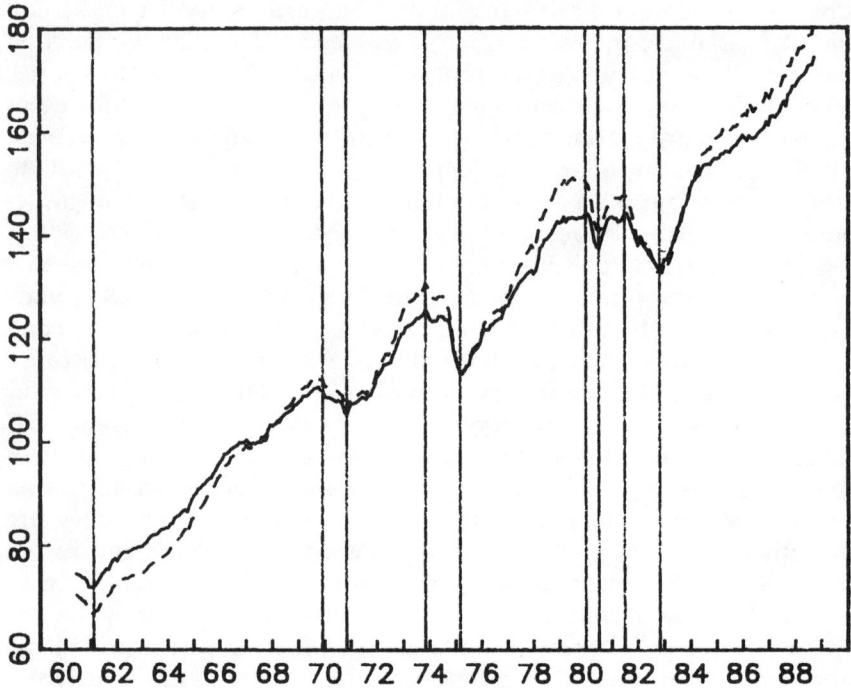

factor model is relatively small, an LEI produced using the unobserved-
components VAR can be approximated by regressing the six-month
growth in the CEI ($C_{t+6|t+6} - C_{t|t}$) on current and past values of the candidate
leading variables. This observation was used to construct several leading
indexes. Starting with a base set of series, indexes were constructed by
including twelve lags of each of the candidate trial variables in the six-step
ahead regression; these were ranked according to a criterion that involved
the full-sample R^2 and the R^2 based on the full-sample performance of the
index when the model was estimated through 1979:9. The series with the
greatest value of the criterion function was added to the index, and the
procedure was repeated until the desired number of variables was added.
The series proposed in Table 1 were obtained by considering those series
that most often were found in the final index, starting from different sets
of base variables. In addition, judgment was used in excluding some
variables that were clearly fitting specific historical episodes in a way that
had no plausible economic interpretation (a sign of overfitting).

Because the growth rates of some of the series contain considerable high frequency noise, some of the series were smoothed. Although this smoothing could in principle be done implicitly by estimating a larger number of regression coefficients, using smoothed series admits the possibility of reducing the number of estimated regression coefficients. The smoothing filter was chosen to be $s(L) = 1+2L+2L^2+L^3$, the filter used by the DOC (until the 1989 revision) to smooth several of their noisy series. This filter has desirable properties from the perspective of producing six-month ahead forecasts using first differences of leading variables. The product filter $(1-L)s(L)$ is a band-pass filter with gain concentrated at periods of four months to one year, zero gain at zero frequency and very low gain for periods less than two months. At a period of six months, the phase lag of this filter is 2.5 months.

The number of lags of each series in the ΔC_t equation of the LEI model (i.e., the order of $\lambda_{CY}(L)$ in (4)) was chosen using the Akaike information criterion (AIC) in a regression of $\Delta C_{t|t}$ on four lags of $\Delta C_{t|t}$ and the selected leading variables. The search was restricted to models with 1, 3, 6, or 9 lags of the variables for computational reasons.[11] Various tests for autoregressive order resulted in setting the orders of $\lambda_{CC}(L)$, $\gamma_{YC}(L)$, and $\gamma_{YY}(L)$ at 4, 1, and 1 respectively. The AIC calculations resulted in a model with six lags of housing starts and the private-public spread and with three lags of each of the other variables. The within-sample R^2 between the resultant LEI and the actual six-month growth of the proposed CEI is .634.

Overfitting the data (and the consequent poor out-of-sample performance) is a risk in any empirical exercise, and the danger is particularly clear here. The first potential source of overfitting—the selection of a final list of leading variables from a much longer list of series—is present both in our procedure and in the traditional NBER/DOC procedure for variable selection (see Zarnowitz and Boschan 1975a,b and Moore 1988). The DOC periodically sponsors a revision of the composite indexes; one interpretation of the need for these revisions is that the underlying relations (and important predictive variables) have changed in the economy, but another is that these revisions are important to correct for previous overfitting.[12] The methodology outlined above introduces a second possible source of overfitting, the estimation of regression coefficients.

11. This entailed examining 4^7 specifications. The AIC is known to overestimate the autoregression order if the order is finite (e.g., Geweke and Meese 1981). As a check, lags were chosen according to the Schwartz information criterion (BIC) and the Hannan-Quinn information criterion. These yielded similar choices of lag lengths, and in particular yielded similar estimated LEIs.
12. Recent revisions occurred in 1975 and 1983. A new set of revisions took effect with the January 1989 data. See Hertzberg and Beckman (1989).

It appears difficult to ascertain the asymptotic properties of this model selection procedure, but these properties can be investigated numerically. Two small Monte Carlo experiments were performed to shed light on the potential overfitting. The first simulated indexes that would be produced if *no* series had any true predictive content for the CEI. Fifty smoothed pseudo-random monthly time series of the form $x_{it} = s(L)\epsilon_{it}$, ϵ_{it} i.i.d. $N(0,1)$ were generated for $i = 1, \ldots , 50$, $t = 1959{:}1, \ldots , 1987{:}12$. The variable and model selection procedure described above was then applied to these time series, and the resultant seven-variable index was calculated. This experiment was repeated twice, and resulted in indexes with R^2's of .228 and .271. The R^2 for a model with no leading variables is .163 over this period (this is non-zero because lagged growth of $C_{t|t}$ predicts its future growth); thus the increment to the R^2 in these Monte Carlo experiments was respectively .065 and .108.

The second Monte Carlo experiment examined a situation where most of the variables have some predictive content, but the chosen series might not be those with the greatest true predictive ability. The estimated seven-variable leading model (4) and (5) was used to generate seven Gaussian pseudo-random leading variables over 1959:1–1987:12, plus a pseudo-random coincident index. For each of the seven pseudo-random leading variables, four more pseudo-random series were constructed by adding various degrees of measurement error to series.[13] Fifteen additional smoothed spurious series like those used in the first experiment were also generated, for a total of fifty pseudo-random potential leading series. The variable and model selection procedure was then used to produce a seven-variable index. The population R^2 for the model generating the data was .65. The average Monte Carlo R^2 of the chosen models across ten replications was .75, and these (suboptimal) models had an average population R^2 of .62. Thus imperfect knowledge of the correct model reduced the R^2 by .03 (.65−.62). Also, on average the sample R^2's were inflated by .13 (.75−.62) above their population counterparts.

These two experiments provide rough measures of the magnitude of the overfitting bias: in the first, approximately .08, in the second, .13.[14]

---

13. For each of the base pseudo-random leading series X_{it}, $i = 1, \ldots ,7$, the four additional pseudo-random series were constructed by setting $X_{ijt} = \Gamma_j(L)X_{it} + u_{ijt}$, where u_{ijt} are i.i.d. $N(0,\tau_j^2)$ random variables, $\Gamma_j(L) = 1, 1, L,$ and L^2, and $\tau_j = 1, 5, 1,$ and 1 for $j = 1, 2, 3,$ and 4, respectively.

14. One reason to suspect that these experiments overstate the bias is that they do not incorporate any researcher judgment, although the construction of the proposed LEI did. In addition, the first experiment fails to recognize that the 55 actual series have many closely related variables (e.g., industrial production of consumer durables and industrial production in manufacturing); thus in actuality the variation across the series is not as great as in the first experiment.

The experimental LEI and its Historical Components. Historical values of the proposed LEI are plotted in Figure 2. A negative value of the index indicates a forecast of negative growth in overall economic conditions over the next six months. This index is negative prior to each of the four recessions since 1960. It is also negative during 1967, a year in which a recession did not occur.

The historical contributions of each of the seven leading variables to the index are plotted in Figure 5. These historical contributions are calculated by setting all series but the series in question to zero, then comput-

Figure 5 HISTORICAL DECOMPOSITION OF THE PROPOSED LEI (A) Total

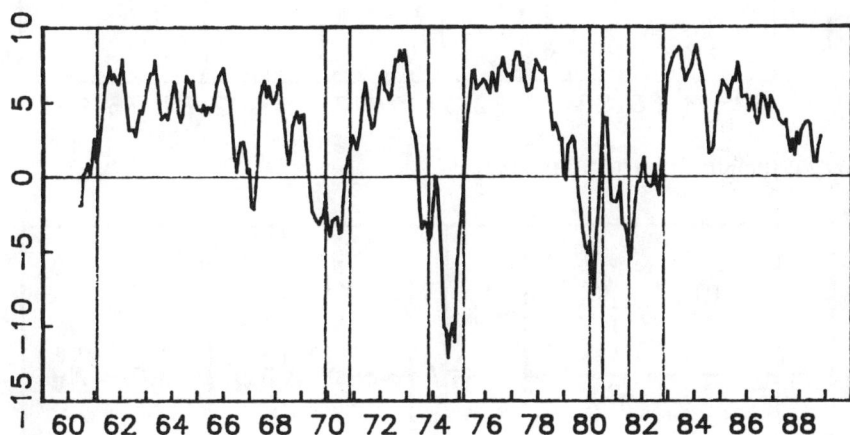

(B) COMPONENT DUE TO HSBP

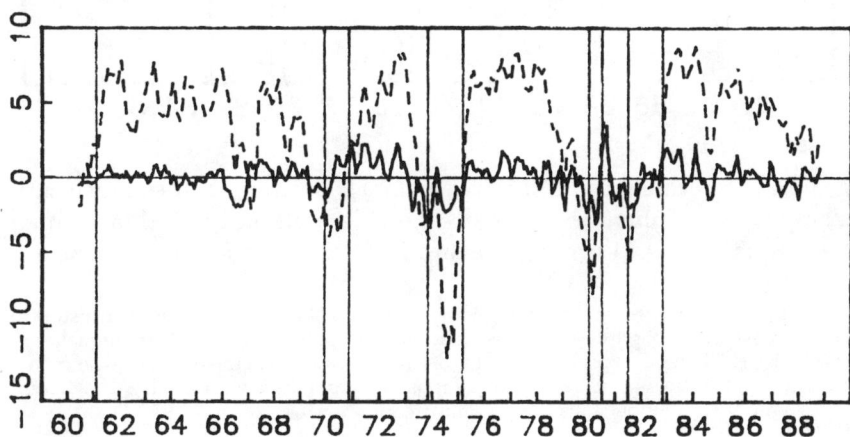

Figure 5 (CONTINUED) (C) COMPONENT DUE TO MDU82S

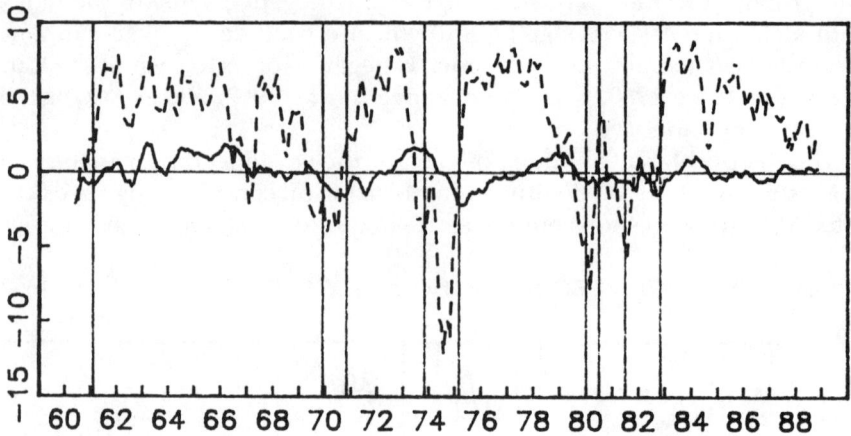

(D) COMPONENT DUE TO EXNWT2S

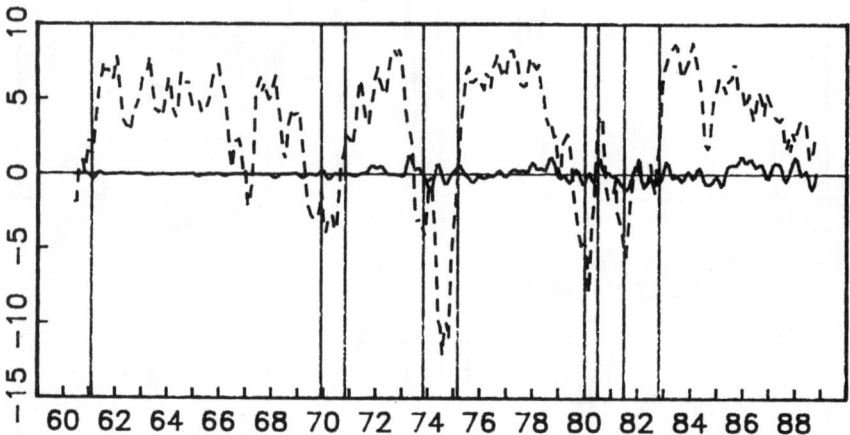

ing the LEI. Because the LEI is linear in Y_t, the sum of these historical decompositions, plus the mean six-month growth in the CEI (at annual rates), equals the LEI (graphed again in Figure 5(a) for convenience).[15]

15. Readers familiar with vector autoregressions (VARs) should not confuse the historical decompositions in Figure 5 with those found in the VAR literature for "orthogonalized" systems. The latter are based on an arbitrary transformation of the original linear model (chosen so that the shocks to each decomposition are mutually uncorrelated), whereas no such transformation is made in producing Figure 5.

Figure 5 (CONTINUED) (E) COMPONENT DUE TO LHNAPSS

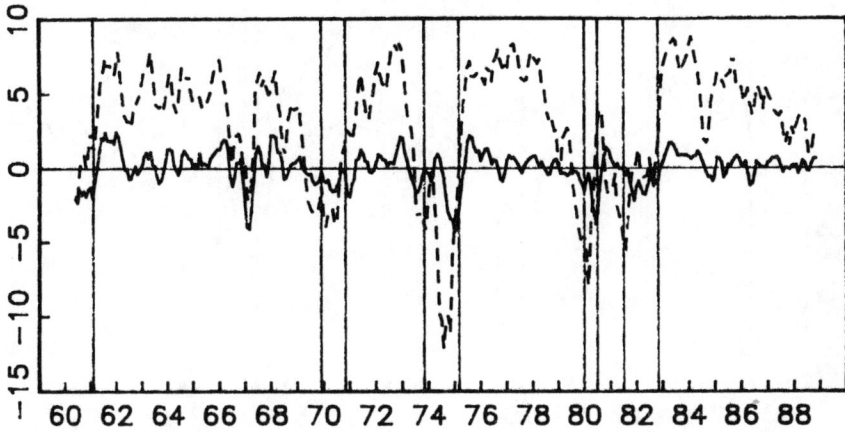

(F) COMPONENT DUE TO FYGT10

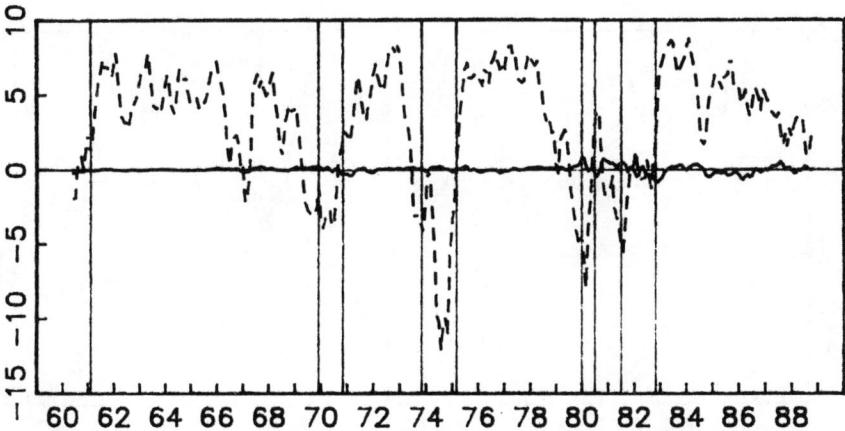

The implicit weights on the variables used to construct the LEI (the implied "distributed lag" coefficients) are plotted in Figure 6; the units are standard deviations of the leading variables.

Each of the series makes a contribution to the total. The largest historical contributions are from the spread between commercial paper and Treasury bills, from the spread between the yields to maturity on 10-year and 1-year Treasury Bonds, from housing starts, from manufacturer's unfilled orders in durable goods industries, and from the growth of part-

Figure 5 (G) COMPONENT DUE TO CP6 _ GM6 (CONTINUED)

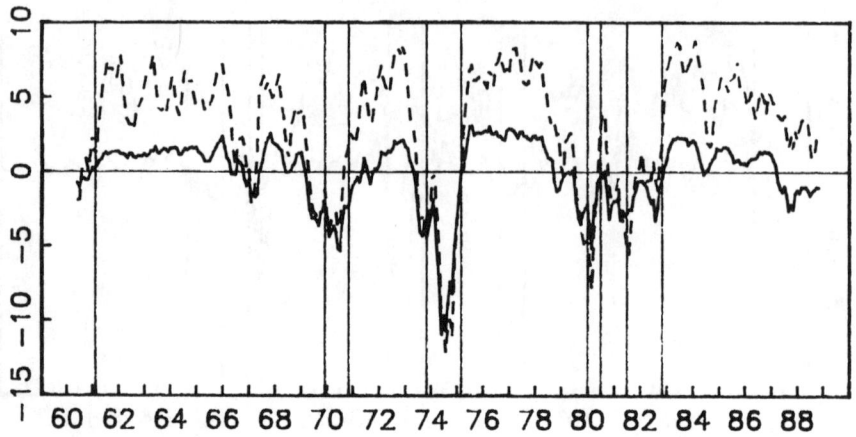

(H) COMPONENT DUE TO G10 _ G1

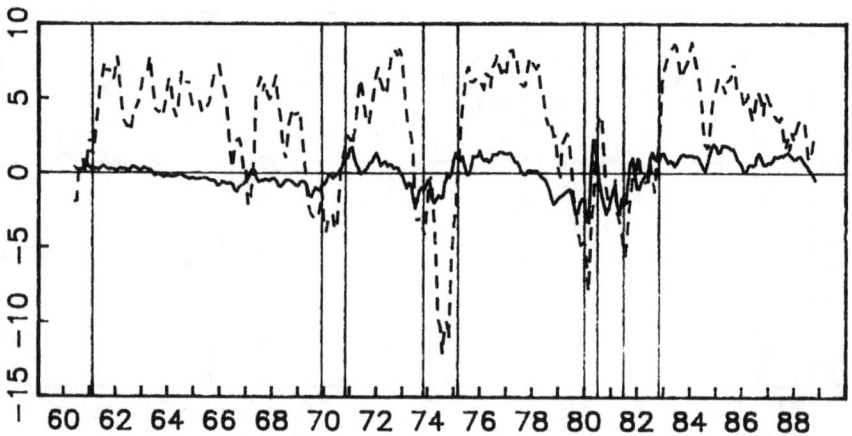

time work due to "slack work." The implied distributed lag coefficients indicate that a rise in housing starts, a low private-public spread, a high long-term/short-term public spread (an upward-sloping yield curve), an increase in durables manufacturers' unfilled orders, and a decline in involuntary part-time work all are indications of strong overall growth over the next six months. To a lesser extent, a depreciation of the dollar and an increase in the long-term Treasury bond yield signify strong future economic activity.

Figure 6 IMPLICIT DISTRIBUTED LAG COEFFICIENTS ON LEADING
VARIABLES

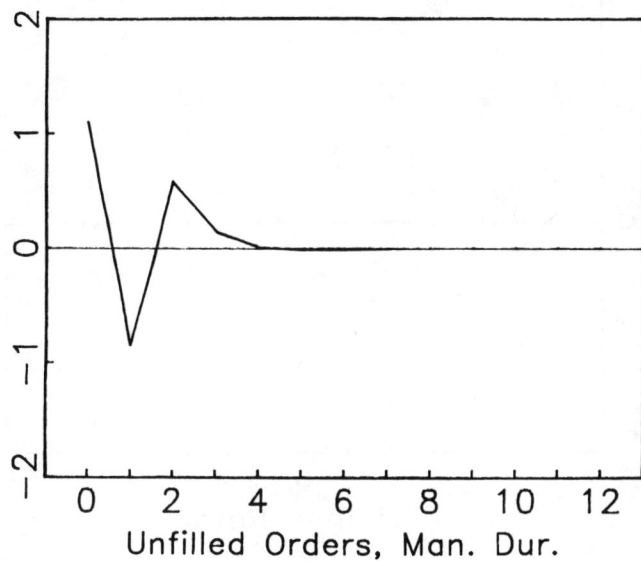

Unfilled Orders, Man. Dur.

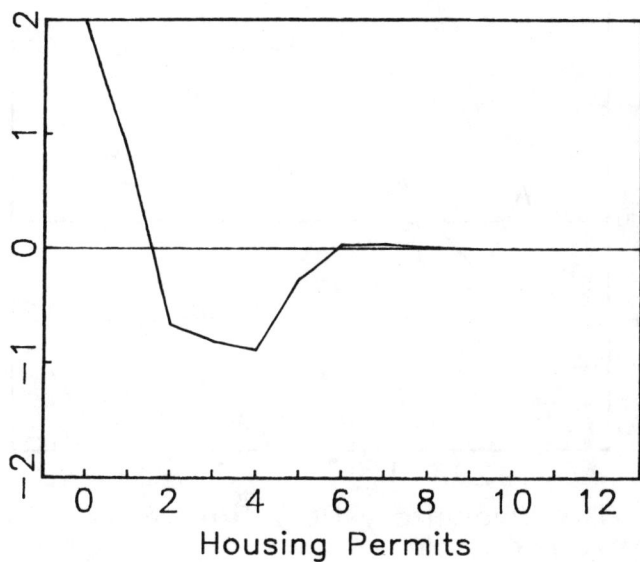

Housing Permits

Figure 6 (CONTINUED)

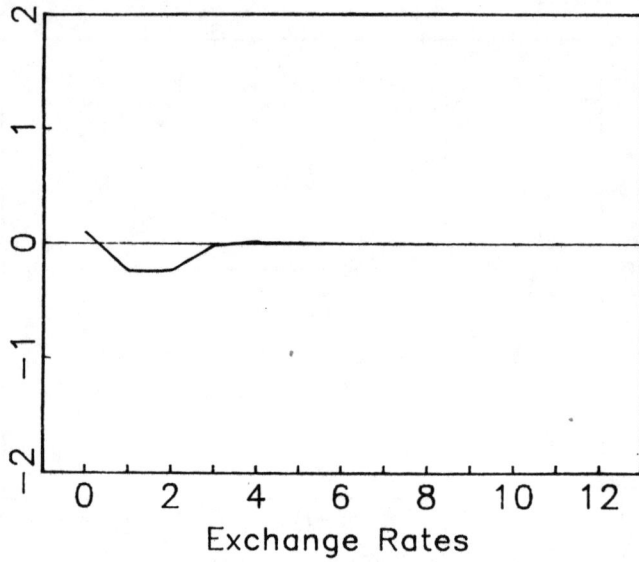

Exchange Rates

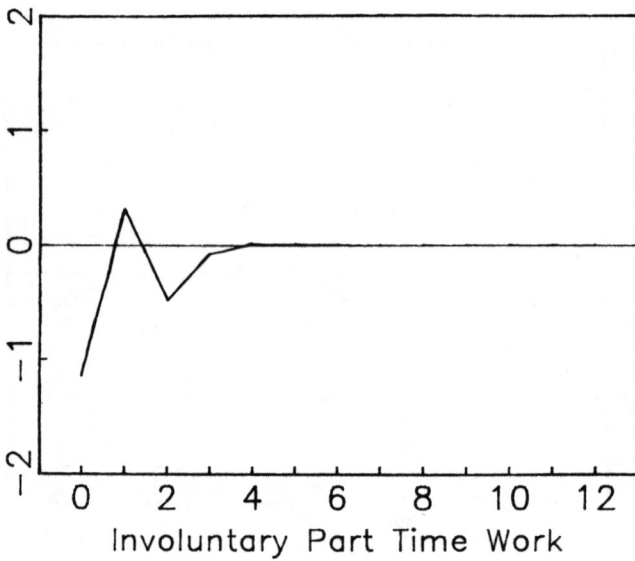

Involuntary Part Time Work

Figure 6 (CONTINUED)

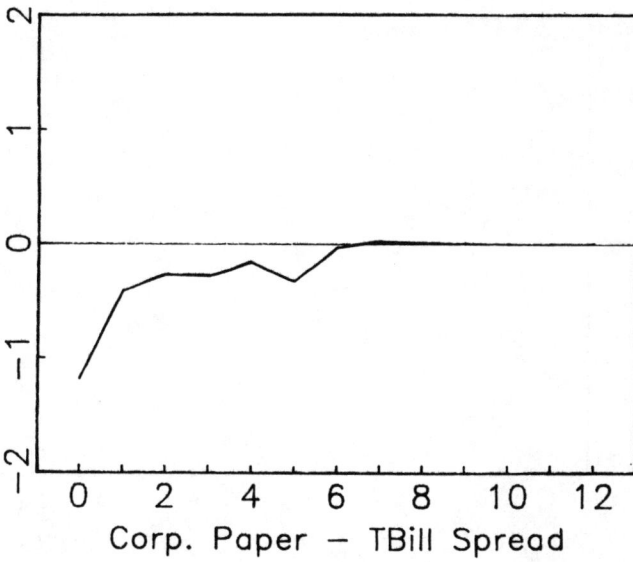

Corp. Paper — TBill Spread

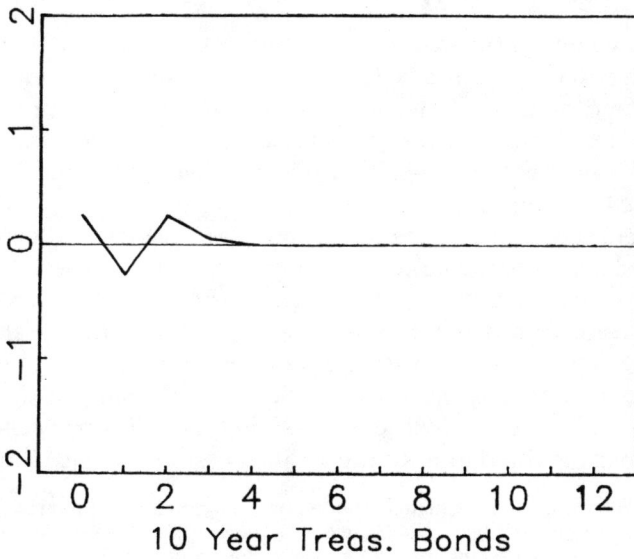

10 Year Treas. Bonds

Figure 6 (CONTINUED)

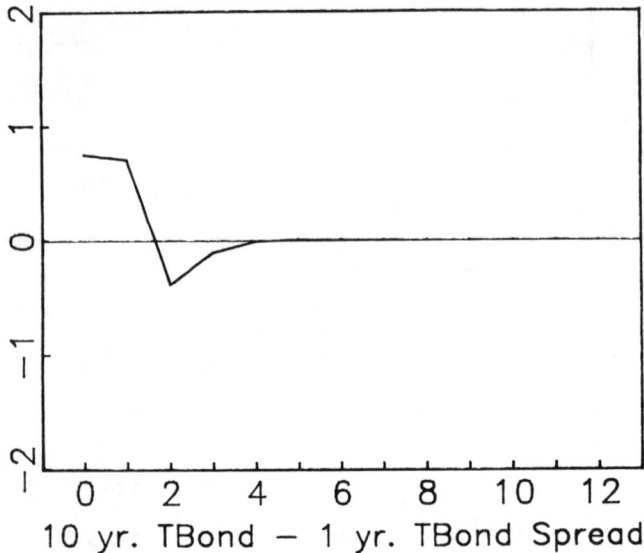

10 yr. TBond − 1 yr. TBond Spread

3.3. THE RECESSION INDEX

Historical values of the experimental Recession Index are plotted in Figure 3. The Recession Index is constructed using the four coincident variables and seven leading variables. Because this is the probability of a recession six months hence, the index ranges between zero and one. Ideally, these recession probabilities would lead the actual NBER-dated recessions by six months.[16]

An important check of the definition of recessions and expansions is the ex post ability of the model to confirm the NBER cyclical dates. Using all the historical data, there is close agreement between the actual NBER-dated recessions and the ex post assessments of whether there was a recession. Figure 7(a) presents the retrospective assessment of whether the economy was in a recession, with the probability calculated using the same definition as in the Recession Index. The greatest point of disagreement is the dating of the 1970 recession: the NBER chronology

16. These probabilities are evaluated by numerical integration over the recession and expansion regions described in footnote 6. The means (μ_e and μ_r) and variances ($\sigma_e = \sigma_r = \sigma$) of the random boundaries (b_{et}, b_{rt}) were chosen to minimize the sum of squared errors between the six-step ahead recession probability and the 0/1 recession-expansion variable six months hence. This criterion was computed over a grid of parameter values, and the resulting estimates are $\mu_e = .25$, $\mu_r = -1.50$, and $\sigma = 0.8$. It turns out that this objective function (and the recession probabilities) are somewhat insensitive to (μ_e, μ_r, σ).

Figure 6 B. SIX-MONTH GROWTH IN THE PROPOSED INDEX OF
COINCIDENT ECONOMIC INDICATORS (SOLID LINE) AND TWO-
QUARTER GROWTH IN REAL GNP (DASHED LINE) (CONTINUED)

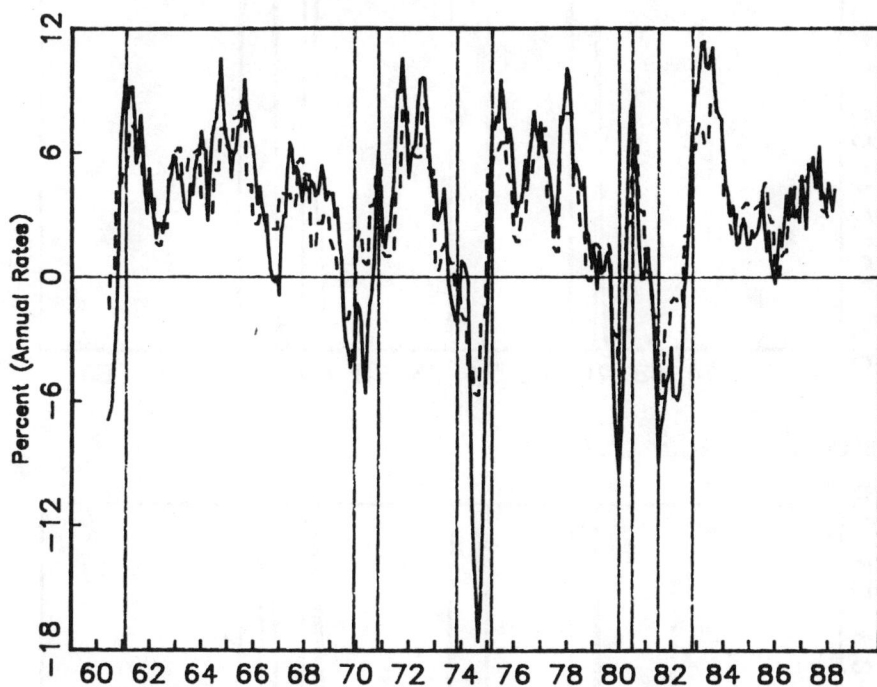

places the peak at December 1969, while this procedure places the peak
at October 1969.

Also presented in Figure 7 are the contemporaneous assessments of
whether the economy is in a recession (Figure 7(b)), the three-month
ahead recession forecast (Figure 7(c)), and the six-month ahead recession
probability (Figure 7(d); this is the proposed Recession Index).

3.4. WITHIN-SAMPLE PERFORMANCE OF THE PROPOSED LEI AND
RECESSION INDEX

The current DOC leading index has been the subject of considerable
ongoing refinement, so one would expect it to be a good predictor of
future economic activity. We therefore compare the within-sample performance of the proposed LEI and Recession Index to two sets of measures
based on the DOC leading index. The first examines the ability of the
DOC leading index to forecast the near-term growth in the CEI; the
second examines the use of the DOC leading index to forecast future
recessions.

Figure 7 RECESSION PROBABILITIES: (A) EX POST

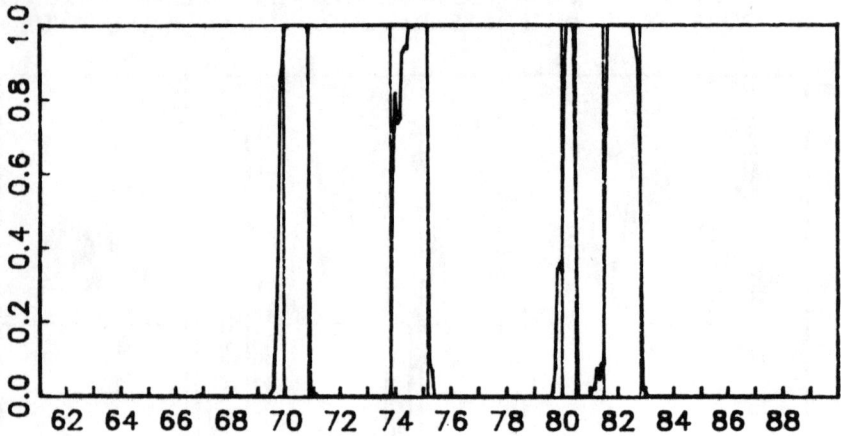

(B) CONTEMPORANEOUS

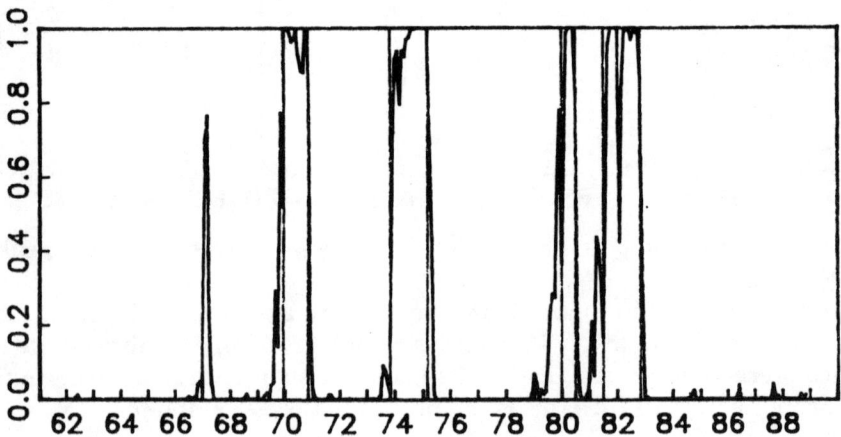

Forecasts of Growth.   The within-sample fit of the proposed LEI is generally good. The within-sample R^2 between the LEI and the true six-month growth of the CEI ($C_{t+6|t+6} - C_{t|t}$) is .634 over 1961:1–1988:4. The LEI and the actual six-month growth of the CEI are plotted in Figure 8(a). The most noteworthy within-sample errors occurred in the middle of the 1982 recession: the LEI was predicting approximately zero growth, while the actual growth turned out to be sharply negative.

Because the six-month growth of the CEI is highly correlated with the two-quarter growth of GNP, one way to measure performance is to com-

Figure 7 (CONTINUED) (C) 3-MONTH AHEAD

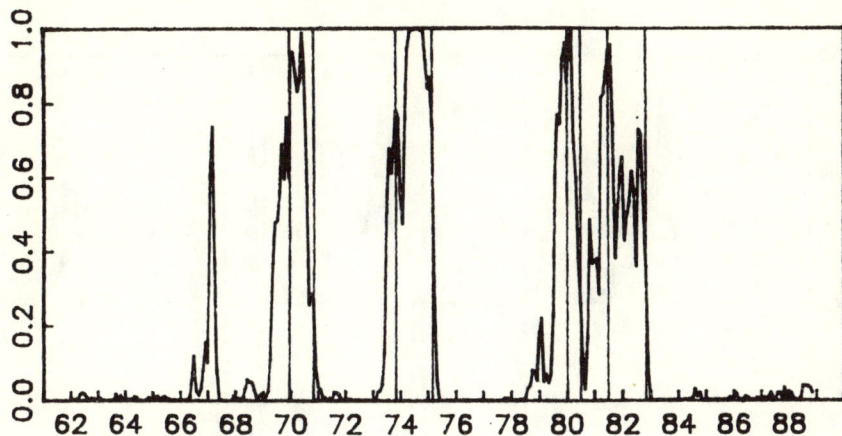

(D) 6-MONTH AHEAD

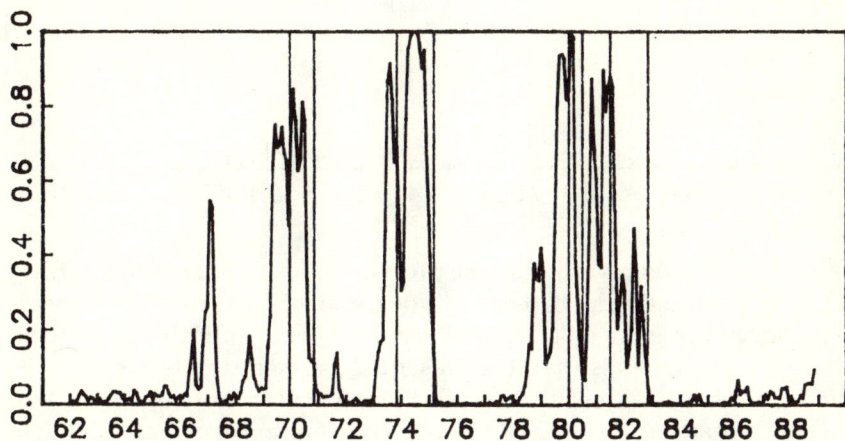

pare the growth forecast of the LEI with historical forecasts of GNP growth. Figure 8(b) presents the two-quarter growth in real GNP (con structed as in Figure 4(b)) and the ASA/NBER median forecast of real GNP growth over the subsequent two quarters.[17] Although the ASA/ NBER median forecast anticipated the 1979–80 recession and contempo- raneously recognized the 1980 recovery, it failed to forecast the severity of the 1974–75 recession and entirely missed the 1982 recession.

17. Prior to 1986, the ASA/NBER survey reports the median forecasts of the GNP price deflator and of nominal GNP, but not of real GNP. For this period the real GNP forecast was constructed as the ratio of these two median forecasts.

Figure 8 SIX-MONTH GROWTH IN THE CEI (SOLID) AND THE LEI
(DASHED)

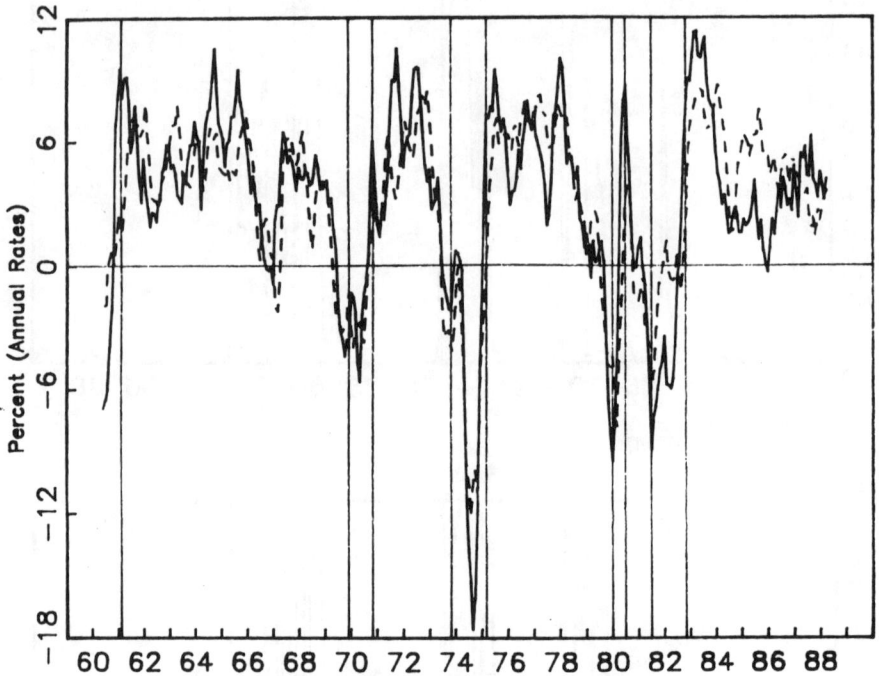

A natural question is whether the proposed LEI represents an improvement over the existing DOC leading index, and whether the DOC series is
itself an accurate estimate of economic growth. One difficulty with evaluating the DOC series is that it is presented as a series in levels, with its
primary mission to signal turning points in overall economic activity. It is,
however, possible to use the DOC series as a forecast of overall growth in
the DOC coincident index. Specifically, if the DOC leading index is a
forecast of the DOC coincident index k months hence, then the percent
difference between the DOC leading and coincident indexes is a forecast
of the growth in the DOC coincident index over the next k months. Let
L_t^{DOC} denote this percent difference. With $k = 6$, the R^2 between L_t^{DOC} and the
six-month growth in the experimental CEI is .410 from 1960:2−1988:4; the
maximal R^2 (as a function of k) is .416, which occurs at $k = 7$.[18]

18. The R^2-s between L_t^{DOC} and $(C_{t+k|t+k}-C_{t|t})$ for $k = 3, 4, \ldots, 12$ are respectively, .364,
.387, .399, .410, .416, .416, .413, .404, .393, and .382. The same results obtain to within
±.02 using the DOC coincident index rather than the experimental CEI. Note that
historical values of the DOC leading index were revised in 1983. This suggests that the

Figure 8 B. TWO-QUARTER GROWTH IN REAL GNP (SOLID) AND ITS ASA/
MEDIAN FORECAST (CONTINUED)

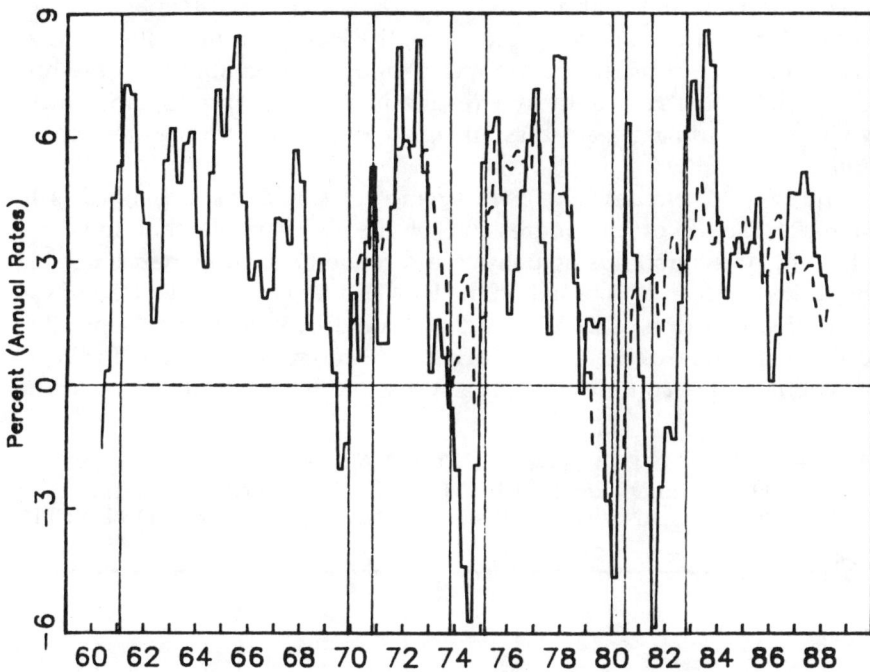

The six-month growth of the proposed CEI is plotted with L_t^{DOC} in Figure 8(c) at annual rates. Although the two series are highly correlated, L_t^{DOC} exhibits somewhat greater fluctuations. In addition, the forecast implicit in L_t^{DOC} has been substantially stronger than the growth in the coincident index (or real GNP) since 1983, a point raised in popular discussions of the existing leading index.[19]

Forecasts of Recessions and Expansions. The DOC produces no series directly comparable to the proposed NBER Recession Index. To provide a basis for comparison, we examine two different recession forecasts based on the DOC leading index: a "three consecutive decline" rule-of-thumb and a limited dependent variable model with the DOC indexes as the predictive variables.

results prior to 1983 should be viewed as within-sample fits, and those after 1983 as out-of-sample forecasting experiments.
19. For example, Hunt (1988) points out that much of the strength in the DOC leading index during the mid-1980s was driven by the strong growth in stock prices.

Popular discussions of the DOC leading index use a three consecutive decline rule-of-thumb as a measure of whether the index is signalling a recession. This rule-of-thumb issues a recession signal (expansion signal) if, during an expansion (recession), the DOC leading index declines (rises) for three consecutive months. Applied systematically to the historical data, this rule-of-thumb results in a series of zeros and ones, where a zero indicates a recession signal and a one indicates an expansion signal.

One way to evaluate the performance of this recession signal is to compute the R^2 of the regression of the 0/1 variable that indicates whether the economy is actually in a recession k months hence against the series of 0's and 1's based on the DOC leading index. At a lead of $k = 0$ months, this R^2 is .289; at a lead of 3 months, it is .116; at 6 months, .028. The greatest of these R^2's is at a lag of 1 month, which is a "forecast" of whether the economy was in a recession in the month prior to the

Figure 8 C. SIX-MONTH GROWTH IN THE PROPOSED CEI (SOLID) AND THE SCALED PERCENT DIFFERENCE BETWEEN THE DOC LEADING AND COINCIDENT INDEXES (DASHED) (CONTINUED)

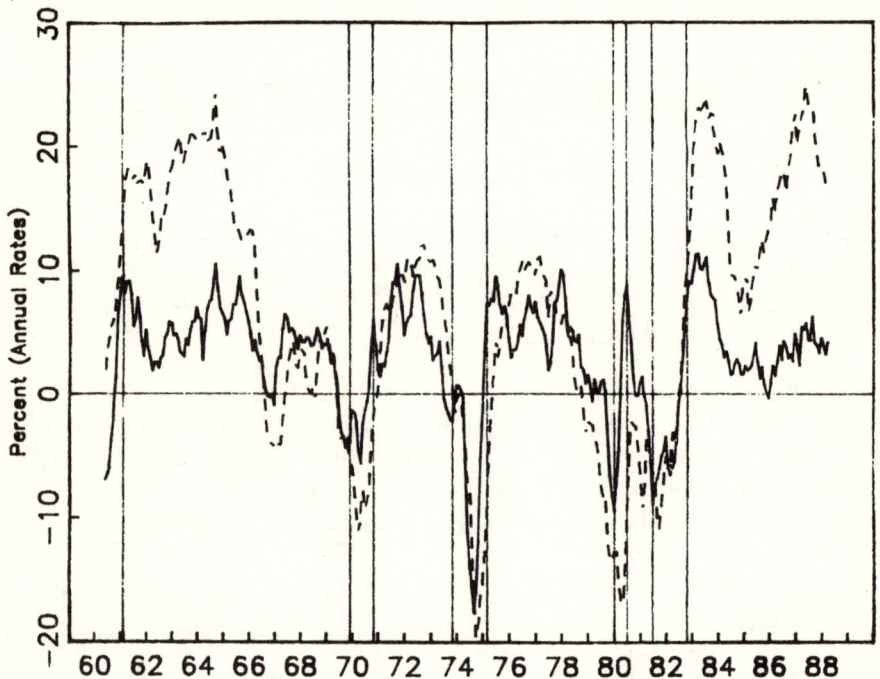

most recent month for which there are data. In contrast, the R^2 for the series in Figure 7(b)–7(d) are respectively .88 at 0 months lead, .64 at a lead of 3 months, and (for the proposed Recession Index) .50 at a lead of 6 months.

Although this rule-of-thumb is commonly used to forecast recessions, it is probably not the most efficient use of the information contained in the DOC index. As an additional comparison, logit models were estimated with the true 0/1 recession indicator six months hence as the dependent variable and with, alternately, lags of L_t^{DOC} and of the growth of the DOC leading index as predictive variables. The greatest of the resulting R^2-s was .292, which obtained in a logit model with eight lags of L_t^{DOC} as the predictive variables.

In summary, these historical comparisons suggest that the proposed LEI and Recession Index are potentially substantial improvements over the existing indexes, both in performance and in ease of interpretation. Whether this potential is realized will, of course, depend on the future behavior of the indexes.

4. Interpretation and Discussion

The construction of the experimental LEI systematically focused on finding a set of macroeconomic variables that jointly have the ability to forecast future economic activity in a reduced-form model. This section examines the resulting index and its components from the perspective of macroeconomic theory.

4.1. DISCUSSION OF VARIABLES INCLUDED IN THE LEI

Long-term/short term treasury bond yield spread. One of the novel features of the experimental LEI is its use of interest rate spreads as macroeconomic predictors. It is generally recognized that a declining yield curve signals a future slowdown in economic activity. The 10-year/1-year Treasury bond spread became negative in 1959, 1966, 1973, 1978, and 1981; with the exception of 1966, each of these inversions in the yield curve preceded an NBER-dated cyclical peak by approximately one year. Similarly, five of the seven cessations of the inversion over this period preceded a cyclical trough by approximately six months to one year. Recent work in financial econometrics has produced the intriguing related result that measures of the slope of the yield curve are useful predictors of a variety of financial variables. For example, Campbell (1987) and Fama and French (1989) document that measures of the slope of the term structure at short horizons have predictive content for excess returns on a variety of assets.[20]

These observations are consistent with a macroeconomic theory in which real rates are temporarily high, perhaps because of tight monetary policy, which in turn results in a postponement of investment and a decline in future activity. Additionally, if market participants expect future growth to be low and believe a Phillips relation to hold, then inflation would be expected to drop and the yield curve would tend to invert. Thus this predictive content is consistent with a theory in which monetary policy works through interest rates and in which inflation and output growth are positively related. It seems to be more difficult to reconcile this finding with a simple real business cycle model in which the marginal product of capital equals the interest rate and in which persistent productivity shocks drive the business cycle: in this case, a positive productivity shock would result in a high marginal product of capital that is expected to decline over time as investment (and output) increases.

Private-public interest rate spread. Although the average spread from 1959 to 1988 is only 60 basis points, during and preceding the 1970 and 1980 recessions it exceeded 150 basis points, and during 1975 it rose to over 350 basis points. The predictive power of similar spreads has been documented by Bernanke (1983), who showed that the Baa-Treasury bond spread forecasted industrial production in the interwar period, and by Friedman and Kuttner (1989), who (independently) concluded that the corporate paper-Treasury bill spread has strong predictive power for industrial production over the period considered here. Like the slope of the yield curve, the private-public spread has recently been recognized as a predictor of various asset returns. Keim and Stambaugh (1986) find that monthly risk premiums on a variety of bonds can be explained with some success by the spread between the yield on long-term low-grade corporate paper and short-term Treasury bills (note however that the maturities in this spread are not matched).

One interpretation of these results is that the private-public spread measures the default risk on private debt. If private lenders can accurately assess increased default risks for individual firms or industries, these changes will, after aggregation, be reflected as increases in the spread. Thus the spread could serve as a useful aggregator of informa-

---

20. In related research, Knez, Litterman, and Scheinkman (1989) identify three common systematic risk factors underlying a variety of money market returns. They associate these factors with shifts in the yield curve, tilts in the yield curve, and changes in the public-private spread. Thus the three factors correspond closely to the three interest rate measures in the proposed LEI.

tion about the prospects of private firms, known best by those buying and selling the debt of those firms. An alternative interpretation would emphasize the allocative role of interest rates: an increase in the spread, all else equal, might induce some firms to postpone investment, resulting in a decline in aggregate demand.

Change in the 10-year Treasury bond yield. Previous research on the predictive content of various financial and monetary variables has emphasized the importance of interest rates or their changes (e.g., Sims 1980), so it is not surprising that changes in the long-term public bond rate have some forecasting content. Interestingly, including a measure of ex ante real rates (with various measures of expected inflation) does not improve the performance of the LEI. In fact, simulated out-of-sample experiments indicate that including a real rate would have dramatically worsened substantially the performance during the 1980s because of the historically high real rates since 1982.

Trade-weighted nominal exchange rate. A depreciation of the dollar relative to the currencies of its major trading partners makes a small positive contribution to the LEI. The sign and the magnitude are consistent with the depreciation being associated with a modest subsequent increase in net demand for domestically produced goods relative to foreign goods.

Part-time work in nonagricultural industries (slack work). An increase in slack work results in a substantial drop in the LEI, holding the components constant. This measure is closely related to indicators in the current DOC index (new claims for unemployment insurance and the average weekly hours of production workers in manufacturing); the procedure described in the previous section indicates that part-time work has preferable statistical properties compared with these other indicators. One interpretation of the predictive value of this series is that the initial response of some firms to productivity and demand shocks is not just to adjust inventories, but to vary labor input. In addition, this is measured better by part-time employment than by layoffs or by average hours.

Housing authorizations. This series, currently in the DOC leading index, could play several roles. Private housing is the most durable of consumer goods. Thus movements in housing authorizations could be a proxy for broader changes in demand for consumer durables, perhaps in response to movements in interest rates or to fluctuations in (the present value of) aggregate income. In addition, changes in housing authorizations could signal more widespread changes in future activity in the construction sector which, to the extent that there is a multiplier mechanism, might spill over into other sectors of the economy.

Manufacturers' unfilled orders (durable goods industries).   The DOC has (independently) decided to include manufacturer's unfilled orders in durable goods industries in the revised DOC leading index starting in January 1989. Unfilled orders are much like negative inventories, and can be used (like inventories) to minimize production costs over time. Thus unfilled orders can be expected to increase in response to unexpected increases in demand or to temporary increases in production costs. The time series properties of unfilled orders will depend on the extent of production smoothing, production times, the relative mix of demand and supply shocks, and the lead-lag relation between new orders for durables and aggregate activity.

B. DISCUSSION OF SELECTED VARIABLES EXCLUDED FROM THE LEADING INDEX

The proposed LEI excludes some variables that appear in the current DOC index or which economic theory suggests could have important predictive power. Summary statistics for the effect of including several such series in the LEI are presented in Table 3. The first column presents the p-value for the F-test of the restriction that the coefficients on lags of the candidate additional leading variable are zero in a regression of the one-month growth of the CEI on the variables in the LEI and on six lags of the candidate variable. The second column contains the same statistic, except that 12 lags of the candidate variable are included in the regression. The third column contains the within-sample R^2 between the six-month growth of the CEI and the LEI, constructed using the base variables and lags described in Section 3 and 12 lags of the candidate variable. The fourth column contains the out-of-sample root mean square error from October 1979 to April 1988 based on an LEI model estimated through September 1979.[21]

Stock Prices.   The present value theory of stock prices implies that movements in the stock market reflect changing expectations of future earn-

---

21. As a simplification, columns 3 and 4 of Table 3 are based on LEI models that were estimated using a conventional multivariate regression specified with $C_{t|t}$, y_t, and the candidate leading variable. That is, C_t was not treated as unobserved as in the estimation of the LEI in Section 3, but rather was replaced by $C_{t|t}$. Now specified in terms of observables, the system was esimated by OLS equation by equation. The numerical error that arises from this simplification is slight because of the small signal extraction in $C_{t|t}$.

Table 3 EFFECT OF INCLUDING ADDITIONAL VARIABLES IN THE LEI: SUMMARY STATISTICS

Candidate Variable	—p-value— 6 lags	12 lags	R^2, 60:2 –88:4	RMSE, 79:10 –88:4
Base Model	—	—	.631	3.64
Base Model plus additional variables:				
Stock Prices				
S&P 500, growth rate	.130	.080	.658	3.57
Money and Credit				
M1 (82$s), growth rate	.662	.854	.635	4.46
M2 (82$s), growth rate	.315	.626	.642	3.64
M2 (82$s), linearly detrended growth rate	.322	.628	.641	3.73
Monetary Base (nominal), growth rate	.981	.353	.631	3.93
Change in bus. and cons. credit as % pers. inc.	.624	.720	.636	3.79
Consumer inst. loans, delinquency rate, >30 days	.260	.556	.635	3.73
Employment				
Avg weekly hours of manufacturing workers	.849	.972	.637	3.85
New claims for unempl. insurance, growth rates	.573	.603	.642	3.68
No. persons unemployed less than 5 weeks	.007	.003	.630	3.62
Sales and Consumption				
IP—consumer durables	.300	.507	.638	4.25
Pers cons expenditures, durable goods (82$s)	.721	.472	.643	3.66
Retail sales (1982$'s, smoothed)	.681	.660	.643	3.63
Retail sales, new cars (smoothed, seas. adj.)	.776	.268	.665	3.43
Inventories				
Mfg & trade inventories, total (82$s)	.497	.265	.640	3.58
Mfg & trade invt's: matl's & supplies (82$s)	.969	.990	.637	3.82
Mfg. & trade invt's: work in progress (82$s)	.258	.017	.634	3.70
Mfg & trade invt's: finished goods (82$'s)	.901	.874	.637	3.75
Additional Leading Indicators				
Contracts & orders for Plant & Eqpt (82$s)	.865	.769	.634	3.70
Mfg new orders, cons. goods & matl's (82$s)	.530	.515	.627	4.12
Construction contracts, comm & indust bldgs	.960	.906	.633	3.88

Notes: The first two columns present the p-value for the conventional F-test (without any additional degrees-of-freedom adjustment) of the hypothesis that the coefficients on the candidate leading variable are zero in a regression of $\Delta C_{t|t}$ on the base set of leading variables (with the same number of lags as are used to construct the NBER LEI), estimated by OLS, using 6 and 12 lags respectively of the candidate variable. The third column presents the within-sample R^2 when the LEI model is estimated using the full sample and 12 lags of the candidate variable. The final column contains the out-of-column RMSE between the LEI and $C_{t+6|t+6} - C_{t|t}$, in which the LEI model (augmented by 12 lags of the candidate variable) is estimated over 60:2–79:9.

ings of publicly traded corporations. Additional theoretical links from
the stock market to future economic activity come through the role of
stock prices as a determinant of the cost of capital (q-theory) and through
wealth effects on consumption. Stock prices therefore ought to be an
indicator of future growth, and indeed were identified as leading indicators by Mitchell and Burns (1938). Fama (1981) and Fisher and Merton
(1984) document the substantial predictive value of stock prices for output. As they do for GNP at longer horizons, stock prices have strong
predictive content for the growth in the CEI; the R^2 of a regression of
$C_{t+6|t+6} - C_{t|t}$ on 12 lags of the growth in the Standard and Poor's 500 is .318,
and the hypothesis that the growth of the S&P 500 does not Granger-
cause $\Delta C_{t|t}$ can be rejected at the .5% significance level.

A result from this research is that the *marginal* predictive content of
stock prices for the six-month growth in the CEI is modest. As reported
in Table 3, the hypothesis that stock prices have no marginal (linear)
predictive content for $\Delta C_{t|t}$ cannot be rejected at the 5% level.[22] Although
the R^2 for the six-step ahead forecast increases somewhat when S&P 500
growth is included, this specification increases the number of estimated
parameters in the $\Delta C_{t|t}$ equation from 28 to 40. Although there is some
evidence that the stock market improves forecasting performance, this
improvement is slight. These findings are consistent with a view that,
from the perspective of forecasting, the expectational aspect of the stock
market dominates its allocative role, and that these expectations can be
captured by examining other variables.

Money and Credit. The marginal predictive content of money for output
is one of the most studied relations in empirical macroeconomics; see
Christiano and Ljungqvist (1988) and Stock and Watson (1989) for recent
results and reviews of the literature. A primary focus of this literature
has been whether the predictive content of money growth in a bivariate
system is eliminated by including an interest rate. The proposed LEI
provides an opportunity to examine the marginal predictive content of
money in a system with measures of real activity and, notably, with a
richer set of interest rates.

The predictive content of real $M2$ growth in a bivariate system with
$\Delta C_{t|t}$ is substantial: Granger non-causality can be rejected at the 0.5%
level, and the R^2 of the regression of $C_{t+6|t+6} - C_{t|t}$ onto 12 lags of real $M2$ is
.435. As the results in Table 3 indicate, however, on the margin real $M1$,
real $M2$, and the monetary base add nothing to the forecasting ability of

22. The large number of variables involved in the search suggests skepticism about the use
of the usual asymptotic distributions for these test statistics. An informal way to correct
for this is to use a more conservative critical value than usual, say 1%.

the LEI. The simulated out-of-sample performance of the index including $M1$ deteriorates substantially, indicating parameter instability. These results hold using either the growth rate of $M2$ or, as suggested by Stock and Watson (1989), the detrended growth rate.

These findings are consistent with several hypotheses. Friedman (1988) argues that even if money had predictive content during earlier periods, its reduced-form relation to output has changed (or vanished) as a result of financial deregulation. This is consistent with the observation that the economy has performed well in the last two years despite the absolute decline of real $M2$ between October 1986 and October 1988. Alternatively, the inclusion of interest rate spreads (in particular the yield curve) might be a more sensitive measure to monetary intervention than is the interest rate alone, the variable typically examined by other authors.

Measures of the quantity of credit have also received some attention as possible predictive variables. The change in business and consumer credit appears in the current DOC leading index; scaled to be a percent of personal income rather than in nominal dollars, this change has no statistically significant predictive content.

Employment. The DOC leading index contains two employment series not in the proposed LEI: average weekly hours of manufacturing workers and new claims for unemployment insurance. Neither make an important marginal contribution to the proposed LEI.[23] While the number of individuals unemployed less than five weeks is a statistically significant predictor of $\Delta C_{t|t}$ at the 5% level, the six-month ahead forecast is not improved by including it in the index.

Sales and Consumption. The Permanent Income Hypothesis and the Life Cycle Hypothesis imply that, like stock prices, changes in consumption reflect changes in expectations of future income. The Keynesian aggregate model suggests that changes in consumption can produce changes in income and employment. In real business cycle models, changes in consumption—even if predictable—reflect optimal responses to changes in productivity or other real disturbances and thus portend future movements in output. The standard versions of these theories refer to service flows from consumption goods, not to consumption expenditures. Theories that explicitly incorporate durability

---

23. New claims for unemployment insurance have the drawback of being sensitive to changes in unemployment insurance regulations and in patterns of application for unemployment insurance among those eligible.

suggest that expenditures on durables might be particularly sensitive to shocks perceived by consumers.

The predictive content of various measures of consumption is, however, slight. Of the four measures listed in Table 3, only real retail sales and auto sales reject Granger non-causality at the 5% level in a bivariate system with $\Delta C_{t|t}$. When the experimental LEI is augmented by the various measures of consumption, they have no statistically significant marginal predictive content. One interpretation of these results is that housing starts are a measure of demand for consumer durables, so that including housing starts (and interest rates) in the LEI reduces the predictive value of other measures of consumption.

Inventories. Theoretical models of inventory behavior variously suggest that inventories will be sensitive to changes in current demand, to innovations in current demand, to expected changes in future demand, or to (changes in, innovations in, expectations of) costs of production. In addition, theory suggests that inventories at various stages of production will respond differently to different types of shocks. A series on smoothed changes in manufacturing and trade inventories appeared in the current DOC leading index (it was dropped in the 1989 revision), and inventories exhibit a strong coherence with the $\Delta C_{t|t}$ at low frequencies. The marginal predictive content of inventories for output is, however, slight. Although the growth in real intermediate inventories makes a statistically significant contribution to forecasting $\Delta C_{t|t}$ when 12 lags are included (based on the conventional 5% level), the improvement in the six-month ahead R^2 is minimal.[24]

Investment variables in the DOC leading index. The Keynesian multiplier-accelerator model gives an important role to investment as a determinant of output. Real business cycle models hold that expectations of future demand and changes in productivity are important determinants of investment. Both theories suggest that measures of investment could help to predict future economic performance. The current DOC leading index includes two variables that measure investment but which have insignificant marginal predictive value when incorporated in the experimental LEI. Neither contracts and orders for plant and equipment nor

---

24. Reagan and Sheehan (1985) use VARs to examine inventories, orders, and production. They conclude that inventories (particularly work-in-progress) have important predictive content for production at the 1–3 year horizon and attribute less of a role to unfilled orders, particularly for non-durables. Their findings depend on the innovation triangularizations for their VARs, and they do not consider interest rates. Still, their results stand in contrast to the limited additional predictive content of inventories found here.

manufacturers' new orders make a discernible marginal contribution. Moreover, these series effectively receive zero weight when entered into the index.

5. Conclusions

A strength of the traditional system of leading and coincident indicators is its examination of many series without imposing too much prior information, and its subsequent identification of those series that appear to have the greatest predictive content for aggregate economic activity. The research reported here has adopted this approach and has attempted to improve upon it by recasting it in a form in which modern statistical theory can be applied. In particular, the emphasis has been on multivariate rather than bivariate predictive content.

This exercise in modern business cycle analysis has focused on forecasting with reduced-form models. We think, however, that the results provide three sets of observations for macroeconomic theory. First, the single-index model imposes restrictions on the joint time series properties of the major coincident series that are not rejected by the data. In principle aggregate shocks could enter these series separately, with different dynamic effects; in practice they appear not to. This does not imply that there is a single source of aggregate fluctuations, but rather that the multiple sources of fluctuations have proportional dynamic effects on these aggregate variables.

The second set of observations concern the variables that are included in the index. In particular, this systematic empirical investigation has identified two potent new variables not in the current DOC list of leading indicators: the spread between interest rates on private and public debt instruments of matched maturities and a measure of the slope of the public debt yield curve.

The third set of observations concerns those variables that are excluded from the LEI. Although arguments can be made in favor of some additional series, in general monthly measures of money and credit, employment, consumption, inventories, investment, and the stock market have little marginal predictive content for the coincident index. This is of additional interest in light of the emphasis placed on these series by modern macroeconomic theory.

*The authors thank Olivier Blanchard, Martin Feldstein, Robert Hall, Christopher Sims, Lawrence Summers, John Taylor, and numerous colleagues for helpful advice and comments on earlier drafts. We also thank the members of this project's technical advisory group for their time and suggestions: Frank de Leeuw, Robert Gordon, Stephen McNeese, Geoffrey Moore, Allen Sinai, and Victor Zarnowitz. Myungsoo Park provided invaluable research assistance. Financial support for this project was provided by the National Bureau of Economic Research and the National Science Foundation.

REFERENCES

Adelman, I. and F. L. Adelman. 1959. "The Dynamic Properties of the Klein-Goldberger Model." *Econometrica* 27: 596–625.

Altug, S. 1984. "Gestation Lags and the Business Cycle: An Empirical Analysis." University of Minnesota. Manuscript. Forthcoming, *International Economic Review.*

Auerbach, A. J. 1982. "The Index of Leading Indicators: 'Measurement Without Theory,' Thirty-five Years Later." *Review of Economics and Statistics* 64: No. 4, 589–95.

Bernanke, B. S. 1983. "Nonmonetary Effects of the Financial Crisis in the Propagation of the Great Depression." *American Economic Review* 73: No. 3, 257–76.

Burns, A. F. and W. C. Mitchell. 1946. *Measuring Business Cycles.* New York: NBER.

Campbell, J. Y. 1987. "Stock Returns and the Term Structure." *Journal of Financial Economics* 18: 373–99.

Christiano, L. J. and L. Ljungqvist. 1988. "Money Does Granger-Cause Output in the Bivariate Money-Output Relation." *Journal of Monetary Economics* 22: 217–36.

Dickey, D. A. and W. A. Fuller. 1979. "Distribution of the Estimators for Autoregressive Time Series With a Unit Root." *Journal of the American Statistical Association* 74: No. 366, 427–31.

Diebold, F. X. and G. D. Rudebusch. 1987. "Scoring the Leading Indicators." Federal Reserve Board, Division of Research and Statistics. Manuscript. Forthcoming, *Journal of Business.*

Engle, R. F. and M. W. Watson. 1981. "A One-Factor Multivariate Time Series Model of Metropolitan Wage Rates." *Journal of the American Statistical Association* 76: No. 376, 774–81.

Engle, R. F. and C. W. J. Granger. 1987. "Co-Integration and Error Correction: Representation, Estimation and Testing." *Econometrica* 55: 251–76.

Fama, E. F. 1981. "Stock Returns, Real Activity, Inflation, and Money." *American Economic Review* 71: 545–65.

Fama, E. F. and K. R. French. 1989. "Business Conditions and Expected Returns on Stocks and Bonds." University of Chicago, Graduate School of Business. Manuscript.

Fischer, S. and R. C. Merton. 1984. "Macroeconomics and Finance: The Role of the Stock Market." *Carnegie-Rochester Conference Series on Public Policy* 21: 57–108.

Friedman, B. M. 1988. "Lessons on Monetary Policy from the 1980s." *Journal of Economic Perspectives* 2: No. 3, 51–72.

Friedman, B. M. and K. N. Kuttner. 1989. "Money, Income and Prices after the 1980s." NBER Working Paper No. 2852.

Geweke, J. 1977. "The Dynamic Factor Analysis of Economic Time Series." in D. J. Aigner and A. S. Goldberger eds. *Latent Variables in Socio-Economic Models.* Amsterdam: North Holland Publishing. Ch. 19.

Geweke, J. and R. Meese. 1981. "Estimating Regression Models of Finite But Unknown Order." *International Economic Review* 22: No. 1 55–70.

Hamilton, J. D. 1987. "A New Approach to the Economic Analysis of Non-stationary Time Series and the Business Cycle." University of Virginia. Manuscript. *Econometrica*. Forthcoming,

Hertzberg, M. P. and B. A. Beckman, 1989. "Business Cycle Indicators: Revised Composite Indexes," *Business Conditions Digest*. January, 1989: 97–102.

Hunt, L. 1988. "An Antiquated, Irrelevant Index." *The Wall Street Journal*. March 29, 1988. p. 28(W).

Hymans, S. 1973. "On the Use of Leading Indicators to Predict Cyclical Turning Points." *Brookings Papers on Economic Activity* 2: 339–84.

Keim, D. B. and R. F. Stambaugh. 1986. "Predicting Returns in the Stocks and Bond Markets." *Journal of Financial Economics* 17: 357–90.

Kling, J. L. 1987. "Predicting the Turning Points of Business and Economic Time Series." *Journal of Business* 60: No. 2 201–38.

Knez, P., R. Litterman, and J. Scheinkman. 1989. "Explorations into Factors Explaining Money Market Returns." Manuscript.

Koch, P. D. and R. H. Raasche. 1988. "An Examination of the Commerce Department Leading-Indicator Approach." *Journal of Business and Economic Statistics* 6: No. 2 167–87.

Koopmans, T. C. 1947. "Measurement Without Theory." *Review of Economics and Statistics* 29: 161–72.

Lucas, R. E. 1977. "Understanding Business Cycles." *Carnegie-Rochester Conference on Public Policy* 5: 7–29.

Mitchell, W. C. and A. F. Burns. 1938. *Statistical Indicators of Cyclical Revivals*. NBER Bulletin 69, New York. Reprinted as Chapter 6 of G. H. Moore, ed. *Business Cycle Indicators*. Princeton: Princeton University Press. 1961.

Moore, G. H. 1979. "The Forty-Second Anniversary of the Leading Indicators." in William Fellner, ed., *Contemporary Economic Problems, 1979*. Washington, D.C.: American Enterprise Institute, 1979. Reprinted in Moore, G. H. *Business Cycles, Inflation, and Forecasting*, 2nd edition. Cambridge, Mass.: NBER, 1983.

Moore, G. H. ed. 1983. *Business Cycles, Inflation, and Forecasting*. 2nd edition. Cambridge, Mass.: NBER.

Moore, G. H. 1988. "Revising the Leading, Coincident, and Lagging Indicators: A Progress Report." Columbia University, Center for International Business Cycle Research. Manuscript.

Neftci, S. N. 1982. "Optimal Prediction of Cyclical Downturns." *Journal of Economic Dynamics and Control* 4: 225–41.

Nelson, C. R. and C. I. Plosser. 1982. "Trends and Random Walks in Macroeconomic Time Series." *Journal of Monetary Economics*. 129–62.

Reagan, P. and D. P. Sheehan. 1985. "The Behavior of Manufacturers' Inventories." *Journal of Monetary Economics* 15: No. 2 217–46.

Sargent, T. J., and C. A. Sims. 1977. "Business Cycle Modeling without Pretending to have Too Much a priori Economic Theory." in C. Sims et al., *New Methods in Business Cycle Research*. Minneapolis: Federal Reserve Bank of Minneapolis.

Sims, C. A. 1980. "Comparison of Interwar and Postwar Business Cycles: Monetarism Reconsidered." *American Economic Review* 70: 250–57.

Singleton, K. 1980. "A Latent Time Series Model of the Cyclical Behavior of Interest Rates." *International Economic Review* 21: No. 3 559–75.

Slutzky, E. 1937. "The Summation of Random Causes as the Sources of Cyclical Processes." *Econometrica* 5: 105–46.

Stekler, H. O., and M. Schepsman. 1973. "Forecasting with an Index of Leading Series." *Journal of the American Statistical Association* 68: No. 342 291–96.

Stock, J. H. and M. W. Watson. 1988a. "Testing for Common Trends." *Journal of the American Statistical Association* 83: No. 404 1097–1107.

Stock, J. H. and M. W. Watson. 1988b. "A Probability Model of the Coincident Economic Indicators." NBER Discussion Paper No. 2772. Forthcoming in Geoffrey Moore and K. Lahiri, eds., *The Leading Economic Indicators: New Approaches and Forecasting Records.* Cambridge: Cambridge University Press.

Stock, J. H. and M. W. Watson 1989. "Interpreting the Evidence on Money-Income Causality." *Journal of Econometrics* 40: No. 1 161–82.

Vaccara, B. N., and V. Zarnowitz. 1978. "Forecasting with the Index of Leading Indicators." NBER Working Paper No. 244.

Wecker, W. E. 1979. "Predicting the Turning Points of a Time Series." *Journal of Business* 52: No. 1 35–50.

Zarnowitz, V. and C. Boschan. 1975a. "Cyclical Indicators: An Evaluation and New Leading Indexes." *Business Conditions Digest.* May 1975.

Zarnowitz, V. and C. Boschan. 1975b. "New Composite Indexes of Coincident and Lagging Indicators." *Business Conditions Digest.* November 1975.

Zarnowitz, V. and G. H. Moore. 1982. "Sequential Signals of Recession and Recovery." *Journal of Business* 55 No. 1, 57–85.

Zellner, A., C. Hong, and G. M. Gulati. 1987. "Turning Points in Economic Time Series, Loss Structures and Bayesian Forecasting." University of Chicago, Graduate School of Business. Manuscript.

Comment

CHRIS SIMS

Textbook classical statistical theory assumes that we begin an inference with a model known exactly except for the values of a few parameters, about which nothing is known. Most classical time series statistical theory is convenient only in "large samples." However, when we set out to forecast macroeconomic time series we find instead that economic theory gives us at best imprecise knowledge of the appropriate model. There are many time series available with plausible connections to the ones we would like to forecast, and the result is so many unknown parameters in any honest model that there are not enough data to determine parameter values well. Samples are not "large," in other words, relative to the level of our ignorance. And it seems apparent that on top of all these difficulties, the stochastic structure of the economy changes over time, not just (or even mainly) because of changes in economic policy, but because of shifts in population, technology, tastes, and resource availability.

In practice, those who forecast regularly understand that textbook statistical theory is therefore only peripherally useful in macroeconomic forecasting. Though the large commercial forecasting models were originally inspired by the elegant simultaneous equations model of statistical textbooks, most of them have come to pay no attention to that theory. They are used largely as deterministic systems of equations and estimated largely by ordinary least squares. When they are used for serious forecasting, they are regularly adjusted by ad hoc judgmental procedures to make their results more reasonable. And of course the Department of Commerce (DOC) leading indicators approach makes no pretense of using any probabilistic modeling in arriving at a predictive index.

Both the standard large-model approach and the DOC approach are useful in bringing data to bear on the forecasting problem, but their heavy use of unreproducible judgmental methods is a drawback. If more systematic and explicit methods could be used, it would be easier to train people to be good forecasters, easier to assess whether and why a model was producing good forecasts, and easier to connect forecasting with analysis of the structure of the economy.

It has recently become practical to use time series models with stochastically time-varying coefficients. It is also possible, as shown over some years now by myself, Tom Doan, Robert Litterman, and others, to work with densely parameterized time series models—models in which the number of unknown coefficients is closer to an honest reflection of our ignorance than in the usual "parsimonious" model appropriate with textbook methods.[1] The idea of this approach is that an explicit Bayesian prior pulls the parameters toward sensible a priori guesses, except to the degree that the data pull them elsewhere. This avoids the problem which otherwise occurs in nonparsimonious models, that ill-determined parameters take on wildly unreasonable values which produce bad forecasts. It also generates a probability model in which our uncertainty about which variables belong in the model, with what lags, is at least partly explicit in the probability structure.

It is therefore disappointing that this paper uses a model without time-varying coefficients, without Bayesian methods, and therefore emerges with what can only be characterized as an unbelievable probability model. It is no more unbelievable than a standard large macroeconomic simultaneous equations model, which also has nonvarying coefficients and a judgmentally restricted parameterization; the opportunity to do better is there and was not taken up.

1. See, e.g., "Forecasting and Conditional Projection Using Realistic Prior Distributions." T. Doan, R. Litterman, and C. Sims, *Econometric Reviews* 3, 1984.

The process of reducing the number of variables has been, apparently, partially formalized, so that it could be simulated on random data to assess its tendency to produce overfitting. This raises the possibility, not explored in this paper, of obtaining realistic estimates of the model's forecast error distribution by recursively re-estimating (incorporating the variable selection process as part of the re-estimate) the model through the sample period. One of the main appeals of explicit Bayesian methods is that they make this form of model validation easy. Here, the variable selection process is probably too time-consuming to be repeated monthly, but surely annually or at least every few years it will in practice be repeated. How would the model, including the implicit model underlying the variable selection, have performed if it had been applied year by year through, say, 1971–88? Showing that it works well would go a long way to answering the argument that the procedure yields an overparsimonious structure which does not take account of parameter drift. Also, in implementing such a test, the modelers would have to be explicit about how often or under what conditions the variable list and/or model structure is to be reassessed in practice. The forecasting procedure is not really complete until these aspects of it have been made explicit.

Winnowing the variable list for the new leading index, until it is shorter than the list in the DOC index, leaves seven variables as the foundation for the new index. Three of these are functions of interest rates. It is undoubtedly true that interest rates are valuable for forecasting: the DOC index is probably mistaken to include no interest rates at all. But interest rates, and especially the public-private spread variable which (as can be seen from Figure 5) dominates the new leading index, have been unusually volatile in the last two decades. A bivariate VAR fit to real GNP and the spread between the six-month commercial paper rate and the three-month Treasury bill rate (my data source, perhaps like that used by Stock and Watson, has six-month Treasury bill rates only back through 1959) shows the public-private spread significant, with marginal significance level .002, for the 1969–88 sample period in the GNP equation, but insignificant, with a marginal significance level of .14, for the 1950–67 sample period. Furthermore, the behavioral interpretation of the predictive power of the public-private spread is problematical. The straightforward reason why such a spread might exist is the presence of default risk on private securities. But the spread, which often has approached or exceeded one percentage point, seems out of proportion to the actual risk of default on these securities. (Bank loan losses, on all types of bank loans, remained under one percent throughout the Seventies and early Eighties, and even prime bank loans earn interest substantially exceeding the commercial paper rate.) The explanation for the size of the spread probably has to do with costs of screening credit risk. Our models of this kind of cost are still rudimentary, however, and in any case a spread from this source would probably be sensitive to the structure of the banking industry.

Is it wise to rely so heavily on a predictive relation that we only partially understand and that appears to be important mainly in the last 20 years? Presumably if interest rates started behaving very differently, the model would be respecified or adjusted; then the criteria for making such adjustments should be more explicit, if we are to have much improvement over the current judgmental DOC procedures in this respect.

In summary, this paper has produced interesting results, especially in reconfirming that interest rates are important forecasting variables and demonstrating that their predictive power is not entirely captured in some single representative rate. By constructing a leading index which is explicitly a forecast of something, it makes a risky, but scientifically valuable, advance over the current DOC methodology. In relying on a probability model which is not nearly a believable characterization of the main sources of forecast uncertainty, it has foregone an opportunity for a more important improvement on existing DOC indicator methodology.

Comment

VICTOR ZARNOWITZ
Graduate School of Business University of Chicago and NBER

PHILLIP BRAUN
Graduate School of Business University of Chicago

On the Background and Scope of the Study

The literature on the meaning, properties, performance, and improvability of cyclical indicators has long been largely a domain of the National Bureau of Economic Research and a relatively few other academic and business economists interested mainly in research methodology and forecasting. The subject is now attracting more and wider interest. Particularly welcome is the growing application of modern time series and econometric methods to the problems of interpreting and evaluating the leading and confirming economic indicators as well as the corresponding composite indexes.

Work on the indicators has in the past added much to our understanding of "what happens during business cycles." It will continue to do so. Stock and Watson (henceforth S-W) are engaged in an ambitious project which promises to make an important contribution to this line of research.

The paper under review lists 40 references, including 17 relating directly to the indicators and dating mostly from the last decade; several more could be added. Many of these papers provide tests of leading indicator forecasts of business cycle peaks and troughs and/or aggregate time series such as real GNP, industrial production, and the index of coincident indicators. The results vary, but most are on balance positive in finding that the Commerce leading index has net predictive value. (See Auerbach 1982; Diebold and Rudebusch 1987; Koch and Raasche 1988; Moore 1983, ch. 25; Neftci 1982; Vaccara and Zarnowitz 1978; Zarnowitz and Moore 1982; Zarnowitz and Braun 1989.) As demonstrated below, the S-W paper does not include adequate tests of the present Commerce index against alternatives such as its own composite of newly selected leading indicators.

The authors proceed by recasting and reinterpreting the index of coincident indicators (CEI). They then present two new and conceptually different forecasting tools. One is called an index of leading economic indicators (LEI) but is really a forecast of the six-month annual percentage change of their CEI. The other, called the recession index, is an estimate of the probability that the U.S. economy will be in a recession six months hence. It is based on the same information as that contained in the CEI and LEI indexes. A recession is defined by a complicated and only sketchily explained formula, which requires a negative growth in the CEI for at least six months.

Coincident Indicators

The S-W CEI index is based on seasonally adjusted, monthly data for the index of industrial production, real personal income less transfer payments, real manufacturing and trade sales, and employee-hours in non-agricultural establishments. These are the same series as those included in the Department of Commerce CEI, except for one rather minor difference: the DOC index uses numbers of employees on non-farm payrolls. The new S-W index has slightly smaller cyclical amplitudes and less of a long upward trend than the DOC CEI index, but otherwise the two series are similar. (See Figure 4(a) in their paper.) S-W offer a novel interpretation of the CEI (C_t) as the "unobserved state of the economy" estimated by a single-index model. In this model, the co-movements of the four component coincident indicators arise solely from ΔC_t. S-W believe that this construction will supplement the old intuitive definition of business or "reference" cycles in Burns and Mitchell (1946) and provide the "precise mathematical content" that the definition lacks (p. 352).

Formal interpretations such as this one can certainly be useful, but they are not unique or demonstrably correct, and may be misleading. S-W are right to stress that the single index specification does not imply that business cycles have a single common cause. Indeed, there is much historical and recent evidence that the sources of fluctuations in the real variables underlying the CEI are multiple and perhaps varying considerably over time in relative importance (for summaries, see Haberler 1964 and Zarnowitz 1985).

The S-W CEI index derives much of its strength from the fact that it is empirically close to being a monthly replica of quarterly real GNP, and so does the DOC CEI (see Figure 4(b)). Neither CEI is sufficiently representative nor reliable to be an adequate proxy for the Burns and Mitchell's concept of "aggregate economic activity." Thus the NBER Business Cycle Dating Committee is likely, for good reasons, to continue monitoring a number of monthly and quarterly time series on output, employment, income, and trade rather than concentrate on the new CEI alone. Here (as elsewhere) mathematical precision is no substitute for careful inference and judgment. However, these cautions do not detract from our basically positive assessment of the S-W work on the coincident index, which is methodologically of substantive interest.

On Selecting Leading Indicators: Search and Prior Beliefs

S-W conducted a massive search to select the components of their LEI. They started with 280 series, reduced the pool quickly to 55 based on univariate tests, and ended up with seven based on multivariate tests. A search of this magnitude, directed specifically to the narrow goal of finding the best indicators for predicting six-month growth rate in the S-W CEI, can be expected to do two things. First, it should go far to accomplish its objective. Second, it will exhaust an unknown but very large number of the available degrees of freedom.

Consequently, a good fit to the sample period chosen must be expected; S-W select their LEI components by examining the data for 1960–88, i.e., the total period covered. They do not, however, have any tests of how well their index would perform outside this sample period.[1] In sum, there is much room for doubt on whether the selected indicators

---

1. All statistics reported by S-W are for 1960–88, except for the root mean square errors in Table 3, column 4, which refer to the sub-period 1979:10–1988:4. But these are not true "out-of-sample" comparisons because of the overlap with the total sample period used in the S-W LEI index construction.

would work with the desired consistency and adequacy for different sample and forecast periods.

Regardless of the extent of the search, any reasonable selection process is inevitably guided by some prior beliefs and judgments based on theory. In this case, to quote, "An important consideration in developing the list was to include the series that have expectational components, that would (under some economic theory) respond rapidly to some shocks in the economy, or that would reflect policy actions" (p. 365). The earlier searches for leading indicators at the NBER and Commerce involved a systematic scoring of the evaluated series for "economic significance." That is, business cycle theories suggested paying special attention to variables associated with early stages of fixed capital investment, changes in inventories, credit, monetary aggregates, and stock prices. The idea that the construction of the leading index is pure measurement without any theory is simply a myth.

In the description of the S-W selection procedure there is a reference to the "desired number of variables" but no explanation how that number was derived. It would appear that the reasons to keep the number of the component leading series small are compelling. The LEI is described as being produced by an unobserved-components VAR system. The extent of the search, the limited length of the postwar series, and the many lagged terms used all combine to reduce sharply the effective number of degrees of freedom left.

The feedback effects from coincident to leading indicators get little attention in the construction of the S-W LEI, which can therefore be said to incorporate few interactive features of a vector autoregression (VAR) model.[2] The presumed reason is that earlier experiments suggested to S-W that such effects are weak. This is consistent with the results of our own work (Zarnowitz and Braun 1989), which finds real GNP to be strongly influenced by the DOC LEI, but not the other way around, in a six-variable VAR-type model, with money, inflation interest rates, and the Blanchard fiscal index.[3] However, it is also clear that in general the component leading series are endogenous variables in any comprehensive model of the economy.

The S-W selection of their LEI components represents a serious challenge to all those whose priors are influenced by long experience with

2. ΔC_t (where C_t is the S-W CEI) is regressed on a constant, ΔC_{t-i}, and X_{t-j}, where X_t is a vector of components of the new LEI; $i = 1, \ldots, 4$, and $j = 1, \ldots, 3$ or 6. X_t is modeled as a VAR(1).
3. We worked with equations that included up to six stationary variables, constant terms, and time trends. Each of the quarterly series used was taken with four (experimentally, also eight) lags.

earlier NBER and Commerce indexes of leading indicators. We are asked to believe that none of the comprehensive series on inventory investment, money and credit aggregates, and stock prices belong in the leading index. Of those series representative of business investment commitments, only the rate of growth in unfilled orders of durable-goods manufacturers makes the grade. The components of the DOC LEI have been chosen as those candidates from the different "economic process" groups (e.g., consumption, investment, money, credit, etc.) that perform best on cyclical conformity or coherence, consistency of leads at business cycles turns, and several other criteria (including timely release and measurement error as revealed by revisions). A series such as the nominal exchange rate, with a short and poor record of cyclical conformity and timing, would never pass these selection criteria.

S-W offer a general description of their elaborate selection procedure (p. 365) but without much of the underlying evidence and specific explanation (no doubt partly because of limitations on the length of the printed paper). Hence, we asked them for some of the information and received prompt and most helpful cooperation. The material which the authors kindly supplied enabled us to make some additional comparisons and tests.

Additional Tests

Table 3 in the S-W paper presents summary statistics for the effects of including individually each of 20 additional variables in the new LEI; six of these series are drawn from the 11 components of the Commerce leading index. We extended this table to cover all ten variables in the DOC index that are different from those in the S-W LEI (housing permits are included in both indexes), and did it using the proper form for each variable (e.g., the series on the average week unemployment insurance claims should be inverted, as in the DOC index). The results are shown in Table 1C and Table 3C.[4]

The first column of Table 1C shows the p-values for the F-tests of the restriction that the coefficients on six lags of the additional leading variables are all zero in a regression of the one-month growth in S-W CEI on the base set of the S-W LEI and four lags of the dependent variable. Only three DOC candidates pass this test at the 5% level (vendor performance, sensitive materials prices, and change in business and consumer credit). When 12 lags are used, only the vendor performance has a very

4. In the limited time available, we could not replicate the unobserved components, modified VAR estimation procedure of S-W, and used instead simple regressions of C_t on the variables in the S-W base model. We also adjusted the S-W series so as not to incorporate the most recently available data.

low p-value. For five variables (those with the lowest p-values in column 1, plus the change in inventories), the $\bar{R}^2$ numbers show (generally modest) improvements (see columns 3 and 4).

Next we essentially reversed S-W's Table 3. Instead of adding assorted components to the S-W base model, as S-W do, we added each of the individual leading S-W components to the DOC base model (see Tables 2C and 4C). Table 2C shows the resulting p-values. Based on the S-W selection procedure, our priors are that all of the S-W components

Table 1C   EFFECTS OF INCLUDING ADDITIONAL VARIABLES IN THE S-W LEI: SUMMARY STATISTICS

Model and Candidate Variables	p-value 1960:3–1988:4		R^2	$\bar{R}^2$
	6-lags	12-lags	1960:3–1988:4	
	(1)	(2)	(3)	(4)
S-W base model	—	—	.652	.622
S-W base model plus additional DOE LEI variables				
Aver. wkly. hours of work, mfg. (DLPHRM)	.778	.782	.657	.612
Aver. wkly. unempl. insur. claims, inverted (ILUINC)	.966	.614	.659	.614
Mfrs. new orders, 82$, cons. goods & mtls. (DMOCM82)	.331	.333	.664	.620
S&P 500 stock price index (DFSPCOM)	.093	.116	.682	.640
Contracts & orders for plant & eqpt., 82$ (DMPCON8)	.762	.641	.663	.619
Change in mfg. & trade inventories on hand & on order (IVMUT8)	.912	.490	.676	.634
Vendor performance, % of cos. receiving slower deliveries (IVPAC)	.001	.002	.678	.636
Change in sensitive mat'ls. prices (PSM99S)	.024	.088	.700	.661
Money supply M2, 1982$ (DFM2D82)	.262	.444	.662	.618
Change in bus. & cons. credit outst. (FCBCUC)	.026	.105	.707	.668

NOTE: Columns (1) and (2) present p-values for the F-tests of the hypothesis that the coefficients on the DOC candidate variable are all zero in an OLS regression of the one-month growth rate in the S-W coincident index on the base set of S-W LEI components, four lags of the dependent variable, and 6 and 12 lags, respectively, of the candidate variable. The DOC base model includes the ten series listed in the table, plus housing permits which are also contained in the S-W LEI. Columns (3) and (4) show the R^2 and $\bar{R}^2$, respectively, within the total sample period, using regressions of $(C_{t+6|t+6} - C_{t|t})$ on the S-W base model plus 12 lags of the candidate variable.

should have small p-values and therefore we need to use a low critical value in evaluating these tests. If we use a 1% critical value, then only part-time work due to slack and the risk premium are significant with six-lags and only the risk premium is significant with 12 lags. None of the S-W candidate variables increase the adjusted $\bar{R}^2$.

Comparing Tables 1C and 2C we see that, for the most part, the addition of the S-W variables to the DOC index produces lower p-values than when the DOC variables are added to the S-W base model. It is difficult, however, to interpret this comparison. A better procedure is to consider out-of-sample forecast performance. The authors choose the root-mean-square-error criterion and apply it to estimates for 1979:10–

Table 2C   EFFECTS OF INCLUDING ADDITIONAL VARIABLES IN THE DOC LEI: SUMMARY STATISTICS

Model and Candidate Variables	p-value 1960:3–1988:4 6-lags	12-lags	R^2 1960:3–1988:4	$\bar{R}^2$
	(1)	(2)	(3)	(4)
DOC base model	—	—	.601	.535
Base model plus additional S-W LEI variables				
Mfrs. unfilled orders, dur. goods indus. (MDU82S)	.643	.036	.633	.553
Trade-weighted nominal exchange rate (EXNWT2S)	.911	.328	.630	.550
Part-time work due to slack, non-agri. indus. (LHNAPSS)	.004	.039	.636	.557
Yield on 10-yr. Treasury bonds (FYGT10S)	.088	.113	.657	.582
6-mo. corp. paper rate—6 mo. T-bill rate, spread (CP6-GM6)	.000	.000	.716	.655
Yield on 10-yr. T-bond—yield on 1-yr. T-bond, spread (G10-G1)	.736	.886	.631	.551

NOTE: Columns (1) and (2) present p-values for the F-tests of the hypothesis that the coefficients on the S-W candidate variable are all zero in an OLS regression of the one-month growth rate of the S-W coincident index on the base set of DOC LEI components, four lags of the dependent variable, and 6 and 12 lags, respectively, of the candidate variable. The DOC base model uses six-month lags for five series (stock price index; real new orders for consumer goods and materials; real contracts and orders for plant and equipment; housing permits; money supply M2 in constant dollars) and three-month lags for six series (average work week; unemployment insurance claims; vendor performance; change in sensitive materials prices; change in business and consumer credit outstanding; change in mfg. and trade inventories on hand and on order). For more detail on these series, see note to Table 2. Columns (3) and (4) show the R^2 and $\bar{R}^2$, respectively, obtained within the total sample period, using regressions of $(C_{t+6|t+6} - C_{t|t})$ on the DOC base model plus 12 lags of the candidate variable.

Table 3C ALTERNATIVE FORECAST HORIZONS FOR THE S-W CEI AND
THE EFFECTS OF INCLUDING ADDITIONAL VARIABLES IN THE
S-W LEI ON FORECAST PERFORMANCE

Dependent Variable Forecast Period	Root Mean Square Error		
	$C_{t+3\|t+3} - C_{t\|t}$ 79:10–88:4	$C_{t+6\|t+6} - C_{t\|t}$ 79:10–88:4	$C_{t+9\|t+9} - C_{t\|t}$ 79:10–88:1
	(1)	(2)	(3)
Model and candidate variables			
S-W base model	4.40	3.66	3.79
Base model plus 12 lags of additional DOC LEI variables			
Aver. wkly. hours of work, mfg. (DLPHRM)	4.49	3.79	3.80
Aver. wkly. unempl. insur. claims, inverted (ILUINC)	4.55	3.76	3.78
Mfrs. new orders, 82$, cons. goods & mtls. (DMOCM82)	4.99	4.23	4.13
S&P 500 stock price index DFSPCOM)	4.66	3.62	4.01
Contracts & orders for plant & eqpt., 82$ (DMPCON8)	4.34	3.82	3.99
Change in mfg. & trade inventories on hand & on order (IVMUT8)	5.37	4.33	4.13
Vendor performance, % of cos. receiving slower deliveries (IVPAC)	4.16	3.80	3.94
Change in sensitive mat'ls. prices (PSM99S)	4.44	3.61	3.97
Money supply M2, 1982$ (DFM2D82)	4.99	3.87	3.75
Change in bus. & cons. credit outst. (FCBCUC)	5.06	3.71	3.72

Note: See Table 1C for description of the S-W base model.

1988:4, which they treat as a forecast period. This procedure is flawed, as noted above (see note 1 and text), but we adopt it for comparability.[5] We extend the S-W tests to consider the forecast performance of not just the six-month annualized growth rate, but also the three-month and

5. We follow S-W in calculating the RMSE over the whole sample because of time constraints. It is obviously more appropriate, however, to use accumulated short horizon forecasts to make comparisons.

nine-month annualized growth rates. These results are presented in Tables 3C and 4C.

From Table 3C it can be seen that adding any of the DOC LEI component series to the S-W base model does not improve forecast performance when we are predicting six or nine-month growth rates. For three-month growth rates the performance is improved in the single case of the vendor performance series. Of the S-W components (Table 4C), only part-time work due to slack and the risk premium improve measurably the RMSE when added to the DOC base model for forecasting six-month growth rates. The yield spread is the only variable that somewhat improves the RMSE for three-month growth rates. None of the S-W variables help improve the RMSE over the DOC base model for the nine-month growth rates.

Since several of the S-W components perform poorly when added to

Table 4C   ALTERNATIVE FORECASTING HORIZONS FOR THE S-W CEI AND THE EFFECTS OF INCLUDING ADDITIONAL VARIABLES IN DOC LEI ON FORECAST PERFORMANCE

	Root Mean Square Error		
Dependent Variable *Forecast Period*	$C_{t+3\|t+3} - C_{t\|t}$ 79:10–88:4	$C_{t+6\|t+6} - C_{t\|t}$ 79:10–88:4	$C_{t+9\|t+9} - C_{t\|t}$ 79:10–88:1
	(1)	(2)	(3)
Model and candidate variables			
DOC base model	4.51	4.16	4.00
S-W base model plus 12 lags of additional S-W LEI variables			
Mfrs. unfilled orders, dur. goods indus. (MDU82S)	5.03	4.55	4.20
Trade-weighted nominal exchange rate (EXNWT2S)	6.54	5.93	4.88
Part-time work due to slack, nonag. indus. (LHNAPSS)	4.48	3.99	4.03
Yield on 10-yr. Treasury bonds (FYGT10S)	5.34	4.27	3.93
6-mo. corp. paper rate-6 mo. T-bill rate, spread (CP6-GM6)	4.33	3.78	3.99
Yield on 10-yr. T-bond—yield on 1-yr. T-bond, spread (G10-G1)	5.14	4.65	4.55

Note: See Table 2C for description of the DOC base model.

the DOC base set, one would wish to exclude them when trying to improve the DOC LEI. This is analogous to what S-W conclude with reference to the inclusion of candidate DOC base variables in their LEI. However, the comparison of the $\bar{R}^2$ and RMSE statistics for the alternative base models suggests that, taken as a whole, the S-W LEI performs better than the DOC LEI over the periods considered.

The same conclusion emerges from an attempt to compare how well the two LEIs perform in forecasting real GNP growth. We produced one-step ahead forecasts of real GNP from a naive AR(3) model, updating the parameter estimates every period, and calculated the RMSE over the period 1979:3 through 1988:1. The RMSE for the naive model was .00997. When we added three lags of the S-W LEI, the RMSE fell to .00863. When we alternatively added three lags of growth rates of the DOC LEI to the naive model, the RMSE only fell to .00935. These results again indicate that the S-W base model taken as a set performs well compared to the DOC LEI.

When the sample period is extended back, from 1960–79 to 1948–79, the RMSE for real growth 1979–88 forecasts from the AR(3) model declines 1.2% to .00985, while the RMSE for the corresponding forecasts with DOC LEI declines 8.0% to .00917. (For lack of data, we could not make a similar calculation for forecasts with S-W LEI.)

Concluding Remarks

Our review of the S-W work and additional tests suggest the following points:
1. The proposed LEI performs relatively well in forecasting the rate of growth in real economic activity (represented either by CEI or GNP) over the periods considered in this study. To some extent, this result reflects the search and other procedures adopted by S-W, and hence, it could well apply mainly to these periods. The S-W LEI is better as a set than are its individual components, but the same can be said of the DOC LEI.
2. Comparisons of the two LEI's are difficult because their objectives and construction are substantively different. When the S-W goal, rates, and time frame are adopted, the S-W LEI gives better results, which may not be surprising and is certainly not conclusive. The DOC LEI has a more comprehensive coverage based on a much longer historical experience. This could well prove an advantage over time inasmuch as the causes of business cycles may vary. On the other hand, the DOC LEI may suffer more from overfitting or redundancies over limited time periods.
3. To assess the predictive performance of the S-W LEI, out-of-sample measures are needed, which are now lacking because the index is con-

structed from data for the entire period covered. The sample and forecast periods must be distinguished, and a sensitivity analysis using different breakdowns of the available data would be desirable. There are indications that the DOC LEI predicts better in a model based on a longer sample period. In any event, it would be well to extend the S-W LEI back ten years as well, to cover the recessions of 1948–49, 1953–54, and 1957–58.

4. Some components of the S-W LEI contribute much, others little when added to the DOC LEI: compare, e.g., the strongly favorable evidence for the risk premium (CP6-GM6) with the poor one for the yield spread (G10-G1). The inclusion of the nominal exchange rate is particularly questionable. Similarly, there are also large differences in performance between the components of DOC-LEI. It is possible that a combination of the best series from both sets would result in significant improvements. This may form a part of a promising research agenda for further study.

5. More components are smoothed in the S-W LEI than in the DOC LEI, which may favor the former. Also, the incorporation of the most recent information available for some of the S-W index components should be on the average rewarding, and the same probably applies to the determination of the lag structures in this index. It would be possible to take advantage of some of these innovations in the DOC LEI as well.

6. S-W have a specific target and focus on six-month growth in their CEI, whereas the DOC LEI has been more flexibly designed and used. This is a basic difference, which has important implications that deserve to be studied.

7. Because of time limitations, we have not been able to examine the S-W Recession Index, an ambitious project growing out of the important work by Wecker and Diebold and Rudebusch. But it may be worth noting that we would expect the Recession Index to share many of the strengths and weaknesses of S-W LEI because of large elements of common coverage.

REFERENCES

Auerbach, A. J. 1982. "The Index of Leading Indicators: 'Measurement Without Theory,' Thirty-five Years Later." *Review of Economics and Statistics* 64: No. 4 589–95.
Burns, A. F. and W. C. Mitchell. 1946. *Measuring Business Cycles.* New York: NBER.
Diebold, F. X. and G. D. Rudebusch. 1987. "Scoring the Leading Indicators." Federal Reserve Board, Division of Research and Statistics. Manuscript.
Haberler, Gottfried. *Prosperity and Depression.* New edition. First published by the League of Nations. Cambridge, Mass.: Harvard University Press. [1937] 1964.

Koch, P. D. and R. H. Raasche. 1988. "An Examination of the Commerce Department Leading-Indicator Approach." *Journal of Business and Economic Statistics* 6: No. 2 167–87.

Moore, G. H. 1983. *Business Cycles, Inflation, and Forecasting,* 2nd edition, Cambridge, Mass.: Ballinger Publishing Company for NBER.

Neftci, S. N. 1982. "Optimal Prediction of Cyclical Downturns." *Journal of Economic Dynamics and Control* 4: 225–41.

Vaccara, B. N., and V. Zarnowitz. 1978. "Forecasting with the Index of Leading Economic Indicators." NBER Working Paper No. 244.

Zarnowitz, V. "Recent Work on Business Cycles in Historical Perspective: A Review of Theories and Evidence." *Journal of Economic Literature,* Vol. 23(2). pp. 523–80. June 1985.

Zarnowitz, V. and P. Braun. "Major Macroeconomic Variables and Leading Indexes: Some Estimates of Their Interrelations, 1886–1982." NBER Working Paper No. 2812. January 1989.

Zarnovitz, V. and G. H. Moore. 1982. "Sequential Signals of Recession and Recovery." *Journal of Business* 55: No. 1 57–85.

Discussion

Watson stressed that the model appeared stable over different samples and that since the equation was only approximate, the six month forecast is appropriate.

Bob Hall stated that this work is NBER-supported but is not an official NBER publication. He also asked what predictive value should be assigned to the different variables in the LEI. Watson replied that the corporate paper/T-bill spread is important but not completely dominant; interest rates and exchange rates are less important. Hall asked what the model currently forecasts. Watson responded that the coincident index is projected to increase 2.6% in the next six months and the probability of a recession in that period is .05; the probability of a recession in the next year is .27.

Ben Friedman noted that monetary policy affects output only if the T-bill rate is used, not the commercial paper rate, as observed by Sims in his monetary policy study. In recent periods, there is no liquidity difference between the two bills, but there is a default premium in the private debt. This is a good economic indicator since defaults tend to occur when the economy is in decline. As a result, the relationship above is rational and furthermore, it is not surprising to find it currently rather than in previous data.

Sims responded that it is unclear why defaults should be cyclical, but Friedman stated that regardless of the real effects of defaults, their cyclicality is well-established.

Olivier Blanchard suggested regressing bankruptcies on the default spread. He then asked if there were a monthly measure of GNP, would this suffice for the coincident indicator. Stock responded that a multi-dimensional measure of aggregate fluctuations is needed. Blanchard asked if the concept needed is really welfare, or if GNP is in fact the relevant aggregate.